C000071441

MARITAL THERAPY IN BRITAIN

Volume 1

Context and Therapeutic Approaches

Markawat
October '06.

PSYCHOTHERAPY IN BRITAIN
A series edited by Windy Dryden

Other titles in the series:
Individual Therapy in Britain
Innovative Therapy in Britain (forthcoming)
Marital Therapy in Britain Volume 2

MARITAL THERAPY IN BRITAIN

Volume 1

Context and Therapeutic Approaches

Windy Dryden
Editor

Harper & Row, Publishers
London

Cambridge
Philadelphia
New York
San Francisco

Mexico City
São Paulo
Singapore
Sydney

Copyright © 1985. Selection and editorial material © Windy Dryden. Copyright for each chapter remains with contributor. All rights reserved.

First published 1985

Harper & Row Ltd
28 Tavistock Street,
London WC2E 7PN

No part of this book may be reproduced in any manner whatsoever without written permission except in the case of brief quotations embodied in critical articles and reviews

British Library Cataloguing in Publication Data

Marital therapy in Britain.
   Vol. 1, Context and therapeutic approaches
   1. Marital psychotherapy
   I. Dryden, Windy
   616.89′156   RC488.5

ISBN 0-06-318331-5

For reasons of confidentiality great care has been taken to disguise the circumstances of the couples discussed so that they will be generally unrecognizable. If, however, any of them should read this book and think they recognize themselves, we hope they do not mind.

Acknowledgement: Harper & Row would like to thank Tavistock Publications and the Tavistock Institute of Medical Psychology for permission to quote from their publications and documents in Diana Daniell's chapter.

Typeset by Mathematical Composition Setters Ltd., Salisbury, UK
Printed and bound by Thomson Litho Limited, East Kilbride

THE EDITOR

Windy Dryden is one of Britain's leading counselling psychologists and counsellor educators. He was lecturer in counselling psychology at the University of Aston in Birmingham from 1975 to 1984 and is at present lecturer in psychology at Goldsmiths' College, University of London. He is an Associate of the British Psychological Society, Fellow of the International Academy of Eclectic Psychotherapists, Diplomate in Professional Psychotherapy of the International Academy of Professional Counseling and Psychotherapy, Associate Fellow and Training Faculty Member of the Institute for Rational-Emotive Therapy in New York, and Director of the Institute for Rational-Emotive Therapy (UK).

He has practised as a counselling psychologist in student counselling, general practice, marriage guidance and private practice settings. He has published over seventy articles, book chapters, and monographs primarily on rational-emotive therapy and cognitive behaviour therapy and is the author of *Rational-Emotive Therapy: Fundamentals and Innovations* (Croom-Helm 1984) and *Therapists' Dilemmas* (Harper & Row 1985). He is the editor of *Individual Therapy in Britain* (Harper & Row 1984) and the forthcoming *Cognitive-Behavioural Approaches to Psychotherapy* (with William L. Golden) also to be published by Harper & Row. He is currently working on a book entitled: *Counselling: A Cognitive Approach* to be published by John Wiley and Sons. He was founding editor of the *British Journal of Cognitive Psychotherapy* and is at present a coeditor of the journal.

LIST OF OTHER CONTRIBUTORS

David Black: Analyst in Private Practice; Clinical Supervisor, Westminster Pastoral Foundation, London.

Robert Chester: Senior Lecturer in Sociology, Dept. of Social Policy and Professional Studies, University of Hull.

Michael Crowe: Consultant Psychiatrist, Bethlem Royal and Maudsley Hospital, London.

Diana Daniell: Senior Marital Psychotherapist, Institute of Marital Studies, Tavistock Institute of Medical Psychology, London.

Jack Dominian: Director, Marriage Research Centre, Central Middlesex Hospital, London.

Patricia Hunt: Tutor Consultant (North-West Region), NMGC.

Dougal Mackay: District Psychologist, Bristol and Weston Health Authority.

Jeanne Magagna: Child and Family Psychotherapist, Dept. of Child Psychiatry, Royal Free Hospital, London.

Thomas Schröder: Tutor Consultant (West Region), NMGC.

Andy Treacher: Senior Clinical Psychologist, Chippenham Child Guidance Clinic, Wiltshire.

Nicholas Tyndall: Chief Officer, NMGC.

To my parents

To my parents

Preface

When I began training as a marriage guidance counsellor, I was disappointed with the available British literature on marital therapy. There existed no comprehensive British text that covered the broad spectrum of therapeutic interventions with married couples. At that time, I was engaged in the task of editing *Individual Therapy in Britain* (Harper and Row 1984) and decided that I would follow up that text with one devoted to marital work. On researching the subject, it quickly become evident that the number of areas that required coverage justified two volumes.

The present volume is divided into two sections. Section 1 covers the *contexts* which frame marital work in Britain today. In Chapter 1, Robert Chester provides an overview of research into marriage in Britain. In Chapters 2 and 4, Jack Dominian considers (a) to what extent values in marriage have changed or remained constant and (b) the patterns that can be discerned in marital breakdown. In Chapter 3, Jeanne Magagna and David Black look at the therapeutic implications of the changing roles of men and women in contemporary Britain; while, in Chapter 5, Nicholas Tyndall reflects on the work and impact of the National Marriage Guidance Council – an organization which provides the context for much of the remedial work with couples in Britain.

In Section 2, the major approaches to marital therapy in Britain are covered. Setting the scene, in Chapters 6 and 7, Patricia Hunt and I first consider the therapeutic alliances that are present in marital work and how these affect help-seeking activities and therapeutic processes. Then, in the next four chapters (8–11), the following approaches are outlined: Psychodynamic (Diana Daniell), Rational–Emotive (Windy Dryden), Behavioural (Dougal Mackay) and Systems (Andy Treacher). There follows Chapter 12, in which comparisons are made among the four approaches. Finally, in Chapter 13, Michael Crowe outlines an eclectic approach to marital therapy which draws predominantly on the behavioural and systems approaches.

For the sake of brevity the therapist is normally referred to as 'him'. The term 'marital' therapy is used in both volumes to reflect the current convention whereby therapeutic interventions with couples who are in committed relationships are given the title 'marital'. I am not entirely happy with this term since it may well offend couples seeking therapeutic help who are not married or who are gay. Since, in my opinion, no acceptable alternative exists, I have reluctantly acceded to convention. However, in so doing, I intend no offence to the afore-mentioned groups.

Windy Dryden
Birmingham, March 1985

SECTION ONE

CONTEXT

CHAPTER ONE Marriage in Britain
An Overview of Research
Robert Chester

Introduction

Contemporary Social Debate

There is much popular, political and media discussion concerning the family in Britain, and in respect of marriage this centres on how far the institution is outmoded, in decline, or at least subject to various troubles. High divorce rates, together with declining rates of marriage and childbearing, increased cohabitation, the greater visibility of homosexual relationships etc., have fuelled a diffuse debate which often polarizes between traditionalist and radical viewpoints.

Traditionalist opinion, viewing stable family life as the cornerstone of individual and social well-being, tends to be pessimistic about contemporary trends, especially the volume of marriage breakdown, and from this quarter may come calls for the remoralization of family life through programmes to preserve marriage (e.g. see Society of Conservative Lawyers 1981). Various shades of radical opinion, however, are perturbed by the persistence rather than the decline of marriage and the family. Conventional family life has been denounced for its alleged suffocating intimacy (Leach 1968), depicted as a system of mystification, scapegoating and violence (Cooper 1972; Laing 1967, 1971), and condemned as a site of female subordination and exploitation (e.g. Segal 1983). The conclusion from perspectives such as this is a need for the transformation (or even abolition) of marriage and the family.

This 'war over the family' (Berger and Berger 1984) is relevant to research in several ways. For one thing it provides the social context in which research is conceived, funded, conducted and evaluated. Some researchers have strong commitments in the debate, while others have developed new sensitivities which have added a further strand to the discussion. This rejects the pessimism and thesis of decline of the traditionalist viewpoint, but picks up the theme of troubles. Simultaneously, it picks up from radical analysis the need for change and adaptation but without adopting the rejectionist position. What emerges is an emphasis on the contemporary pluralism of family life, an analysis of the disjunctions between traditional forms and current social conditions, and a prescription for policies which acknowledge and legitimate diversity and change (e.g. see Study Commission on the Family 1980, 1982, 1983). Beyond all this, the social debate is often able to proceed undisciplined by empirical evidence because the necessary research is scarce, or inconclusive, or simply has not been done.

The term 'research' here refers to work which is grounded in systematic investigation and social scientific procedures of verification, and it thus precludes a class of work which arises from the therapeutic milieu. Many analyses of marital interaction rely for their force upon detailed elucidation of case histories by way of concepts which are the postulates of a therapeutically oriented theory, generally of a psychodynamic kind. Such work looks for validation not so much to amassed empirical data as to assessed clinical outcome and contribution to the elaboration of the therapeutic theory concerned. Writings of this kind have their own justifications, but they are a matter for later chapters rather than this one. Within the definition of research thus given there exists a literature which is not inconsiderable in its constituent parts but which does not in total offer a comprehensive or cohesive body of knowledge, and its nature thus merits some comment.

Marriage research

It has to be said that we are not well-endowed with systematic knowledge of marriage in Britain, or of how married life is carried out on a day-to-day basis. Reviews of literature are apt to comment on its paucity, sporadic nature and gaps in coverage, and policy agencies frequently find that there is little empirical evidence upon which to draw. A consultant's report to the Economic and Social Research Council (Chester 1983) recently recorded a widely held view that past research on marriage and the family has been fragmented and non-cumulative, and the contents of an associated research register (Chester 1984) suggest that such qualities may still persist. From the viewpoint of practitioner agencies it has also been said that there is a dearth of research by those in professional services or by people who collaborate with them, and that practitioners often find that published research material does not address their preoccupations and dilemmas (Working Party on Marriage Guidance 1979). In observing that research has a poor record judged by the extent to which it has influenced practice, the Working Party was referring primarily to research on marital problems, but the paucity of research on ordinary marital functioning is also of relevance to practitioners, since it means that they cannot situate their case experience in a wider framework.

Despite such judgements, however, there is a volume of research achievement, and the purpose here is to provide an overview of this. Clearly a single chapter cannot note in detail all the potentially relevant items, especially since they exhibit such a diversity of interests, intentions and styles. Some more general approach is required, and this chapter is therefore developed along the following lines. Comments drawn from researchers and their reports indicate the existence of certain perceived impediments affecting the nature and volume of research, and consideration will therefore be given to some possible reasons why research effort has not been more substantial and diverse. Following this, brief attention will be given to the theoretical orientations which can be seen to underlie empirical studies, even though perhaps few studies have a strict theoretical derivation. Next there will be exploration of an important theme which emerges from research: the relationship between the private world of marriage and the public world of institutions. Finally the substance of research will be approached under two headings. The first of these is the research debate on the changing nature of conjugal roles, while the second is the more diffuse category of 'marital problems'. Many studies specifically focus on problematical aspects of marriage, and others which were not necessarily conceived in such terms can nevertheless be seen in this way, so that a problem focus facilitates the marshalling of otherwise diverse material.

Impediments and deterrents to research

It is possible to cull from research communications some issues perceived to act as constraints on family research, and these form a useful background consideration in evaluating the field. Some of these points may apply to other research areas, but they are felt to have particular force in the sphere of marriage and the family.

Status   Researchers on family relationships often seem to sense that this specialism has low disciplinary status. How this perception might be verified is not fully clear, but some pointers can be indicated. Few members of the British Sociological Association, for instance, record marriage and the family amongst their interests, and analysis of research activity and journal publication suggests that the field ranks low with professional sociologists.

Psychologists, although much concerned with, say, infant–caregiver relations (note the terminology), seem to have a lack of interest in the family as such, and possible reasons are suggested by Gale and Jolly (1982). Regarding legal studies, there is no university chair in family law, and few professors specialize in it. More generally, the field lacks the attributes of high status such as specialized journals, permanent and well-funded institutes, and attention from senior scholars. Inability to command substantial institutional focus and sustained commitment is a source of weakness which may be self-maintaining, since young researchers are not much drawn to fields which do not attract their seniors.

Theoretical underdevelopment   Although some theoretical orientations are described later, research on family issues often springs from practical rather than theoretical concerns, and fragmentation comes about partly because practical concerns are diverse and unpredictable. There has thus been a low level of theoretical development in the field and a relative lack of interchange with general theoretical and conceptual developments in the disciplines. A consequent 'applied' flavour may contribute to low status, and may also make research seem to be an apologie for the *status quo* in a manner which is uncongenial to some. Certainly, as Morgan (1975) trenchantly argues, there has been lacking the kind of critical tradition which fosters theoretical elaboration by redefining boundaries, challenging assumptions, and making new connections. One issue here is whether 'marriage', which is grounded in social and legal definitions, is an appropriate rubric for the conduct of research, since strictly speaking it precludes attention to other phenomena which may be theoretically comparable, such as informal cohabitation, homosexual pairing, and experimental forms of living. There might be arguments, therefore, for reconstitution of the field under some heading such as 'intimate environments' (Skolnik 1973), 'networks and processes' (Morgan 1977) or 'long-term close relationships' (Argyle et al. 1984).

Methodological issues   Theoretical underdevelopment also has a methodological dimension. Cumulative investigation requires the development of common concepts and indicators but, as Orford and Edwards (1977) complain, concepts and instruments are frequently developed in isolation from existing work. There are few operational measures in general use, so that even when common concepts are employed they are often diversely measured, and the outcome can be a congeries of apparently conflicting findings which defy comparison and cumulation. Reasons for this situation may include the diverse locations of research reports, the intellectual and institutional isolation of many researchers, and the general lack of work concerned with testing and refining methodology.

There are other methodological issues apart from insularity, and one concerns the dimension of time. Many marital topics of research interest involve dynamic phenomena which work themselves out over long periods of time. The well-known problems of longitudinal research mean that prospective studies are less common than would be desirable, and the use of partial alternatives both has its own hazards (Walker 1977) and results in reliance for data upon uncomfortably high degrees of retrospective recall. More generally, there has been only a limited development of data-gathering methods, with the interview retaining pride of place. Other observational techniques frequently raise practical or even ethical difficulties, but recently there has been some innovation, such as the use of unobtrusive video cameras to record domestic interaction (Argyle et al. 1984) and residential participant observation with new recording techniques (Reynolds 1982), and these give access to actual behaviour rather than accounts of behaviour.

Intellectual boundaries Interest in marriage is widely dispersed over the disciplines, and because many topics cross intellectual boundaries they require an interdisciplinary approach. This is not often found, and there are problems in adopting it, including trained incapacity and institutional segregation of researchers. There is a need for linking concepts which can span disciplines, but specialist researchers tend to restrict attention to selected issues and to employ a limited repertoire of favoured perspectives and methods. Furthermore, where no particular discipline lays particular claim to a field, it tends, in the absence of facilitating institutions, to become marginalized.

Privacy The intense privacy which surrounds marriage erects barriers to research and imposes special demands upon investigators. Strong social images concerning the family may lead people to present a facade of 'normality' (Burgoyne and Clark 1984; Voysey 1975) which can render research on sensitive issues particularly vulnerable to false findings, especially in social survey work. For many research topics it is necessary to penetrate the intimacy of domestic life, which not only requires special aptitudes but also ensures that much marriage research will be qualitative and small-scale in nature. The more personal nature of such research means that researcher effects may be more elusive and harder to assess than in other approaches.

Access   For many topics of research on intimate relations an appropriate sampling frame cannot be delineated, and inordinate time and energy may be required to identify and locate any respondents at all (see Baum 1982; Burgoyne and Clark 1984). Samples are often perforce self-selected or defined by their availability rather than by other desiderata, and this precludes claims for generalizability except via experimental design or replication. In sociology and anthropology, at least, experimental design is unusual, and replication is rare, perhaps because it seems unexciting to research principals, inappropriate to research students, and unnecessary to funding agencies. In consequence, knowledge of a topic may rest upon a very limited and perhaps dated base.

Restricted informants   Researchers often have access to only one family informant, commonly the wife/mother, and there are problems in this. There is sufficient evidence of discrepant perceptions (Brannen and Collard 1982) to indicate that the type of informant colours the research, and persistent use of a single informant type will colour the whole field, so that the regular use of female respondents constitutes a research hazard. Certainly it can be said that past research has been insufficiently sensitive to gender, and while this is now changing under feminist tuition there still remains a lack of knowledge of male perspectives on marriage.

Ethical issues   The privateness and sensitivity of marriage mean that ethical issues may be particularly salient in this sphere (Vetere 1982). Requirements of informed consent and non-violation of respondents may be difficult to achieve, since complete frankness about objectives would probably deter consent in many cases, and penetration of the compact of privacy which normally surrounds marriage may perturb the well-being of the individual or the relationship of the couple. Research procedures sometimes elicit new perceptions from respondents, and these may feed back unpredictably into their marriage, while delicate interviews sometimes occasion unanticipated distress. Being permitted into the domestic backstage imposes special obligations on researchers, and ethical considerations can deter or limit research.

One consequence of the considerations outlined above is that marriage research often falls short of ideal procedural canons, and researchers may feel methodologically vulnerable. In evaluating research, however, critics must accept that sometimes the alternative to methodological solecism would be no research at all.

Theoretical orientations

The theoretical approaches which have influenced British research on marriage are American in origin, and mostly stem from broader theoretical perspectives rather than from within family research. Research studies themselves range from being atheoretical in conception to being formally constituted in theoretical terms, with many in fact lying only somewhat loosely within a theoretical orientation and intended to advance empirical knowledge rather than to contribute to theoretical development. However, explicitly or implicitly, and singly or in combination, the approaches described below provide a means of locating the orientation of research studies which otherwise might seem to be relatively free-floating.

The functionalist approach

Until recently this approach has been the most influential, and is inseparable from the writings of Parsons (1943, 1964; Parsons and Bales 1956). Its attention is directed primarily towards the macrosocial context of marriage rather than towards marital interaction, but it contains two themes of particular relevance. The first is that the marital dyad is internally differentiated on sex-related and relatively fixed lines. The husband is the 'instrumental leader', meaning that he is the principal breadwinner, authority and gatekeeper to the outside world, while the wife is the 'expressive leader', concerned with nurturant functions and tension management. The nuclear family has become a relatively isolated unit, anchored in the conjugal bond, and marriage has evolved from a prescriptive institution into a committed and voluntaristic relationship, dependent for stability on internal resources rather than external props. The second theme is that while marriage is a personal relationship it is also a structure which harmonizes individual needs with the functional imperatives of society. Marriage provides for the socially necessary functions of legitimizing and socializing children, stabilizing adult personality and maintaining adult morale. The needs of the spouses are also harmonized via the sexual division of function, which creates interdependency and mutual reliance. Clear role specification is significant for psychological security, while role uncertainty is threatening to personalities, relationships, and ultimately to the social system. To both individual and social benefit, marriage affords a more or less optimal basis for finding identity, emotional and sexual satisfactions, and stable motivation.

The functionalist approach has been much criticized, in Britain most systematically by Morgan (1975), as static and overdetermined, and as failing to recognize both the complexity of marital patterns and the impact of social change on conjugal roles. Particular exception is taken by feminists to the assumptions about the fixity of the traditional division of labour, and antagonism to these assumptions has generated some research. Other criticisms concern the emphasis on harmony and stability, which is held to deflect attention from conflict and from gender differences in experience. Nevertheless, the approach has much relevance to research in Britain. It is the starting point for the research debate on conjugal roles described below, and it provides the impetus behind recent research emphasis on pluralism in marital form and functioning. Again, the functionalist emphasis on the family's crucial significance for child socialization, adult personality and social continuity implies that untoward consequences could be expected to flow from marital disruption. Departures from the model family form tend to be seen as deviations rather than variations (Chester 1977a), and they generate the kinds of anxiety and social concern which underlie some research on marital problems.

Conflict theories

There exists a cluster of approaches to marriage that revolve around conflict, bargaining and power. In such views, conflict inevitably arises in marriage, either from the spouses' differing perceptions, needs and goals or from their differential access to resources (Scanzoni 1979; Sprey 1979). Each partner therefore bargains in search of a favourable balance of costs and rewards, and the outcome is conditioned by power. The partner with the greatest control over mutually valued resources tends to acquire the most power in the marriage.

Approaches based on opposition, competition and inequality undoubtedly portray aspects of social reality, but they can also lead to a reductionist view of marriage, as when Leonard (1980) conceptualizes the conjugal bond as a mere labour relationship. Conflict approaches tend to present an over-rational view of human action, to underrate the subjective aspects of rewards and costs, and to ignore the possibility of mutual projects and non-conflictual differences. To see the marital relationship as consisting of metered exchanges is to miss the fact that it is also grounded in the emotional lives of the partners and the feelings which they invoke in each other, and a narrowly economistic view of resources underrates the significance of such factors as love and respect. Relevant here is some current research (described in Argyle et al. 1984) which is testing the theory that cognitive and deliberate action relates to middle-run and medium-scale patterns of interaction, while longer-run and global patterns are more compellingly shaped by affective processes.

Symbolic-interactionist approaches

Boundaries around theoretical orientations are hard to draw, but this heading refers to a further cluster of approaches which in their general form are conveniently discussed by Rock (1979), and which involve certain common tenets. Applied to marriage, the first of these is that understanding must be founded upon how married persons themselves define and interpret their actions and situations. Furthermore, while conformity to cultural prescription plays a part in marital behaviour, it does not determine the nature of marriage. Individuals always have scope for the exercise of preferences, and they have their own interpretations of norms and expectations, so that the nature of the marital relationship varies from couple to couple. Implicit here is the notion that marriage is a process, so that the relationship is formed and re-formed over time, within the flux of daily interaction, life experiences and developments in the spouses' conceptions of self and the couple. Contradictions may occur between the expectations and hopes of the two partners, or between marriage and other spheres of life, and while these may lead to conflict they do not necessarily do so because other ways of resolving them are available. The task of research is to capture and understand the subjective meanings which people accord to their marital experience and the values and imagery by which they evaluate and guide their married lives.

Some branches of this approach shade over into phenomenology, and it is convenient to note here the conceptualization of marriage presented by Berger and Kellner (1977). These authors argue that amongst the complex, rationalized and pluralistic structures of modern societies life may be experienced by individuals as atomized and without secure meaning. In the process of making sense of the world and achieving personal identity the private sphere of life assumes crucial significance, and marriage, as the central form of long-term intimate relationship, has become *par excellence* the setting in which the individual may find identity and a means to link past, present and future into a meaningful whole. Marriage is thus envisaged as a kind of continuing conversation by which the couple create a joint life world based on shared understandings. Berger and Kellner see this as an inherently precarious exercise, and they also recognize that there is in fact a dialectical relationship between the private sphere and the public world. However, the primacy which they give to subjective meanings results in overemphasis on the autonomy of private life (Morgan 1981),and this consideration has influenced some British research (e.g. Askham 1984; Burgoyne and Clark 1984; Hart 1976).

The developmental approach

This approach seeks to encompass the dynamic processes in the life of the family from courtship up to eventual dissolution, and the cycle of development is viewed as a routine succession of differentiated stages, each precipitated by a critical event, such as the birth of a child, or by a new phase in individual development. Each transition requires the accomplishment or reaccomplishment of developmental tasks, both by individual members and by the family group collectively. Transitions are not always made without conflict, indeed are sometimes experienced as crisis, and patterns of development at one stage may have significance for future stages. As the cycle proceeds the family acquires a history and a culture, shaped partly by personal factors and partly by circumstances. Within the overall approach there can be analysis at the subsystem level, for instance via the marital career (Aldous 1978).

In Britain, research has been informed less by full developmental theory than by the more restricted concept of the family life cycle. Rapoport et al. (1977) used the concept as an organizing principle in summarizing a wealth of material on the nature and course of marriage at various stages of the cycle (although much of this is American), and the same authors have studied discrete stages of the cycle (Rapoport R. 1963, 1964, 1967;

Rapoport, R. N. 1975; Rapoport and Rapoport 1965). Although not necessarily from within the same framework, other writers have studied particular transitions, such as from courtship to marriage (Leonard 1980; Mansfield 1982) or from married pair to parental couple (Clulow 1982; Simms and Smith 1982).

Despite its attractions as a means of comprehending the processual aspects of marriage, the developmental approach has certain weaknesses (Chester 1977b). One is the absence of a standard depiction of the family life cycle, which varies from having four stages to twenty-four in different versions, and another is that transitions are typically described as being triggered by child-related events, so that the implications of significant adult events are masked. Most importantly, perhaps, its picture of routine and predictable progression is misleading today, when large numbers of people progress not through *the* family life cycle but rather through a series of irregular and part cycles.

The private and the public

Although with varying emphasis, the orientations outlined above all recognize the family as simultaneously a bounded system in its own right and a part of the wider social structure, so that the private negotiation of marriage occurs within a framework of regulation and constraint. A pertinent understanding of marriage, therefore, must include an illumination of such constraints together with the ways in which couples overcome, avoid or adapt to them, and this theme has been addressed by a variety of researchers.

Some constraints are structural. In a pioneering study of stepfamilies, Burgoyne and Clark (1984) sought also to shed light on contemporary marriage in general, and they centred their analysis on the public/private issue. Many of the remarried couples wished to be seen as 'ordinary', but pursuit of this goal was conditioned by assumptions and definitions of marriage and the family which are built into legal and social provisions and the practices of agencies. The extent to which these could be gainsaid varied with the material and interpersonal resources of the couple, and questions concerning capacity to preserve privacy and autonomy apply equally to the generality of married couples. Circumstances arising in the world of work also affect marital patterns. Finch (1983), for instance, argues that the present structure of employment depends upon a particular kind of marriage relationship and household organization, and that this militates against the development of egalitarian marriage, whatever the wishes of the couple. There are also research findings concerning the influence on marriage of intermittent work-based absence of husbands (Clark et al. 1985; Cohen 1977; Frost 1975; King 1967; Morrice and Taylor 1978); the 'greediness' of particular occupations for time and resources (Edgell 1970, 1980; Finch 1983; Pahl and Pahl 1971; Young and Willmott 1973); special occupational characteristics (Banton 1964; Hollowell 1968; Noble 1970; Tunstall 1962); unemployment or redundancy (Fagin and Little 1984; Hakim 1982; Marsden and Duff 1975; Morris 1985); and dual-career patterns (Rapoport and Rapoport 1976). More generally, the size and stability of income from work influences the attainment of some domestic goals, and is related to financial relationships within marriage (Gray 1979; Pahl 1980) and to marital stability (Chester and Streather 1972; Thornes and Collard 1979). Recognition of the influence of public structures has led the Economic and Social Research Council (ESRC) to focus its proposed initiative on family research upon the interrelationships between domestic life, social policies and economic structures (ESRC 1984).

Public constraints on marriage are ideological as well as structural. In interpreting their experiences and reconstructing their lives, Burgoyne and Clark's remarried couples encountered strong social images and concepts of the family which actively shaped their arrangement and presentation of private life. Exploring the impact of a handicapped child, Voysey (1975) found the same projection of positive images by her couples as did Burgoyne and Clark by theirs, and she concluded that couples tend to stress aspects of experience which accord most closely with what they take to be normal, and play down aspects which may differentiate them from others. Similarly, Busfield and Paddon (1977) found that public ideologies of marriage and reproduction were potent in shaping family-building attitudes and behaviour. Askham (1984) broke new research ground by investigating the possibility that the process of creating a sense of stability in marriage may conflict with the creation of each partner's sense of personal identity. She concluded that such a conflict does exist but that most couples are skillful in maintaining a balance. More relevantly here, she also found that the constraints which people felt in marriage they attributed not to their spouse but to the fact of being married and the corollaries of this which they took for granted. Again, that is, people employed socially generated images of normal marriage in evaluating their own.

The relationship between the public and the private is not all one way, because private decisions and aspirations can affect public institutions. There is evidence, for instance, that the pursuit of expressive and affective satisfactions at home is for many workers a primary focus of economic striving, and that this affects their industrial attitudes (Goldthorpe et al. 1969). Again, 'private troubles' may become 'public issues' (Mills 1967) if the incidence of some disvalued behaviour such as divorce increases to a point where cherished social values seem threatened. Thus the personal experience of marriage breakdown, when aggregated, animates various kinds of moral entrepreneur, engages the energy of therapeutic experts, and evokes political and administrative action. Widespread divorce and other changed patterns of marital behaviour are consequential for tax and social security systems, legal arrangements, housing policy, personal social services and therapeutic agencies of various kinds. The size and nature of case-loads of service agencies reflect private decisions about whether and where to seek help with troubled marriage, and the process of becoming a client is channelled by social factors and public images (Brannen and Collard 1982).

For various reasons, therefore, research on this interplay between the inner and outer worlds is highly relevant to marital therapists. Much evidence suggests that older values and typifications concerning marriage are deeply rooted in individual consciousness, and these provide the images of normal marriage which influence attitudes and behaviour. If these are inappropriate to modern conditions in general, or to the conditions of particular couples or groups of couples, then there is ground for tension and confusion over marital expectations. Moreover, individuals have been differentially exposed to or affected by changing conceptions of marriage, and some therapeutic implications of this are indicated in research by Kiely (1984a, 1984b). According to this, some who present for marital therapy are emotionally mature and without individual personality problems, even if they initially show 'clinical' symptoms arising from their marriage troubles. Kiely's reasoning is that such couples often stand at different points on the continuum from traditional/institutional to modern/companionate conceptions of marriage, and their difficulties spring from incompatible role expectations rather than intrapsychic tribulations. The research showed that couples could be selected on this basis for a distinctive counselling approach and treated with success. Obviously, too much should not be made of a single study, but from wider evidence there are good reasons to suppose that recent research interest in the interrelationships between the private milieu and the public domain has potential benefit not only for social scientific understanding but for therapeutic practice, since therapeutic experts are significant mediators of moralities and images concerning the family.

Conjugal roles

Despite the points made above, the modern family is nevertheless considerably privatized in historical comparison. Viewing both the longer run (Shorter 1975; Stone 1977) and nineteenth-century developments (Anderson 1971; Hobsbawm 1977), historians describe a complex process of closure and separation which includes the rise of domesticity, intimacy and romantic love, the idealization of parenthood, and the eroticization of marriage. This process was sociologically summarized by Burgess and Locke (1953) as a shift in marriage from 'institution' to 'companionship', meaning from marriage as the enactment of culturally specified roles, with spouses having differentiated activities and associations, to marriage as a personal relationship involving shared activities, common interests and mutual association. This evolutionary theme is continued in research on the more recent period. Young and Willmott (1957) spoke of a 'great transformation' involving new kinds of companionship and equality, and later (1973) they saw marriage as becoming 'symmetrical'. Gorer (1971), in comparing data from 1951 and 1969, found an increase in companionship values, with a minimization of differences in temperament, functions and skills, while Rosser and Harris (1965) noted a recent 'marked change' in marital patterns. Such research contrasted older patterns with the new, but Bott (1957, rev.1971) shifted discussion from its evolutionary focus to examination of current variation in conjugal role patterns, and opened what is perhaps the most substantial debate in British research on marriage.

Bott distinguished two polar patterns of role relationship: *segregated*, where spouses have clearly demarcated roles, act relatively independently within their own spheres, and have more or less separate social lives; and *joint*, where domestic roles are not sharply distinctive, there is much collaborative decision making, and the couple operate socially as a pair. The distribution of these patterns, Bott believed, was mediated by the nature of the social networks in which couples were involved, close-knit and highly interconnected networks being associated with segregation and loose-knit networks with jointness.

Bott's study was seminal in stimulating research on marital roles, but findings have been diverse, and the accompanying debate has sometimes been confused. One part of this is methodological, since different researchers have taken an independent line in defining 'jointness', in choosing whether to study it via behaviour or attitudes or a mixture of these, in selecting which behaviour or attitudes to measure, and in methods of measurement. Such differences, together with measures which are anyway imprecise, mean that comparison of findings can be difficult and that contradictory findings sometimes may have a methodological source. Other research has shown that jointness is an overgross category, and that it may apply differentially in different aspects of the couple relationship (Harrell-Bond 1969; Platt 1969). Edgell (1972) claimed that there are cultural biases in some definitions of companionship, and that in some form it exists in most marriages. Some studies have found greater jointness amongst younger as against older couples, but because they are based on cross-sectional rather than longitudinal design it is unclear whether the findings represent generational differences or life cycle effects. Other studies have specifically sampled for couples in the child-rearing phase when, as Cohen (1977) observes, departures from symmetricality are particularly likely to occur. These methodological issues have not precluded useful research, but they do illustrate how cumulative research can be hampered.

A further source of confusion is social class. The categories joint and segregated are often taken to refer to middle-class and working-class patterns respectively, but this is not consistent with research findings. Bott herself did not see conjugal role patterns as directly determined by class, although she supposed that type of social network might be class-linked. In fact a segregated division of household labour has commonly been found amongst middle-class groups (e.g. Cohen 1977; Edgell 1980; Pahl and Pahl 1971;Robertson 1975), and companionate values have been found amongst the working class (Gorer 1971; Toomey 1971; Young and Willmott 1957, 1973). Bott's revised conclusion (1971) is that the segregated-role hypothesis continues to hold for cases of high network density, but that with loose-knit networks, in whatever class, role patterns are not predictable because couples have more latitude in adopting their own form of marital relationship. It should be noted that Bott's own study found in *all* families a basic division of labour by which husbands were the primary breadwinners and wives were responsible for child care and the home, so that, for her, jointness consisted of a variation on this theme rather than a major departure from it.

Perhaps the major confusion, however, stems from the conflation of concepts which in fact are analytically distinct. The literature contains a profusion of overlapping terms, such as jointness, sharing, companionship, partnership, closeness and equality, and of these, equality has proved the most troublesome. A common pattern of findings is that marriages exhibit intimacy, closeness, discussion, mutual sociability and some participation by husbands in housework and child care, but that this participation is markedly limited, and that basic domestic responsibility still falls to the wife. Some researchers therefore conclude that their evidence disproves the belief that modern marriage is *egalitarian* (e.g. Leonard 1980; Mansfield 1982; Oakley 1974; Pahl and Pahl 1971). This is to falsely assume, however, that jointness and equality are synonymous or entailed in each other, whereas really they are separate categories, as Edgell (1980) and Harris (1983) point out. Bott actually distinguishes the two, and observes that male authoritarianism is often confused with segregation. It seems possible that researchers may sometimes pick up this misidentification from their respondents. Even if men's domestic participation is circumscribed, the evidence is totally convincing that there is much home centredness, 'closeness', sharing and mutual sociability. Possibly in contrast with their parents' marriages, spouses sense these trends as tending towards egalitarian marriage, but they are not inconsistent with either the continued subordination of one partner or with the retention of one-sided responsibilities to the household. There is thus no necessary conflict in findings that men's actual domestic participation is disproportionately less than women's while couples nevertheless express norms of equality and sharing, or that men's domestic participation is greater than hitherto but that they remain dominant in marriage. According to Edgell (1980) and Harris (1983), the key to understanding this is the way in which domestic role relationships are articulated with the sexual division of labour in society.

On this analysis, a consequence of the historical separation of home from work was to assign men to the labour market while women were confined to the domestic sphere, with the dependency which this implies. This situation of dependency means that the woman's psychologically most salient roles, as wife and mother, are subject to determination and control by the husband, but he in turn finds that his providing role is determined by occupational exigencies. Work demands energy and time, and acceptance of hours and rhythms of attendance, geographical mobility etc. which have domestic significance. This is the private/public issue again, and, as noted earlier, there is research showing how home and work demands may be in rivalry. Any conflict must typically be resolved through accommodation by the wife because she is less situationally constrained than the husband, but such accommodation may require adjustment of marital expectations and aspirations. Any conflict between marital expectations and occupational demands is thus also a potential source of conflict between the spouses.

The wife may be content with domestic roles and an accommodative relationship, although equally there may be ambivalence or resentment concerning the erosion of wished-for marital standards. Where, however, the wife wishes for identities outside the home there is a different potential for conflict. To forgo external activities in deference to domestic obligations may cause a sense of constriction or unfulfilment, whereas to take employment may cause guilt and anxiety about domestic performance. There is a minority pattern of dual-career marriage, but according to Rapoport and Rapoport (1976) this creates dilemmas of overload, normative conflict, identity, social-network demands and role-cycling. The kind of demanding career implied in the concept is anyway unavailable to most women, making it unlikely that symmetricality of this kind could serve as a model with a social trickle-down effect as Young and Willmott (1973) seem to expect. On the evidence, wives more typically seek employment which is adapted to the primacy of their domestic responsibilities. Part-time work and underemployment in relation to capacity are common, and even at the very beginning of marriage wives tend to shape their occupational activities in relation to anticipated domestic arrangements (Mansfield 1982). Again the wife may be content, but any wish for more domestic relief or greater occupational involvement creates a potential for conflict.

What may be said in conclusion, on the basis of research on conjugal role relationships, is that couples commonly do find an accommodation and an interpretation of 'equality' which is acceptable to them (if not always to the sensibilities of researchers), but that the combination of contemporary marital expectations and values, the changing aspirations and opportunities of women, and the continuing occupational constraints on marital roles contains a disruptive potential which should be of interest to marital counsellors and therapists.

Marital problems

The notion of 'marital problems' is not without conceptual difficulties, because what is problematical can be defined only against some idea of what is normal. Concepts of 'normal' marriage are likely to contain unexamined cultural assumptions, so that marital problems are usually taken to consist of conditions or situations which threaten the stability of a marriage or the happiness of the partners. This may not be unreasonable, although the value implications should be noted – that marriage should be lasting, for instance, and that failure in this respect represents 'breakdown'. In practice, much research has been directed towards such issues as divorce, separation, lack of marital satisfaction etc., and the intention here is to sketch some of the topics which have received attention.

The incidence of troubled marriage   Some research has sought to quantify the extent of marital problems, and attempts to do this by exegesis of official statistics are exemplified and summarized in Chester (1972a, 1977c). Results show that there are procedural and conceptual difficulties in using routine statistics for this purpose, and that while divorce figures may offer a minimal measure they are unsatisfactory as an index of broader categories of troubled marriage. However, since projections indicate that one marriage in three may now end in divorce (Haskey 1982), and since to this must be added separated marriages and discordant but persisting marriages, it is evident that marital problems are widely experienced. This is confirmed by some limited and dated survey evidence from Pierce (1963) and Schofield (1973), who respectively reported 48 per cent and 64 per cent of couples as experiencing problems of some kind. Housing, money, and in-laws predominated over personal difficulties as a source of these, although 25 per cent of Schofield's respondents acknowledged problems of sexual adjustment.

Another approach to incidence, common in the USA but limited in Britain, is via measurement of marital satisfaction. Walker (1977) and Walker and Chester (1977) reported 8 per cent of women 'very dissatisfied' and 15 per cent 'a bit dissatisfied' with their marriage taken as a whole, but the figures were 50 per cent higher than these in ratings of particular dimensions of marriage such as companionship, confiding, and love and understanding. Dissatisfaction was thus concentrated on the expressive sphere, which is precisely where the modern emphasis in marriage lies (Gorer 1971). Elsewhere, Brown and Harris (1978) observed that 40 per cent of working-class wives with a child at home expressed either considerable dissatisfaction with marriage or notably little enthusiasm for it. Evidence on male marital satisfaction is even scarcer than that for women, but among graduate marriages Bailyn (1970) found only 55 per cent of cases where both spouses reported the marriage as happy. Thus, although the material is limited, the impression is repeated that many marriages experience difficulties of some sort.

Duration of marriage   Investigation of the time distribution of marital problems may assist in discovering periods of particular vulnerability and clues to causation. Statistics show that divorce is concentrated in the earlier years of marriage, but several studies have stressed the important difference between de facto and de jure length of marriage, and they show that actual breakup is significantly earlier than is revealed by divorce statistics (Chester

1971; Gibson 1980; Murphy 1984; Thornes and Collard 1979). Further data from Thornes and Collard confirm the vulnerability of the early years in a different respect. Of their divorced respondents, 37 per cent claimed that marital problems were manifest within one year of marriage, while 52 per cent said within two years, and 61 per cent within three years. Women claimed earlier recognition of onset than did men, and other data linked early onset with experience of premarital difficulties and with youthful marriage (especially where the bride was pregnant at marriage). However, early recognition did not lead to precipitate action, because typically there was a lengthy interval from onset to parting, just as there was from parting to divorce.

American marital satisfaction studies generally agree in finding a progressive temporal decline from an early peak, and limited British data confirm this (Walker 1977). The coincidence in time of peak marital satisfaction and peak breakup of marriage appears paradoxical, but Chester (1977b) argued that while most couples may experience their peak satisfaction at the beginning, there is also a substantial minority of marriages which are of dubious viability from the outset and which are soon aborted by divorce. Thereafter, divorce rates and satisfaction levels decline together because any disruptive push from decreasing satisfaction is countered by such factors as increasing interhabituation, pessimism over alternative futures, adjustment of expectations, alternative sources of satisfaction etc. Marital survivors are selected for other qualities besides marital satisfaction, including reluctance to divorce or separate, and this raises the unstudied issue of stable but low-satisfaction marriages, an area where research might prove profitable.

The developmental approach considers duration not as a simple time measure but as an index of family life cycle transitions and their implications for marital quality. Rapoport et al. (1977) should be consulted for an extended discussion and bibliography of relevant research findings, but note can be made here of their conclusions regarding the later developmental phases (parenting with adolescent children and the postparental phase). The authors find a potential here for strain, disenchantment and problems, because marital relationships may have become hollowed through decline in sexual relations, companionship and affection, and the partners may be facing different mid-life experiences. Reviewing similar material, Chester (1973) also concluded that many middle-aged marriages may be devitalized. However, Walker's data suggested some upturn in satisfaction levels at the postparental stage, and Rapoport and her colleagues noted a reconstructionist perspective in some research and were optimistic concerning the potentialities for revitalization in mature marriages. A cautious conclusion would be that middle-aged marriage is potentially subject to problems and low satisfaction, but that evidence on outcomes is neither plentiful nor consistent.

Age at marriage Statistics indicate an enhanced risk of divorce where brides are aged under 20, and a compounded enhancement where the husband is also a teenager (Leete 1979). Research evidence also links youthful marriage with very early breakup (Chester 1972b), early matrimonial proceedings before magistrates (McGregor et al. 1970), earlier decline in marital satisfaction (Walker 1977), earlier onset of perceived marital problems (Thornes and Collard 1979), and violence against both wives (Gayford 1975a) and children (Smith 1975). Counterfindings to this bleak picture are rare, but the meaning of such associations is uncertain because they do not necessarily demonstrate the causal influence of age per se. Some writers do accord direct significance to chronological age, referring to barriers to satisfying interaction created by emotional immaturity (Rutter and Madge 1976) and insecure identity (Hooper and Sheldon 1969), or to precocious marriage precipitated by stressful relationships with parents (Dominian 1968). Other authors, however, have been sceptical of youthful personality factors as primary explanations (e.g. Chester 1972a; Gibson 1974; Ineichen 1977).

Demographic statistics show that teenage brides tend to be of working-class origin and to have as husbands unskilled or semiskilled young workers. Such brides are also more likely to be pregnant at marriage (Gill et al. 1970; Ineichen 1977), and there is evidence of briefer courtship duration and less ritual preparation for marriage (Ineichen 1977; Thornes and Collard 1979). In consequence, youthful spouses experience financial disadvantage through low occupational skills, absence of asset-accumulation, and loss of the wife's earnings through early fertility (Ineichen 1977). Moreover, there is a high incidence of housing difficulties, showing in inferior accommodation (Ineichen 1979), shared accommodation and involuntary residential mobility (Thornes and Collard 1979), and homelessness (Glastonbury 1971). Over and above such material factors, there is American evidence that premarital pregnancy may be independently divorce-disposing (Bumpass and Sweet 1972). Youthful marriage is thus surrounded by a constellation of social-class, economic, housing, reproductive and marriage preparation factors, the effects and interactions of which have not been unravelled in respect of marital instability. It is for this reason that some researchers have reservations concerning the *intrinsic* influence of age at marriage.

Social class Since class is one of the commonest social research variables, the paucity of information on class patterns of discordant marriage is perhaps surprising. Official statistics do not report on divorce by social class, and the generally quoted view is derived from research by Gibson (1974), using the Registrar General's classification running from Class I (major professional and managerial occupations) to Class V (unskilled workers). This showed that Class I had the lowest divorce rate and Class V the highest, but the class gradient was not a smooth one because Class III (non-manual) had the second highest figure, so that clerical workers and similar grades had higher rates than both skilled and semiskilled manual workers. Explanations of this pattern have been attempted (e.g. Thornes and Collard 1979), but subsequent research suggests that Gibson's results may be misleading. Haskey (1984) and Murphy (1985) were each in different ways able to use more refined data and methods, and both found a more or less continuous upward gradient from Class I to Class V, with the latter having a particular excess of divorce. Other measures of marital problems accord with this picture, since an inverse class gradient has been found in respect of matrimonial proceedings before magistrates (McGregor et al. 1970) and marital dissatisfaction (Walker (1977).

Because social class summarizes so many social differences, the overall distribution is somewhat uninformative about how class membership is actually mediated in respect of marital problems. Some writers contend that social network type and specific occupational characteristics may be more relevant than gross class category (Noble 1970), while Thornes and Collard explored some aspects of material disadvantage, but it cannot be said that the mechanisms by which class membership influences the incidence and outcome of marital problems are well specified.

American research has investigated the implications for marital relationships of interclass marriage and lifetime social mobility, but British work is lacking here. The major modern study of social mobility (Goldthorpe 1980) dealt with kinship and sibling relations but not with the marriages of the male respondents. It is evident (Coleman 1977) that marriage in Britain is markedly homogamous by social class, although interclass marriage does obviously occur, and there is some anecdotal evidence that this may contain a potential for marital difficulty (e.g. Hart 1976). In general, however, there is little knowledge in these areas.

Children and marriage There is a substantial volume of research which bears in various ways on the impact of children (or the absence of children) on the quality and stability of marriage. However, the literature has recently been extensively reviewed elsewhere (Chester 1982), and it would be redundant here to do more than indicate the headings under which research exists. These are:

(1) the relationship between childlessness and divorce;
(2) the impact of both voluntary and involuntary childlessness on the quality and nature of the marital relationship;
(3) the relationship between the presence of children and levels of marital satisfaction over the marital career;
(4) the impact of the transition to parenthood on the quality of marriage.

The amount of research under these headings is variable, and its nature permits of few firm conclusions. However, review suggests that empirical research in many cases fails to confirm, or even contradicts, ideas about children, marriage and marital problems which are widely held both in popular and professional circles.

A significant research finding which postdates the review mentioned above is provided by Murphy (1984). Chester concluded that those views were mistaken which asserted a positive association between childlessness and propensity to divorce, because other research showed them to be based on procedural defects and fallacious reasoning. This may be so, but using new data from the General Household survey, and more appropriate procedures than were available to previous authors, Murphy now shows that an enhanced propensity to divorce is indeed associated with childless couples, although it is also associated with above-average fertility. To quote his conclusion, '. . . the well-spaced two-child family is seen to have a lower risk of breakdown than either childless or large-family couples' (p. 498). However, this still leaves open the question of mediation, and it may be that having a 'well-spaced two-child family' is not directly causal but itself an index of other qualities which are relevant to marital stability.

Violence in marriage In 1975 the Parliamentary Select Committee on Violence in Marriage complained that its inquiry was handicapped by what it called a remarkable paucity of information. The literature which has developed since then is scarcely prodigious, but there are two collections of papers which summarize extant knowledge from various disciplinary perspectives (Borland 1976; Martin 1978), and more unified reviews of evidence and conceptualizations are provided by Freeman (1979) and Dobash and Dobash (1979).

Estimates of the incidence of violence have varied wildly, and research on this is bedevilled by definitional and other problems (Borkowski et al. 1983), although it may safely be concluded that real incidence exceeds observed incidence, possibly by a considerable factor. Some researchers have studied the nature of assaults and injuries in search of analytical implications (Dewsbury 1975; Dobash and Dobash 1979; Fonseka 1974; Gayford 1975a, 1975b; Marsden and Owens 1975), and most of these also attend to the sources of conflict out of which violence may arise.

With regard to explanatory analysis, the literature exhibits a number of distinct although sometimes overlapping approaches. Some studies are oriented towards pathology, and emphasize the qualities of the assaulting husband, the victim wife and/or the nature of their interaction (e.g. Faulk 1974; Gayford 1975a, 1975b; Levine 1975). Other approaches, while not necessarily ignoring such factors, focus equally or more on structural aspects of the social environment (e.g. Dobash and Dobash 1979). There is also a radical approach which rejects the focus on individuals, on the grounds that this unduly constricts the concept of violence, ignores the structures in which violence is embedded, and fails to grapple with why the flow of violence is towards women. On this view research should centre not on the spouses but on the forces which generate and sustain female subordination, and on the part played by force and threat in maintaining male authority (e.g. Hanmer 1978). Such an approach may also subsume marital violence into a more general conspectus of physical, mental and symbolic violence against women (e.g. Wilson 1983). It will be evident that this is an area where research may be heavily politicized, although this may not be detrimental if controversy generates additional or alternative perspectives on an issue which most authorities concede to be not really understood.

Conclusion

Other topics of research

The discussion above is not exhaustive of British research relevant to marriage, although it includes the main topics covered by work which takes marriage as its primary focus. However, there is a further range of work, mostly clinical in origin, which considers various aspects of ill health, handicap or disorder in relation to marriage – work, that is, which is motivated as much or more by interest in the condition concerned as by interest in marriage per se. The literature is too scattered and diverse for review here, but some of its headings may be noted. One of these is psychopathology and marriage, with an emphasis on neurosis and personality disorder rather than psychosis, and prominent attention to the phenomenon of conjoint psychiatric disorder of the spouses. Psychiatry has also provided the framework for most research on alcoholism and marriage. Handicap has been another focus of research, in respect both of the marriage of mentally or physically handicapped people and of the impact on parental marriage of a handicapped child. There has also been limited attention to marriage in relation to chronic and critical medical conditions. A general comment which may be made on work of this kind is that it is prone to be insulated from research on marriage in the social sciences.

Emergent issues

Contemporary social conditions have brought to the fore several issues which must increasingly be attended to in the sphere of research on marriage: cohabitation, remarriage, and ethnicity.

Cohabitation There is some information on the extent of cohabitation (summarized by Kiernan 1983), but no research reports have yet appeared. Sufficient is known to indicate that cohabitation is a complex and heterogeneous form of behaviour, and it is likely that research will find differentiation of relationships according to whether cohabitation is before marriage, between marriages, or an alternative to marriage. More generally, since cohabiting unions are marriagelike relationships which are growing in frequency and social legitimacy they will have to be incorporated into the agenda of marriage research if a significant aspect of contemporary behaviour is not to be missed.

Remarriage Rising divorce rates have meant a great increase in remarriage, so that one marriage in three now occurring is a second or subsequent union for at least one of the partners. Research has begun to appear (e.g. Burgoyne and Clark 1984; Clark 1982) from which it is evident that there are differentiated patterns and that the dynamics of remarriage differ in important ways from those of first marriage. As with cohabitation, there is a need for marriage research to pay heed to a newly significant form of relationship.

Ethnicity It is a commonplace that Britain is now a multiracial society, but so far there has been no large volume of research either on interethnic marriage or on marriage within the various ethnic minority groups. There is literature on the family, but this relates more to kinship and intergenerational relations than to marriage. From the viewpoint of marital therapy as well as others there is a need for research on ethnicity and marriage, and it is important that this should respond to the true diversity of ethnic groups rather than to gross categories such as 'Asian' or 'Afro-Caribbean'.

Coda

Therapeutic utility is not the only justification for research on marriage, but it is an important one, and to be effective in work with clients, practitioners need access to the kind of knowledge which research can provide. From this review it will be evident that marriage research in Britain is not without substance, but that much remains to be done, in volume, in coverage, and in the development of a coherent and comprehensive body of knowledge. In making such advances a major contribution could come from greater communication and collaboration between the research and the therapeutic communities, both to inform research with practitioner needs and perspectives and to enable research results to have practical effect.

References

Aldous, J. (1978) *Family careers: developmental changes in families.* New York: Wiley.

Anderson, M. (1971) *Family structure in nineteenth century Lancashire.* London: Cambridge University Press.

Argyle, M., Clarke, D. and Collett, P. (1984) The psychology of long-term relationships. *Fourth annual report to ESRC: September 1983–August 1984.* Mimeo.

Askham J. (1984) *Identity and stability in marriage.* London: Cambridge University Press.

Bailyn, L. (1970) Career and family orientations of husbands and wives in relation to marital happiness. *Human Relations, 23(12),* 97–113.

Banton, M. (1964) *The policeman in the community.* London: Tavistock.

Baum, F. (1982) Voluntary childless marriages. *International Journal of Sociology and Social Policy, 2(3),* 40–54.

Berger, P. L. and Berger B. (1984) *The war over the family: capturing the middle ground.* Harmondsworth: Penguin.

Berger, P. L. and Kellner, H. (1977) Marriage and the construction of reality. In P. L. Berger *Facing up to modernity*. Harmondsworth: Penguin.

Borkowski, M., Murch, M. and Walker, V. (1983) *Marital violence: the community response*. London: Tavistock.

Borland, M. (ed.) (1976) *Violence in the family*. Manchester: Manchester University Press.

Bott, E. (1957, rev. 1971) *Family and social network*. London: Tavistock.

Brannen, J. and Collard, J. (1982) *Marriages in trouble: the process of seeking help*. London: Tavistock.

Brown, G. W. and Harris, T. (1978) *The social origins of depression: a study of psychiatric disorder in women*. London: Tavistock.

Bumpas, L. L. and Sweet, J. A. (1972) Differentials in marital stability. *American Sociological Review, 37(6)*, 754–766.

Burgess, E. W. and Locke, H. J. (2nd edn. 1953) *The family: from institution to companionship*. New York: American Book Co.

Burgoyne, J. and Clark, D. (1984) *Making a go of it: a study of stepfamilies in Sheffield*. London: Routledge and Kegan Paul.

Busfield, J. and Paddon, M. (1977) *Thinking about children: sociology and fertility in post-war England*. London: Cambridge University Press.

Chester, R. (1971) The duration of marriage to divorce. *British Journal of Sociology, 22(2)*, 172–182.

Chester, R. (1972a) Current incidence and trends in marital breakdown. *Postgraduate Medical Journal, 48*(Sept), 529–541.

Chester, R. (1972b) Some characteristics of marriages of brief duration. *Medical Gynaecology and Sociology, 6(3)*, 9–12.

Chester, R. (1973) Marital satisfaction and stability in the postparental years. *Marriage Guidance, 14(11)*, 338–348.

Chester, R. (1977a) The one-parent family: deviant or variant. *In* R. Chester and J. Peel (eds) *Equalities and inequalities in family life*. London: Academic Press.

Chester, R. (1977b) Divorce and the family life cycle in Great Britain. *In* J. Cuisenier (ed.) *The family life cycle in European societies*. The Hague: Mouton.

Chester, R. (ed.) (1977c) *Divorce in Europe*. Leiden: Martinus Nijhoff.

Chester, R. (1982) Children and marital problems. *International Journal of Sociology and Social Policy, 2(3)*, 5–27.

Chester, R. (1983) *Research on the family*. A report to the Social Affairs Committee of the Economic and Social Research Council. Mimeo.

Chester, R. with McGlaughlin, A., and Pashley, B. (1984) *The family: a register of research in the United Kingdom*. London: Economic and Social Research Council.

Chester, R. and Streather, J. (1972) Cruelty in English divorce: some empirical findings. *Journal of Marriage and the Family, 34(4)*, 706–712.

Clark, D. (1982) Restarting a family: having children in second families. *International Journal of Sociology and Social Policy, 2(3)*, 55–68.

Clark, D., McCann, K., Morrice, K. and Taylor R. (1985) Work and marriage in the offshore oil industry. *International Journal of Social Economics 12(2)*, 36–48.

Clulow, C. F. (1982) *To have and to hold: the first baby and preparing couples for parenthood.* Aberdeen: Aberdeen University Press.

Cohen, G. (1977) Absentee husbands in spiralist families. *Journal of Marriage and the Family, 39(3)*, 595–604.

Coleman, D. A. (1977) Assortative mating in Britain. *In* R. Chester and J. Peel (eds) *Equalities and inequalities in family life.* London: Academic Press.

Cooper, D. (1972) *The death of the family.* Harmondsworth: Penguin.

Dewsbury, A. R. (1975) Family violence seen in general practice. *Royal Society of Health Journal, 95*, 290.

Dobash, R. and Dobash, R. (1979) *Violence against wives: a case against the patriarchy.* New York: The Free Press.

Dominian, J. (1968) *Marital breakdown.* Harmondsworth: Penguin.

Economic and Social Research Council (1984) Information Sheet I 4/84, June.

Edgell, S. (1970) Spiralists: their careers and family lives. *British Journal of Sociology, 21(3)*, 314–323.

Edgell, S. (1972) Marriage and the concept companionship. *British Journal of Sociology, 23(4)*, 452–461.

Edgell, S. (1980) *Middle-class couples: a study of segregation, domination and inequality in marriage.* London: George Allen and Unwin.

Fagin, L. and Little, M. (1984) *The forsaken families: the effects of unemployment on contemporary British life.* Harmondsworth: Penguin.

Faulk, M. (1974) Men who assault their wives. *Medicine, Science and the Law, 14*, 180–183.

Finch, J. (1983) *Married to the job: wives' incorporation in men's work.* London: George Allen and Unwin.

Fonseka, S. (1974) A study of wife beating in the Camberwell area. *British Journal of Clinical Practice, 28*, 400–402.

Freeman, M. D. A. (1979) *Violence in the home.* Westmead, Farnborough: Saxon House.

Frost, P. (1975) The work on a rig. *New Society, 32*, 701.

Gale, A. and Jolly, C. (1982) Introduction: Ecological studies of family life. In *Papers presented at a symposium during the annual conference of the British Psychological Society.* Mimeo.

Gayford, J. J. (1975a) Wife battering: a preliminary survey of 100 cases. *British Medical Journal, i*, 194–197.

Gayford, J. J. (1975b) Battered wives. *Medicine, Science and the Law, 15*, 237–245.

Gibson, C. (1974) The association between divorce and social class in England and Wales. *British Journal of Sociology, 25(1)*, 79–93.

Gibson, C. (1980) Childlessness and marital instability: a re-examination of the evidence. *Journal of Biosocial Science, 12(2)*, 121–132.

Gill, D. G., Illsley, R. and Hoplick, L. H. (1970) Pregnancy in teenage girls. *Social Science and Medicine, 3(4),* 549–574.

Glastonbury, B. (1971) *Homeless near a thousand homes.* London: George Allen and Unwin.

Goldthorpe, J. H. (1980) *Social mobility and class structure in modern Britain.* Oxford: Oxford University Press.

Goldthorpe, J. H., Lockwood, D., Bechhofer, F. and Platt, J. (1969) *The affluent worker in the class structure.* London: Cambridge University Press.

Gorer, G. (1971) *Sex and marriage in England today.* London: Nelson.

Gray, A. (1979) The working class family as an economic unit. *In* C. C. Harris (ed.) *The sociology of the family: new directions for Britian.* Sociological Review Monograph No. 28.

Hakim, C. (1982) The social consequences of high unemployment. *Journal of Social Policy, 11(4),* 433–467.

Hanmer, J. (1978) Violence and the social control of women. *In* G. Littlejohn et al. (eds) *Power and the state.* London: Croom Helm.

Harrell-Bond, B. (1969) Conjugal role behaviour. *Human Relations, 22,* 77–91.

Harris, C. C. (1983) *The family and industrial society.* London: George Allen and Unwin.

Hart, N. (1976) *When marriage ends: a study in status passage.* London: Tavistock.

Haskey, J. (1982) The proportion of marriages ending in divorce. *Population Trends, 27,* 4–7.

Haskey, J. (1984) Social class and socio-economic differentials in divorce in England and Wales. *Population Studies, 38(3),* 419–438.

Hobsbawm, E. J. (1977) *The age of capital.* London: Abacus.

Hollowell, P. G. (1968) *The lorry driver.* London: Routledge and Kegan Paul.

Hooper, D. and Sheldon, A. (1969) Evaluating newly-married couples. *British Journal of Social and Clinical Psychology, 8(2),* 169–182.

Ineichen, B. (1977) Youthful marriage: the vortex of disadvantage. *In* R. Chester and J. Peel (eds) *Equalities and inequalities in family life.* London: Academic Press.

Ineichen, B. (1979) Housing factors in the timing of weddings and first pregnancies. *In* C. C. Harris (ed.) *The sociology of the family: new directions for Britain.* Sociological Review Monograph No. 28.

Kiely, G. M. (1984a) Social change and marital problems: implications for marriage counselling. *British Journal of Guidance and Counselling, 12(1),* 92–100.

Kiely, G. M. (1984b) *Finding love in marriage.* Dublin: Turoe Press.

Kiernan, K. E. (1983) The structure of families today: continuity or change. *In* Office of Population Censuses and Surveys Occasional Paper No. 31, *The family.* London: HMSO.

King, E. (1967) Resident hospital doctors' families. *Lancet, i,* 559–560.

Laing, R. D. (1967) *Politics of experience and the bird of paradise.* Harmondsworth: Penguin.

Laing, R. D. (1971) *The politics of the family and other essays*. London: Tavistock.

Leach, E. (1968) *A runaway world*. London: BBC Publications.

Leete, R. (1979) *Changing patterns of family formation and dissolution 1964–1976*. Studies on Medical and Population Subjects No. 39. London: HMSO.

Leonard, D. (1980) *Sex and generation: a study of courtship and weddings*. London: Tavistock.

Levine, M. B. (1975) Interparental violence and its effects on the children: a study of 50 families in general practice. *Medicine, Science and the Law, 15*, 172–176.

Mansfield, P. (1982) A portrait of contemporary marriage: equal partners or just good companions? *In* National Marriage Guidance Council, *Change in marriage*. Rugby: NMGC.

Marsden, D. and Duff, E. (1975) *Workless: some unemployed men and their families*. Harmondsworth: Penguin.

Marsden, D. and Owens, D. (1975) The Jekyll and Hyde marriages. *New Society, 32*, 333–335.

Martin, J. P. (ed.) (1978) *Violence and the family*. Chichester: Wiley.

McGregor, O. R., Blom-Cooper, L. and Gibson, C. (1970) *Separated spouses: a study of the matrimonial jurisdiction of magistrates' courts*. London: Duckworth.

Mills, C. W. (1967) *The sociological imagination*. London: Oxford University Press.

Morgan, D. H. J. (1975) *Social theory and the family*. London: Routledge and Kegan Paul.

Morgan, D. H. J. (1977) Alternatives to the family. *In* R. Chester and J. Peel (eds) *Equalities and inequalities in family life*. London: Academic Press.

Morgan, D. H. J. (1981) *Berger and Kellner's construction of reality*. Occasional Paper No. 7, Department of Sociology, University of Manchester.

Morrice, J. K. W. and Taylor, R. C. (1978) The intermittent husband syndrome. *New Society, 43*, 12.

Morris, L. (1985) Responses to redundancy: labour-market experience, domestic organisation and male social networks. *International Journal of Social Economics 12(2)*, 5–17.

Murphy, M. (1984) Fertility, birth-timing and marital breakdown: a reconsideration of the evidence. *Journal of Biosocial Science, 16(4)*, 487–500.

Murphy, M. J. (1985) Marital breakdown and socio-economic status: a re-appraisal of the evidence from recent British sources. *British Journal of Sociology 36(1)*, 81–93.

Noble, T. (1970) Family breakdown and social networks. *British Journal of Sociology, 21(2)*, 135–150.

Oakley, A. (1974) *The sociology of housework*. London: Martin Robertson.

Orford, J. and Edwards, G. (1977) *Alcoholism*. Institute of Psychiatry Maudsley Monographs No. 26. Oxford: Oxford University Press.

Pahl, J. (1980) Patterns of money management within marriage. *Journal of Social Policy, 9(5)*, 313–335.

Pahl, J. M. and Pahl, R. E. (1971) *Managers and their wives*. London: Allen Lane.
Parsons, T. (1943) The kinship system of the contemporary United States. *In* T. Parsons (ed.) *Essays in sociological theory*. New York: The Free Press.
Parsons, T. (1964) *The social system*. London: Routledge and Kegan Paul.
Parsons, T. and Bales, R. F. (1956) *Family: Socialisation and interaction process*. London: Routledge and Kegan Paul.
Pierce, R. M. (1963) Marriage in the fifties. *Sociological Review, 11(2)*, 215–240.
Platt, J. (1969) Some problems in measuring the jointness of conjugal role relationships. *Sociology, 3*, 287–297.
Rapoport, R. (1963) Normal crises, family structure and mental health. *Family Process, 2(1)*, 68–80.
Rapoport, R. (1964). The transition from engagement to marriage. *Acta Sociologica, 8*, 36–55.
Rapoport, R. (1967) The study of marriage as a critical transition for personality and family development. *In* P. Lomas (ed.) *The predicament of the family*. London: Hogarth Press.
Rapoport, R. N. (1975) Home and school at the launch: some preliminary observations. *Oxford Review of Education, 1(3)*, 277–286.
Rapoport, R. and Rapoport, R. N. (1965) Work and family in contemporary society. *American Sociological Review, 30*, 381–394.
Rapoport, R. and Rapoport, R. N. (1976) *Dual career families re-assessed*. London: Martin Robertson.
Rapoport, R., Rapoport, R. N. and Strelitz, Z. (1977) *Fathers, mothers and others*. London: Routledge and Kegan Paul.
Reynolds, S. (1982) Participant observation in families. In *Papers presented at a symposium during the annual conference of the British Psychological Society*. Mimeo.
Robertson, F. (1975) *Work and the conjugal family*. Unpublished Ph.D. thesis, University of Edinburgh.
Rock, P. (1979) *The making of symbolic interactionism*. London: Macmillan.
Rosser, C. and Harris, C. (1965) *The family and social change*. London: Routledge and Kegan Paul.
Rutter, M. and Madge, N. (1976) *Cycles of disadvantage*. London: Heinemann.
Scanzoni, J. (1979) Social processes and power in families. *In* W. Burr et al. (eds) *Contemporary theories about the family*. New York: The Free Press.
Schofield, M. (1973) *The sexual behaviour of young adults*. London: Allen Lane.
Segal, L. (1983) *What is to be done about the family*. Harmondsworth: Penguin.
Shorter, E. (1975) *The making of the modern family*. London: Collins.
Simms, M. and Smith, C. (1982) Young fathers: attitudes to marriage and family life. *In* L. McKee and M. O'Brien (eds) *The father figure*. London: Tavistock.
Skolnik, A. (1973) *The intimate environment*. Boston: Little, Brown and Co.
Smith, S. M. (1975) *The battered child syndrome*. London: Butterworth.
Society of Conservative Lawyers (1981) *The future of marriage*. London: Conservative Political Centre.

Sprey, J. (1979) Conflict theory and the study of marriage and the family. *In* W. Burr et al. (eds) *Contemporary theories about the family*. New York: The Free Press.

Stone, L. (1977) *The family, sex and marriage in England 1500–1800*. London: Weidenfeld and Nicolson.

Study Commission on the Family (1980)*Happy families*. London.

Study Commission on the Family (1982) *Values and the changing family*. London.

Study Commission on the Family (1983) *Families in the future*. London.

Thornes, B. and Collard, J. (1979) *Who divorces?* London: Routledge and Kegan Paul.

Toomey, D. M. (1971) Conjugal roles and social networks in an urban working-class sample. *Human Relations, 24,* 417–431.

Tunstall, J. (1962) *The fishermen*. London: McGibbon and Kee.

Vetere, A. (1982) Ethical problems in research with families. In *Papers presented at a symposium during the annual conference of the British Psychological Society*. Mimeo.

Voysey, M. (1975) *A constant burden*. London: Routledge and Kegan Paul.

Walker, C. (1977) Some variations in marital satisfaction. *In* R. Chester and J. Peel (eds) *Equalities and inequalities in family life*. London: Academic Press.

Walker, C. and Chester, R. (1977) Marital satisfaction amongst British wives. *Marriage Guidance, 17(1),* 219–227.

Wilson, E. (1983) *What is to be done about violence against women*. Harmondsworth: Penguin.

Working Party on Marriage Guidance (1979) *Marriage matters*. London: HMSO.

Young, M. and Willmott, P. (1957) *Family and kinship in East London*. London: Routledge and Kegan Paul.

Young, M. and Willmott, P. (1973) *The symmetrical family: a study of work and leisure in the London region*. London: Routledge and Kegan Paul.

CHAPTER TWO Values in Marriage
Change and Continuity
Jack Dominian

Historical introduction

The pattern of marriage which we have inherited and which will be discussed in this chapter is an expression of the Judaeo-Christian heritage of Western society. Much of the current debate about values in marriage is taking place in our post-Christian civilization, but their roots lie in the unfolding history of Christian marriage over nearly two thousand years. This is not to say that marriage did not exist throughout the world, but the particular issues we are facing today in Britain and the West depend on an understanding of this history. Its beginnings can be traced to Genesis, the first book of the Bible, written some three thousand years ago.

There we find that man and woman were created in the image of God and were meant to have a personal relationship for the purposes of procreation and companionship (Genesis 1 and 2). Given the later attitude of Christian thought, it is worth noting that the reaction of the Jews to sexuality was positive and the Song of Songs is a beautiful description of erotic love. However, sex was primarily for procreation. An abundance of children, particularly boys, was a blessing, and sterility was considered a curse from God. Above all, the history of the Old Testament was one that placed marriage within a context of something that was sacred and holy because it took place between people who acknowledged God as the creator of their union and fruitfulness. Despite this, divorce was permitted, but it was not approved and the ideal of indissolubility remained (Malachi 2: xiv).

The advent of Christianity can truly be said to have started with Paul, whose letters were the earliest documents of the New Testament. Paul introduced a mixture of attitudes. On the one hand he confirmed that marriage is good and holy; on the other he took an ambivalent position on sex and declared that he would like everyone to be single like him (1 Corinthians 7: vii). Paul also confirmed Christ's repudiation of divorce, one of the most basic teachings of Christianity. Thus, at the end of the first century, marriage was an essential part of Christian life and was considered a permanent institution for the sake of children. The Jewish principle of the essential goodness of sex was still influential.

During the next five centuries we see one of the momentous shifts in values and attitudes, namely the gradual degradation of sexuality and with it the devaluation of women, who were considered to be man's seducers and therefore potentially dangerous and evil. The adverse impact on sexuality continued till this century, and it is only now that a basic revaluation is occurring. What caused this profound transformation in the early centuries?

There is no clear answer, but at least three factors can be cited. The first was internal to Christianity: the mother of God was described as a virgin and this, coupled with the advocacy of the single state, made celibacy a virtue. The other two factors were external. One was the presence of Manicheism as an adjacent religion which competed with and influenced Christianity: Manicheism held that the body was evil, trapped the soul and therefore intercourse which resulted in continuation of this situation was evil also. The other was the impact of Stoicism in Hellenic thought. This philosophy advocated intellectual tranquillity and contemplation as the highest achievement of man, giving him an inner peace called ataraxia. This peace was shattered by the disturbance of sex which therefore was to be deprecated.

These three reasons are greatly simplified but between them they explain, at least partially, the growing hostility towards sexual intercourse manifested by the early theologians of the Church which culminated in the utterances of St Augustine. Augustine is easily the most influential figure in the history of marriage. He wrote a treatise on the subject which has left its indelible mark to this very day. Augustine summarized the purpose of marriage in three words – children, fidelity and permanency. Marriage was for children, based on an infrastructure of permanency and mutual fidelity. The avoidance of children, particularly through contraception, adultery and divorce, was a heinous sin, and the impact of this thought has governed moral standards in Western society ever since. Furthermore, sex was deprecated and was only legitimate, that is free of serious sin, when used for the intention of procreation. The idea of enjoying the experience for its own sake or using it for the sake of mutual love was utterly incomprehensible and these concepts were only to be redeveloped in recent times. The Church has, over time, slightly softened its attitude to sex, but never by any substantial degree, and the sex/guilt connection is certainly at least partially a powerful Christian influence.

There were no major changes in Christian thought between the sixth and eleventh centuries and then there followed five centuries of intense deliberation in the Mediaeval Church on this topic. The details are extensive and exhaustive but the principal result was a change in the theological status of marriage. It now became a Sacrament and therefore all its characteristics were drawn further towards the concept that it represented something divine; in strict theological terms, that it was a source of grace.

This view of marriage was a point of division between the Roman Catholic Church and Protestantism, the former accepting the Sacramental nature of marriage while the latter did not. But the gulf between the two is being reduced today.

The sixteenth century, which saw the rise of the divided Church, saw also the beginnings of the secular thinking about life and marriage with which we live today. Books like *The world we have lost* (Laslett 1971), *Household and family in past time* (Laslett 1972), *The making of the modern family* (Shorter 1976), *The family, sex and marriage in England 1500–1800* (Stone 1977) are beginning to unravel the history of marriage in the last three to four hundred years. Of the many changes that have occurred, three are important. The first is the gradual emergence of secular thought which has questioned the religious absolutes of the past. The second is the diminishing impact of parents and the community upon the choice of spouses which is left increasingly in the hands of the partners. The third is an extension of the second, namely the diminution of the concept of marriage as an institution for external purposes, such as children, heritage, economic reasons, political and social alliances, and an increasing emphasis on the fulfilment of the individual. This ideology has come of age in our times but its roots are deep. Stone (1977) calls it 'affective individualism', and he summarizes what he means in this way:

> In the 16th century and earlier, the standard world view was that all individuals in society are bound together in the Great Chain of Being, and are all interchangeable with each other. One wife or one child could substitute for another, like soldiers in any army. The purpose in life was to assume the continuity of the family, the clan, the village or the State not to maximise the well being of the individual...
>
> The second view, which developed in the 16th and 17th centuries, was that each individual thinks of himself as unique and strives to impose his own will on others for his selfish ends...
>
> The third view, which developed in the late 17th century and early 18th century, was that all human beings are unique. It is right and proper for each to pursue his own happiness, provided that he also respects the rights of others to pursue theirs... (pp. 257–258).

This gradual development of individualism has found its most concrete expression in the twentieth century, during which several movements have been gathering momentum. These include the emancipation of women, the pursuit of happiness by both men and women, with greater emphasis on divorce, and the commitment of women to work rather than to stay at home or to take exclusive care of children. At one end of the scale all these changes evoke a cry of selfishness, and at the other the fulfilment of the potential of the individual is seen as something essentially good. The conflict between these competing priorities is at the very heart of the present discussion of changing values.

More specifically during this century the following have had a major impact on the fundamentals of marriage: (1) the widespread advent of contraception with its impact on the size of the family; (2) the increasing rate of divorce; and (3) the liberation of sexuality. All of these have important implications for values and will be considered in this chapter.

Perhaps the single most important change in marriage, which has been occurring in the last thirty years, is the change in the character of marriage itself. This change has been described as a shift from institutional to companionship type (Hicks and Platt 1970). The institutional variety has been described as the traditional one in which spouses have clearly delineated roles. The husband goes out to work and is the provider. He has external responsibilities vis-à-vis the rest of the world in paying the bills, taking the initiative, and dealing with crisis. He is the source of authority and the head of the household. The wife is the childbearer, the caretaker of the children, the manager of the house and the person who ensures the affective integration of the family. In this type of marriage the husband has instrumental responsibilities and the wife procreative and affective ones. Provided they each fulfil their role, the marriage is considered to be a good one.

The companionship variety is different. Now the emphasis is on intimacy, communication, sharing, expressing feelings, equity and mutual decision making. This is not to say that some of the institutional characteristics are not present: for example the husband is expected to be a provider when the wife withdraws from work and has young children. But the emphasis is on the personal and the affective. Equally, the change does not mean that affective elements were not present in the institutional variety. But the difference there was that, although love was welcomed when present, it was not considered essential and the marriage could proceed in its absence. Today, the absence of love or happiness is considered to be a ground for dissolution, for the shift towards companionship has also brought about what are described as increasing expectations of marriage.

These expectations are connected with the understanding of love in marriage. Men and women are increasingly judging the viability of their marriage by the absence or presence of love. They often use the word, though not always. What they do is point to the absence of loving feelings, of expressions of affection and sex, of mutual socialization, and to their alienation over intellectual and spiritual goals. In fact, these five dimensions, the social, emotional, physical, intellectual and spiritual, form the basic framework on which marital relationship rests (Dominian 1980).

Whatever the changing character of marriage, its three main features enumerated by Augustine remain its foundations, namely children, fidelity and permanency. Augustine took it for granted that women were meant to be solely mothers. The modern evolution of women has changed this thinking and so the status of women has become an essential fourth feature.

Women

There is little doubt that the status of women has changed considerably for the better in the last hundred years, but particularly in the last fifty years. Changes in education, employment, autonomy and contraception have advanced the position of women considerably. There is a vast literature to document all these changes.

One key feature in women's emancipation has been their increased employment in work which is independent from that of their husbands in the labour market. The percentage of married women in the labour force rose between 1951 and 1971 from 40 per cent to 64 per cent. Married women's employment shows a sharp fall immediately after marriage which is accounted for by childbearing, stabilizes around five to seven years' duration of marriage, and then increases progressively later on (Briton 1975). On a broader front, in 1921 only one in three of the labour force were female and the majority were not married. In 1979 two in five were female and of these a quarter were married (Rimmer and Popay 1982). Of course, since 1979 there has been increasing unemployment and women have suffered as well as men.

What is the impact of this increased employment on marriage? The combined income of spouses has undoubtedly meant greater material standards and at times of hardship, if the husband is unemployed, the wife's salary may keep the home going. The wife's economic independence gives her a greater status vis-à-vis her husband, and her contact with the outside world offers the possibility of friendship, stimulation and a growth in self-esteem which undoubtedly can enhance the quality of marriage. When the marriage is in difficulties, the wife's income means that she is not totally dependent on her husband for survival and, if she wants to leave, she may be able to survive economically.

The objections which have been raised about a woman working relate to her availability to her children. Many people still believe that young children under school age should have their mother with them. In fact the majority of women give up work when their children are young. Only 6 per cent of those with preschool children work full-time.

Mention has already been made of the shift towards companionship marriage. Does this mean that men have accepted an equal responsibility for childcare and housework? The overwhelming evidence suggests that, whilst husbands do more, they still consider their wives primarily responsible for these activities. This continuity of expectation on the part of the husbands puts heavy burdens of tiredness on women and certainly contributes to marital stress.

Nevertheless, the changes in the position of women have undoubtedly meant alterations in the man–woman relationship in marriage. This is now an encounter between people with greater educational, financial and social equality. On a personal basis, this equality leads to greater intimacy. The social and emotional distances created by the traditional roles of the past are gradually disappearing. In the depths of this personal intimacy, however, couples gradually come to expect other qualities (Dominian 1981): sustaining, which is material and emotional; healing, which is physical and psychological; and the facilitation for personal growth, which is social, emotional, sexual, intellectual and spiritual. This is part of the silent inner change in contemporary marriage which is seen by those who handle marital breakdown where failure to meet the sustaining, healing and growth leads to divorce.

Children

Children and marriage are linked throughout the world and no less so in our society. For Augustine, they were the primary justification for intercourse, and to this very day the Roman Catholic Church makes the link between marriage, sex and children a fundamental and primary one. However, for a long time the achievement of the required number of children was a difficult task due to the dangers for the mother in pregnancy, at birth and in the postpuerperium, and infant and child mortality was exceedingly high. In 1764, the city of London recorded that 49 per cent of its children were dead by the age of 2 and 60 per cent by the age of 5 (Stone 1977). In 1911 infant mortality (dead under one year) was 129.4 per 1,000 live births, whereas in 1982 it was 10.8 (*Population Trends* 1984). The equivalent reduction is also seen in stillbirth, and it is now exceedingly rare for women to die during pregnancy and childbirth. Thus, as far as the physical factors are concerned, the increased safety means that multiple births are no longer required in order to achieve the desired family size, which in turn has been considerably reduced. The average number of children born to a married women in the 1860s was 5.7 and for those women married between 1955 and 1959 it is approximately 2.4.

The reduction of family size is a significant change, but it must be remembered that nearly 90 per cent of married couples have children so that there is no repudiation of childbearing as such. Nevertheless, there is an opinion that women are being selfish in this reduction. It should be remembered that the decision regarding the size of the family is a mutual one between spouses, and that the reduction is an expression of powerful social changes influenced by economic and emotional reasons, including the desire to give the children a better education and to give them more attention.

There is also an increasing awareness that the traditional view that children make a marriage, bind it, facilitate the well-being of parents, is not accurate in every aspect. There is no doubt that children elicit a matura- tional and integrative response, but they can also have an adverse impact. Evidence presented in the USA (Feldman 1971; Rollins and Cannon 1974) and in Britain (Walker 1977) suggests that marital satisfaction declines with the advent of children and continues to remain low until the children have reached adolescence and later leave home.

Despite the adverse impact on the parents, procreation continues albeit at a reduced level. This reduction is undoubtedly associated with the advent of another major change, namely contraception. Contraception is approved of by the vast majority of society, with the single exception of the Roman Catholic Church which nevertheless approves of family regulation by natural means. In 1976, 83 per cent of ever-married women had used some form of contraception (Dunnell 1979). The use of contraception means that not only the size of the family but also the timing of pregnancy can be controlled.

The extensive and continuous use of contraception has posed some fun- damental questions of value. It seems evident from such wide utilization that the vast majority of sexual acts are performed consciously and deliberately with non-procreative intention. The question arises that, if the intimate physical and traditional link between coitus and procreation is severed, what is the purpose of sexual intercourse? Some would object to the question being raised at all. The answer for them is pleasure, and that exhausts its meaning. For many others, pleasure certainly exists, but it serves the intimate world of love of the couple. So we are left with the question whether sex is in the service of love or only for pleasure.

The spontaneous expression of couples is that sexual intercourse is for love-making, but in what way is love served in its unitive achievement? Little discussion has taken place on this subject. An analysis of the meaning of sexual intercourse (Dominian 1981) offers five possible goals. Dominian describes coitus as a body language in which the couple communicate with each other through the pleasure experienced. The communication is one of *thanksgiving* for the joy experienced, *hope* through the desire for repetition of the act, *reconciliation* and the removal of pain after conflict, *affirmation* of sexual identity and *confirmation* of the personal meaning for each other.

The significant change in relation to children is the rise of abortion. Abortion is not a new phenomenon and has been known since ancient times. In recent times, it has become much safer and the grounds for its use widened since the Abortion Act of 1967. Abortion, unlike contraception, still mobilizes strong feelings, for and against it. The feminist movement has proclaimed strongly the right of women to control their bodies, to regulate the number of children they will have by contraception, and if necessary by abortion, and have asked for the greatest possible freedom and safety for this procedure. The opponents maintain that life is an indivisible unity which begins at fertilization, and should be respected and preserved at all costs. This debate involves some of the most profound values and continues with emotional intensity. It has been estimated that in the year 1966 there were about 6,000 abortions in the NHS and some 17,000 privately (Gardner 1972). These estimates, however, do not include illegal abortions for which there are no reliable figures. After the 1967 Act abortions had to be reported compulsorily and the figure for 1982 was 128,000. For those who approve of terminations this figure may be large but it is acceptable; for those opposed to it, it represents a continuing tragedy. Nowhere is the division of values more marked than over this Act.

Faithfulness

The traditional view, embedded as it has been in Christian morality, expected men and women not to indulge in premarital intercourse, and to remain faithful to each other after marriage. This ideal has never been attained in the whole history of Christianity, but in the last twenty-five years it has been breached as a deliberate policy.

As far as premarital intercourse is concerned, two views have been taken. The first suggests that sex is fun and should be thoroughly enjoyed as long as no one is hurt and no unwanted child is conceived. The presence of widespread contraception has given a sense of safety and has facilitated this approach. The second is concerned with marital stability and happiness, and holds that premarital experience enhances the knowledge of the individual and removes the ignorance which prevailed in previous generations.

There is considerable evidence that premarital intercourse has increased. Studies in the USA (Kinsey 1948, 1953) and in Britain (Schofield 1965) showed comparable results. By the age of 20 some 40 per cent of males had experienced intercourse and approximately 35 per cent of girls. Ten years later a marked increase was noted in that 69 per cent of 18-year-old boys had experienced intercourse and 55 per cent of 18-year-old girls (Farrell 1978).

The question that has to be asked is to what extent this rise in premarital intercourse is indiscriminate and promiscuous and to what extent already partly anticipating marriage. The changes, of course, are more marked in women, but the evidence suggests that there is no increase in promiscuity amongst teen-age girls (Bancroft 1983).

The increase in premarital intercourse is also shown to a certain extent in the *Family formation* study (Dunnell 1976). Women who married in the 1971–75 period and who were under 20 reported an incidence of 82 per cent of intercourse with their future husbands, those between 20 and 24 of 72 per cent, and those aged 25 and over of 64 per cent. These high percentages of premarital coitus are associated with the future husband and suggest further that intercourse is not of a promiscuous nature.

The next stage in premarital sexual behaviour is to live together with the partner. Cohabitation has also increased. Women marrying between 1956 and 1960 reported an incidence of 1 per cent of living together with the future husband. This percentage had increased to 9 per cent for those marrying between 1970 and 1975. Of those who cohabited, 26 per cent reported a period of less than three months, 15 per cent between three and five months, and 24 per cent between six months and a year. Thus nearly two-thirds of those who had lived with their future husband before marriage had done so for less than one year. Cohabitation therefore appears to be a step towards marriage.

Despite the increased use of contraception, pregnancies do occur before marriage. Once again this is not a new phenomenon but there has been an increase in illegitimate births. In 1961, the number of these was 48,000. In

1983, there was an increase to 89,900 (*Population Trends* 1984). However, once again there is a trend showing a more responsible attitude in that the proportion of illegitimate births jointly registered increased from 49 per cent in 1974 to 55 per cent in 1979. This suggests that parents, although unmarried, are likely to be living in stable relationships (Rimmer 1981).

Finally, there is the question of extramarital sex. The Kinsey data (Gebhard and Johnson 1979) showed that 34 per cent of married men and 20 per cent of women had experienced extramarital relationships. Recent studies in the USA do not show any major change. In Britain, figures are not easily available but they indicate a lower incidence (Gorer 1971). The *Sunday Times*/MORI survey of March 1982 indicated that adultery is still taken seriously and is considered wrong by two-thirds of the total sample. In fact, over 70 per cent of the 18 to 25-year-olds and 80 per cent of the 65-year-olds surveyed subscribed to the view that it is morally wrong. However, the same study has shown that, whilst adultery is still considered improper, it is not felt that sexual fidelity is the most important ingredient in a good marriage.

This survey finding is in agreement with clinical experience which suggests that couples are paying much greater attention to the quality of the personal relationship, and that an act of extramarital intercourse does not constitute a major assault on the marriage provided the relationship can recover and it is satisfactory. In the past, any act of adultery was considered a ground for divorce. Now couples can distinguish between at least three forms of adultery:

(a) First there is adultery which occurs when either spouse is lonely, away from home or the other spouse cannot provide sex; which is carried out as an experiment; or which reflects an acting out of anger or retaliation. In all of these situations, there is usually no threat to the marital relationship. The spouse involved expresses regret, is forgiven and the marriage is not severely damaged. There are marriages where the spouse, usually the wife, tolerates more than one episode of adultery in the knowledge that her husband is not really betraying her as he has no intention of leaving her.

(b) The second type is totally different. Here the situation has altered and the extramarital relationship is a symptom of the deteriorating or non-existent marital relationship. The spouse is seeking an alternative partner, and adultery in fact signals the end of the marriage.

(c) The third variety is an intermediate one. Either spouse may have an extramarital affair which is significant and emotionally important.

During its duration the partner falls in love with the third party and wants to be with them continuously. Deceit, lies and mistrust are introduced into the marriage, making the relationship very difficult. Even so the extramarital affair often ends and the spouse returns to the commitment of marriage, although in some instances he or she wants to have a concurrent relationship with both the spouse and the third party.

Whatever the circumstances, spouses are much more likely nowadays to be understanding of each other's extramarital behaviour and make allowances for it.

Thus, in the field of sexual behaviour there are marked changes indicated by the increase of premarital sexual activity and cohabitation. It is doubtful whether there are major alterations in the frequency of extramarital activity, although attitudes have certainly changed. Those most pessimistic and concerned see in these changes occurring in the last twenty-five years the possibility of chaos, a rise in promiscuity and the breakdown of containing and expressing sexuality in marriage where it can be linked with love. The evidence available does not suggest that the results of change are so destructive. Gynaecologists and venereal disease specialists are warning us about the dangers of carcinoma in the genital tract of women, associated with sexual activity with different men, of venereal diseases, and of the particular scares associated with AIDS. These are serious warnings, but there is no evidence that sexual changes are in general of a promiscuous variety, and in particular have undermined marriage and the commitment of fidelity. Commitment in fact has taken on a stronger meaning, and from the time when a couple take each other seriously, through mutual sexual activity and cohabitation, there is a commitment which is the equivalent of faithfulness which is no more nor less precarious than the fidelity exhibited in marriage in the past. There is still much room to discuss the value of premarital sexual activity and cohabitation in terms of supporting the future marriage, but what is absolutely clear is that marriage has in no way been seriously replaced by these alternatives.

Marriage

The crucial test remains the popularity of marriage itself. What do people feel and think about it? In the Social Science Research Council's Survey

Unit national survey conducted in 1975 the largest single reference to quality of life was to family, home life and marriage (Hall 1976). Similarly, in the 1979/80 survey of Colchester, which involved interviews with 461 people, marriage and the family were seen as the most important things in their lives (Nicholson 1980). A *Sun* newspaper survey of teenagers' attitudes showed that most teenagers want marriage, parenthood, and a happy home (*Sun* 21 October 1980). In a 1977 survey by McCann Erikson Advertising Limited of 15 to 19-year-olds only 9 per cent said they would not marry. In a NOW/MORI survey in 1979, the vast majority of the slightly older age group, 15 to 25, said they wanted to marry. Thus, there is no lack of evidence that marriage is popular and remains, with work, the most important goal for young people.

Given that this is the hope and aspiration of young people, how many translate it into action? How many actually marry? On the basis of a thousand couples who married in England and Wales in 1979, Haskey (1983a) made a calculation of the number of men and women who would marry in each social class. Overall 88 per cent of men and 92 per cent of women would marry, with the lowest marrying rate being found in men of social class V, of whom only 81 per cent are likely to marry. Thus the current evidence suggests that some 90 per cent of men and women are likely to marry and therefore we have to draw the conclusion that marriage remains highly popular.

But given the divorce rates, do the participants of these marriages intend to enter into permanent relationships or not? Is the concept of permanency still influential in the type of marriage that is being discussed? The evidence suggests that, although some people are now prepared to consider divorce, the overt intention of those who marry is still to remain together for life. At the heart of contemporary marriage is the state of being in love, that is to say, the desire to be together with the spouse for as long as possible. Spouses do not enter marriage with the intention of splitting up. In a NOP survey in 1980, 87 per cent of divorcees had expected their marriage to last forever. In a NOW/MORI sample of 15 to 25-year-olds, only 13 per cent thought they would actually divorce.

Thus, the evidence available does not suggest that couples marry less or do so more frivolously despite the drop in church weddings. In fact, church weddings are no guarantee against marital breakdown. Many people marry in church as an appropriate social event without accompanying religious commitment which would act as a potential barrier to divorce. When the religious commitment is high, there is a greater chance that the marriage will not end in divorce.

Divorce

Perhaps the single most obvious change in marriage is the rise in divorce in the last twenty-five years. The statistics are familiar, but are worth repeating. In 1960 there were nearly 24,000 divorces, and in 1982 some 146,000 in England and Wales. This is nearly a 600 per cent increase. At the current level, one in three marriages is expected to end in divorce (Haskey 1982), and this involves not only the couple but also their children: approximately 160,000 under the age of 16. Thus, a total number of some 450/500,000 men, women and children are involved annually in divorce.

This high figure is not confined to Britain. Most Western countries, and now increasingly countries from the Third World, are showing evidence of high divorce. Why should this be the case? There are no definitive answers, but it is likely that the following factors are involved. First, as already indicated, there is the emancipation of women. Increasingly women are no longer prepared to stay in marriages that either do not fulfil their expectations or actually cause them harm. There is evidence that wives are aware of marital problems much earlier than men and want to do something about them. It is men who find it difficult to recognize the emotional difficulties in a marriage and are very reluctant to seek help until the last moment when it is often too late (Thornes and Collard 1979; Brannen and Collard 1982). In support of the important role played by wives in seeking divorce, it should be noted that seven out of ten petitions are filed by them (*Population Trends* 1982). Solicitors claim that there are technical reasons for this ratio, but clinically the evidence suggests that it is wives who become aware of problems before their husbands, and finally, if no redress is made, want to terminate the relationship.

The wives' contribution is by no means the sole reason for the marked increase in divorce. For both spouses these last twenty-five years have seen a dramatic rise in material standards. Expectations in food, shelter, job fulfilment have risen. Unemployment is a relatively recent phenomenon. In the hierarchy of values there is a tendency for a descending scale in which personal fulfilment, love and affection, follow the presence of material security. In the presence of material sufficiency, both wives and husbands are likely to seek a greater degree of fulfilment in emotional and sexual satisfaction and, when this is not present, to seek it in a second marriage.

Thirdly, marriage is changing from the institutional to the companionship variety. The new type of marriage which emphasizes feelings, their expression, communication, mutuality, consultation, joint decision making and attentive listening is one which causes difficulties for both partners, but particularly for men. Women, on the whole, are stronger in their affective appreciation and its expression, and clinical experience suggests that the mobilization of feelings is a continual problem for men.

These and other factors suggest that marriage is in a stage of transition. It now requires a whole variety of skills which society has not acquired on a large scale. The absence of education and support for the new type of marriage is filled by divorce. Is this an indication of the moribund state of matrimony or one which indicates that men and women are seeking a new ideal for which they have to pay the price of divorce? These possibilities are examined exhaustively, for the importance of marriage remains unquestioned by the vast majority of people. The evidence on the whole points to the second, more positive hypothesis.

This view is supported by the rate of second and subsequent marriages. There is no suggestion on current evidence that marriage is any less popular for those whose first marriage ends. Remarriages are common. A study of 2,000 people divorced in 1973, who were followed up for an average of four and a half years, showed that the proportion remarrying was higher for men than for women: some 55.5 per cent compared to 48.0 per cent (Leete and Anthony 1979). The proportion remarrying declined with age. It was highest for those divorcing before the age of 30, of whom some 60 per cent had remarried by the end of 1977, with only a small difference for the sexes. After the age of 30, women remarried less than men. Of those aged 40 and over, only 33 per cent divorced women had remarried against 50 per cent men.

Remarriage occurs quickly after divorce. By the end of the first year, 60 per cent of those who remarried within four and a half years had done so. This ties in with what has been said before, namely that in marriages which have ceased to exist in all but name the existence of an extramarital relationship is not the cause of this but an indication of the searching for a new partner, who is married soon after the divorce is obtained.

As has been said, in the same study about 50 per cent of both sexes remarried within four and a half years of divorce, and the ultimate remarriage rate is higher. The next question that has to be asked is how stable are these second marriages? In the 1960s it was fashionable to state that second marriages were indeed stable and the answer for those divorced. At that time, the numbers of divorced were less than now and studies were hardly available. As the number of remarriages has increased and extended over the years, there is an opportunity to study more precisely the rate of breakdown of second marriages. The rate in fact differs for men and women. A recent study (Haskey 1983b) sums up the likelihood of divorce in a remarriage as follows: 'The chance that the marriage of a divorced man would again end in divorce is $1\frac{1}{2}$ times that of a single man who marries at the same age. Analogously, a divorced woman who remarries is approximately twice as likely to divorce as a single woman who marries at the same age' (p. 14). Thus, we are now beginning to see that subsequent marriages are more vulnerable.

Finally, divorce leads to one-parent families. The vast majority of these families are headed by women since in most instances custody of the children is given to the mother. The first estimation of one-parent families was made in 1971 when it was calculated that there were 570,000. This increased to 750,000 in 1976, and in 1980 the figure is estimated to be nearly 1 million. Currently about one in eight families is headed by a single parent.

The life of a single parent is undoubtedly difficult, socially, economically and psychologically. When the single parent has to work as well as look after the children, the usual outcome is a serious level of tiredness. When the single parent is not working, then the level of income may fall seriously to the detriment of both parent and child.

Divorce inevitably has an impact on the children. In one-parent families the quality of the relationship between the child and the departing parent is a vital contribution to the amelioration of the adverse effects of the separation. The key to the welfare of the children is the relationship of the parents and what really matters is the likelihood of stability and happiness in the life of the parents.

Conclusion

The conclusion of this chapter is that marriage remains the ultimate goal of the overwhelming majority of young people, and that, in wishing to marry, young people still retain the ideals of permanency and faithfulness as worthy moral aims. Yet, although on the surface the externals of marriage remain essentially unchanged, its internal world is changing substantially, and the problem in Western society is the difficulty in examining marriage in depth, beyond its externals, and appreciating those internal changes which call for a different education, preparation and support for it. There is on the one hand a basic continuity of values, and yet, on the other, profound changes in values, and for the time being society has to live with this ambivalence.

References

Bancroft, J. (1983) *Human sexuality and its problems.* Edinburgh: Churchill Livingstone.

Brannen, J. and Collard, J. (1982) *Marriages in trouble.* London: Tavistock Publications.

Briton, M. (1975) Women at work. *Population Trends, 2,* 22–25. London: HMSO.

Dominian, J. (1980) *Marital pathology.* London: Darton, Longman and Todd/British Medical Association.

Dominian, J. (1981) *Marriage, faith and love.* London: Darton, Longman and Todd.

Dunnell, K. (1976) *Family formation.* London: Office of Population Censuses and Surveys.

Farrell, C. (1978) *My mother said: the way young people learn about sex and birth control.* London: Routledge and Kegan Paul.

Feldman, H. (1971) The effects of children on a family. *In* A. Michel (ed.) *Family issues of employed women in Europe and America.* Leiden: E. J. Brill.

Gardner, P. F. R. (1972) *Abortion.* Exeter: Paternoster Press.

Gebhard, P. H. and Johnson, A. B. (1979) *The Kinsey data.* Philadelphia: Saunders.

Gorer, G. (1971) *Sex and marriage in England today.* London: Nelson.

Hall, J. (1976) Subjective measures of quality of life in Britain 1971 to 1975. *Social Trends, 7,* 47–59.

Haskey, J. (1982) The proportion of marriages ending in divorce. *Population Trends, 27,* 4–7. London: HMSO.

Haskey, J. (1983a) Social class patterns of marriage. *Population Trends, 34,* 12–19. London: HMSO.

Haskey, J. (1983b) Marital status before marriage and age at marriage: their influence on the chance of divorce. *Population Trends, 32,* 4–14. London: HMSO.

Hicks, M. W. and Platt, M. (1970) Marital happiness and stability: a review of the research in the sixties. *In* C. B. Broderick (ed.) *A decade of family research and action.* Cleveland, Ohio: National Council on Family Relations.

Kinsey, A. C., Pomeroy, W. B. and Martin, C. E. (1948) *Sexual behaviour in the human male.* Philadelphia: W. B. Saunders.

Kinsey, A. C., Pomeroy, W. B., Martin, C. E. and Gebhard, P. H. (1953) *Sexual behaviour in the human female.* Philadelphia: W. B. Saunders.

Laslett, P. (1971) *The world we have lost.* London: Methuen and Co.

Laslett, P. (1972) *Household and family in past time.* Cambridge: Cambridge University Press.

Leete, B. and Anthony, S. (1979) Divorce and remarriage: a record linkage study. *Population Trends, 16,* 5–11. London: HMSO.

McCann Erikson Advertising Ltd. (1977) *You don't know me.* London.

Nicholson, J. (1980) *Seven ages.* London: Fontana.

Population Trends (1982) *30*, 5. London: HMSO.

Population Trends (1984) *35*, 42. London: HMSO.

Rimmer, L. (1981) *Family in focus: marriage, divorce and family patterns*. London: Study Commission on the Family.

Rimmer, L. and Popay, J. (1982) *Employment trends and the family*. London: Study Commission on the Family.

Rollins, B. and Cannon, K. L. (1974) Marital satisfaction over the family life cycle: a re-evaluation. *Journal of Marriage and the Family, 36*, 271–282.

Schofield, M. (1965) *The sexual behaviour of young people*. London: Longman.

Shorter, E. (1976) *The making of the modern family*. London: Collins.

Stone, L. (1977) *The family, sex and marriage in England 1500–1800*. London: Weidenfeld and Nicholson.

Thornes, B. and Collard, J. (1979) *Who divorces?* London: Routledge and Kegan Paul.

Walker, C. (1977) Some variations in marital satisfaction. *In* R. Chester and J. Peel (eds) *Equalities and inequalities in family life*. London: Academic Press.

CHAPTER THREE Changing Roles for Men and Women
Implications for Marital Therapy
Jeanne Magagna and David Black

Introduction

Like their patients, therapists are often confused by the social changes they live through. They are unable to see them clearly and certainly are unable to have an authoritative 'right attitude' in relation to them. The current changes in sex-roles are a good example of this: the newspapers insist that a whole generation is changing; the therapist, seeing a small number of couples in some depth, finds that a few are consciously pioneering and experimenting with new styles of relationships, others are adapting to current changes, and others again might be living in the days of Queen Victoria. It is impossible to know exactly which of these groups are the trend-setters for the future.

Already the 'revolution' of the 1960s has been declared officially 'over' by *Time* magazine (9 April 1984). For the first time in twenty years, the number of divorces in America dropped in 1982, whereas the number of US weddings was at an all-time high. Such evidence suggests that therapists can only remain uncertain about the duration and depth of the change of roles seen to be occurring at present. Moreover, the fact that more women work, and more men wash dishes and look after the children, may have had only a small impact on sexual behaviour, roles in parenting and perceptions of gratifying roles for the self. Certainly the sexual fantasies of both sexes appear to have changed little in response to 'liberation'. Women retain an unconscious desire to submit to a 'romantic repressor' (Marrin 1984), a fact seemingly confirmed by David Barlow's research (Goleman 1984) which showed that the second most common sexual fantasy in heterosexual women is of a forced sexual encounter, such as rape.

Despite this relative lack of change in the inner world of the sexes, in the last thirty years there has been a recognizable trend towards diminishing the differentiation of sex-roles, and asserting the similarity of male and female 'persons'. Even where roles have not conspicuously changed, they are experienced as less God-given and more man-made. Such a shift is both challenging and liberating for couples. But it is not the task of the marital therapist to say whether social trends are 'good' or 'bad'; what has to concern the therapist is the way in which changing trends may collude with the couple's conscious or unconscious defensive systems. These typically involve a denial of feelings, in particular those to do with the need or fear of dependence and intimacy. Equally, it is important that the therapist be aware of how these changing trends may promote the growth of the couple.

It will be with these strictly limited concerns in mind that we approach the issues in this chapter.

Alongside the trends towards diminishing the differentiation of sex-roles is an increasing tendency to see the individual (rather than, for example, the family) as the essential unit. We shall discuss this later, in the section entitled 'The influence of psychotherapy on social change'. Consequences of these two tendencies include the following:

(1) *Divorce* is seen as an acceptable phenomenon, both by society at large and by the couple themselves. Of those under 45 in America, one-third will divorce. In Britain, the corresponding figure is one-quarter. In Britain between 1965 and 1980 divorce figures rose from 37,785 to 148,000 (divorces per annum); in America, between 1965 and 1979, from 393,000 to 1,170,000 (Gathorne-Hardy 1981).

(2) *Cohabitation*, frequently for years, and frequently without any clear statement of commitment to one another, is acceptable too. Often one partner is unhappy with the situation, but does not feel on secure ground (does not feel socially supported) in protesting about the failure to get married or to solidify the cohabitation agreement in some way.

(3) *Single parenthood* is not only acceptable but in some cases actually the mother's choice. More frequently it is a result of divorce or the breakup of an uncommitted couple. In Britain one out of three children, and in America two out of five children, spend their formative years in one-parent families (Gathorne-Hardy 1981).

(4) *Work by married women and mothers*, now built into the economic structure of many families and of the country as a whole, is one of the most striking changes. In the propaganda of social revolution it was typically linked with the idea that men might work less, and perhaps take on the traditional 'housewife' role. Except under pressure of unemployment, this has occurred to only a very limited extent.

(5) *Social and sexual experiments* are somewhat acceptable. Homosexual relationships and activity are presently much more widely tolerated than they were, and experiments such as same-sex gay people marrying, or adopting a child, enjoy some measure of acceptance. Cross-cultural and cross-racial marriages, remarriages of divorced people

with and without children, are all increasingly accepted. The struggle by some groups, such as the Anglican and Roman Catholic Churches, to maintain 'traditional standards' are felt to be reactionary and legalistic. Since the mid-1970s, however, it is likely that the trend towards sexual permissiveness has stabilized. For example, premarital sex, laden with guilt and excitement in the revolutionary years of the 1960s, is now taken largely for granted, but expected to occur in a somewhat enduring relationship. Sexually 'open' marriages, group sex and one-night stands no longer attract public advocacy. Gathorne-Hardy (1981) reports that, in a survey by the American magazine *Redbook*, 38 per cent of married couples had had extramarital sex. Of these 20 per cent of the women and 27 per cent of the men said they had very satisfactory marriages, including very good sex. They saw love affairs as something they should have in addition to marriage.

Marital therapists see the people for whom change has caused difficulty, not those who have found change possible and liberating. In this chapter we shall be looking at some typical difficulties, and the way in which marital therapists need to be alert to the influence of sex-roles on both therapist and couples. We shall begin by considering the limitations of traditional sex-roles, and look at some wider questions concerning role-models: the effect of their absence and the nature of the desire to change them. Next we shall consider how changing sex-roles also affect the expectations of the partner. Finally, we shall consider how having theories about intimacy has consequences. We shall then go on to illustrate, more psychodynamically, the way in which some of these difficulties spring from the interaction of the couple's personal dynamics with the possibilities made available or denied to them by their roles. The basic orientation we shall adopt in this chapter derives from a mixture of object-relations theory (see Chapter 8) to understand the workings of the individual, and systems theory (see Chapter 11) to understand the interaction of the couple.

The limitations of traditional sex-roles

Thus far we have indicated the possible dangers of changing sex-roles. To correct the balance, however, we want to emphasize that traditional roles offer no security either. Osborne (1983), suggesting that therapists acknowledge the new acceptable trends for couples, quotes the fact that married women more frequently suffer from emotional distress than either men or financially secure women who have never married. Married men, however, show a lower level of mental distress than never-married or widowed men. Clearly, married men experience the need to consult mental health professionals far less than married women.

This disquieting fact can readily be understood in the light of traditional sex-roles. The Swiss psychologist, Willi (1982), describes a revealing experiment. When men and women, separately, do Rorschach tests, psychologists are unable to deduce the sex of the testee with any accuracy from the results. When men and women do the same tests, but in couples, they at once adopt the traditional stereotypes: men become forceful and take the initiative, while women become retiring and supportive, and their sex becomes deducible from their responses. Understood psychodynamically, what has occurred reflects a process of splitting and projective identification in both partners. The men have split off their vulnerable, sensitive qualities and projected them onto the women; the women have projected their initiative and independent judgement onto the men. In this process, mental distress is part of the burden that falls to the women.

It is necessary for the marital therapist to recognize the limitations as well as the assets of both traditional and new roles in marriage. Stereotypes, for certain individuals, particularly those with poorly differentiated gender identity, can have a very real value in providing consolidation and support. In a couple with greater capacity for psychic development, however, stereotypes sooner or later prove inhibiting. The sex of the therapist (another factor stressed by Willi) will also elicit stereotyped responses from couples. And finally, since change is also very difficult for therapists, the therapist too will need to be aware of his or her own tendency to fall into detrimental stereotyped reactions in the presence of the two sexes.

Effects of the absence of an accepted role-model

The conventional analytic understanding of how children come to adopt desires and modes of behaviour appropriate to their sex and gender, and thus acquire the capacity to relate satisfactorily to the opposite sex, is that in the Oedipal phase the boy's desire for the mother, or the girl's for the father, is recognized but not allowed to 'succeed'. In response to this disappointment, the child accepts his position as a child, and identifies with the parent of the same sex. This enables him to acquire a partner like the parent of the opposite sex when he comes to maturity.

A full picture of the development of gender identity would also require that constitutional factors be taken into account. They are the unknown element in any discussion of sex-roles. But the Oedipal theory is of special significance because of its emphasis on the role-modelling by the parents: a child not only identifies with the parent of same sex (a notion which includes using the parent as a role-model), but does so in a way that 'anticipates' (in inverted commas because there is not necessarily any conscious intention involved) choosing a partner like the parent of opposite sex. In this sense, the parent of the opposite sex is also perceived as a role-model, not for the self, but for the future spouse or sexual partner. We shall be dealing with some of these further issues in the section entitled 'Expectations of the partner'. By the time the child leaves home, he has internalized a pattern of the parents relating to one another, an 'internal couple'.

When socially accepted sex-roles are undergoing rapid change, confusion emerges: the roles identified with and anticipated by the child are no longer socially approved or intellectually accepted by the time he arrives at sexual maturity. It is as if a whole generation is put in the position of the child from a neurotic family, who has radically to relearn the elementary basis of intimate relations. But the intrapsychic conflict experienced by such a transitional generation is wrongly seen if it is seen as merely neurotic.

For example, a woman with a responsible job and a demanding family life decided one busy Christmas that, contrary to her custom, she would *buy* the Christmas cake. Although she knew the good sense of this, and was under no pressure from her family, she found herself, having bought the cake, standing in tears in the supermarket. Guilt and sadness at departing from an internalized role-model often need to be faced before change is possible: she had to stand still for a moment and mourn.

The power of the unconscious role-modelling derived from the Oedipal stage is so great that it acts as a major hindrance to conscious attempts at change. No doubt that is one reason why many 'revolutions', despite their conscious aims, tend within a generation to revert to something close to the status quo. In terms of the mental health of the couple, it seems clear that internalized good role-models (which may be seen as one aspect of good internalized parents) allow a resilience and healthy resistance to excessively rapid change; those in a transitional generation who suffer most are those who lack such models, and are either especially vulnerable to social pressures or else resistant to them so that they adopt compensatory attitudes of rigidity.

Example 1   Mrs A was a young woman who had made a 'masculine identification' in adolescence. She was aided in this by her intelligence and cheerful, frank, outgoing manner. Her father had been a war hero, a courageous, vigorous barrister, with whom she went on long camping expeditions as a girl. She described herself as 'the son he never had'. She married first a very sensitive, penniless poet, whom she supported. When that broke up, she moved in with a bisexual musician, who first idolized and then neglected her in a manner that contained a strong element of sadism. When their first son was born she returned home to find her husband in bed with another girl.

Mr A's background was in a sense complementary. The only child of a mother who adored him, brought up without a father, he had found himself a provisional identity by being gifted artistically. He made a precarious living on the fringes of the musical and theatrical professions. With a powerful need for intimacy, but terrified of continuing closeness, his phobic reaction to marriage took the form of sadistic withholding and unconcealed sexual acting out with partners of both sexes. Unsupported by reliable internal role-models, the marriage tended towards a role-reversal in which she earned the main income for the family and he expressed the dependent, sensitive aspects of the couple, in an increasingly chaotic way. In the late 1960s, the fashionable attitude of experiment and 'openness' offered neither any support in understanding their increasing distance from one another. The marriage drifted towards shipwreck.

Such a story is typical of the transitional generation. Disregarding constitutional factors, it shows a characteristic mixture of personal elements – deriving from the individual family histories, both of which perpetuated neurotic modes of relating – and social influences – which at that time fostered unusual, 'sexually liberated' modes of relating. Although both partners consciously 'saw nothing wrong' with a role-reversed marriage, unconscious pressures then asserted themselves: she became resentful of the role she found herself in, and wanted him to be responsible towards her; he felt angry and trapped by her demands. The real and symbolic transitions of marriage, for him, and the arrival of the first child, for her, triggered attitudes of a traditional kind against which the conscious 'liberated' beliefs were powerless.

Example 2 Mr and Mrs B were both successful economists in their early 30s. Both had full-time jobs while rearing their three children. Both advocated feminist ideals of equal responsibility, together with equal opportunity and sexual freedom for both partners. They had a clear notion that mothers and fathers could replace each other in all aspects of taking care of the children. As each baby was born, they took turns to leave work for nine months in order to look after the new child. When the youngest child was eighteen months old, an interesting work opportunity arose for Mrs B, requiring travel to Russia for three months. She did not hesitate to take this opportunity, although her husband was by then working full-time and they had only part-time child-minding assistance.

This couple can be well understood in terms of shared fantasy. They shared both the illusion that they were independent of one another, and the fantasy that they were androgynous parents (i.e. that each individually was capable of fulfilling the whole of the children's need for parenting). As long as one parent was at home, Mrs B felt that the children would manage their lives satisfactorily. Quite unacknowledged, however, were the intense feelings of dependency and the separation anxiety which the children, and to some extent the couple, experienced at Mrs B's departure. Their belief in an androgynous super-parent was used by them as a defence against their guilt at failing to meet the family members' individual needs.

One issue for the marital therapist is how much to 'know'. Many fashionable theories can be used by a couple to do a great deal of damage to the marriage. At the same time, like the feminist movement or the sexual revolution of the 1960s, these new ideas will often contain something that society needs to learn. The therapist is not a prophet, and is not qualified to pronounce on the direction in which society needs to evolve. Nevertheless, he cannot with a good conscience go along with the glib acceptance of 'shared parenting' ideas which ignore children's dependency needs.

A useful guideline for work with couples is to help them to perceive the actual consequences of the behaviour they are choosing, and to enable them to develop the capacity to face the emotional reality, for themselves and their family, of what they are doing. Almost invariably, when a fashionable trend in behaviour (such as 'open marriage') is seen to be destructive to a particular couple, one can trace how the couple has adopted the 'popular' notion because it fits in with their shared manic defence. That is, it is being used to obliterate painful feelings such as jealousy, sadness, and concern for the harm done to the other. Example 3, below, illustrates such a case.

The desire to change role-models

The conscious desire to change role-models has itself to be brought under scrutiny. Even the most heartfelt political conviction can act in the service of an unconscious neurotic motive. Psychological ideas especially can be misused. The feminist movement, for example, has been apt to misuse the psychoanalytic idea of constitutional bisexuality. A distinction has to be observed between an immature bisexual identity, characteristic of an adult who has failed for neurotic reasons to make commitments and go forward into life, and what might be called mature androgyny, characteristic of an adult who has entered life, undertaken his life tasks, and established a definite gender identity while also keeping in touch with traits stereotypically characteristic of the opposite sex. Much feminist propaganda fails to make this distinction, and creates an uneasy feeling in consequence.

Most of the running, in the urge to change role-models, has been made in recent years by feminists and Marxists, both activated by a concern for equality. Much of this, in our view, has been timely, and more remains to be done. However, the motive of equality may be enlisted by neurosis both, fearfully, to avoid acquiring a distinct role and identity oneself, and also, enviously, to prevent others from achieving distinction or excellence. We propose the following check-list of such neurotic motives.

(1) A desire to undermine authority in general. This might stem from hatred or envy towards an authoritarian parent, or from envious loyalty to an inadequate parent which will not allow anyone else to be an adequate authority.

(2) A desire to undermine the authority of the man. This is linked to hatred or envy of the authority and sexual power of the father in particular.

(3) Defensive determination by a woman who is very frightened of her little-girl feelings (wanting to find the man wonderful, wanting to depend on him completely, wanting to be adored etc.) and prefers to remain in a world of ideas, feeling 'I can do everything on my own'. The male version of this is very similar, and reflects a feeling of shame at being seen as small, dependent, and needy.

(4) A desire to remain in a self-centred world, ignoring one's connectedness to others and one's responsibility to be concerned for their needs.

(5) Among some extreme feminist propagandists are infantile or homosexual women who harbour an envious desire to spoil the intimate relationships or pleasure in childbearing of others. A similar motive is perceived in Marxism in the common phrase 'the politics of envy'.

Expectations of the partner

The theme of expectations of the partner is closely related to that of role-models. In healthy development such expectations derive from the resolution of the Oedipal phase. When the social definition of sex-roles changes, the new spouse finds it extremely difficult because he does not feel free to follow the model of the same-sex parent, and cannot expect the partner to follow the model of the parent of the opposite sex. Acceptance of a change of role for oneself need not imply a reciprocal acceptance of a change of role for the other.

For example, a man who is quite at ease looking after the baby, cooking meals etc., may still resent the fact that his equally liberated wife wants to work and relate to colleagues, and not be at home to attend to him. He may want appreciation of his 'liberatedness' as if it were another old-style masculine achievement. Or a woman, competent in the world of work, may, like Mrs A in Example 1, be upset to find herself feeling contempt for her stay-at-home, domestically skilled husband. Very often such reactions express themselves in sexual failure. Sexual response and fantasy are very conservative, and often such couples find it easier to have an extramarital affair than to acknowledge their "unfashionable" possessive or dependent desires. A great deal can be achieved in therapy if the couple can be enabled simply to acknowledge that they have such feelings, which are experienced as quite disproportionately shameful or destructive.

Deliberate education is another source of expectation which may be over-taken by changes in adult roles. One girl, taking to heart her headmistress's admonition, 'Don't flaunt yourself', felt too guilty to wear sexy or revealing clothes. A man, who had been through an all-male boarding education, said: 'I was brought up to be a warrior – and look: society is composed of children playing!' Dynamic psychotherapists do not usually regard education as part of their function, on the grounds that essential learning takes place by experience in the transference. Marital therapists are often more flexible. They will sometimes explain to couples some basic principles of interaction, for example the importance of facing anger, or may make suggestions about how important it is for the couple to express their feelings of jealousy. It can on occasion be appropriate to speak directly about expectations of the partner, and to indicate how tenaciously they can be held even at a time when changing social roles have made them manifestly obsolete. Such interventions can have the advantage of involving the more mature part of the couple in thinking about the issues. For example, it is often stabilizing to realize that one's miserable resentment at an unsatisfactory spouse is not only that, but is also part of a general response to difficult social change. Men actually do find it hard to come to terms with having their wife out to work all day; women do find it difficult to be a professional one minute and a loving wife the next.

It is appropriate here to repeat that the therapist too has expectations, derived from his own background, which if not dealt with will colour his responses. How does he react, for example, when the couple tells him that:

(1) when the baby was born, the oil company granted Mr Harrison eight weeks maternity leave, while his wife returned after four days to her work as a top geneticist;
(2) Mrs Harrison spent Sunday morning changing the cam-shaft, while her husband stayed indoors to bath the baby;
(3) they are arguing whether to dismiss the 18-year-old au pair, as Mrs Harrison has taken to sun-bathing with him on the lawn?

The effect of having theories

Having fully conscious theories about how relationships should diverge from the sex-roles of the past, has a powerful influence on couples. One may have correctly identified an element which needs to be changed in intimate relationships, but totally fail to notice that other crucial elements get changed in the process. Of no field is this more true than intimacy.

Example 3 Mr and Mrs C had married in their early 20s, neither having much significant previous sexual experience. It was the heady days of the early 1970s, with much talk of sexual freedom, 'open marriage', and so on. They decided that in deference to one another's autonomy each must be free to have relations outside the narrow couple. When Mrs C started to get friendly with a man at work, Mr C found himself having acute feelings of rage and jealousy. Convinced that these were an unwarranted and 'childish' response on his part, he refused to intrude on his wife's freedom by acknowledging them. Mrs C experienced him as becoming unaccountably aloof and withdrawn. Partly in consequence, her new friendship became increasingly attractive to her. Mr C became extremely depressed and would lie on the floor for long periods of time, unable to summon up the energy to go to work. He was unable to understand his depression; he could see nothing to be depressed about.

It is clear that the new ideas played a central role in the failure of this marriage. However, what is also clear is that, at a more basic level, this couple were unable to handle feelings. Mr C was unable to revise his ideas about marriage in the light of his experience; Mrs C did not enquire into her husband's unhappiness, but responded manically to his aloofness by going off into a new relationship. Consequently, instead of a dialogue developing between liberated ideas and actual experience, which might have resulted in both partners understanding better what was possible for them and what they each wanted, the liberated ideas colluded with their defences and both were able to avoid facing the underlying fear of having to acknowledge their dependency needs.

In our experience, such a case is typical. The effect of theories about sex-roles is to highlight certain facets of need and behaviour, casting others into shadow. But the resulting difficulties need not be catastrophic unless, more fundamentally, there are also neurotic personal factors at work to prevent the couple learning from their experience.

The influence of psychotherapy on social change

One of the central determinants of these changes in social attitudes has derived in part from psychotherapy itself. It is the notion of 'self-development' (also met with in such guises as self-actualization, individuation, self-sufficiency, and personal growth). Sometimes, the apparently mature concern with self-development may be a disguise for narcissistic self-absorption, an inability to experience concern for another, and a withdrawal from life rather than an encounter with it. Disregarding such misuse, however, the assumption implicit in the emphasis on self-development is that the basic human unit is the individual, not the couple, family, extended family, or political or religious community. For example, part of the rationale for the acceptability of divorce stands on the premise that human beings can split from those with whom they are intimate, can mourn, and can then be free to enter into new intimate relations without having caused or suffered irretrievable damage. If the goal, or one of the goals, of life is 'self-development', such separations can even come to be regarded as a duty (not, as they would normally have been considered a century ago, a reprehensible self-indulgence). These ideas derive in particular from the more optimistic 'popular' psychotherapies.

We shall now look more psychodynamically at the sort of defences which most readily collude with some of the prevailing theories about men and women, and then, in our final section, go on to show how, in the practice of marital therapy, the awareness of changing social roles has to be related to the actual stage of psychic development reached by particular couples.

Social trends or defensive manoeuvres?

The attitude that minimizes the difference between men and women is liable to collude with the following psychological difficulties.

(1) *Projective identification.* Here the man, for example, fails to develop his manliness but instead seeks a woman with 'masculine' qualities of initiative, practicality and competence (cf. Example 1, Mr and Mrs A).

(2) *Envious undermining.* Here neither partner is allowed to have a clear sphere of influence but each interferes with everything the other does.

(3) *Defensive withdrawal or withholding.* Here, one partner refuses to play a full part in the life of the other. The base of this is normally fear and denial of dependency needs, but it may include variations on the theme, e.g. sadistic exacerbation of the other's dependency (cf. Example 3, Mr and Mrs C).

Some implications for marital therapy practice

It is part of the task of the marital therapist to evaluate continually the couple's joint capacity to bear anxieties relating to nurturance, life/death and individuation issues. To bring the capacity to bear anxiety into focus, we shall postulate four types of relating, corresponding to four levels of psychic development in the individual. The couple's joint psychic life can often be seen to progress through these stages of development, but obviously the emotional capacity of each spouse affects the fluctuations in the psychic development of the couple.

Stage One – the 'delusion of fusion'
Stage Two – adhesive clinging
Stage Three – the jack-in-the-box marriage
Stage Four – ideal marriage

We shall try to show how 'liberated' views can be used by couple and therapist to assist or to thwart the couple's development at each of these four stages.

Stage One – the 'delusion of fusion'

When two people 'fall in love' and come together, they often have the delusion of being in some way inseparable. Couples in this state often describe how a day apart feels like a month; a week apart, like a year. The wish for union with the other promotes a regressive wish for part of the self to have a permanent parasitical residence inside the other. For example, a man in tears joins his new lover saying, 'I have come home at last'. What one sees here is his wish to reside passively inside his lover, while projecting onto her the wished-for love and power-to-protect that he wanted from his parents. Encapsulated in his word *home* is the suggestion that he has identified her with parents possessing an infinite capacity to meet the needs of a parasitical person.

In 'falling in love', each person at times has this fantasy of 'coming home'. The partner is expected to be 'the parent'. There is present in such moments an early euphoria, a sense of oneness, a sense of the commonality of self and others.

The couple experience extreme reactions at the time of separation when they sustain, rather than experiencing only momentarily, the belief that the partner will be a replacement for the parents. These separation reactions may include feeling that:

(1)   They cannot survive outside the relationship because it is too painful to do so.
(2)   They are rejected when the partner is absent. The fantasy is often of being rejected for some fault that the partner could not bear. This fantasy may be held even though the partner has merely gone to work or chosen to see some other friends.
(3)   They are bad, or felt to be cruel, if they leave the partner temporarily.

One woman who existed in this 'delusion of fusion' faced separation anxiety when her boyfriend went off on a business trip. She said: 'When you are not here, the relationship disappears like a soap bubble becoming air and I fear I will be left with nothing.'

The imagined early infancy of partners who continually succumb to the regressive fantasy of 'coming home' is one in which good enough mothering did not occur, and therefore could not be internalized. The possessiveness and greed to have the whole of the other person's life have resulted from the lack of good internal parents. Typically, in such couples, difficulties that they experienced as babies were dealt with by the parents in a manic way, often by providing food or dummies rather than comfort and emotional containment at a deep level.

The liberated views of the 1960s, advocating communal living, often attracted people wishing to regress in this way. Careers and work outside the commune were abandoned. The fact that other people were always present, and often sexually available, meant that extreme separation anxieties could for a time be avoided. 'Open marriages', too, were often based on fear of infantile dependence which might occur in a monogamous relationship. Extreme separation anxieties were fended off with affairs to deny separation. Other liberated views, however, particularly those of more recent feminists addressing the 'Doll's House' phenomenon in women, present a more mature point of view. In *Women and Mental Health* the feminist editors agree that an infant does appear to behave and function as though he and his mother were an omnipotent system, a fused dual unity with a common boundary. However, they attempt to counteract the Cinderella fantasy of marrying a prince and living happily ever after by emphasizing that experiences in marriage can never fully compensate for inadequacies in the primal relationship. This means that each partner is required to take responsibility for keeping in touch with his or her adult capacities, both to cope with anxiety and also to maintain relationships outside the family (Howell and Bayes 1981).

Stage Two – adhesive clinging

One third of the couples who divorce in Great Britain and America split up within a year of marriage. It is during this first year that the 'delusion of fusion' collapses. Some couples become so shattered that they divorce, others progress to further stages of development. It is at this point that the partners may resort to 'adhesive clinging' to various aspects of the other's personality or social functioning. For example, partner choice may have arisen partly because of the woman's wish to have a husband who is successful in his profession, politically and intellectually aware, and proficient in handyman tasks. Similarly, the man may have chosen his wife partly because of her gregariousness, her domestic skills, and her physical charm and appearance. Such choices may be made in lieu of sustaining or developing these capacities in oneself. The chooser then clings adhesively to these chosen aspects in the partner. For example, the man having chosen his wife for her gregariousness, may not dare to socialize except in her presence. The wife, adhering to her husband's political awareness, may never develop her political consciousness sufficiently to vote according to her own judgement.

Other forms of clinging are far less obvious. It is often only when the partners are apart that extreme reactions tend to appear, indicating that adhesive clinging is part of the relationship. The partners, when apart, may appear suddenly collapsed, flat, as if torn off and discarded by the absent partner. Here are two examples illustrating adhesive clinging:

A husband, away on a business trip, telephoned home to find his wife terrified to be alone. She was full of worries about burglars, peeping toms, and the indistinct noises outside the house. Clearly, she had been relying too much on her husband's protective 'big-daddy' function, and was not acknowledging her own lack of security and anger about separation. Her hostility to her absent husband had been projected into the burglars and peeping toms who now haunted her.

A second example of adhesive clinging is seen in a very narcissistic novelist, who adhered to the notion that his wife was essentially a satellite whose life was destined to revolve about his as the moon revolves about the earth. When they had a child, and later, when she pursued her own studies, he suffered severe attacks of anxiety and depression, fearing that her independence made him a lesser man and threatened him with unendurable solitude.

The imagined infancy of such partners would be one in which they did not internalize parents who could adequately tolerate their infantile anguish and hostility. Perhaps because their mothers provided the necessary physical care but not an 'ordinary devoted' understanding of the baby's infantile anxieties, the baby was left to bear intolerable stress alone. Although the baby would continue to relate to the mother, he would need to develop a variety of defensive manoeuvres such as holding on to external objects in order to replace the internal security which his experience of mothering had not enabled him to establish. Preoccupation with the surface of objects (their colour, texture, or shape), clinging to objects or sounds, and even intellectual precocity, can all be used as defences in such a case. Such clinging to objects instead of the relation to the mother also is detrimental to establishing good relationships in the future.

In later life, such people may well need to cling adhesively to stereotyped sex-roles – how mother was, how father was, or how men are, how women are – in order to avoid the insecurity of having to discover their own unique pattern of relating. Any deviation from role-typical behaviour threatens them with a loss of identity. Many feminists have suggested a change in the employment possibilities for women, with women relinquishing the place they now have in the family, and men sharing in the parenting (Eichenbaum and Orbach 1982). However, for 'adhesive' partners, who are internally so unrooted that they have to cling to external frameworks, such as role definitions, any such change threatens an increase rather than a decrease of emotional disturbance: panic, guilt and depression being likely consequences. For them, only if there is an emotionally 'holding' environment within the couple, or in therapy or a self-help group setting, can this transition to new roles take place without excessive and damaging emotional upheaval.

Stage Three – the jack-in-the-box marriage

The 'jack-in-the-box' marriage is characterized by one partner's feeling of being imprisoned (the jack-*in*-the-box). All sorts of unwanted bits of the personality (e.g. weakness, incompetence, insensitivity) are projected onto this imprisoned partner, while the other partner is identified as a super-competent spouse or parent. This second partner, 'jack-*out*-of-the-box', has little knowledge of his true self, and suffers from a feeling of emptiness because so many aspects of the self have been projected out into the imprisoned partner.

Here is an example taken from psychotherapy with a couple, described by Halton and Magagna (1981):

> For thirty years this couple (both from very traumatic and deprived backgrounds) had been developing a psychic structure for surviving together. The structure which had evolved was heavily reliant on the notion of a 'super-parent/spouse', a father/mother or husband/wife who was highly idealized as successful, capable, impervious to criticism or self-doubt, able to tolerate and administer to the needs of the whole family ... This identification with a 'super-parent' was a way of coping with helplessness, neediness and rage ... identification with a person who is a model of tough self-sufficiency, one who could bear anything, was a way of avoiding the pain of mourning the lost parents (p. 87).

For men, the cultural stereotype of adult sex-roles is the reverse of what they experience in the early helplessness and dependency of infancy. Generally men are designated to be the 'super-parent', while women are imprisoned as the jack-in-the-box and laden with the man's projections of unwanted weakness. The image of the jack-in-the-box has been chosen because in an emotionally frail couple, unable to bear anxiety, frequently one partner springs up to be the 'super-parent', without problems, while the other partner is burdened with his own depression and the partner's projections of depression. Cultural stereotypes frequently employed in this pattern include the following:

(1) Assertiveness belongs to the man, while the woman is viewed as dependent and helpless without him. If a woman is 'the assertive one', the fear is that her husband will be labelled as 'feminine'.

(2) The woman bears the projection of being less intellectually able and less competent. If she has more ability there again arises the fear that she 'wears the pants' and her man is feminine.
(3) Weakness and naivety belong to the woman. If her partner is seen as less strong, she is again labelled as 'masculine', and has the feeling of badness associated with a failure to maintain her sexual identity.
(4) Hysterical, overemotional, tearful are all descriptions of what women 'are'. They are typically not ascribed to men.
(5) Passivity is attributed to women. Being feminine implies not being active in the courting process, in the sexual relationship or in the struggle for power in the couple's relationship.

The difficulty with these stereotypes is that if women assume the more positive characteristics, they immediately experience the fear of being, and may actually be, labelled 'the masculine one'. Hence, women often keep out of sight in the 'home-box'. When the jack-up-and-out-of-the-box is the man, it is likely to be the woman who cracks, under the load of undesirable projections from the man.

There are no easy solutions to the jack-in-the-box marriage. The best hope lies in the fact that, however much 'jack-out-of-the-box' may seem in a strong position, he is in fact 'emptied' by this use of projective identification. Both partners stand to gain by a withdrawal of the projections, but usually they will need the security of therapy to contain their anxieties if they are to face the fears involved in changing and actually make a change in their relationship.

Stage Four – the ideal marriage

Gathorne-Hardy (1981) says that in an ideal marriage men and women must be equally responsible for looking after both children and home and earning the family wage. Otherwise, there will be no fundamental change in marriage. No matter if it takes decades, an economic and social revolution of apparently some magnitude must be the ultimate goal.

This change of roles is taking place, but meanwhile an ideal marriage in the 1980s requires that both partners take on male and female functions while having a secure identification with the parent of the same sex. This is important in order to fulfil certain roles in the family designated as 'being a mother' or 'being a father'. The partners in such a marriage can be autonomous, but must be able to be intimately related without intensely fearing separation. They also require a sufficient frequency and depth of interchange to develop a satisfying internalization of a trustworthy relationship with the partner. Such an internalization involves experiencing a partner who can be trusted to love his spouse despite the spouse's difficulties.

Gathorne-Hardy quotes several studies showing that marriages where women work are happier, in particular sexually more successful, than ones in which women confine themselves to the home. We assume that at present a variety of home/work patterns can be found in good marriages. The essential ingredient, however, is that the partners are able to think about their experiences and bear emotional pain, without having to evacuate parts of their weak or competent selves into the other, or deny their experiences.

Osborne (1983) adds that it is important for the couple to acknowledge that it is impossible for all their emotional needs to be met within the couple. Friendships with others outside the family can support the psychological maturity and stability of the couple.

Conclusion

Our discussion has shown that 'progressive ideas' about sex-roles may be of great value in promoting liberation from infantile or detrimental patterns of relationship, or may collude with neurotic defences in individuals to keep the couple stuck in neurotic interaction. Which of these effects progressive ideas have depends not so much on the ideas themselves as on the level of psychological development the partners have reached when they come to make use of them. We have illustrated this theme with a number of examples, and more specifically have outlined a fourfold scheme of 'stages of psychic development' in couples, based on how the two partners handle their anxieties to do with separation and feared inadequacy in themselves or the spouse. In the final section, we have ventured to outline some of the requirements of an 'ideal marriage'.

References

Eichenbaum, L. and Orbach, S. (1982) *Outisde In/Inside Out*. Harmondsworth: Penguin.

Gathorne-Hardy, J. (1981) *Love, Sex, Marriage, and Divorce*. London: Jonathan Cape.

Goleman, D. (1984) Sexual fantasies and their meanings. *International Herald Tribune*. Paris, 8 March.

Halton, A. and Magagna, J. (1981) Making space for parents. *In* S. Box et al. (eds) *Psychotherapy with Families*. London: Routledge and Kegan Paul.

Howell, E. and Bayes, M. (1981) *Women and Mental Health*. New York: Basic Books Inc.

Marrin, M. (1984) Article in the *Guardian*, 5 March.

Osborne, K. (1983). Women in families. *Journal of Family Therapy, 5(i)*, 1–10.

Willi, J. (1982) *Couples in Collusion*. New York and London: Jason Aronson.

CHAPTER FOUR Patterns of Marital Breakdown
Jack Dominian

Introduction

The marked increased of marital breakdown in Britain is leading to a search to understand the reasons and in particular to comprehend the clinical manifestations of marital conflict. Little work has been carried out in discussing *patterns* of marital difficulties and, up to the present, therapy without an underlying theoretical framework of pathology has been the established practice. The most influential books on mechanisms of marital interaction have been those by Dicks (1967) and, later, by Skynner (1976). The impact of this dynamic thinking on the conceptualization of marital pathology has been extensive and has influenced the practice of marriage counselling in Britain. It provides a rich framework of thought and has been immensely useful but has also considerable limitations, particularly in the therapeutic situation where the couple concerned have to engage at a level of comprehending their difficulties, which are often extremely hard to grasp. In some ways this theoretical difficulty has been overcome by compensating with a rich array of therapeutic techniques, which include developments of the dynamic, behavioural, existential and eclectic approaches, and ignoring the underlying complexity of marital situations (Segraves 1982). One of the many hazards of this approach is that it is very difficult to compare the efficacy of various kinds of intervention because what is treated does not consist of a single entity but of different patterns of marital difficulties. Thus at the present moment there is an abundance of therapeutic frameworks with which to comprehend the underlying presentation of the problems.

In this chapter I shall offer an examination of this problem with particular reference to a framework of looking at patterns of marital breakdown developed by the author but not yet subjected to vigorous scientific examination. The patterns proposed are still at the theoretical level. Before discussing the author's model, it is necessary to look at marital problems on a larger scale.

Global social factors

The increase in divorce is a worldwide phenomenon, particularly well documented in the West (Chester 1977; Cherlin 1981). If that is the case, global factors are in operation. These have been examined elsewhere in this book and only a brief mention will be made here.

The first factor which has to be considered is the gradual emancipation of women and the changing nature of the man–woman relationship, moving towards equity.

The second is the progressive change of the nature of marriage from an institutional to a companionship or symmetrical variety. This change has fundamental implications for marital conflict. At the heart of marital problems is the failure of the couple to meet mutual needs. These mutual needs are likely to depend on the expectations of the couple, particularly the provision of what is essential for the survival of the marriage and its inherent quality. In a study by Levinger (1966) where 600 divorced couples had a mandatory interview with a marriage counsellor, middle-class marriages were found to be more concerned with psychological and emotional interaction while the lower-class spouses saw financial problems and violence as more important. This finding, which corresponds to clinical experience, can be interpreted to mean that until the material needs are met in marriage the partners cannot entertain the psychological and emotional ones. This is a fundamental piece of research because it draws our attention to the fact that, even though the whole of society is able to seek redress through divorce, the factors which lead to marital discontent are different. Thus at the beginning of every counselling interview one must be open to assess the priorities of the couple according to their needs, for, unless the couple are engaged at the level of their priority, counselling will be off target. The real difficulty is that so many couples present themselves at a point of marked transition in their expectations that both instrumental and affective needs have to be considered.

The third factor is related to the above. As material standards have risen rapidly in the last twenty-five years, at least until recently, both men and women have had their expectations deepened, in particular in terms of sexual and affective fulfilment. In the past these were bonuses to a materially successful marriage and were considered good fortune; today material survival has become a necessity, indeed a right. When material success is taken for granted, the emotional and sexual expectations in marriage increase.

Finally, all these changes are taking place against a background of diminishing influence of religion, the main prohibitive influence on divorce. The combination of increasing expectations and decreasing prohibitions, coupled with public acceptance of divorce, have undoubtedly increased its incidence.

Section One: Context

Specific social factors

These major social factors combine with more specific ones which have been studied in some detail, and include age at marriage, premarital pregnancy, social class, religion, and mixed backgrounds.

As far as age is concerned, marriages where the bride is under the age of 20 are more vulnerable, and the risk is increased when the groom is also under the age of 20. This finding has been widely confirmed (Glick and Norton 1971; Thornes and Collard 1979). The reasons for this are not far to seek. Young people may marry to escape from their parents, to find their separate existence, and, when this has been achieved, there is no reason to continue with the marriage. At this early age physical and intellectual maturity may have been reached, but not emotional. Emotional immaturity is a grave handicap in maintaining an emotional relationship, and it may collapse under the strain of two people needing an excess of support and affection which neither of them is able to give. In dynamic terms, one or both partners regress to an earlier stage of childhood and expect their partner to support them emotionally, which they cannot do, and the relationship ends in mutual recrimination of unmet needs. Most important of all, as we shall see later, the process of maturation means that one spouse may develop at a much greater pace, leaving the other behind, an outcome which is often interpreted as falling out of love. What this phrase indicates is that the needs for which the partner was married are no longer present and he or she has become redundant. In the past marriage not only marked a phase in the life of the couple, characterized by separation from parents, but also tolerated the different rate of growth of the partners. Today this is no longer acceptable and unless both partners develop at similar rates one spouse may be discarded.

Premarital pregnancy and its impact on marriage has been extensively examined and found to have an adverse impact on the outcome of marriage (Christensen 1963). In Thornes and Collard's (1979) study of premaritally pregnant marriages which ended in divorce, it was found that these were different from marriages in which there was no premarital pregnancy in that the former had a short courtship, lacked kinship support and were economically disadvantaged. Thus these marriages were starting with little mutual knowledge of each other, little support from relatives, and limited resources. These social strains require particularly strong and flexible spouses to overcome them and in the absence of such tenacity it is not surprising that the ensuing emotional stresses overwhelm the young partners.

If youthful marriages and those which start with a premarital pregnancy are individually vulnerable, then the combination of the two is particularly risky and this is exactly what has been shown (Rowntree 1964; Thornes and Collard 1979).

As far as social class is concerned, repeated studies in the USA have shown an inverse relationship between social class – and its component constituents, education and income – and divorce. The lower the socio-economic status, the greater is the risk of divorce (Bernard 1966). In Britain, the results were similar but not identical. The results of Thornes and Collard (1979) suggest that social classes V and III (non-manual) are the two most vulnerable classes. Social class V is the group that contains an increase in the number of marriages with brief courtship, a greater number of youthful marriages and of premarital pregnancies, and, linked as it is with material disadvantage, the combination is particularly vulnerable. What about social class III (non-manual)? Thornes and Collard suggest that members of this class are in a particularly unstable position. They do not belong to the upper echelon of society, nor to the lower, and have particular difficulty in establishing their own identity with all the con-sequent tensions that this involves.

The traditional dictate of the Judaeo-Christian religions is to enter into and stay in a permanent relationship. Religious adherence, however, may be in name only and so the crucial factor is whether a deeper commitment indicated by church attendance prevents divorce. The findings suggest that this is the case (Thornes and Collard 1979).

Finally, all research has shown that couples are attracted by social similarity. Partners are likely to marry someone with a similar background of age, social class, religion, education and intelligence. The evidence is overwhelmingly in favour of homogamy, that is like marrying like. When people of mixed backgrounds marry, the risks of marital conflict increase. These risks arise not only because of different expectations but also because the differences are held responsible for problems which have alternative reasons, e.g. psychological. For example, in the past a combination of a Roman Catholic with a non-Catholic partner might have blamed their difficulties on the difference in contraceptive practices, omitting to see that there were sexual and emotional difficulties which were being displaced onto the subject of contraception.

The combination of major and universal social factors with these specific social ones provides the background for interpersonal conflict. Understand-ing such conflict is the key to therapy and, as already mentioned, it is important to recognize both material and emotional needs and their interac-tion with each other.

It is here that the author's model fits in and it will now be described.

Model for interaction

The model under consideration is based on two crucial factors. The first is the phase of the marriage and the second is the dimension of the relationship involved. The phase of the marriage is part of a continuing tradition of research which sees marriage divided into several phases of a life cycle. These include the period before the arrival of the children, the advent of the children, their preschool phase, children at school, the presence of adolescents, their departure from home, leading to the stage where the couple are left on their own (the empty nest period) until the death of one spouse. This life cycle research is mainly American and has several phases. The present model has reduced these phases to three.

The first phase includes the first five years of marriage. If the average age of marriage for a man is 25 and for a woman 23 (*Population Trends* 1984), then the first five years of marriage bring the couple to about the age of 30. This division of the first phase is not arbitrary. It has been established that the first five years are critical for marriage. Both Chester (1971) and Thornes and Collard (1979) found that between 30 and 40 per cent of all those who divorce have ceased living together by the fifth anniversary of their marriage. Furthermore, the problems that start during these early years are often the ones that contribute to divorce whenever it occurs.

The second phase is between the ages of 30 and 50. These are the years which cover the growth of children, promotion at work, the children's adolescence, the death or illness of parents, but above all, personal change and maturation. Men and women change during these years, outgrow each other and find each other no longer relevant in their lives.

The third phase is characterized by the menopause for women, the departure of children, the cessation of work and ultimately the death of one partner, statistically the chances being high that it will be the husband. But often the couple can have twenty or more years together to enjoy a new degree of satisfaction with each other and with their children and grandchildren. On the other hand the departure of children may reveal an underlying emptiness which has existed for a long time but which is now acted upon by separation and divorce.

These are the three phases of the schema roughly indicating the sort of problems that might be occurring at each stage of the marriage. But what constitutes the problems? In this theoretical model there are five dimensions involved: the social, emotional, physical, intellectual and spiritual. As one is listening to the couple, their difficulties are assessed in a sequence of importance with the various factors taken into consideration. These dimensions tell a practitioner very quickly the viability of a marriage. For example, if the couple have not engaged in any common social activity for years, nor had sexual intercourse, nor shown affection to each other for the same period of time, then it is obvious that in most instances there is no longer a marital relationship left. This evaluation is particularly important in trying to handle the question that every counsellor or therapist has to face, namely the seeking of advice as to whether the participants should terminate their marriage or not. Clearly, direct advice should not be given. It is up to the couple to decide. But if one goes over the ground of these dimensions, and finds that none is present in any meaningful sense, then the couple usually draw their own conclusion and realize the emptiness of their marital relationship. In practice the story unfolded reveals which dimension or dimensions provide the key issues that should be focused on. There are two essential parts in marital therapy. The first is to offer insight by appropriate interpretation or explanation of the nature of the problem. With this information, which can be achieved in as little as one interview, the couple can then work out what needs to be done. The second is to help the couple achieve the desired change, completely or partially.

The evaluation of and focusing on these five dimensions helps in structuring and directing the therapy.

Given this model which acts as a basic framework, is there a series of patterns of marital difficulties that can be discerned? Such patterns do appear and in the second half of this chapter a description will be given of such recurrent marital problems.

Patterns of marital breakdown

Before we look for specific patterning of marital difficulties leading to marital breakdown, it is important to note that, whatever the underlying problem may be, the presenting manifestations of marital difficulties are usually the following. The first is an escalation of arguments, accompanied by verbal or physical violence. The second is the opposite, namely a growing indifference and non-involvement. The third is the deterioration or absence of sexual activity or the presence of a third party. The fourth is a complaint about alcohol and its various complications. The fifth is a complaint of deceit in its various manifestations. The task of the therapist is to trace the marital interaction from its inception and see which of the five dimensions have led to the present complaint.

Phase I: the first five years

Social dimension   There are five social factors that appear repeatedly in the complaints of this phase, or in later phases, when one partner looks retrospectively at the behaviour of their spouse. These factors are:

1. Separation from parents or key friends.
2. Housing and household arrangements.
3. Money.
4. Work.
5. Leisure.

The normal process of development for the vast majority of men and women involves a gradual physical and emotional separation from parents, an interlude of a few years followed by marriage. Marriage implies a distinct social, physical and emotional separation from parents. The spouse becomes the crucial person in the partner's life and it is with him or her that the main communication, discussion and decision making takes place in the overwhelming majority of marriages.

There are two patterns of marital problems that are seen at frequent intervals. The first one is characterized by the inability of the husband or wife to really detach themselves from their home. Despite the fact that the spouses are married, one or the other spends most of the time in the parents' house. Sometimes all the leisure hours are spent there. Alternatively they are in constant communication with the mother or father by telephone, and their main discussions and decisions are taken with them rather than with their partner. Sometimes the husband of the wife who acts like this is taken into the family business and the parents appear to be totally unwilling to let go. Alternatively, when the couple have an argument, the one who is attached to the parents runs to them seeking shelter, protection and support against the other. In all these situations the spouse begins to realize that he or she is bypassed in favour of the partner's parents and remonstrates with the partner, to no purpose. The strong attachment to the parents remains and is reinforced if one of the parents dies. The mother is often the key parent, and mother–son or mother–daughter attachments that exclude the partners are frequent ones. Sometimes the son or daughter will go on visiting the parent for many years, long after he or she has ceased to take any interest in the partner.

The second pattern is somewhat different. Here a husband or wife is so insecure that he or she will not allow the partner to visit the family at all. There will be violent rows in which the possessive or jealous spouse will attack the partner for the slightest evidence of friendship with the parents. Such a spouse is often extremely anxious and unable to cope with any degree of aloneness, and gradually tries to imprison the partner to the ultimate detriment of marriage.

The same jealousy may also apply to any contact with an ex-girlfriend or ex-boyfriend. The jealous spouse needs to banish such people from the circle of friends, long after they have ceased to have any erotic, personal meaning. Gradually such a spouse will try to prohibit other friends of the partner with some excuse or other, but on the basis of the reality that they cannot tolerate any competition for attention.

As far as housing is concerned, there is evidence that a separate abode is a facilitating event in the life of the newly married. Divorced populations show a much greater degree of sharing and frequent changes of housing (Thornes and Collard 1979). But whether a couple have independent accommodation or not, who does what in it can become important. With the current social changes, men are expected to undertake more household chores than in the past. During courtship they may make generous promises but when they marry often the husband returns to a traditional pattern of doing the minimum whilst his wife does the majority of the work. As in all marital situations, the outcome of such loss of support from the husband depends on the personality and resources of the wife. Normally she is irritated but accepts a good deal of the traditional role of cooking, cleaning, etc. However, sometimes when she is working herself or when she feels strongly about her independence and the equality of sharing responsibility, such unwillingness on the part of the husband becomes totally unacceptable and the relationship founders on this issue.

Money often features as a symptom in serious marital difficulties, and the conflict over it takes three forms. The first applies to the situation where the husband usually provides insufficient funding for the household needs. If the wife is working, she may make up the difference through her income, but she resents this and a sense of grievance is built up. This grievance may stand on its own or become part of a wider series of problems. For example, the husband may accuse her of incompetent housekeeping, which adds insult to injury. Not only is she not receiving enough money, but on top of this she is regarded as a defective manageress. The second financial problem concerns the responsible handling of money. Here the husband may not be able to cope with bills, which are either left unpaid, unopened or pushed on to the wife to deal with. If the wife is financially insecure or excessively worried about financial order, then her husband's financial incapacity will make her lose her trust in him, to the point where she wants to go. Thirdly, money not only has an economic value; it also has an emotional one. In giving money to each other spouses feel that through the money they are being taken care of, protected and even appreciated. So often wives say 'If you loved me you would not keep me short of money'.

Perhaps one of the commonest complaints of wives, but sometimes of husbands, is the excessive work that husbands undertake, as a result of which they are not available to their wives, who feel that the only reason for existence is to be a housekeeper and a source of sex. This absence of attention may produce a bitter reaction on the part of the wife, who feels annihilated as a person.

Intimately linked with work is leisure. Another repeated pattern is the man who marries and spends all his leisure time playing the games of his bachelor days, dragging his wife to soccer, rugby or cricket, whether she likes it or not. Worse than this is his regular attendance at his pub where he meets his pals, never taking his wife with him.

Any of the above social patterns of difficulties may exist alone or in combination, and may be sufficient at times to precipitate the dissolution of the relationship as the spouse recognizes that the ceremony of marriage has not made any impression on the partner who continues to act as if he or she were a single person.

Emotional dimension   In the early phases of describing marital difficulties the emotional dimension was largely related to such psychodynamic principles as projection, collusion, projective identification and so on. These mechanisms, established by Dicks (1967) and other workers at the Tavistock, dominated thinking about marital problems for several decades, yet, though they undoubtedly occur, they are not invariably present, and explaining them to couples can be fairly difficult. A rule that most marital therapy tries to follow is to interpret situations to people at the point where they are with their experience so they can understand and assimilate the dynamics of their behaviour.

At this simple level the commonest emotional complaint that spouses make is that their partner does not show enough affection. In practice this means that often he, sometimes she, will not talk to them, discuss things, say anything affirmative or exhibit physical contact. The story of the man who comes home, reads the paper, has his meal, watches TV and says very little or anything to his wife is one of the most common in marital breakdown. A variant of this pattern is that he will say very little to his wife but at a social gathering he will not stop talking.

Another major problem is not the lack of demonstration of affection but the inability to register and receive it. This is often a complaint made by men that their wife cannot tolerate being touched, kissed or hugged. When the wife is asked about this the commonest excuse is that the 'affection' leads to sex. But a closer look at the problem indicates that she cannot accept loving feelings from her husband. The inability to receive loving feelings may arise from a background in which feelings were not shown at home, or in which the person grew up feeling unloveable; or it may be that they have a make-up which cannot handle feelings, a rather cold, detached personality in which the cognitive may be more important than the affective. As has been mentioned before, the behaviour of one partner may or may not be tolerated, depending on the needs and personality of the spouse. If the spouse is an emotionally needy person who wants a demonstration of affection, marrying someone who is undemonstrative may be intolerable. If the spouse is someone who feels urgently the need to be needed and cannot find the spouse interested in this demonstration of affection, then equally they find the situation intolerable.

The next emotional pattern frequently associated with difficulties is the way a couple quarrel. Usually one or the other is highly and consistently critical of the other's achievements. Whatever they do is wrong, leading to the situation where apparently they cannot do anything to please. The wife who is often the victim of this behaviour feels constantly put down, ultimately looking elsewhere for recognition and appreciation.

If the couple quarrel, then normally one or the other recognizes that they are in the wrong and apologizes. There are husbands and wives who find it impossible to apologize. Even if they are in the wrong, apology is out of the question. They withdraw into themselves in a protracted sulk, and their spouse has constantly to take the initiative to resume conversation.

The husband or wife who is highly critical, rarely if ever satisfied with the spouse's efforts, constantly complaining, entering quickly into a frenzy of abuse and never able to accept responsibility is a stock figure in serious marital conflict.

In these early years another pattern may be present, in which a man and woman have come to each other as a way of gaining their freedom and independence from parents. They marry only to find that their partner makes demands on them like their parents. Both of them want to live in an autonomous manner, only to find that they are no more free now than before. These marriages do not last because the object of the marriage was not a man–woman relationship but a means for obtaining freedom. Having achieved that, they are not prepared to be chained to each other and they go their separate ways.

Physical dimension   The physical dimension involves both the health and the sexual activity of the couple. Beginning with the physical health of the couple, one meets at regular intervals in hospital referrals men and women who started their marriage with a serious physical illness or were struck by it shortly afterwards. Here the spouse often ceases to be a husband or wife in that there is no possibility for sex or affection to be demonstrated. Time passes, measured in months or even years. The healthy spouse has now become a nurse and no longer treats the other as a marital partner. When the time comes for resumption of sex, this is no longer possible – the husband–wife relationship of the start of the marriage has become a deep friendship without the sexual dimension – and indeed such marriages die because their character has changed in the course of the illness.

Sexual patterns can be divided into two. The first is concerned with the sexual difficulties of function where the affective relationship is good. These problems do not often conclude with marital breakdown because they can be helped. These problems include functional difficulties, such as non-consummation, premature ejaculation, partial or incomplete impotence and vaginismus.

The patterns of sexual difficulties that are associated with marital breakdown are often associated with the deterioration of the relationship. This deterioration may occur over the quality of sexual intercourse or other factors. As far as the quality of sexual intercourse is concerned, the commonest complaints by wives are that their husbands are indifferent lovers, showing no affection or preparation before the act, and, more rarely, that they want unacceptable sexual variations. The other complaint by wives is that their husbands want too much sex. Husbands complain that their wives are unresponsive or frigid. These complaints are frequently involved in petitions for divorce, and imply a deteriorating relationship between the couple. The presence of an extramarital affair in these early years is not common but when it does occur it can jeopardize the marriage.

Finally, there is one rare pattern in which a couple have had successful intercourse prior to marriage, or when living together, but the moment they marry the wife ceases to be interested totally. A couple that I treated had lived together for four years with successful intercourse. They married, only to find that the wife completely lost interest in coitus. After four years of this total abstinence the wife realized, and he admitted it, that her husband was having an affair. The moment she knew this her sexual desire returned and intercourse was resumed. In this instance the wife only wanted companionship, and when she made certain of this, through marriage, she lost interest in sex, only to recapture it when she felt threatened that she might lose her husband. Other women lose interest in sex because deep inside them they feel unattractive or unwanted, and they cannot really believe that anyone wants them. Unless these patterns of complete loss of sexual desire are appreciated the marriage does not survive.

The advent of children provides a familiar pattern of problems. These include an excess of tiredness and loss of sexual desire. Many couples trace the beginning of their difficulties to the deterioration of sexual activity after the birth of a particular child. This loss of sexual activity may be accompanied by the husband having an affair. The reaction of the wife to the affair may be the key to the outcome of the marriage.

Another pattern of difficulties after the birth of children is the change in life-style for the couple, with heavier demands placed on the wife. At this point, with sexual life at a lower peak, tiredness a major factor, the wife needs the active support of the husband. If this is not forthcoming the wife feels actively neglected. The advent of children thus places considerable pressure on the couple and part of the well-being of the marriage depends on the resilience of the couple, in the face of this challenge, to come together and support each other.

The postpuerperal period is not only marked by tiredness for many women but for some it is clouded with a depressive reaction. A picture of a depressed, tired woman with no libido is a familiar one and here the outcome of the marriage depends on the patience of the spouse and the recovery of the wife's spirits.

Intellectual and spiritual dimension   Couples are interacting constantly at the cognitive and value level. They need to make sense of each other with words and ideas.

One pattern that is seen is the hasty marriage in which a couple decide to get married after a few weeks. They do not really know each other but become infatuated, that is to say their attraction is mainly physical. When they come to live together they find they have very little in common and their relationship cannot be sustained.

Assuming, however, that their intelligence and cognitive level of communication is similar, there may be difficulties in the way two people try to make sense of each other. There is, for example, the spouse who wants to discuss the most minute details. No conversation is deemed complete until the last little point has been clarified. If this is not achieved then the points left undiscussed will be raised repeatedly. This type of approach has an obsessional quality about it, although it is interpreted by the other partner as harassing or nagging.

Another pattern which presents difficulties is the situation where one talks and emphasizes the literal or rational meaning of words. For example, one of the partners states that they do not want to go out, meaning that, with a bit of coaxing, they will be prepared to go out. If the emotional under-tones of the communication are missed, then the cross-exchange between the rational and the affective, both of which are misinterpreted, can play havoc. Spouses complain that their partners do not say what they mean or stick to their words, and these complaints are countered by the criticism that they in turn are insensitive to emotional signals. A classical example is the husband or wife who has just become hurt and is upset. Their partner wants to make up and goes to embrace them. They are told in a temper to 'Go away and leave me alone'. In fact the last thing they want is to be left alone and they really want their objections overruled. This example is given to show the poor empathy of the spouse.

Lack of empathy has further complications. Unless spouses recognize the affective motives of their partners they will accuse them of dishonesty, deceit, lying, cheating and all sorts of other moral accusations. It is impor-tant for the counsellor to disentangle these moral judgements and show to both partners that the intention and motivation are in fact more authentic. Silence, for example, may be interpreted as deceit. Spouses insist that they want to know everything, and when their partners withhold information they accuse them of deceit. When some event is interpreted differently they are accused of lying. Classically the major task of a therapist has been to interpret the differences of couples or their instinctive behaviour camou-flaged in neurotic symptoms. What is suggested here is that the major role of counselling is to interpret negative moral terminology which is accusatory. Spouses have to be rescued from being declared lazy, selfish, liars etc. If that does not happen, the couple spend all their energy in an arid exchange of 'You are lazy' – 'No I am not....'. These sterile vicious circles have to be interpreted and the real cause of the problem elucidated.

Phase II: 30–50 years

The second phase of marriage is characterized by two features. The first is the acknowledgement that persistent problems will *not* change, and the second is *change*. Change is a major feature of this phase, contributing considerably to marital difficulties, and here the emphasis will be placed upon it.

Social Social change is primarily an alteration in the status of the individual. Social mobility can be upward or downward. Upward social mobility by either spouse implies that they move into a new circle of affluence, friends, interests or activities. In the past the person who moved upwards has usually been the husband who has made a success of his job. By doing so he moves into a new world to which he aspires but to which his wife may not. His new circle of friends may leave her cold and she may feel that she no longer belongs to her husband. He is preoccupied with his new contacts and may be critical of his previous pattern of living, whilst his wife still feels at home with it. If the friends are business associates, the discussions may be limited to the theme of work, leaving the wife uninterested and an outsider. Increasingly these priorities may occur in the life of the wife, and it is the husband who has to adapt to a new circle of friends. The point may be reached with either partner where they feel they have nothing in common any more and decide to go their separate ways.

The downward movement is brought about by unemployment, drink, drugs or illness. Most of these features are associated with loss of work, poverty, and rise in tension and conflict with each other. If the conflict becomes worse, there is violence, and the combination of violence and drink is very damaging to marital life.

During the second phase there are two other social events that impinge on marriage. The first is the impact on the spouses of their parents' deteriorating health and the second is the presence of adolescent children.

When the spouses reach their 40s their parents are likely to become ill or die. During illness either spouse but particularly the wife may have to be extra supportive to the ailing parents. The wife may be expected to support her own parents or those of her husband. Normally, this help is given without any acrimony but it does present an extra burden to the wife and this in turn requires additional support or facilitation from her husband. When this is not forthcoming, or when the husband resents the time spent by his wife helping her parents, the situation produces marital stress. This in itself is not a cause of marital breakdown but if there are already pre-existing stresses the parental illness may bring matters to a head. If one of the parents dies there is often pressure to bring the other parent into the matrimonial home. When this happens it may set up a constant source of friction. Since often it is the mother that survives, there is almost a return to the early years of marriage when a mother and daughter act together and the husband feels excluded.

The presence of adolescent children does not necessarily imply stress in the family. Most adolescents go through this period without provoking their parents. A minority, however, act out their problems and cause strain. The two usual areas of conflict are sexual and the flouting of authority. Sexual acting out on the part of the daughter raises the level of anxiety of parents. The mother turns to the father for an authoritative lead and, if he does not give it, the unresolved sexual situation with the daughter stirs up the residual unresolved sexual problems of the parents. Occasionally the wife will accuse her husband of having a sexual interest in the daughter which is vehemently denied. The daughter's active sexual behaviour worries the mother regarding the possibility of pregnancy, and the husband is blamed for not exerting more authority.

Both the illness of the spouses' parents and the adolescent problems aggravate preexisting difficulties and may be the straw that breaks the camel's back.

Emotional   The growth from emotional dependence to independence is perhaps the single most important factor in patterns of marital breakdown. A typical story is that of a woman who marries at the age of 18. At that time she is content to play a secondary role to her husband. She tries to please him, do his will, and sacrifices herself for him. She may stick to his friends, allow him to drive her, accept his decisions, and do things his way. Then imperceptibly, little by little, she changes within herself. She has her children and feels that she can cope with them. She begins work and finds that she is good at it. She even begins to take her own decisions and finds that they are wise and sound. Thus she begins to live a life of gradual independence. Now she wants to take the initiative in her life. She decides she wants to drive her car, have her own circle of friends, do things in her own way and decide for herself her priorities. She wants to have a say in her husband's life, know how much he earns and have some control over the money.

Most couples develop through this phase from dependence to independence, and most spouses adjust to each other's growth. There are partners, however, usually husbands, who resist this drive for independence. Instead of cooperating they resist every change and block it. They tell their wives they see no reason for change. Indeed, they maintain that things were much happier when they were in charge. This intransigence of the husband brings resistance from the wife. She feels that she is trapped in a relationship where her husband has changed from being a lover into a father. She longs for her independence and freedom and insists on it. There may be blazing rows or a quiet withdrawal on her part. A wife said, in these circumstances, 'When

I was young my father told me what to do, then it was my teachers, and now it is my husband. I have had enough of being told what to do. Now I want to run my own life.' The most powerful weapon in her resistance is withdrawal from sexual intercourse. This is a severe attack on the husband who tries to overcome her defiance by further attempts to manipulate her. In the end such a wife decides to leave her husband. She may or may not have formed an alternative relationship. When she does, there is somebody next door or at work who is prepared to treat her in accordance with her present, newly found independence. She is no longer a child but an adult, and wants to be treated as such.

Physical The same changes can be seen in the sexual field. Often a woman, sometimes a man, may carry on having intercourse for a number of years in order to please their partner, but without enjoying it. Then they have an affair and discover that there is nothing wrong with their sexual ability. In the affair they respond with genuine sexual enthusiasm. In a sense they have come of age sexually. They realize that sex is not a mere passive manipulation to give pleasure to their partner but an adult experience in which they can participate to the full.

In these circumstances they may leave their spouse or often they stay in the marriage and approach sexual intercourse with a feeling that they have the capacity and the right to enjoy it for themselves. It ceases to be a passive experience. It becomes an active participation in which they contribute as much of their personality as possible. They have now discovered that they are a fully sexual person.

In this phase an extramarital affair is not uncommon. From what has already been written, it can be seen that such an affair is either a definitive alternative choice, signifying the end of the marital relationship, or it is an attempt to discover something outside marriage which is missing inside it. The outcome of such affairs depends on the underlying integrity of the marital relationship. If that is sound, then the affair is worked out to a satisfactory end. However, if the affair signals the seeking of an alternative partner, then the marriage is unlikely to survive.

Intellectual Just as men and women come to discover their adult, independent feelings in the emotional and social fields, so they discover their own separate ideas, values and goals in life. This is a phase where spouses may go their separate ways. In particular this is the time when wives may decide to try their hand at a new business career, or begin to feel frustrated with the routine of housekeeping and care of children. Men may find that their job no longer satisfies them and they want to try a new career. The ability of the marriage to survive depends on the spouses' capacity to absorb their differences on the strength of their underlying affection and sexual fulfilment.

Spiritual   During their 40s the spiritual development of people takes a special turn. Spirituality in Western society is expressed in a minority form by those attending church, and by a majority who are concerned with transcendental, ultimate values without being committed to the practice of any particular faith.

A number of spiritual changes take place which can be summarized in two main forms. The first is the abandonment of the practice of faith accompanied by widespread disillusionment. Those who pursue this line are often men and women who follow the dictates of their faith through the persistence of childhood fears, through habit and the presence of an unquestioning attitude. There is a parallel growth of autonomy and confidence which makes the remnants of childhood religion unnecessary. Once again the abandonment of religion is not a cause of marital breakdown but what happens is a gradual erosion of common life and the couple find that they have less and less common interests to bind them together.

There is, however, an opposite trend in which the spiritual side unfolds and deepens. Having completed the tasks of successful work and family formation, men and women are in a position of asking, at the beginning of the second half of their life, the meaning and purpose of it all. For a number this is the time when a deeper spiritual purpose is sought. If this outlook is not shared by both spouses, a tension is created regarding the ultimate values to be pursued. Wives often complain that their husbands remain too attached to material and power ends whilst they want to spend more time together, doing good works, pursuing spiritual objectives or even engaging in active religious preoccupations. But in general there is a change in values, moving from the material to the transcendental, and, if this is not shared by the couple as a couple, the underlying unity is diluted.

Phase III: 50 years to death of one spouse

Social   The commonest pattern of marital breakdown of this phase is that after the children have departed the parents split up. The reasons for the separation have usually been present for a long time. There has been a lack of affectionate, sexual and intellectual bonds and they have stayed together for the sake of the children. When they grow up and leave there is no common bond to hold the parents and they go their separate ways.

Another pattern, seen particularly in the upper socioeconomic group, is the discarding of a wife who has played a particular social role. For example, I have met a number of ambassadors who have needed their wives as social partners in the course of their careers. Then at retirement they have sought a divorce and formed a new relationship with a younger woman because they are free to concentrate on a personal emotional encounter. Businessmen and other professional men who have been busy all their lives with their work may decide, on retirement, to enjoy a different style of life with a new partner. Needless to say, such breakdowns cause much hardship to the discarded wife who feels that she has given the best years of her life to her husband only to find that now as she looks forward to a rewarding retirement, she is dismissed.

The pattern applies not only to men but to women too, who have had children but never enjoyed the raising of a family. These are people who are seeking an exclusive, close relationship and believe that now they are free of their career and family obligations they can pursue intense emotional relations.

Emotional The process of emancipation proceeds into the early part of this phase and now, as with the social dimension, it is the turn of the husband to consider leaving the home. Husbands who have spent thirty years in the same relationship now discover the desire to experiment with a new relationship. This behaviour of a middle-aged man is often interpreted as the desire to find a younger partner. This is not always the case. The existing sexual life of such a couple may be good. The change is an internal one and the husband's emotional desire is to make a free choice for the first time in his life. So far life has been a social and moral routine which has required compliance. Now a newly found independence makes the husband seek a new relationship which reflects his own choice, rather than continue in a relationship which was foisted on him by compliance with familial, social and religious obligations. The dilemma of these men is immense. They have a deep sense of moral righteousness and are torn between their obligations to the past and the intense drive inside them to find a new meaning in their life.

Sexual The sexual difficulties of the menopause and male impotence problems span the late phases of the second phase and the beginning of the third phase. They are often physiological events and rarely lead to emotional difficulties responsible for marital breakdown.

Nevertheless some well-established features should be mentioned. For example, it is generally agreed that the menopause itself does not threaten sexual activity. The majority of women sail through the menopause without any impairment of the frequency of intercourse. Women, however, who find intercourse unacceptable before the menopause, often use this physiological event as an excuse for not continuing with coitus. They withdraw from their husbands sexually and in doing so often offer little affection to their spouses. Men in their fifties, deprived of sexual activity and affection, find the situation frustrating and intolerable. They may have an extramarital affair which renders them liable to marital breakdown.

As far as impotence is concerned, Kinsey (1948) showed that impotence begins in the middle 40s and thereafter rises steadily. But between 50 and 65 it is of the order of 10 to 20 per cent so that, in those who present in this age group with impotence, psychological causes that are reversible should not be excluded. In particular men lose the capacity to attain spontaneous erections but may do so with the assistance of their spouses. When there is good will between spouses this is precisely what is attained. But when the relationship between them has deteriorated the wife may refuse to be cooperative and marital problems may arise. The lesson in this age group is that impotence is not necessarily irreversible. In particular men of this age group who marry for the second time may be initially anxious and alarmed at the prospect of intercourse which renders them impotent. Reassurance may be cost-effective.

Intellectual Freed from the constraints of work, after retirement, men in particular may change the direction of their lives. If they were active before, they may want solitude and peace now, or if they were leading an introverted life, they may want excitement and activity. If marital stress is to be avoided the spouse who changes needs to carry the partner along with them. At other times the wife has been patiently waiting for retirement in order to do things together with her partner. If he, however, wants to put his feet up, refuses to socialize, then there is much marital stress.

But in general these are the years when the couple pursue common objectives of mutual satisfaction. Marital breakdown occurs only when one spouse realizes that the much wanted changes will never be possible because the personality of the spouse continues unaltered during retirement.

Spiritual As in the second phase, so in this, one partner may take an exceptional interest in religion or some new value. If their partner cannot share it with them then this becomes a divisive experience.

Summary

Patterns of marital breakdown are relative to a particular culture and its expectations. In this chapter, for example, the point has been made that woman's emancipation has played a crucial role in the current themes of marital tension. Equally, sexual fulfilment is now considered to be more important and its absence is considered a major loss to the marriage relationship. But throughout the history of man marital breakdown has ensued when some particular need or value is not met or flouted.

As far as contemporary marriage is concerned, it is important to appreciate the priority which couples give to the various areas of their relationship. For example, in the past an extramarital affair carried a much greater social censure than it does today, although fidelity still remains an important expression of mutual trust.

Because the patterns outlined in this paper reflect current social and psychological priorities in marriage, they are valuable indications of the central issues facing counsellors. By identifying correctly the main focus or thrust of the disturbance, there is little danger of wasting time on secondary phenomena. The couple are directed at once to the central issues and in this way the spouses are encouraged from the start of counselling to appreciate the main difficulty and focus on it. For example, much time is wasted by couples who call each other lazy, selfish, self-centred; accusations which are then denied by the partner. The counsellor translates these accusations into a main theme of marital conflict. In this way both the couple and the counsellor can work at the problem with the certainty that they are tackling the main issues with the minimum waste of time and energy.

Finally, if these patterns are accurate clinical observations of marital breakdown they hold out the hope that preventive work can be done in time before the situation gets out of control.

References

Bernard, J. (1966) Marital stability and patterns of status variables. *Journal of Marriage and the Family, 28,* 421–424.

Cherlin, A. J. (1981) *Marriage, divorce, remarriage.* Cambridge, Mass. and London: Harvard University Press.

Chester, R. (1971) The duration of marriage to divorce. *Britsh Journal of Sociology, 22,* 172–182.

Chester. R. (ed.) (1977) *Divorce in Europe.* Leiden: Martinus Nighoff Social Sciences Division.

Christensen, H. T. (1963) Timing of first pregnancy as a factor in divorce: a cross-cultural analysis. *Eugenic Quarterly, 10,* 119–130.

Dicks, H. V. (1967) *Marital tensions.* London: Routledge and Kegan Paul.

Glick, P. C. and Norton, A. J. (1971) Frequency, duration and probability of marriage and divorce. *Journal of Marriage and the Family, 33,* 307–317.

Kinsey, A. C. (1948) *Sexual behaviour in the human male.* London: Saunders.

Levinger, G. (1966) Sources of marital dissatisfaction among applicants for divorce. *American Journal of Orthopsychiatry, 36,* 803–907.

Population Trends (1984) *35,* 46. London: HMSO.

Rowntree, G. (1964) Some aspects of marital breakdown in Britain during the last thirty years. *Population Studies, 18,* 147–151.

Segraves, R. T. (1982) *Marital therapy.* New York and London: Plenum.

Skynner, A. C. R. (1976) *One flesh: separate persons.* London: Constable.

Thornes, B. and Collard, J. (1979) *Who divorces?* London: Routledge and Kegan Paul.

CHAPTER FIVE The Work and Impact of the National Marriage Guidance Council

Nicholas Tyndall

Historical context

The NMGC is the main specialist marital agency providing a national service throughout the United Kingdom[1]. Its roots lie in the British Social Hygiene Council which set up a Marriage Committee in 1937 in response to concern about marriage breakdown, as the divorce rate had grown from 4,000 per annum at the end of the 1920s to 8,000 by the end of the 1930s. The Marriage Committee sought to explore alternative ways of providing help to couples facing the prospect of marriage breakdown at the same time as A. P. Herbert's Matrimonial Causes Act of 1937 greatly extended the grounds for divorce.

The first Marriage Guidance Council was thus formed in London, under the chairmanship of The Reverend Dr Herbert Gray who was author of many books on sex education and a great pastor. His fellow founder members were practitioners in medicine, social work, the law and the magistracy. Though strongly committed to the institution of marriage, their wide experience of working with unhappy couples caused them to give preeminence to the pastoral aspect in their work rather than to the preservation of marriage at all costs.

The Council suspended activities for three years at the beginning of the Second World War. As the end of hostilities drew in sight, it became apparent that the disruption in family life caused by servicemen's long separations would create a greater need than ever for advice on marriage problems. From 1944 MGCs were formed in many towns, and in 1947 about a hundred local councils formed the National Marriage Guidance Council to supervise the rapid developments. Shortly afterwards the Catholic Church parted company over the issue of contraception and established its own Council.[2]

The present pattern of the service was established in these early postwar days. A small but fervent central staff encouraged the birth of new councils, published popular sixpenny booklets on all aspects of marriage and family life and assumed responsibility for the selection and training of counsellors. These early counsellors had no body of theory or practice to guide them but were strongly motivated to respond to couples in distress, and 'as nobody else was trying, we must needs try' wrote Herbert Gray (quoted by Sanctuary 1968, p. 15). Records show that at that time they acted primarily as a source of reference to doctors, psychiatrists, lawyers and family planning. Only gradually did it become apparent that as 'someone to turn to' they could themselves often be the main therapeutic agent, merely by offering a shoulder to cry on. As the body of counselling experience has grown, so has the number of referrals to other services diminished. John Wallis's writings as Training Officer chart this slow awareness of counselling as an end in itself. He emphasized the necessity for the counsellor to be an attentive listener, not butting in or giving advice, but 'accepting the confused feelings of another who is troubled and trying to find a way out of his difficulties...' (Wallis and Booker 1958, p. 32).

Recognition of NMGC's role was given by the Denning Committee on Matrimonial Procedures in 1947, and financial support from central government was granted the following year. Since then the Home Office, which was the government department most closely connected with matrimonial work through its oversight of probation officers in Domestic Courts, has continued grants-in-aid to the three recognized marital agencies.[3]

NMGC now consists of some 160 constituent MGCs and has headquarters and a training college in Rugby. It remains essentially a voluntary organization, providing a marriage counselling service primarily through voluntary counsellors, backed up by a small number of paid professional staff based at Rugby and in six regional centres. The study undertaken by the Home Office in conjunction with the Department of Health and Social Security, and published as *Marriage Matters* in 1979, acknowledged the key role of NMGC as a non-medical, non-statutory agency, and commended it as a voluntary service with professional standards. That Working Party saw no reason for major changes, but recommended that ways should be found of making further use of the expertise of existing counsellors and that closer liaison should be formed with those professions and agencies which provide other doors on which people knock for marital help.

The work of NMGC must be seen against the changing social mores of its time. The Council first declared ten general principles as the basis of its work, and required all counsellors to assent to them. They included the statements that 'the right foundation for the (family) unit is permanent monogamous marriage...', that 'the right basis for personal and social life is that sexual intercourse should not take place outside marriage', and that 'everything possible should be done to promote fertile unions' (NMGC Annual Report 1950). By 1968 the principles had become no longer acceptable and were abandoned. A more neutral 'objective' was then adopted that 'the Council believes that the well-being of society is dependent on the stability of marriage' (NMGC Annual Report 1968). This was amended again in 1983 to read that 'the Council is concerned with marriage and with family and personal relationships, and believes that the quality of these relationships is fundamental to the well-being of society' (NMGC Annual Report 1984). It is in the context of that belief system that the current work takes place.

Administrative structure

Marriage Guidance Councils

The present marriage counselling service is provided through some 160 marriage guidance councils. They are autonomous bodies, electing their own committees, managing their business affairs, engaging administrative staff and raising their own finances. Generalizations about them are not easy to make, because some are large urban councils, with perhaps fifty to a hundred counsellors, others are small rural or isolated councils with perhaps six counsellors, and yet others cover a large county area with several widespread counselling outposts and members who rarely come together centrally. Some employ full-time paid managers, with ancilliary staff. Some, by contrast, rely heavily on an appointments secretary who mans the office telephone, with the organizational function being undertaken by an Honorary Secretary.

What they have in common is that premises are provided in which counselling can take place in comfort and confidence. Only on rare occasions, such as handicap or illness, do counsellors visit the homes of clients. Office-based counselling not only respects that one's home is one's castle and not to be trespassed upon, but it protects counsellors, and by extension clients also, from getting drawn beyond the boundaries of the counsellor/ client relationship. In the counselling room neither has to contend with intrusions of family members, television distractions or worries about exercising hospitality. Both can feel free to work within the limits of the counselling contract.

In practice, most clients make appointments by phone to the office. The local management is responsible for making an adequate and, if possible, speedy response to clients, and for deploying the work force of counsellors.

National Marriage Guidance Council

The national body retains responsibility for ensuring a minimum standard of work. It lays down criteria which MGCs are required to meet before being granted constituent status, and it monitors their work through regional staff who consult with, and provide training for, the MGCs in each of the six regions. Increasing emphasis is being given to professional standards of organization through management training and reviews of MGC performance.

The main way, however, in which NMGC has controlled standards of work is through the central system of selection, training and supervision of counsellors. No educational or therapeutic work can be undertaken in MGCs except by workers who are acceptable to NMGC supervisory staff. At any time tutors may, for good reason and after consultation, suspend a counsellor. These formidable powers tend to be considered in local MGCs as somewhat undermining, but they have proved an effective way of safeguarding a standard of counselling that is recognized to apply nation-wide, and they provide a protection for clients who make a great personal investment in an agency which must respect that trust.

Selection and training of counsellors

Throughout its history, NMGC has recruited counsellors to work in a voluntary capacity. Though some counsellors with experience are now undertaking additional counselling to their voluntary commitment on a paid basis, and though salaried counsellors have been employed recently in areas of special need on a pilot basis, potential counsellors apply for a voluntary activity. From the early stages, emphasis has been placed on a centralized selection system which accepts only those with a clear aptitude for counselling.

Selection

The selection process is in two stages. The first stage is the responsibility of the local MGC in whose catchment area the applicant lives. This results, if desired by the council and the candidate, in the sponsoring of the applicant.

The aim of this first stage is to familiarize the potential counsellor with the agency, giving maximum information about counselling and its require-ments. The candidates should gain sufficient 'feel' of the commitment to make an informed decision about whether to persevere with the application. At the same time the council will assess informally whether the applicant is a candidate who would be acceptable locally. How this stage is carried out will depend on local practice and on the previous experience of the candidate. The process is completed by a formal interview of the applicant by a sponsoring committee whose task is to elicit certain information about practical matters, such as time availability, and to make a fairly superficial assessment as to motivation, suitability and personal standing in the community. The committee completes a form with this information, and asks the candidate to complete a detailed open-ended form aimed at eliciting personal history, education and career, family relationships, interests, attitudes and values. The candidate nominates two referees who must be close acquaintances, and they are sent an extensive questionnaire for completion confidentially.

Composite records are not kept of the numbers of applicants who do not complete the sponsoring stage. Many people who express interest fall by the wayside as they learn of the requirements. The majority of those who are interviewed by the sponsoring committee are successful at that stage. Currently some 500–600 are sponsored each year, though about 10 per cent of these do not subsequently pursue their application through to a selection conference.

Each selection conference is arranged by the national organization. Eight candidates and three selectors meet for a seven-hour day of intensive interaction. Two of the selectors are tutors of NMGC. The third selector has experience of selection in some other field such as social work, medicine, education or industry, or may be a practising psychiatrist, so is likely to bring a different perspective to the conference. Their collective responsibility is to assess candidates for the qualities of 'accurate empathy', 'creative openness' and 'non-possessive warmth' (Truax and Carkhuff 1967).

The selectors have four measurements for making their assessments. They have, first, the forms completed by the sponsoring committees, referees and the candidates themselves. These already give a fairly intimate picture of the applicant's intelligence, openness and personal relationships – indeed it is surprising how often reservations are expressed by the referees who have been nominated by the candidates themselves.

Secondly, additional written tests are completed early in the programme of the day. Ten minutes are allocated for candidates to write a self-description which reveals their level of insight. Then tape-recordings of client 'stories' are played, and the participants are assessed on their perception and on the emotional level of their response.

Personal interviews during the day with one of the internal selectors and the external selector give opportunity for exploration of any areas of doubt raised in the written material, and test for personal defences and vulnerability. Each selector gets a feel of whether candidates are at home in one-to-one interaction, and of their capacity to respond to training. In particular, those applicants with a disabling degree of personal stress can be identified and turned away.

Fourthly, throughout the day one selector works in a group setting with those participants who are not being personally interviewed at that time. A series of topics are presented for group discussion – case material, statements on social or moral issues, and questions relating to marriage guidance. The setting provides an indication of how the members interact in groups, uncovers personal concerns and prejudices and displays leadership potential.

Finally, the candidates themselves also use the day to test whether they want to continue with their application. Sometimes they disclose uncertainty in interview. And some 5 per cent of those who are 'accepted' at a conference decide themselves to opt out.

The selectors accept all those they consider to have an aptitude for counselling and to be able to respond positively to training. Acceptance rates differ considerably but, on balance, some 45 per cent of candidates are offered the chance to enrol for training.

Though there are no specific educational requirements, the majority of successful applicants have received tertiary education and about half have undergone professional training. Women outnumber men by four to one. This regrettable imbalance arises from the difficulty of combining full-time work and voluntary counselling, but more subtly, one senses, it also suggests that the necessary sensitivity and insight are more female than male characteristics.

Successful candidates are preponderately aged 30–50, with an average age around 36. Almost all are, or have been, married. Those who have been through the trauma of marital breakdown or bereavement may well be accepted if they have shown that they have come to terms with, and learnt from, the experience. One in twenty selected have previously been MGC clients.

Training

Training aims to build on the personal strengths which have been revealed during the selection process. It is based on the fundamental principle that learning is maximized when combined with practice. New counsellors therefore begin counselling on their own after attendance at two introductory residential week-ends, separated by a period of observation of experienced counsellors. Subsequent training all takes place against the background of personal experience as a counsellor. A second fundamental principle is that training, which consists of residential training, personal supervision, in-service tutoring and follow-up training, is a process which continues throughout a counselling career.

Basic training   This runs concurrently with the first two years of practice. It provides a trainee with '...opportunity to be introduced to, or to revise what he has previously learnt about human growth and development by demonstrating the effect of earlier experiences on later adult relationships and their transformation within marriage and family' (*Marriage Matters* 1979, p. 64). The aim is to build on the trainees' experience gained in their own families of upbringing and their own marital or intimate personal relationships; increase their understanding and awareness of psychological and social influences on current experience; and introduce them to the knowledge and skills needed for marriage counselling.

The residential part of basic training consists of six 48-hour sessions at NMGC's training college in Rugby, spread out over two years. It is based on small-group work, with maximum personal involvement. The clear message is that the counsellor's main tool is himself, and his ability to improve his art lies in extending his listening and sensitivity.

The objectives of this formative training have been laid down by Joan Sullivan, who played the key role in developing the training and supervisory system during the 70s and early 80s, as:

(1)   To ensure that trainee counsellors have knowledge of MGC...and its relations with other agencies...

(2)   To enable [them] to ground their initial practice in the client-centred model, and to introduce them to a range of counselling approaches.

(3)   To focus attention on relevant theoretical frameworks and concepts in psychology and sociology related to marriage...

(4)   To ensure [they] become aware of ... skills needed in relationship counselling ...

(5)   To enable [them] to achieve a greater awareness of self ... and to increase their sensitivity to clients' experience ... (NMGC 1984, p. 3).

The main teaching is achieved through case discussion, role-play, video recordings, awareness groups and skills practice. In a setting which often seems unstructured and unsafe, the new counsellors gain a flavour of the tension and subsequent anxiety which they are beginning to sense in their clients. The tutors who staff the courses can be seen as something of a model by acting as facilitator rather than controller, creating an atmosphere for the group to gain maximum learning through a free expression of thoughts and feelings.

At the time of writing (summer 1984) the basic training syllabus is being revised to place more emphasis on sexuality and on developing skills in problem exploration, goal setting and contracts in counselling (see Volume 2, Chapter 12 for an evaluation of NMGC Counsellor training).

In-service training   All marriage guidance counsellors receive continuous in-service training.

Each counsellor is allocated to a tutor, who is himself an experienced counsellor who has undergone training as a trainer/supervisor. Individual tutorials, reinforced in certain instances by group tutorials, take place with the tutor, who supervises the counsellor's case-load, discussing the counselling and reviewing the case notes kept by the counsellor. This may be a close relationship between tutor and counsellor based on appropriate dependence as in a counselling relationship. The tutor is available to talk through difficulties, test hunches or hypotheses, and provide an objective shaft of light particularly on counselling which seems 'stuck'. However, tutors strive not to undermine the autonomy of their counsellors. At the end of the day, the counsellor is on his own and must do the best he can in the light of his own intuition and experience.

As counselling often places counsellors in vulnerable positions, or creates anxieties and feelings of isolation, all counsellors meet in a discussion group in their local council about once a fortnight. The primary purpose of these groups is to provide a forum for presentation of casework to one's peers. The insights of a group may well provide a rich source of inspiration in dealing with clients. Most groups are led by a tutor or a relevant professional with links with MGC, who may also use the opportunity for teaching, experimental projects or indeed free discussion of relevant local issues.

Counsellors may attend other courses from time to time, ranging from regional induction courses to specialist residential courses such as ones on family therapy or sex problems, or general refresher courses. The aim is that counsellors take responsibility for their own development once they have completed basic training. As a minimum they are expected to attend a refresher course every five years.

The theoretical base of NMGC counselling

Counselling in MGC is seen primarily as a natural, warm, understanding response to individuals or couples in stress. The process involves the seeking of help by one (the client) of another (the counsellor) in the setting of the MGC office. But the counsellor is first and foremost an artist chosen for his instinct and temperament acting in the role of sophisticated good neighbour. It is not just for financial reasons that NMGC continues to rely on the services of voluntary counsellors. The 'voluntary' element reflects the important truth that offering sympathy is a basic human reaction, not the preserve of any profession; that difficulties in marriage and other intimate relationships spring from the ebb and flow of life, and not from medical, social or psychiatric disorder; and that the person who can come closest to understanding may well be not a detached expert but someone deeply aware of the vagaries in their own marital relationships.

Each counselling relationship is unique, for each individual is unique. A basic belief in the worth and individuality of every human being is an essential element in the 'faith of the counsellor', and belief also that humans are 'helpable' and helpable by the work of 'caring – listening – prompting' (Halmos 1965).

Though unique, there are recognizable strands in the relationship – identified by Anthony Mann (1974) as four factors:

First the client's feelings towards the counsellor are bound to be ambivalent whatever their outward appearance; second, the client's attitudes in counselling are a reflection of his other relationships, especially his interaction with his partner; third, the counsellor's own reaction to his client's behaviour may be an indication of how other people react to it; last, the client's wish for a change (may) be opposed by an equally strong resistance to change ... (p. 104).

The influence of the work of Carl Rogers

MG counsellors gain awareness through training of this ambivalence in the helping process, an awareness which owes much to Freudian concepts of unconscious motivation and to the theory of marital interaction. More is owed explicitly, however, to Carl Rogers's (1951) framework of client-centredness; with its hypothesis that 'the individual has a sufficient capacity to deal constructively with all those aspects of his life which can potentially come into conscious awareness' (p. 24). The resulting 'non-directiveness' which Rogers advocates is not, and never was, a mere passive listening which suggested a laissez-faire outcome. Its implications still hold valid in counsellor training that the counsellor must 'lay aside his preoccupation with diagnosis ... and his tendency to make professional evaluations, must give up the temptation subtly to guide the individual, and must concentrate on ... providing deep understanding and acceptance of the attitudes of the client ...' (Rogers 1951, p. 30, quoting Raskin).

Imbued with this Rogerian outlook, the counsellor becomes a 'significant other' to his client, for a period establishing a relationship of sharing secrets, compensating for lost satisfactions or good parenting. It can be a relationship of strong emotional attachment, with clients feeling free to explore unexpressed feelings or safe enough to change their pattern of behaviour, gaining courage and confidence from the security of the counsellor. As in all loving relationships, both sides put themselves at risk. Clients may find their hopes unfulfilled. Counsellors may have their loving concern rejected. A successful counselling relationship is one where counsellor is closely involved with client, but yet retains an objectivity and detachment from which he can throw light on hidden problems and help to bring some order out of confused or overwhelming emotions.

It is more complex to counsel dyads than individuals. In the former the focus must be on the pair, the marriage, whether or not both partners attend. By the simple device of keeping a chair for each spouse, the counsellor has a visual reminder of the marriage relationship and of his responsibility to both spouses, even if one chair remains vacant throughout the period of counselling. This is recognition that each client is not just an independent individual with a sense of separation, nor just a spouse with a wish for attachment, but is also one of the partners influenced by, and influencing, the marriage bond. This marital interaction between the spouses at conscious and unconscious level may become the main therapeutic tool in restoring love and communication between them, or may prove to be the irrational sunken rock on which the counsellor's best endeavours fail.

The influence of the work of Gerard Egan[*]

Recent developments have been to graft on to this essential client-centredness a sharper focus, adapting the contract-making approach of

---

[*]*Editor's note:* Since this chapter was written, NMGC decided to place more emphasis on Robert Carkhuff's work than Gerard Egan's in their new counsellor training scheme.

Gerard Egan (1975) when appropriate. It seems possible to integrate the vital acceptance of clients, and all their stress and confusion, with the often laborious process of goal setting. At times the goal may be to tackle some overt explicit problem in the marriage – perhaps difficulties with children or stress following retirement. In other cases it may be to set, say, six sessions for further exploration of all the complexities of the marital relationship, with renewed goal setting at the sixth session. Establishing a contract of work, however ill-defined, between counsellor and client not only provides a focus for work but also enables joint decision on frequency of meeting, client contributions if any, and whether to use one or two, and male or female, counsellors.

The theory of marital interaction

Fundamental to marriage guidance counselling is an understanding of the concept of marital interaction. This theoretical basis has been most fully developed in the Institute of Marital Studies, as elaborated by Daniell in Chapter 8. Marriage is viewed as the constant paradox of two separate persons, yet at the same time a couple, one flesh. The couple's relationship is a continual tension between the wish for intimacy and the need for isolation. Morley (1982) identifies four strands in this struggle: attachment versus detachment; commitment versus disengagement; intimacy versus alienation; and similarity versus difference. 'Relationships are very complex matters in which the partners are attempting to find a comfortable position for themselves, in which the fears aroused by the presence of the intimate other are at a minimum and the gratifications are at a maximum' (p. 20).

The couple consciously or unconsciously use each other, seeking in their choice of partner someone who will make up for deficiencies in themselves or compensate for losses experienced in their family of upbringing. The more an individual feels a lack in himself, the more he may have unrealistic expectations of how his partner can made good the loss, or the greater his need to blame his partner for his own inadequacies.

Counsellors must be alive to these problems of interaction in marriage. It is not that the individual influences the marriage, it is that the marriage is the sum total of both individuals and the electric current that constantly flows between them. These strong forces are often cruelly exposed in the counselling room. A marriage can then present itself as 'either a process facilitating growth (where the partners cherish and respect each other as individuals and have no desire to possess or restrict one another), a substitute for personal growth (where the partner is used to contain the lost aspects of self, without attempt at reintegration), or a defence against growth (where they rely on each other's defences to maintain the status quo and seek comfort and security only)' (Skynner 1976, p. 128).

Counsellors work within this dynamic framework not with a one-person psychology but constantly asking what the couple are doing to each other, why they chose each other and why the relationship has gone wrong. They seek to reconcile in the couple the wish for separate identity and the need to be a couple with 'good enough' functioning.

Translating theory into practice

With such a large counselling force, recruited over many years and working throughout the country in many types of environments, it is not surprising that there is diversity of practice. Through the personal supervision provided by the tutor system, efforts are made to ensure minimum standards are maintained. But, face-to-face with clients, counsellors are on their own and call upon their own individual capacities, experience and preference in style. They may borrow as they think appropriate from family therapy or transactional analysis, systems theory or Gestalt, in a fairly eclectic way. But the MG house-style is well grounded in the client-centred approach. The basic assumption that man can be free to change and grow, that he is basically 'good' but that he may have been warped or distorted by 'bad' experiences and that his autonomy must be respected encourages counsellors to concentrate on the 'inner world' of clients. Strong emphasis is placed on exploration and articulation of feelings. Counsellors struggle to enter 'into the clients' shoes', to understand and then guide them out of their confusion and distress. Client-centredness recognizes the existence of unconscious defences, but may deal explicitly with 'here-and-now' material, varying the approach to the sophistication or immediacy of each client. Counsellors may seek to be 'good parents' providing a positive model of parenting to those who have suffered without one, or 'significant others' exercising a supportive good-neighbour role; reflective agents enabling clients to explore their own inner conflicts at depth, or teachers offering programmes of behaviour modification. The goal is not that counsellors should range experimentally at will over a variety of approaches, but that they sensitively adopt the most appropriate response to each client.

Sex therapy

Sexual difficulties and ignorances are commonly presented by couples to marriage guidance counsellors. Often sex is but one part of the complex array of problem areas, and it is not easy to solve the chicken–egg conundrum of whether poverty, in-laws, inadequate housing or whatever torpedoes satisfactory sex, or whether sexual incompetence promotes discontent about other aspects of the marriage. MG counsellors have traditionally enabled couples to talk freely about their sex lives, encouraging them to express their feelings to each other, seek relevant information, or consult with doctors or family planning experts where necessary.

In 1973 behavioural methods based on the research and practice of Masters and Johnson were introduced in the marital sexual therapy project, the history of which has been elsewhere recorded by Heisler (1983). Under the direction of a clinical psychologist, Paul Brown, a group of experienced MG counsellors undertook training in cotherapy with a programmed approach to those dysfunctions identified as treatable by Masters and Johnson (1970) – premature ejaculation and impotence in the male, orgasmic inadequacy, dyspareunia and vaginismus in the female.

The counsellors who undertake this additional training are required to be competent in marital work and confident about their own sexuality. In the beginning, six women counsellors embarked on the two-year project of training and practice. Thereafter, the project was extended by those therapists training other cotherapists, until now the ripple effect has spread through all regions, and over 130 counsellors are working in 68 MST clinics.

There are several features which differentiate the clients taken into the sex therapy programme from other marriage guidance clients. There is first the requirement that couples, either married or in a committed relationship, should be willing to attend together. Unlike in counselling where the counsellor may be the main therapeutic agent, in sex therapy the couple are very much their own therapists. The therapist is there to educate and instruct but the couple, under his guidance, learn mutually about their own sexuality, exploring each other's physical emotions, communicating about their own feelings and responses. So it is essential that both spouses are committed to attending together and undertaking any homework tasks set by the therapist.

Secondly, there is an extensive diagnostic stage, with comprehensive questions and answers, and forms to be completed. Diagnosis is necessary to ensure that only couples with treatable dysfunctions are accepted into the programme, and also to screen out couples who are also incapacitated by other personal problems which need to be resolved first. A woman who is deeply inhibited by early incestuous experiences, a couple with low sex drive, a man with strong homosexual inclinations or a couple with a history of violent rows are not suitable cases for this form of treatment – though some may become so after a spell of ordinary counselling.

Thirdly, the nature of the helping relationship is that of educator giving instruction to a couple who have committed themselves into the hands of the competent expert. In practice about half the couples who undertake this commitment complete treatment. Twenty-five percent are referred elsewhere before the end of treatment: the majority for straight counselling (after which some return to sex therapy) and the remainder to medical or psychiatric services.

Though this programme is founded on the Masters and Johnson model, there are significant differences. The American therapy was based on an intensive two-week period of residence, when couples were freed from all other distractions to concentrate solely on themselves. This has not been thought to be feasible in Britain. The NMGC programme therefore requires attendance non-residentially at weekly sessions. That does not demand the same high level of commitment (or indeed expense) as in the States. Also, the British programme often uses single therapists once their training is complete. Research into the outcome of sex therapy in MG shows that the results of using a single therapist correlate closely to those of cotherapy, so the extra expense of the former is not justified (Crowhurst 1982).

Inter-agency relationships

Referrals

The bulk of MG counselling takes place on MG premises, but links exist with other agencies in terms both of making and taking client referrals and of joint working in other settings.

Seventy percent of MG clients are self-referred. They know of the existence of the MGC through the media, from friends or users of the service, or merely by knowing marriage guidance as a household name. Surveys show that over 90 percent of the population have heard of the MGC and see it as a service of help with marriage problems.

The remaining 30 percent of clients report that they have been advised to make application by medical practitioners (13 percent), solicitors (3 percent), other voluntary agencies such as Citizen Advice Bureaux and Samaritans (7 percent) and 'others' (7 percent) (Heisler 1984). Most of these are people who make appointments themselves acting on the advice received, indeed MGCs have traditionally been reluctant to accept referrals through third parties, be they friends, relations or other agencies. However, the closer links created through working in other settings, particularly in health centres and GP surgeries, have undoubtedly increased the number of direct referrals.

The more counselling itself has become the therapeutic agent, the more the number of referrals from MG to other agencies has decreased. In 1975 only 4 per cent of clients had their counselling terminated by referral to another agency, and by 1982 only 3 percent. Referral is most likely to take place where the client demonstrably requires help other than counselling, or where there is a case of mistaken identity – some clients, indeed, mistake MGC for a marriage bureau in their search for a partner! Nowadays clients may be encouraged to seek help from family planning clinics, solicitors or medical sources, but it is likely to be done within the context of continued counselling, so will not be classified as 'counselling terminated by referral'. That is less likely to happen in the case of clients who are referred to Marital Sexual Therapy within the MG setting.

The referral rates for MST are somewhat different. Of the first 1,000 cases, 351 were referred by MG counsellors and 405 by GPs and hospital gynaecologists. Only 20 percent were self-referred. However, referrals from the MST clinics to other agencies were also 3 percent though an additional 20 percent of the clients were referred within MGC for counselling before being considered for entry into the MST programme (Heisler 1983).

Joint working

The last decade has seen the development of MG counsellors working in a part-time capacity in health centres and GP surgeries as part of a medical team. About a hundred counsellors are working in this way, effectively 'on secondment'. Though they are primarily trained for marital counselling, they receive a wider range of clients, with some doctors referring patients with all sorts of stress-related conditions. This work not only provides an additional service for referral and treatment of patients for their doctors, but it also enables feedback for doctors in helping them spot those clients who can benefit from talking therapy, with emphasis on ameliorating the marital relationship. Medical training does not adequately equip doctors for recognizing marital problems and responding appropriately. The Institute of Psycho-sexual Medicine provides in-service training for some GPs, and the marriage counsellor in the surgery is now a means of educating other doctors and giving effective alternative treatment to some patients.

Recent studies have reported beneficial effects in terms of inter-disciplinary cooperation, more appropriate treatment and savings on drug prescriptions. Shooter (1981) concluded that an important gain was 'the learning experience for practice doctors and auxiliary workers. Both professions gained from sharing each other's viewpoint, and for the doctors there was much satisfaction for gaining insight into the dynamics of marriage and its problems.' She identified this process as 'learning to deal with unrealistic hopes of "repairing" marriages; shedding perhaps long-standing fixed views or judgements about the clients; coping with the inevitable anxieties concerned by these complex problems: objective listening rather than actively advising or prescribing; and being willing to suspend the habitual pressure for rigid diagnosis and treatment' (p. 14). Clients also view the availability of counselling in surgeries favourably. Keithley (1982) found that 78 of the 82 clients in her study were in favour of this provision.

Marriage counsellors have worked in other settings to a small degree. A few have been attached to social service teams, where they have been used either as consultants to their colleagues on marital cases or to work directly with couples. Others have been used in penal institutions, generally to run groups with young fathers or sex offenders, or participate in predischarge courses. Though such activity originates as an educational venture, it also leads to therapeutic work with individual inmates.

Training other workers

Many studies have shown that help with marital problems is sought, overtly and covertly from many agencies (Borkowski, Murch and Walker 1983; Brannen and Collard 1982; *Marriage Matters* 1979). The concept of the need for many doors on which to knock, with a different style of service behind each door but with mutual understanding among the workers behind all the doors, was propounded in *Marriage Matters*. People in marital difficulties experience their pain in different ways and seek help which seems appropriate and most relevant. The help-seeking path for most individuals going through the process of marriage breakdown leads to a doctor's surgery. Others seek help from ministers of religion or voluntary organizations which are less overtly concerned with marriage. Those who do not actively seek help may show signs of distress to health visitors, school teachers or nurses. Those couples who do not seek help for themselves may well make their stress apparent through their children or parents, so that social workers or school counsellors may become aware of the marital tensions.

NMGC provides training for all such groups of workers. This training is on similar lines to that provided for MG counsellors, but it has a different focus, one appropriate to the work setting of those attending. The understanding of basic counselling skills forms the core of any training. But practitioners are encouraged to develop their own model of help-giving in the context of their main task. For doctors, this entails using their six minutes with a patient more effectively. For ministers of religion, health visitors and social workers, it means responding to the disordered marriage rather than just to the anguished individual. For youth workers and teachers, it encourages them to be open to interpreting the wayward behaviour of youngsters in the light of the relationships between the parents and children and between the spouses themselves.

The main purpose is to improve the practitioners' understanding and competence. A secondary purpose is to make them conscious of the potentiality for referral, with appreciation of the sensitivity needed to make useful referrals and the pitfalls involved. These sorts of workers are both the main therapeutic agents and the potential gate-keepers using referral to specialist agencies. Training gives the participants a better awareness of when they can be one, when the other.

Liaison with other marital agencies

NMGC is the major partner in the network of government-funded marital agencies. The Institution of Marital Studies, as a small, highly specialist agency, undertakes its own intensive therapy programme with 100–150 couples annually, but its major contribution to the voluntary marriage guidance bodies is through training key personnel.

The Catholic Marriage Advisory Council has a similar pattern of organization and work to that of NMGC, and its percentage clientele in proportion to the Catholic population corresponds with that of NMGC, i.e. one couple per thousand population. The Jewish Marriage Council provides a small counselling service on similar lines for the orthodox Jewish community. In Scotland, the Scottish Marriage Guidance Council provides an independent but similar service. The main links between these bodies are through shared training of some tutors, though in-service training, secondment and shared work may happen in response to local initiatives.

NMGC clients

Regular client data is not kept comprehensively. A detailed study was made of clients in 1952/53 (Wallis and Booker 1958). It is now planned that occasional detailed surveys will be made of all clients, and the first two took place on the total monthly intake in April 1975 and October 1982 (Heisler 1984). Comparison with other samples gives confidence that these months give results which are representative of the total client population.

Age and length of marriage

The client population falls into approximately equal thirds – those in their 20s, those in their 30s and those 40 + . Very few clients are under 20.

Half the clients have been married for more than nine years and half for less. In 1982, 70 percent of male clients were in their first marriage (69 percent of women), 16 per cent had been married once before (17 percent of women) and 1 percent had had two previous marriages. In the previous survey of 1975, 78 percent and 79 percent of men and women clients respectively were in their first marriage.

Social class and occupation

The evidence of the surveys is of a striking correlation between the social class of MG clients and of the general population. Nine percent of clients are in social class I, 26 percent in class II, 39 percent in class III, 8 percent in class IV, 4 percent in class V, and 14 percent students, armed forces and 'others'.

Seventy-eight percent of the male clients are in full-time employment, while, of the female clients, 40 percent are in full-time employment, 35 percent are primarily housepersons and a further 13 percent are part-time employees. The percentages unemployed –9 percent of men and 3 percent of women – are lower than the current national rates.

Client problem

Analysing the problems brought by clients is notoriously difficult, because so many clients present with multiple symptoms – what degree of severity must be present for an irritant to become a problem? Given broad categories of classification, the counsellors in the 1975 survey assessed that 39 percent of client problems were due to 'personal traits', 22 percent to sexual difficulties, and 16 percent to infidelity. The 1982 counsellors noted infidelity as a problem in 26 percent of cases, violence in 16 percent and alcohol-related difficulties in 8 percent.

Interviews

First interview

Women have consistently been more ready to approach MGCs than men: 53 percent of first interviews are conducted with women, which shows little change from 56 percent in 1975 and 58 percent in 1953. The percentage of men having solo first interviews has dropped from 37 percent in 1953 to 25 percent in 1975 and 19 percent in 1982. By contrast, first interviews with both spouses together have increased from 5 percent in 1953 to 19 percent in 1975 and 27 percent in 1982.

Further interviews

The total number of interviews in 1983—4 were 215,000: 94,000 (44 percent) with women, 42,000 (20 percent) with men, and 79,000 (36 percent) with couples. The increasing percentage of joint interviews reflects a more open approach in society to help-seeking, and a greater encouragement within NMGC for couples coming together, arising partly from the emphasis in sex therapy on conjoint work. The new research into sex therapy rediscovered the old truth that the couple are their own best therapists, if they can be enabled to be so by an external catalyst.

A small number of cases are undertaken by two counsellors in 'four-somes', where a series of individual interviews in which the spouses each have their own counsellor, are followed by sessions in which counsellors and clients together share the individual work they have been doing and build on it.

Reception interviewing

Though no national policy exists about how to manage the intake process, many MGCs have resorted to offering clients an immediate short 'reception interview'. This has primarily arisen in areas where a long waiting list has grown, and clients have been unable to get help with pressing problems.

Reception interviews enable clients to gain a clearer perception of what sort of help is available from marriage guidance. At the same time those who interview can make some initial assessment of the clients' difficulties, can suggest referral if the problem may be better responded to elsewhere, or estimate how long the waiting period for counselling will be.

As well as reducing time between application and being seen, reception interviews have merits of their own. Some research suggests that many clients are confused by their initial contact with counsellors, and that the expectations of client and counsellor are sometimes widely disparate (Hunt 1985). Reception interviewing can act as a form of preparation and/or self-selection; indeed one MGC found that only 50 percent of clients who had reception interviews came later for regular counselling (Gaunt 1981). Nationally, one-third of all clients are one-interview clients. Reception interviews may increasingly provide a formal screening procedure which will cut down the number who try counselling but do not find it helpful.

Counselling outcomes

A body of knowledge is now being acquired about the effect of counselling. As Hunt (1985) and Keithley (1982) have shown, research into this area is beset by unknowns and qualifications. For many years there were fears that client follow-ups might break confidentiality, so assessment was merely that of estimation by counsellors. Now the doubts lie far more in methodological questions concerning the accuracy of data collected, the inability to measure against control groups, and the expense in time and money of the enterprise.

Counsellors' estimates

The earliest attempts at measuring outcomes were made by asking counsellors to assess their clients' improvements. In the 1953 study counsellors rated 'no improvement' in 30 percent of cases, 'outcome unknown' in 37 percent and 'relationship improved' or 'difficulty overcome' in 33 percent. In the 1975 survey, the same questions elicited change and improvement in 41 percent of cases, 25 percent no improvement and 34 percent 'don't knows'. Similar answers were forthcoming in 1982, by when some MGCs were carrying out their own research. A postal survey by Leicester MGC recorded that 80 percent of those replying felt that counsellors had done a good job, and 90 percent affirmed that they would talk freely to the counsellor (Heisler 1980).

Clients' assessments

A fairly consistent pattern that half the clients are well served emerges from the recent more sophisticated client follow-up studies. Keithley's (1982) interviews with clients counselled by MG counsellors in a North-East GP surgery during 1975–8 led her to the conclusion that 'over half of the interviewed clients reported that they had found it to be of substantial and lasting help. About one-quarter reported some degree of help, but this had been limited in nature. The remaining one-fifth had not found the counselling experience a helpful one. Overall . . . the responses of counsellors and the GPs . . . were similar with reference to their clients and patients' (p. 337). She goes on to warn against too uniform an interpretation of these results, pointing out that clients, counsellors and GPs did not always concur in their assessment of satisfaction!

Brannen and Collard's (1982) sample was a small one, but their results were similar. They compared the MG clients with a control group treated in a non-MG setting. They found 'about half of the fourteen couples who were MG clients described their experiences as being very positive, with most of the others having mixed feelings and only three respondents expressing entirely negative views' (p. 187). They found women more appreciative than men, particularly of being able to express bottled-up feelings.

The most comprehensive follow-up of MG clients counselled in MG offices is Hunt's (1985). Her findings on intensive interviews with 51 clients six to twelve months after completion of counselling show 49 percent were satisfied with their counselling, 25 percent were satisfied in some ways but not in others, and 25 percent were dissatisfied with counselling. She attempted to draw a distinction between being satisfied with counselling and benefiting from it, and in this regard the findings were less encouraging, with 50 percent of the clients recording that they had not benefited from counselling. She notes, however, that the degree of 'benefit' appeared to correlate with the clients' satisfaction with their present condition. If they were living in a state of separation or divorce which was not of their choosing, they were likely to rate counselling as unhelpful. One surprising finding in Hunt's survey is that her counsellors' assessments did not concur with those of most previous studies in which counsellors' views of outcomes are more pessimistic than their clients. Hunt found that her counsellors were over-optimistic in their assessment of outcomes.

Sex therapy outcomes

Measurement of sex therapy is easier, not only because successful sex functioning can be more accurately assessed, but also because there is a clearer point of entry into treatment. In fact, of the first 1,000 cases, 46 percent completed treatment to the satisfaction of clients and therapists. The therapists rated these clients achieving 'total improvement' in 391 interviews, 'sufficient improvement' in 89 and 'some improvement' in 204. After six months, 328 clients made themselves available for follow-up, 204 reported continued improvement in functioning or no change, and 124 reported deterioration. That 38 percent of the follow-up group regressed suggests a more intensive 'after-care' service might be beneficial (Crowhurst 1982).

Looking forward

Present role

NMGC is a product of its history, with the consequent strengths and weaknesses. Its strength lies in its community roots, a body brought into being by concerted action in localities throughout the country by individuals, professions, churches and community organizations prepared to work for and give financial support to action on behalf of marriages under stress. A broad base of funding from many sources still shows that that concern is there, and furthermore, counsellors are still recruited to work voluntarily, largely drawn from the educated professional classes with a tradition of voluntary work.

The drawbacks are evident. The joint Home Office and Department of Health and Social Security Working Party on Marriage Guidance commended NMGC, but suggested that reliance on voluntary workers would unduly restrict its rate of growth. Some critics expressed surprise that in its report *Marriage matters* (1979) the Working Party did not conclude that marriage counselling was now too skilled work to be left to unpaid volunteers. In fact *Marriage matters* commended the NMGC's standard of work, and saw no evidence that a better or more cost-effective service could

be sustained by any other means. The present service attracts high commitment from its workers, maintains a freshness which derives from low case-
loads, and develops skill through specializing in marital relationships.

It is the quantity of work rather than the quality which is inadequate.
Many MGCs are not providing a sufficient volume of work to meet current
demand. What the potential demand might be is hard to assess. Comparison can fairly be made with Australia whose service is modelled on
Britain's. The combined case-load of Australian marital agencies is mar-
ginally less than NMGC's, yet Britain's population is three times that of
Australia. This disparity may well be primarily accounted for by the backing and financial support levels of the respective governments. The federal
government grant in Australia is two and a half times that of the UK
government, yet the Australian counsellors undertake two-thirds of the
number of interviews in the UK!

Marriage and family education

In addition to providing a counselling service, MG has always been committed to marriage and family education. Education is needed for youngsters
growing towards adult roles and responsibilities, and it is needed for adults,
including middle-aged and elderly ones, who find themselves facing problems in their own or their children's marriages with which they do not feel
competent to deal. Traditionally MG has used group discussion methods to
make children, couples and parents aware of developmental and relationship issues, and discover ways of coping with them.

Such groups enable people to get in better contact with their own feelings
and emotions, become more aware of their own value systems and those of
their contemporaries, learn social skills such as listening and joint decision
making, develop sensitivity to others, and assimilate factual knowledge
about parenting, sexuality or budgeting.

Education programmes take place as opportunity offers in many different
settings. The first education courses were with engaged couples, preparing
them for marriage. It became apparent that this form of social education
should begin much earlier, before couples committed themselves to marriage. For a while priority was given to work with young people in schools
and youth clubs where talking together about relationships with an uninvolved adult can prove a very liberating experience. More concentration is
now placed on work with adult groups, in churches or community centres,
through women's groups or other voluntary organizations, or in special

settings such as prenatal clinics, penal establishments or vocational training courses. Work with trainee medical students, social workers or clergy can be particularly rewarding, as they struggle with learning a counselling approach in their new vocations at the same time as they become more aware of their own personal development.

This face-to-face education is carried out mostly by experienced marriage counsellors with some teachers from other backgrounds. It is supplemented by the publication and dissemination of leaflets, booklets and magazines on all aspects of personal relationships. The recent 'MG Lifeguides' series, which includes *Preparing to marry, Money and marriage, The divorce book* and *Parents and teenagers,* is an indication of the range of marriage and family education and is a response to the experience of counsellors that ignorance can be a contributory cause of much marital unhappiness.

Marital focus

Despite the above, counselling traditionally achieves preeminence, absorbing the highest proportion of resources and presenting MG primarily as a marriage counselling service. Some pressures exist to develop counselling into wider aspects of family life – into other sexual problems, such as homosexuality or rape crisis, into abortion counselling, youth counselling, redundancy or mid-life crisis counselling. Clearly all these are related to intimate personal relationships, but NMGC continues to focus on the marital relationship for fear of wasting the specialist skill of marriage counsellors by too great diversification. Present policy is that NMGC's work will be primarily though not exclusively with marriages. Differences of opinion remain, however, and doubtless the debate about focus will continue.

An associated tension continues over 'professionalism' – a word which is used in various senses. There is agreement that MG counsellors are trained to work to a professional standard. At present they mainly work unpaid. Those who believe that there is now such a large body of theory and experience to draw on that additional training is required are pressing for payment for counsellors and for an accreditation system based on regular assessment followed by some form of qualification. It is evident that an accreditation system will be introduced during the 1980s, but it is likely to be one which builds on the present structure of counsellor recruitment and deployment.

Future developments

NMGC's workload has doubled in the last ten years. With its objective of strengthening family life, its use of volunteers and its cost-effective service, the Council has maintained its level of government support throughout the financial hazards of the late 1970s and early 1980s. There is no reason why such support should not continue.

However, NMGC is keen to extend its activities in order to provide a range of services that truly constitute 'Marriage Guidance'. Renewed initiatives are currently being taken to extend education for marriage and family life, by providing it in the community throughout the life cycle. The training of non-MG workers in sensitivity to marital problems will be developed.

The newest marriage-related activity to emerge is conciliation – the process of assisting separating couples to face their joint responsibilities and make the most advantageous decisions, particularly relating to the custody and access of children (see Volume 2, Chapter 10). MGCs have cooperated in establishing such services. MG counsellors may be used as conciliators and they require extra training in helping couples with negotiation and joint decision making. MG may be well placed to develop conciliation services in some areas, and certainly close links must be kept between MG and the staff and management of conciliation services.

As for the counselling service itself, it will remain as the most significant arm of NMGC – the clients demanding help over the telephone will continue to see to that. The evaluation studies show the present service is meeting important needs. The escalating rise in divorce and in second marriage and reconstituted families is causing additional work, both in counselling and in education, with stepfamilies. NMGC must increasingly be ready to respond to calls for marriage help in a variety of ways. The marriage guidance network needs to publicize itself more and give birth to new services.

Britain must take a more serious approach to mass marriage breakdown. *Marriage Matters* (1979) proposed the establishment of a Central Development Unit for Marital Work to develop services, practice and training. It would encourage collaboration between agencies, promote research and liaise between the various government departments responsible for aspects of marital work. Without such a central development unit efforts to provide marital services will remain piecemeal. This recommendation has not yet been accepted by the government. NMGC cannot itself undertake the necessary coordinating role. It will however strive to work in active partnership with the other agencies involved in marital work.

Notes

1 In Scotland this service is carried out by the Scottish Marriage Guidance Council which is fully autonomous though based on similar principles and practice to NMGC.
2 The Catholic Marriage Advisory Council has some seventy centres in England and Wales, eight in Scotland and sixty in Northern Ireland and the Republic of Eire. Close links exist with NMGC, and counsellors and tutors from NMGC and CMAC share some training events.
3 NMGC, CMAC and the Institute of Marital Studies (formerly the Family Discussion Bureau, and now under the auspices of the Tavistock Institute of Medical Psychology).

References

Borkowski, M., Murch, M. and Walker, V. (1983) *Marital violence: the community response.* London: Tavistock Publications.

Brannen, J. and Collard, J. (1982) *Marriages in trouble: the process of seeking help.* London: Tavistock Publications.

Crowhurst, H. M. (1982) *The NMGC client in sexual dysfunction clinics 1976–80.* Rugby: NMGC.

Egan, G. (1975) *The skilled helper: model, skills and methods for effective helping.* Monterey, California: Brooks/Cole.

Gaunt, S. (1981) *Reception interviewing.* Birmingham: MGC.

Halmos, P. (1965) *The faith of the counsellors.* London: Constable.

Heisler, J. (1980) The client writes. *Marriage guidance, 19(3),* 115–125.

Heisler, J. (1983) *Sex therapy in NMGC.* Rugby: NMGC.

Heisler, J. (1984) *The NMGC client 1982.* Rugby: NMGC.

Hunt, P. (1985) Clients' responses to marriage counselling. Rugby: NMGC.

Keithley, J. (1982) Marriage counselling in general practice: an assessment of the work of marriage guidance counsellors in a general medical practice. Unpublished PhD thesis, University of Durham.

Mann, A. (1974)*The human paradox: counselling in the context of human experience.* Rugby: NMGC.

Marriage Matters: a consultative document by the working party on marriage guidance (1979) London: HMSO.

Masters, W. H. and Johnson, V. E. (1970) *Human sexual inadequacy.* Boston: Little, Brown.

Mattinson, J. and Sinclair, I. (1979) *Mate and stalemate: working with marital problems in a social services department.* Oxford: Basil Blackwell.

Morley, R. (1982) Separate but together – the essential dichotomy of marriage. In *Change in marriage.* Rugby: NMGC.

National Marriage Guidance Council (1950–1984) Annual Reports.

Rogers, C. (1951) *Client-centered therapy : its current practice, implications and theory.* Boston: Houghton Mifflin.

Sanctuary, G. (1968) *Marriage under stress: a comparative study of marriage conciliation* London: George Allen and Unwin.

Shooter, A. (1981) *Counselling in medical practice.* Reading: MGC.

Skynner, Robin (1976) *One flesh: separate persons: principles of family and marital psychotherapy.* London: Constable.

Sullivan, J. P. L. (1984) *Basic counsellor training prospectus.* Rugby: NMGC.

Truax, C. B. and Carkhuff, R. R. (1967) *Towards effective counselling and therapy.* Chicago: Aldine.

Wallis, J. H. and Booker, H. S. (1958) *Marriage counselling: a description and analysis of the remedial work of the National Marriage Guidance Council.* London: Routledge and Kegan Paul.

SECTION TWO

THERAPEUTIC APPROACHES

CHAPTER SIX Therapeutic Alliances in Marital Therapy
1 Pretherapy Influences
Windy Dryden and Patricia Hunt

While there are different theoretical perspectives on marital therapy, the effectiveness of all approaches to marital work depend on the establishment and maintenance of a sound working relationship between therapist and clients. In this and the following chapter we wish to focus on therapeutic alliances as they pertain to the practice of marital therapy, and to consider some of the issues that emerge from taking this perspective. In the present chapter, we will consider the concept of the therapeutic alliance and explore the pretherapy influences that are exerted on the development and maintenance of therapeutic alliances in marital therapy. In the following chapter we will focus on matters pertaining to these alliances as they unfold during the therapeutic process.

The practice of marital therapy involves the therapist attending to a complex set of alliances with a number of client systems. Barker (1984) has argued that the marital therapist has to be mindful of serving at least seven different client systems: (1) the marital dyad; (2) the wife as an individual; (3) the husband as an individual; (4) those dependent on the couple; (5) society; (6) the authority that sanctions the work of the marital therapist; and (7) the therapist him or herself.

What does it mean to have a therapeutic alliance with the marital dyad? Harper (1981) considers that the couple is an abstraction and that it is nonsensical for therapists to have a therapeutic alliance with an abstraction. Gurman (1981a) disagrees and notes:

> While the couple does not, of course, have a palpable organismic existence as a psychological entity apart from the separate existence of each partner, they do share a behavioral and dynamic relatedness which must be considered functionally in its own right. Thus the therapist must identify early the unspoken language, implicit agreements, and unconscious contracts ... which simultaneously bond the partner together and create the medium for the emergence of the current continuing conflict. (p. 85)

Most marital therapists would probably concur with Gurman's view and would consider that the alliance they are most concerned with in marital therapy is that with the marital dyad. However, there are six other systems to consider and there *may* be times when the basic desires of these other systems conflict with those of the couple system.

First, there may be occasions when the interests of the marriage conflict with the interest of one of the individual partners. For example, a woman may wish to pursue a career which threatens her husband. If she takes this course of action she may jeopardize her marriage, whereas if she does not she remains unfulfilled in a significant area of her life.

Second, there may be situations when the interests of those dependent on the couple are not served if the couple pursue their interests. Thus, a couple may agree that the best way to bring up their children is to subject them to frequent beatings to teach them a lesson. The children will thus suffer if the couple put their values into practice.

Third, society's interests may be threatened by the couple pursuing their interests. Thus, a couple may preserve that relationship by pursuing a 'career' in drug trafficking. The risks to members of society are obvious if they do so, whereas, if they do not, their relationship may dissolve.

Fourth, marital therapists have to be mindful of the views of their sanctioning authority which may conflict with the wishes of the couple. The therapist may work in an agency which regards divorce as 'sinful'. How, then, does such a therapist respond to a couple who mutually agree to divorce?

Finally, the values of the couple may seriously conflict with those of the therapist. The couple may support the views and causes of the National Front and seek help from a therapist who finds these values abhorrent.

In all these situations the marital therapist's interventions are going to be coloured by his or her decision concerning to which system to give priority at any point in time. The practice of marital therapy cannot therefore be a value-free exercise and is likely to often pose searching dilemmas for its practitioners (Dryden 1985).

The concept of the therapeutic alliance

The concept of the therapeutic alliance was first employed in the psychoanalytic literature, although in recent years it has been used to consider the complex of attachments and shared understandings formed and activities undertaken by therapists and clients as the former attempt to help the latter with their personal problems. In psychodynamic psychotherapy, the therapeutic alliance has been used to refer to the non-transferential or more rational aspects of the therapeutic relationship. Sterba (1934) was one of the first to write of an ego-level identification with and positive attitude towards the therapist which helped the patient to work towards the accomplishment of common therapeutic tasks. Since then the concept has been considered from a variety of different perspectives, which has led to a situation of conceptual confusion. For example, while most writers make the two-part distinction between the therapeutic alliance and the transference relationship, Greenson (1967) and Weiner (1975) refer to three aspects: (1) the real relationship, (2) the working alliance, and (3) transference.

The theoretical work of Bordin (1979) has done much to elevate the 'therapeutic alliance' to a position of greater conceptual clarity and we shall draw heavily upon his work in both this chapter and the next. Bordin argued that the therapeutic alliance is made up of three major components: (1) bonds, (2) goals, and (3) tasks. The *bonds* refer to the quality of the relationship between the participants, the *goals* are the ends of the therapeutic journey, while the *tasks* are the means for achieving these ends. Disruption to the therapeutic journey might occur because the 'travellers' (a) do not get on or have a relationship which is not conducive to the goals or tasks of therapy (weak or inappropriate bonding); (b) disagree on journey's end (non-agreement about goals); and/or (c) prefer different ways of reaching the therapeutic destination (non-agreement about tasks). These three components will be considered separately in greater detail in the following chapter.

It is important to note that both the therapist and clients make contributions to the development and maintenance of therapeutic alliances in marital therapy. Failure to develop sound alliances, then, may be due to therapist factors, client factors or both sets of factors as they interact with each other. For example, a therapist may be poorly skilled in the technical aspects of the practice of marital therapy, the clients may not be capable of meeting the demands of the particular type of marital therapy being offered (Hartley and Strupp 1983) or clients and therapist may seek to form a different type of relationship with one another. In addition, agency factors (the setting in which therapy takes place) play their part in this interaction. When failure in marital therapy occurs, it is important to scan the complex set of contributions made by participants, and their interaction with each other and with the agency on each of the three components of the alliance, to gain a full understanding of the failure.

Some research studies have shown that when therapists in individual therapy pay attention to alliance-related problems and intervene accordingly, then poor outcome can be avoided. For example Lansford (quoted in Bordin 1983) found that therapists' sensitivity to weakening of the alliance and their effectiveness in repairing those 'breaks' were positively correlated with a good therapeutic outcome. Furthermore, Lehrke (1978) found that a therapist's failure to respond, except by listening, to patients' expressions of interest or concern regarding alliance-related issues was predictive of alliance failure. These findings echo Hartley's (1978) view that in individual therapy 'problems in the alliance take precedence over all others; the therapist must recognize them and intervene before further progress can be made' (p. 8). Thus, while threats to the alliance may come from each of the participants' contributions or their interaction, it is incumbent upon the therapist to intervene accordingly. Failure to do so augurs poorly for therapeutic outcome. Whether this conclusion applies to marital therapy awaits further inquiry.

Finally, there are probably different types of helping alliances. Luborsky (1976) distinguished between an alliance in which the client experiences the therapist as supportive and helpful, with himself as the recipient, and one where a sense of collaboration is developed between therapist and client, where both join forces and work together in a joint struggle against what is impeding the client. In the latter type, the client is more of an active participant in the therapeutic process, whereas he is more passive in the former. Luborsky's work was based on individual therapy, and it remains to be seen whether the same two helping alliances emerge in marital therapy or whether other types are reliably found in this therapeutic arena. Additional research is required to determine whether particular types of alliance endure throughout the course of marital therapy or whether particular types become salient at different times for different couples.

Pretherapy factors affecting therapeutic alliances in marital therapy

The practice of marital therapy takes place neither in a vacuum nor in isolation from what the couple and the therapist bring to the endeavour. In the rest of this chapter we will focus on factors that influence the development and maintenance of the therapeutic alliances in marital therapy before the couple even meet their therapist. First, we shall cover the contributions that the couple are likely to bring to therapy which have an influence on the set of therapeutic alliances. Then, we shall outline the therapist's contributions. Finally, we shall consider how the agency in which marital therapy takes place plays its part in framing therapeutic work and how such factors may affect the alliances that emerge and are sustained in such work.

Couple factors

The ways in which couples define their problems and the processes by which they decide to seek help both have an important effect on the way therapeutic alliances may develop. If we consider problem definition, couples may seek help after arriving at a mutually agreed definition of their marital problems to which they both contribute. This situation is the marital therapist's dream in that the couple's definition of their problems is congruent with the way the therapist is likely to define their concerns and thus the latter is likely to have few problems in moving from problem definition to problem assessment. Alternatively the wife, for example, may consider that the couple have problems to which they both contribute whereas the husband's view may be that the wife is 'sick' or that her unreasonable behaviour has led to tension between them and that her actions are due to hormonal changes associated with the menopause. In this scenario, the danger is that since the wife's definition of their problem is probably more congruent with the therapist's definition than is her husband's, the therapist may more easily form an alliance with the wife than with the husband. In so doing the therapist may alienate the husband, further entrenching him in his definition of their problems.

The way the couple decide to seek help is also of relevance when alliances are studied in marital therapy. Hunt (1984) in her research on clients' reactions to marriage guidance counselling found that for 50 percent of her sample it was a particular event that triggered them to seek help. 'For the other 50 percent . . . the trigger event was hard to define and contact seemed more to be a response to mounting pressure and an inability to make a decision, or to an accumulation of stress that was perhaps affecting their health' (p. 74). While there is no research which deals with the question concerning the effect of specific or non-specific problem triggers on the development and maintenance of marital therapy alliances, some speculation is in order. It may be more difficult for marital therapists to shift the focus of exploration from overt to underlying issues in cases where specific triggers have prompted the couple to seek help for their difficulties than in cases where less specific triggers exist.

Garvin and Seabury (1984) also note that the events leading to couples applying for help have implications for their view of clienthood and their expectations of the role of their helpers. A crisis may encourage the couple to enter marital therapy with productive views about clienthood or it may lead them to expect instant help from the therapist who at the same time may be prepared for a long-sustained period of on-going therapy. In the latter situation the resulting discrepancy threatens the marital therapy alliances between couple and therapist at the outset of the work.

Another pertinent issue concerning a couple's decision to seek help for their marital problems relates to the extent to which both partners have applied for help voluntarily. It often happens that one partner willingly

seeks help while dragging their reluctant partner with them (metaphoric-
ally and occasionally literally!). The threat to the three-person alliance is
ever present as long as one partner feels coerced to participate in the marital
therapy process. When both partners are seeking help voluntarily then this
augurs well for the development and maintenance of the various alliances
between the participants. Occasionally, both partners seek help involun-
tarily. They may have been recommended such help by an authority and
perceived the suggestion as an order, or they may have been referred to a
marital therapy agency by a helping professional who has previously failed
to help them. In such instances, the skills of marital therapists to avoid
unproductive alliances with reluctant couples are severely tested. Indeed,
sometimes it would be an error to offer marital help to such clients.

When a couple decide to seek help from a marital therapist they bring to
this enterprise general attitudes towards seeking help and specific attitudes
towards seeking marital therapy in particular. These attitudes may be well
developed and easily verbalized or they may be vaguely defined and not
available to the person's awareness. In the latter cases such attitudes may
be inferred from the person's behaviour, although this, of course, is a
hazardous enterprise.

General attitudes to seeking help are productive when the person can
freely admit to having problems, believes that seeking help is a legitimate
activity, not a source of shame or embarrassment, and brings a healthy
scepticism to what the therapist has to offer. The person is able to take what
is helpful from the therapy process and reject what is unhelpful without losing respect for the therapist. Examples of unproductive attitudes to seeking
help are demonstrated when the person assumes an overly dependent stance
in therapy or when the person's sense of autonomy is easily threatened by
the act of applying for help. In the former case, the person is likely not to
utilize their own potential for solving problems and will look to the
therapist as the sole source of help. The person is likely to ask the therapist
frequently what they should do and remain in therapy for a long time rather
than use therapy as an opportunity to develop resources and skills which are
then applied to their everyday marital experiences. In the latter case, the
person brings a compulsive self-reliance to therapy and tends to deny that
problems exist, or that they are as bad as they are, or that they are unable
to cope with them. The person may attempt to call into question the
therapist's qualifications as a helper or their ability to provide effective
assistance. It is important to reiterate that these are attitudes to help that
such persons *bring with them to* the therapeutic enterprise. While these
attitudes may be less problematic in marital than in individual therapy

(given that there is less scope in the former for intense attachments between clients and therapist), they do exert an important influence on the type of alliances that develop in marital therapy. When the therapist is faced with a situation where both partners have unproductive attitudes towards help, then again their skills to develop appropriate and helpful alliances are severely tested. When one partner has a productive attitude to help while the other has an unproductive attitude, the danger exists that the marital therapist will ally himself with the former and thus further alienate the latter.

Couples' specific attitudes to marital therapy depend heavily on their expectations of such therapy. Duckro et al. (1979) have made the telling point that it is important to distinguish between anticipations and preferences when considering these expectations. Couples may correctly anticipate what might happen in marital therapy but prefer a different kind of process. Frequently couples do not have clear anticipations of what marital therapy will be like (Brannen and Collard 1982; Hunt 1985). Barker (1984) has argued that this is because (a) marital therapy has a vague public image, and (b) there is so much variation in the way marital therapists work. Brannen and Collard (1982) further speculate that this may be so because clients are so preoccupied with their painful feelings that this may interfere with their thinking about their anticipations.

Research carried out on clients' expectations of marital therapy has been problematic for two reasons. First, such studies (Brannen and Collard 1982; Hunt 1985) have tried to ascertain what clients expected to receive from marital therapy *after* they have been exposed to such help; thus experience has probably coloured their responses. Second, these studies fail to make the important distinction mentioned above between clients' anticipations of and preferences for marital therapy. While Brannen and Collard's and Hunt's data show that clients seeking help from MG and a hospital-based marital therapy agency had unclear anticipations concerning what would actually occur, their findings indicate that clients' preferences for what they hoped to receive were better formed although quite diverse. Data from MG clients show that their preferences for help range from independent, unbiased commentaries on their marriage, to help in tracing missing spouses, to advice on specific topics (Heisler 1980; Hunt 1985). Brannen and Collard (1982) and Hunt (1985) also refer to the tacit widespread assumption amongst clients that MG is a 'mending service'. One of Hunt's interviewees said in this regard:

'It might be a wrong assumption on my part but I assumed that if you set up marriage guidance it must be basically to try and help couples stay together

... Well I don't think either of us would have gone there unless we wanted to. I can't see that anyone would go to marriage guidance if they didn't want to save their marriage.'

Thus a good proportion of MG clients hope that Marriage Guidance will provide advice on helping them stay married, whereas, as Tyndall (see Chapter 5) notes, MG counselling is largely non-directive and counsellors generally refrain from giving advice and do not as a matter of course share the assumption that their first priority is to help clients mend their marriages. These discrepancies if unmodified remain threats to the therapeutic alliances in marital therapy. Not only do some clients drop out from MG counselling when their preferences are not met, but other clients remain in the hope that if they are 'good clients' such advice may be eventually given to them (Hunt 1985). The name of the agency 'Marriage Guidance' may be partly responsible for the perpetuation of the widespread assumption that advice will be provided (Keithley 1982), given that clients often confuse the terms guidance and advice.

There is some research evidence to suggest that men are more likely to prefer more directive help and advice from their MG counsellors than women, who tend to prefer a more non-directive, reflective style of help (Brannen and Collard 1982). Hunt (1984) found a small trend in this direction but noted that men who were willing to stay in counselling for a while, and thereby learned how to use a less directive form of help, were more satisfied with the process than Brannen and Collard's (1982) male respondents. This data although retrospective would suggest that the working alliance in the task realm between MG counsellors and wives may be stronger at the outset of therapy than between counsellors and husbands.

Another area worthy of study and having implications for the development and maintenance of therapeutic alliances in marital work concerns the anticipations of and preferences for help among clients of different social classes. There is some evidence that lower-class persons are more likely to prefer their therapists to be active and to give advice than middle-class persons (Irwin 1980; Lazare, Eisenthal and Wasserman 1975; Mayer and Timms 1970; Overall and Aronson 1963). These preferences may make it more difficult for MG counsellors to form productive alliances with their lower-class clients since these helpers (who are predominantly middle-class women) are likely to favour a more non-directive form of help (see Chapter 5). It is probable that clients' preferences for particular forms of help in marital therapy are closely linked to the problem-solving styles that these clients typically employ in their everyday experiences (Maluccio 1979). Thus, those men who employ an active, behavioural-focused style of problem-solving in their lives may prefer the same style of approach in marital therapy. This remains a fruitful area for future empirical inquiry.

Couples' views about marital therapy may be further influenced by their experiences of the referral process, although Brannen and Collard (1982) found that referral agents rarely give precise information concerning what help couples can realistically anticipate from marital therapy agencies. However, couples do place interpretations on what referral agents say even if the latter do not give precise information, and these interpretations have relevance for the type of marital therapy alliances couples anticipate. A young couple seen by one of us (WD) in a marriage guidance setting were quite distressed by their GP's suggestion that they seek help from their local MG council for the wife's dyspareunia (pain on sexual intercourse). Although the doctor explained that MG had a special sex therapy programme, the couple were upset because they thought that the doctor had spotted some hidden marital problem that they were not aware of, since they believed that MG was 'the place to go if you had marital (as opposed to sexual) problems'. Furthermore, the husband anticipated that treatment would take place in a group setting and had been quite anxious about this prior to their appointment.

The final set of client factors to be considered in relation to the types of alliances that are likely to emerge in marital therapy concerns what personal resources and personal motives partners bring with them to the therapeutic enterprise. Concerning clients' resources, a recurrent finding in the therapy outcome literature is that clients who benefit most from therapy are those who need it least, i.e. those who already have strong personal resources. Moras and Strupp (1982) found that clients in individual therapy who formed collaborative and positively toned alliances with their therapists were those who were judged to already have basically adequate interpersonal relationships prior to embarking on therapy. Their positively toned involvement in therapy was more productive of good outcome than therapist technique and those therapeutic relationship factors that are commonly believed to be primary agents of change. If this finding is replicated in marital therapy it means that the strength of the alliance between therapist and clients is to some degree predetermined by what clients bring to the therapeutic process. If one member of the couple has had a history of adequate interpersonal relationships and the other partner has not, the therapist may well find it easier to develop a sound alliance with the former, thus again possibly further alienating the latter.

A number of writers on marital therapy have considered the various personal motives partners bring to the therapeutic process. While much of this work is derived from clinical experience rather than empirical research, it

is likely that these motives have already been formed prior to partners entering therapy. Indeed, these writers argue that such motives and the therapy
roles that partners develop based on them are designed to elicit responses
from therapists that confirm partners' implicit or explicit *pretherapy* ideas
about their marriage, who is to blame for the marital distress and whether
they want their relationship to continue or not.

Smith and Grunebaum (1976) and Broderick (1983) have written on the
motivations and consequent roles brought by partners to the therapy situation that are likely to sabotage the establishment of working alliances in
marital therapy. It is important to reiterate at the outset that partners rarely
disclose these motives spontaneously. They are either available to the partner's awareness but not disclosed or are outside that person's awareness.
These motivations have also been described as 'hidden agendas' (Irwin
1980). The most common motivations are the following.

'I want out'   Here one or both partners come to marital therapy with a
strong investment for it to be unsuccessful and thus seek to avoid developing a lasting alliance with the therapist. They can then say, 'Our relationship
is hopeless, look even therapy was of no help', and start divorce
proceedings with a minimum of guilt. Some of these partners can actually
'appear' to be 'model' clients and the therapist may leave the first few
therapy sessions highly encouraged about the prospects of an effective
therapy outcome. Then the partner who is 'looking for an exit' (Smith and
Grunebaum 1976) will cancel or fail to attend further appointments much
to the puzzlement of both the therapist and the spouse who is left abandoned in the hands of the therapist. Other partners who 'want out' are
highly negativistic in their attitude at the outset of therapy, and may
demonstrate this by attacking the therapist overtly or by covertly undermining his attempts to establish triangular rapport.

'Could *you* live with him (or her)?'   Here one or both spouses consider that
they are on the receiving end of their partner's unreasonable behaviour and
that their own conduct is either exemplary or only poor because they have
to put up with such unfair treatment. These partners seek to get the
therapist on their side either by asking direct questions such as 'would *you*
put up with it?' or by making similar appeals non-verbally. They will direct
most of their remarks to the therapist and resist attempts to speak directly
to the spouse. If asked to reflect on their own contribution to the marital

distress they will bring up further evidence of their spouse's unfair treatment. Some partners who enter therapy with this motivation attempt to play the role of cotherapist, joining forces with the therapist to help the 'sick' or 'bad' spouse.

'Help me to stay married – I'm sick'   This motivation is held by those partners whose spouses have left them or are on the brink of leaving them. Often this is in response to the first partner's newly discovered affair or long-standing drink problem. Such spouses who are seeking the 'sick' label may try to convince both the therapist and their partner that their behaviour is out of their control or due to severe intrapsychic problems. They seek to be pitied rather than blamed because they consider that guilt or compassion will stop their partner from abandoning them. In doing so they tend to praise their spouse, whom they consider to be a wonderful person, 'for putting up with a wretch like me'. This self-damning attitude is phony and as soon as these clients obtain their objective they quit therapy. They promise to be 'good hard-working clients' but rarely are. Similar to this pattern is one best called 'I'll change, I really will'. Here the person is not seeking a sick role but admits to causing the marital distress and promises to be different in the future. This enthusiasm is often not backed up with real attempts to change. The motive is once again to save their marriage and return to the status quo.

'It's her hormones (his mid-life crisis)'   In this scenario, one partner comes to therapy believing that they are blameless and that their spouse's dissatisfaction with their marriage is due to 'a phase they are going through'. These partners either deny that there is anything wrong with their relationship from their perspective, or admit that there is marital discord but insist that this is caused by the problems of their partner which are due to the normal stresses of aging such as the menopause or the mid-life crisis. They strongly resist considering that they may play a part in the marital discord and, if they remain in therapy, strive to avoid self-observation (Smith and Grunebaum 1976). Another version of this motivation is displayed by partners who say, 'Ours isn't a perfect marriage, but whose is nowadays?'

'I'll make someone pay for this'   Sometimes one partner issues the other an ultimatum: 'Come to marital therapy or I'll leave you.' Occasionally, particularly in our experience, in the case of men, this can be the stimulus for productive involvement in therapy. More frequently, however, the partner resents being placed in an ultimatum situation, and responds by adopting a difficult role in the therapeutic process. Such partners may challenge the therapist for control of the session, sabotage the alliances that the therapist seeks to establish with both spouses and adopt other blocking tactics. Basically the partner feels trapped and seeks to make someone pay for his or her plight.

While marital therapists of different persuasions will choose to respond to these threats to the therapeutic alliances in different ways, it is clear that, unless these 'hidden agendas' are dealt with in some way, effective marital therapy will in these circumstances rarely take place.

Having reviewed some of the pretherapy couple factors that influence the ways in which in marital therapy alliances develop and are sustained, we will now consider therapist factors.

Therapist factors

Marital therapists bring to their work a host of factors that may affect the alliances that emerge during therapy.

With respect to the personal qualities of marital therapists, Broderick (1983) in an informal survey noted that his own pool of (American) trainees over many years had personality profiles that were very similar to those of marital therapy clients. Both were different from the average person in the street and from individual therapy clients. Summarizing these profiles, he wrote that marital therapists tend to have:

> (1) a high level of interpersonal needs or dependency (this person is sensitive to people and their approval and has a greater than average need for strokes from significant others); (2) a resentment of authority and restrictive social rules; (3) a history of hurts received in intimate relationships starting in childhood; (4) a tendency to utilize the defense mechanisms of denial, that is, putting a good face on things as a means of dealing with problems. (p. 170)

It is important to note that this list of qualities has been derived from informal research on American marital therapists and needs to be more formally replicated in Britain. However, Broderick's list is surprisingly similar in certain respects to Ellis's (1983) list of the irrational beliefs which may be held by marital therapists more frequently than one would ideally expect from helping professionals.

(1) 'I have to be successful with all of my marital therapy clients practically all of the time!'
(2) 'I must be an outstanding marital therapist, clearly better than other marital therapists I know or hear about.'
(3) 'I have to be greatly respected and loved by all my marital therapy clients.'
(4) 'Since I am doing my best and working so hard as a marital therapist, my clients should be equally hard working and responsible, should listen to me carefully and should always push themselves to change.'
(5) 'Because I am a person in my own right, I must be able to enjoy myself during marital therapy sessions and to use these sessions to solve my personal problems as much as to help clients with their difficulties.'

How might these qualities and beliefs affect marital therapy alliances? A marital therapist's need for approval may distract him from the tasks of marital therapy, particularly if couples find them painful or onerous. Such therapists' prime concern is to keep couples happy, they are often highly regarded by their clients but tend to keep couples in therapy for a long time and to collude with them in avoiding the exploration of painful and difficult issues. In the latter respect, utilization of the defense mechanism of denial aids this collusive process. Resenting authority and restrictive social rules, some marital therapists may have ambivalent feelings about the traditional institution of marriage and thus give undue weight to different alternative life-styles. This attitude may lead such therapists to abuse their traditional therapeutic role in ways suggested by Ellis. Having a history of childhood hurts may lead some marital therapists to use the arena of marital therapy as an opportunity to work out their childhood problems in a setting which resembles the nuclear family. Object-relations theory would hypothesize that for this to happen such marital therapists would first have to recreate the circumstances of these hurts in order for them to be resolved. Thus, therapists may seek unconsciously to achieve bonds similar to those that were formed with their parents in childhood. These 'countertransference' issues are well documented in the therapeutic literature and may be more prevalent in marital therapy given the similarity between this setting and that of the nuclear family. The needs of marital therapists to be competent and successful may lead them to be intolerant of their clients when the latter fail to improve or fail to carry out suggested homework tasks. Such therapists would tend to blame couples for the therapeutic impasses that result, instead of acknowledging their own contribution to the resistance, since were they to admit such responsibility they would condemn themselves.

It is important to stress that the forementioned qualities and beliefs do not inevitably lead to the above problems in marital therapy alliances, but the potential for such disruption is present given their existence. It is to be hoped that marital therapists are in an on-going supervisory relationship where these tendencies can be discussed so that harm can be minimized in circumstances where therapist and couple characteristics interact in such a way for these tendencies to become overtly expressed.

Another set of factors that may influence the complex set of therapeutic alliances in marital work concerns the values of the therapist. Therapists who prioritize the desires of the couple system above those of each of the individuals in that system are likely to focus most of their therapeutic attention on the therapist–couple alliance. Conversely, workers who put the individuals before the couple, may well attend first and foremost to the therapist–wife/therapist–husband alliances. Marital therapists who believe that marriages should be preserved at all costs and construe their role as intervening against this backdrop are likely to form very different alliances from those who believe that their major role is to facilitate (but not influence) the couple's decision to remain married or to separate. Surprisingly there is no research which links marital therapists' values with the formation and maintenance of marital therapy alliances. However, one of us (WD) once rated all the interventions made by a marital therapist during his work with a couple. This therapist was selected because he saw his major alliance responsibility was to the couple rather than to the individuals involved. The case was selected by the therapist as being a good example of the strength of the therapist–couple alliance. In fact 70 percent of the therapist's interventions were addressed to the wife with the remaining 30 percent being evenly distributed between the 'couple' and the husband. At face value one might conclude in this case that the therapist–wife alliance was strongest in the alliance matrix, yet since there is a difference between objective and subjective measures of alliances in marital therapy any research programme studying the relationship between therapists' values and marital therapy alliances needs to employ both sets of measures. There is some speculation that objective alliance measures would not be good predictions of this relationship. For example, McDonald (1975) notes:

> A strong possibility in the therapeutic situation is the likelihood that a therapist will respond more readily and empathetically to one partner who more nearly represents the therapist's value system. The reverse is also possible, such that the therapist may attempt to compensate for this overidentification by isolation of that person with whom he identifies. (p. 146)

This 'increased attention – decreased attention (through compensation)' pattern may occur on other variables such as therapist–partner gender, race and class matching. Marital therapists would do well to observe deviations from their habitual modes of responding in the therapeutic process and reflect on the meaning of these deviations. In summary, as Coyne and Widiger (1978) and Hadley and Hadley (1976) have warned, marital therapists need to guard against any tendency to project their reformist values, sex-role expectations and life-style preferences onto their clients. To what extent they can do this remains a matter for private reflection and detailed supervision.

Another influence on the alliance matrix in marital therapy is particularly relevant for those therapists who have a strong background in individual therapy and have a history of working with disturbed individuals. Gurman (1981b) has noted that the therapist may become so intrigued by the psychopathology of one spouse that he or she may imply that this spouse is the 'sick' partner. This may result in the therapist non-therapeutically avoiding the second spouse's problems or in that spouse feeling excluded from the special alliance that has developed between the therapist and the 'sick' spouse. Gurman argues that therapists who have been initially trained to view clinical matters from an interpersonal perspective are less likely to fall into this trap of developing special alliances than are those therapists whose initial training was intrapsychically oriented. Again this is a matter for research.

As shown above, a further therapist factor influencing marital therapy alliances concerns the therapeutic orientation of the marital therapist. As shown in the final chapters of this volume, marital therapists have different approaches to marital work. It is likely that even therapists who take an eclectic approach to such work are guided by specific principles so that eclectic marital therapists will differ from each other. In terms of the marital therapy alliances, the various approaches to marital therapy outlined in the rest of this volume advocate different therapeutic bonds, suggest different levels of therapeutic goals and demand that different therapeutic tasks are carried out by both therapists and couples. As will be explored in the following chapter, strong therapeutic alliances will be forged between therapist and clients when the participants involved form mutually compatible bonds, have a shared understanding of the couple's goals and are able to perform their mutual tasks in the service of achieving these goals. These alliances can be weakened to the extent that there are mismatches on any of these three dimensions. The point of relevance here is that therapists are limited by the perspective on marital therapy that they bring to this work, and that threats to the development and maintenance of therapeutic alliances in marital work can be explained, in part, by the therapeutic orientation variable.

Marital therapists differ in the level of therapeutic skill and expertise that they bring to marital work and, even if their clients share their perspectives on alliance-related issues, threats to these alliances may still be present because therapists may poorly handle bond, goal and task-related interventions.

It is often asked what effect the marital therapist's gender, age and marital status has on the marital therapy alliances. There is little research evidence to show that these factors have any discernible or reliable impact on these alliances but undoubtedly they do have some impact on certain couples. Broderick (1983) has put this point well. 'I have ... known a number of members of Catholic religious orders, several homosexuals and a number of other never-married people who were top notch [marital] therapists by any measure' (p. 176).

In conclusion, it is important to reiterate that the foregoing factors may interact with the couple factors outlined in the previous section for better or worse with respect to the marital therapy alliances.

Agency factors

The agency's response to the couple's application for help is also important in facilitating or hindering the development and maintenance of marital therapy alliances as well as in influencing the type of alliances that may be fostered. First, the speed of the agency's response is an important factor. If there is a long period between the couple's first application and their first therapy session or initial interview, marital therapy may get off to a bad start in that the couple's first experience of the agency has been a negative one. It should be borne in mind in this regard that what constitutes a 'long' and thus unhelpful waiting period is subjectively experienced rather than objectively determined. Second, the kind of initial response from the agency is influential mainly in determining what types of therapeutic alliances are favoured in the agency. Writing about psychiatric outpatient clinics (but with direct implications for marital therapy services), Levinson, Merrifield and Berg (1967) have outlined four models of agency response to persons applying for their services before formal therapy begins.

1. The diagnostic model   Here the couple submit themselves to a rigorous diagnostic examination of their problems and personalities hoping that it will somehow help them to overcome their difficulties. The therapist offers treatment on the basis of the couple's (diagnosed) need, not on the basis of their feelings and preferences.

In this model, the couple has begun to be socialized into a therapeutic alliance where their therapist knows best and where his expertise carries more weight than their desires and notions.

2. The suitability model   Here the agency staff select couples deemed to be most qualified to accept and sustain the client role, much as applicants are selected for college, business or government positions.

In this model the agency has clear and firm ideas about the type of marital therapy they are able to offer and which couples can best utilize such services. Couples who are deemed unable, or find it very difficult, to contribute productively to the types of therapeutic alliance implicit in that form of therapy are turned away or referred elsewhere (if there are other agencies offering different forms of marital therapy). Such an agency is likely to have a good record of successful outcomes (since only 'suitable' couples are offered therapy) but this may be misleading if judged independently of the numbers of couples turned away. In this model the couple are also seen as passive recipients of an agency-managed activity – in this case selection rather than diagnosis. Again the couple are not seen as having capacity for affecting the course of their applicancy. They are deemed either as suitable for the predetermined therapeutic programme and thereby accepted, or as unsuitable for the therapy and thereby rejected.

3. The help-seeking applicant model   Here the burden of decision making is passed to the couple. The agency adopts a take-it-or-leave-it attitude after their services are explained.

The success of this model depends upon (a) the clear and detailed exposition of the therapeutic services on offer to enable the couple to make an informed decision, (b) the ability of the couple to make an informed decision at the time, and (c) the availability of alternative resources. This latter point is important. If there are no actual or perceived credible alternative therapeutic services in the community, the couple may decide to accept the offer of help, not because they believe that they can make productive use of it but because they believe they have no other options. This may lead the therapist to overestimate the extent to which he will be able to develop productive therapeutic alliances with the couple and thus the helper may be less alert to signs that there are problems in the alliance matrix. As Levinson et al. (1967) note, 'the help-seeking applicant model is insufficient in itself; it takes no account of the appropriateness of the application, the agent's part in the process, the prerogative of the clinic to ultimately offer or withhold treatment, and the multiple priorities and practical problems of treatment allocation in the clinical facility' (p. 403). In short, what is missing from this model is any real transaction between the couple and the agency.

4. The negotiated consensus model Here the agency and the couple engage in a process of negotiation where each takes seriously the views of the other. They try jointly and cooperatively to reach a consensus in their understanding of the couple's problems and in their decision about how these problems are going to be tackled.

In this model a process of negotiation is established and the couple are shown that their views are taken seriously. This open dialogue is central to a frank discussion of matters pertaining to the development and maintenance of productive therapeutic alliances between the partners involved. It is particularly important for the participants to keep this channel of communication open when alliances are threatened so that facilitative repair work of alliance breaks can be achieved (a point which will be underscored in the following chapter).

It is our view that in marital agencies that adopt a policy of negotiated consensus with their applicants therapists are likely to be more successful in developing and maintaining productive alliances suitable to particular couples than therapists working in agencies that have different policies. This, of course, awaits empirical inquiry. However, it should be noted that this model may match or be discrepant from how couples anticipate being received by the agency they approach. Some couples, for example, may anticipate and prefer an agency which operates a diagnostic system and definitely not prefer an agency which favours the negotiated consensus model.

Another way in which agency factors can affect the marital therapy alliances concerns the house-style of counselling advocated by the agency. Thus, the house-style of the NMGC has up to very recently been an amalgam of client-centred counselling and object-relations therapy. Here the emphasis is on exploration, talking and understanding, processes which seem to more closely approximate to women's preferences for counselling (Brannen and Collard 1982). More recently a focus on action-oriented counselling methods has been introduced into the new MG training curriculum (see Chapter 5 in this volume, and Volume 2, Chapter 12) and this development may be more congruent with men's preferences. This latter conclusion stems from the finding that the approach adopted by therapists in the hospital marital service studied by Brannen and Collard (1982) had a more goal-oriented focus and a more professional ambience than MG. These factors provided a closer approximation to men's preferences for counselling. As long as marital therapy agencies are going to favour a particular house-style of counselling they had better accept the possibility that they will find it difficult to engage a large minority of their clientele. As a corrective measure there appears to be a pressing need for an agency in Britain which can offer potential clients a wider range of marital therapy services than is the case at present.

Preparing couples for marital therapy

Are there any productive steps that agencies and therapists can take to better prepare couples for marital therapy before the formal process of therapy begins? Such a question is perhaps most pertinent for therapists who work in agencies which adhere to a help-seeking applicant model where the couple are given an explanation of the services being offered before they are asked to choose whether or not they are going to avail themselves of these services. However the question is also an apt one for therapists working in agencies operating different models of responding to clients.

There have been a number of research studies investigating the effectiveness of techniques of systematically preparing clients for therapy, the results of which have been encouraging (McCaskill and McCaskill 1983). However, only one of these studies (Gaunt 1981) has focused on the marital therapy modality and further research in this area is called for.

McCaskill and McCaskill (1983) suggest that the aims of systematically preparing couples for marital therapy are to (1) provide couples with an easily understood rationale for marital therapy and the range of problems for which this modality is indicated, (2) explain important theoretical concepts central to the therapeutic approach offered, (3) describe the respective roles of therapist and clients that have been found to be helpful in the therapeutic approach being outlined, (4) detail the potential difficulties in marital therapy so that the couple can be appropriately forewarned, and (5) suggest reasonable expectations for the outcome of marital therapy.

A number of methods have been used to achieve these aims. First, written instructions have been employed. These are generally sent to couples before they meet their therapists (Barker 1984). Second, a number of agencies have employed a semistructured interview. In this interview, initial interviewers take a brief history of the couple's problems, partly to establish rapport, and then question them on their understanding of marital therapy, expanding this knowledge with additional clearly comprehensible information relevant to the couple's particular difficulties on each of the topics outlined in the preceding paragraph on aims. The major purpose of this interview is to dispel unrealistic expectations and to induce a productive set for marital therapy on the part of the couple (Orne and Wender 1968). Gaunt (1981) carried out a study in the Birmingham MGC comparing clients who received a similar interview to that described above (known as a 'reception interview') to clients whose first contact with the agency was a counselling interview. She found that those receiving a reception interview remained in counselling longer than those who did not have such an interview. However, this finding must be tempered by the fact that the time between clients' first telephone contact and first interview contact was a contaminating variable. Gaunt (1981) further interviewed eighteen clients who had received a reception interview. She found that the effect of the interview was to engender a feeling of hope in clients, but that most clients did not fully understand what the interviewer said on the subject of what might happen in the counselling process. They did, however, notice quite a lot about the interviewer as a person. Gaunt also found that most interviewers had great difficulty in explaining the nature of MG counselling to clients. It is apparent that extensive training may be necessary for interviewers to skilfully implement the tasks of the induction interview.

Third, group lectures can be employed. Here a lecture is given and couples are provided with an opportunity to ask questions about the therapeutic process thus described. Fourth, audio and video-tapes have been used to describe relevant details of the marital therapy process and to model productive client behaviours.

These methods vary in the amount of interaction provided between the couple and the agency representative. Most workers prefer the semistructured interview since this format provides the greatest opportunity for such interaction and allows the interviewer to tailor the information to be provided to the couple's own situation.

Recently work has been done on preparing therapists to more adequately meet clients' preferences for therapy and their therapeutic needs (Yamamoto et al 1984). This is an important area to be considered in Britain, if clients from different cultural and socioeconomic backgrounds are going to be effectively helped with their marital problems.

Summary

In this chapter the concept of the therapeutic alliance was described. The point was made that a number of alliances are present in marital therapy and a number of pretherapy influences on these alliances were discussed – couple factors, therapist factors and agency factors. The point was made that these sets of factors interact – often in subtle and elusive ways. Finally, a number of ways of preparing couples for marital therapy were discussed. In the following chapter the emphasis will be shifted to the alliances as they unfold throughout the process of marital therapy.

References

Barker, R. L. (1984) *Treating couples in crisis*. New York: Free Press.

Bordin, E. S. (1979) The generalizability of the psychoanalytic concept of the working alliance. *Psychotherapy: Theory, Research and Practice, 16*, 252–260.

Bordin, E. S. (1983) Myths, realities, and alternatives to clinical trials. Paper delivered at the International Conference on Psychotherapy, Bogota, Colombia.

Brannen, J. and Collard, J. (1982) *Marriages in trouble: the process of seeking help*. London: Tavistock.

Broderick, C. B. (1983) *The therapeutic triangle: a sourcebook on marital therapy*. Beverley Hills, California: Sage.

Coyne, J. C. and Widiger, T. A. (1978) Toward a participatory model of psychotherapy. *Professional Psychology, 9*, 700–710.

Dryden, W. (1985, forthcoming) *Therapists' dilemmas*. London: Harper and Row.

Duckro, P., Beal, D. and George, C. (1979) Research on the effects of disconfirmed client role expectations in psychotherapy: a critical review. *Psychological Bulletin, 86*, 260–275.

Ellis, A. (1983) How to deal with your most difficult client – you. *Journal of Rational-Emotive Therapy, 1*, 3–8.

Garvin, C. D. and Seabury, B. A. (1984) *Interpersonal practice in social work: processes and procedures*. Englewood Cliffs, New Jersey: Prentice-Hall.

Gaunt, S. (1981) The Birmingham Marriage Guidance Council reception interview scheme. Unpublished report. Birmingham: BMGC.

Greenson, R. R. (1967) *The technique and practice of psychoanalysis*. New York: International Universities Press.

Gurman, A. S. (1981a) Creating a therapeutic alliance in marital therapy. *American Journal of Family Therapy, 9(3)*, 84–87.

Gurman, A. S. (1981b) Integrative marital therapy: toward the development of an interpersonal approach. *In* S. H. Budman (ed.) *Forms of brief therapy*. New York: Guilford.

Hadley, R. G. and Hadley, P. A. (1976) Response to task force report. *American Psychologist, 31*, 613–614.

Harper, R. A. (1981) Limitations of marriage and family therapy. *Rational Living, 16*, 3–6.

Hartley, D. E. (1978) Therapeutic alliance and the success of brief individual therapy. Unpublished PhD dissertation, Vanderbilt University.

Hartley, D. E. and Strupp, H. H. (1983) The therapeutic alliance: its relationship to outcome in brief psychotherapy. *In* J. Masling (ed.) *Empirical studies of psychoanalytic theories*. Hillsdale, New Jersey: The Analytic Press.

Heisler, J. (1980) The client writes. *Marriage Guidance, 19*, 115–125.

Hunt, P. (1984) Response to marriage counselling. *British Journal of Guidance and Counselling, 12*, 72–83.

Hunt, P. (1985) Clients' responses to marriage counselling. Unpublished PhD thesis, University of Aston in Birmingham.

Irwin, R. S. (1980) Client and counselor expectations of the therapeutic alliance. Unpublished PhD dissertation, University of Michigan.

Keithley, J. (1982) Marriage counselling – general practice: an assessment of the work of marriage guidance counsellors in a general medical practice. Unpublished PhD thesis, University of Durham.

Lazare, A., Eisenthal, S. and Wasserman, L. (1975) The customer approach to patienthood: attending to patient requests in a walk-in clinic. *Archives of General Psychiatry, 32*, 553–558.

Lehrke, S. A. (1978) Working alliance development early in psychotherapy. Unpublished PhD dissertation, University of Florida.

Levinson, D. J., Merrifield, J. and Berg, K. (1967) Becoming a patient. *Archives of General Psychiatry, 17*, 385–406.

Luborsky, L. (1976) Helping alliances in psychotherapy. *In* J. L. Claghorn (ed.) *Successful psychotherapy*. New York: Brunner/Mazel.

Maluccio, A. N. (1979) *Learning from clients: interpersonal helping as viewed by clients and social workers*. New York: Free Press.

Mayer, J. E. and Timms, N. (1970) *The client speaks*. London: Routledge and Kegan Paul.

McCaskill, N. D. and McCaskill, A. (1983) Preparing patients for psychotherapy. *British Journal of Clinical and Social Psychiatry, 2*, 80–84.

McDonald, G. W. (1975) Coalition formation in marital therapy triads. *Family Therapy, 2*, 141–148.

Moras, K. and Strupp, H. H. (1982) Pretherapy interpersonal relations, patients' alliance, and outcome in brief therapy. *Archives of General Psychiatry, 39*, 405–409.

Orne, M. T. and Wender, P. H. (1968) Anticipatory socialization for psychotherapy. *American Journal of Psychiatry, 124*, 88–98.

Overall, B. and Aronson, H. (1963) Expectations of psychotherapy in patients of lower socio-economic class. *American Journal of Orthopsychiatry, 33*, 421–428.

Smith, J. W. and Grunebaum, H. (1976) The therapeutic alliance in marital therapy. *In* H. Grunebaum and J. Christ (eds) *Contemporary marriage: structure, dynamics and therapy*. Boston: Little, Brown and Co.

Sterba, R. (1934) The fate of the ego in analytic therapy. *International Journal of Psychoanalysis*, *15*, 117–126.

Weiner, I. B. (1975) *Principles of psychotherapy*. New York: Wiley.

Yamamoto, J., Ascosta, F. X., Evans, L. A. and Skilbeck, W. M. (1984) Orienting therapists about patients' needs to increase patient satisfaction. *American Journal of Psychiatry*, *141*, 274–277.

CHAPTER SEVEN Therapeutic Alliances in Marital Therapy 2   Process Issues
Windy Dryden and Patricia Hunt

In this chapter, we will consider a number of issues that emerge from considering the practice of marital therapy from the vantage point of the alliances that are formed and sustained between the therapist and the couple on the one hand and between the partners on the other. In doing so, we will raise issues and suggest solutions to particular problems from the perspective of alliance theory rather than from any one therapeutic orientation, although we recognize that such solutions are to a degree dependent upon marital therapists' allegiances to particular orientations. The hypothesis that guides our analysis is that effective marital therapy occurs when there are strong working alliances among the participants on the three major dimensions of bonds, goals and tasks. To reiterate the point made in the previous chapter, this means that in effective marital therapy participants form and sustain sound working bonds, share a common understanding concerning the goals of the couple and agree on task-related issues (here participants (a) agree that each have tasks to accomplish in the therapeutic endeavour and agree to accomplish these tasks, and (b) understand how the execution of these tasks will lead to the attainment of the couple's therapeutic goals). Since the application of alliance theory to marital therapy is a recent development, the reader should note at the outset that the forementioned hypothesis awaits full, empirical inquiry.

The processes of negotiation and renegotiation

The view advanced above stresses the importance of the participants reaching certain agreements on alliance-related matters. These agreements can be explicit or implicit. While it is unlikely that the participants are going to spontaneously agree at the outset on alliance-related matters, there has to be some way in which they can arrive at such agreements. For this to occur a process of negotiation has to be initiated at the beginning of therapy. We will focus first on how participants arrive at a shared understanding of the couple's problems, one which provides the basis for constructive change. The therapist initiates the negotiation process by striving to understand each partner's viewpoint concerning the nature of the couple's problems and what has given rise to these problems. The therapist has to take these views seriously but also has to put forward, at some point in the process, an alternative perspective on these issues, one that not only can be used by both partners but will help them to solve their problems. In doing so, the therapist does not insist that the couple accept this view but offers it as a possible focus for the therapeutic work. In this respect, Elton (1982) has said 'it seems to me very helpful to be able to formulate the focus in such a way that the family cannot only accept it, which is essential, but also make sense of it, enlarge on it and broaden the area of work themselves' (p. 198).

As shown above, there are two major components of the negotiation process: (1) understanding and (2) persuasion (Smail 1978). In this context persuasion means offering the couple different versions of an alternative perspective until one becomes acceptable to all concerned. The therapist takes the couple's view into account in formulating this alternative perspective and the couple take the therapist's views into account while making sense of their difficulties. The focus (or several foci) of the work should be the natural result of this process. In this respect Gurman and Kniskern (1981) argue that it is important for the therapist to offer the couple a different and unaligned view to allow them to mutually adopt a common framework and vocabulary as a starting point for change. Broderick (1983) argues that to enable a productive focus to be achieved this should incorporate the rules that appear to govern the marital system rather than emphasize the individuals' behaviours, perceptions or feelings. The negotiation process is more complex in marital therapy than it is in individual therapy, since the therapist has not only to negotiate a shared meaning framework with each partner, but also has to help the partners achieve a workable consensus.

In this process of negotiation it is legitimate to ask which of the participants does the most of the accommodating. Some interesting research by Pearlman (1977) showed that continuance in marital therapy was positively correlated with the participant's agreement on goals after four sessions of therapy (rather than at the end of the first session). Much of this goal convergence was explained by couples coming to agree with the therapist's viewpoint rather than the therapist radically changing his perspective. Couples who did not make this shift terminated therapy 'prematurely'.

Future study of couples' shifts in their definitions of their problems and what occasions such changes is needed. It may be that such shifts will not occur (a) if therapists attempt to *impose* an alternative explanatory perspective on the couple, (b) if they offer implausible alternatives (that are *too* discrepant from the couple's present definitions of reality), or (c) if they refrain from offering any perspectives at all. Conversely such shifts are likely to result when the therapist, after communicating empathic understanding of both partners' viewpoints, offers an alternative perspective that is *moderately* discrepant from these views.

In sum, the therapist's role in the process of negotiating about problems seems to be twofold: (1) to communicate understanding of each person's phenomenal reality, and (2) to offer an alternative viewpoint that the couple can constructively use in the therapeutic work. Similar points can be made when considering how the participants negotiate constructively about therapeutic goals and tasks which will lead to the attainment of these goals.

If the therapist succeeds in establishing a 'negotiating' set with a couple, a particular attitude has been communicated and accepted. This can be summarized thus: 'Let us see if we can arrive at a way of viewing your problems that will help you to achieve the changes you want. Furthermore let us see if we can find mutually acceptable ways of reaching these goals.'

This 'let us see' attitude is also central to the process of *renegotiation* which occurs when obstacles to therapeutic progress arise. Here the therapist's view can be summarized thus: 'Let us see if we can determine what is happening to account for this situation we find ourselves in. Perhaps our focus needs to be reconsidered. Perhaps we had better look again at what we are working toward. Or could it be that we need to find different ways of achieving these goals?' Here the therapist invites the couple to join with him or her to work out what has gone awry in the process and how it can be put right in a manner which minimizes the couple's 'resistance' to therapy. When the therapist is able to forge this kind of alliance with a couple they frequently can begin to use these principles of negotiation and renegotiation in their own life situation.

There are couples, however, for whom these processes are quite alien. For example, some couples come to marital therapy expecting to be diagnosed and treated by an 'expert'. Their attitude is: 'Tell us what to do, and we'll do it.' Numerous therapists make the error of confronting this attitude *too* early in the therapeutic process. They may say: 'That is not how I see my role. My job is to help you decide for yourselves what to do.' Alliance theory would predict that the couple may drop out of treatment when they receive such a clear rebuttal of their therapeutic preferences. A different response in this instance might be to say something like: 'First, can you help me to understand what you have already tried in attempting to solve your problem and why you think these haven't worked.' The therapist can then begin to help the couple piece together a picture of what strategies have not been helpful which can in turn lead to constructive discussion about more effective alternative solutions. The therapist in effect goes along with the couple's expectations in the first instance – 'Yes I am an expert but I need to know more about what you have tried' - and then in the process of gaining information – 'What have you tried that hasn't been helpful?' – begins to implicitly educate the couple that they can begin to work out different solutions based on their own responses to such questions. Thus the therapist might say: 'So you both found that way unhelpful because it was too passive. What kinds of more active ways might suit you both?' The point is that sometimes a therapist may have to accept *a portion* of a role he would rather not adopt in order to relinquish it more effectively later.

This raises an important dilemma in the negotiation/renegotiation process where to be directly open may lead to the dissolution of the therapeutic relationship. The tension here is between the 'ethical' and the 'pragmatic'. Do I, as a marital therapist, be directly open in the negotiating process and (as shown above) risk losing this couple? Or do I adopt the 'pragmatic' approach and dodge the issue but deal with it indirectly and thus preserve the therapeutic relationship? Different marital therapists will respond to this dilemma in different ways, but it is one that has to be faced. As Mattinson and Sinclair (1979) put it: 'The need to be straightforward in the initial negotiations with clients . . . is limited by the need to take into account what the client is in a position to hear' (p. 186).

When a channel of communication about alliance issues has not been established, then discrepancies between the therapist and couple cannot be resolved. This may mean that the couple may drop out of therapy or continue in treatment but with on-going frustration (Maluccio 1979).

Bonds, goals and tasks

In this section we will consider the three components of the marital therapeutic alliance.

Bonds

It takes time to establish therapeutic bonds and the bases of such bonds between clients and therapist may be different in different therapeutic relationships. Strong (1978) has noted that an initial facilitative therapeutic relationship may be based on *credibility* – where the client sees the therapist as having legitimate expertise to provide help for marital problems – or on *liking* – where the client perceives the therapist to be attractive in a way that facilitates the development of a working relationship. Marital therapists should preferably attempt to meet the initial bonding preferences of clients which means emphasizing different facets of themselves in the therapeutic interaction. This is more difficult, of course, when each partner has different preferences on this dimension.

Broderick (1983) has referred to the marital therapist–couple relationship as the 'therapeutic triangle'. The development and maintenance of triangular rapport is one of marital therapists' principal tasks on the bond dimension. Perhaps the main initial component of triangular rapport concerns the degree to which partners feel deeply understood by the therapist. Here, the task of the therapist is to try and achieve 'empathic symmetry' in the triangle – each partner must feel equally accepted, supported and understood. The degree to which clients feel understood is significantly related to positive therapeutic outcome (see Garfield and Bergin 1978), although this needs to be further studied in marital therapy. Some corroborating evidence, however, in marital work comes from Hunt (1985) who studied the retrospective accounts of clients concerning their responses to MG counselling. Hunt found that the clients in her study who expressed a positive attitude towards counselling and what they gained from it made statements like 'I felt the counsellor understood me', 'There was an understanding between us', 'We got on well together and I felt that she understood and accepted me'. By contrast, clients who expressed a negative attitude about counselling referred to 'not being understood or accepted' or 'not having established a rapport with the counsellor'. Here we note that it is not sufficient for therapists to identify the distress of clients or even to respond to their distress but to really get into the skin of their clients and respond to the underlying issues upon which their distress is based.

In addition to 'empathic symmetry', the marital therapist has other components to attend to in the therapeutic triangle so as to achieve and maintain a well-bonded relationship with the couple (Broderick 1983). First, the therapist should preferably develop and sustain 'spatial symmetry' between the three participants. Broderick advocates the following:

> If the arrangement of furniture in the office permits it, most therapists choose to sit in a position facing the couple and equidistant from them. If the relationship seems to be veering in one direction or the other, he or she may want to shift positions somewhat like a sailor leaning to adjust the balance in a crosswind. In our practice should we feel a husband becoming more and more

distant and withdrawn as his wife recites an embarrassing inventory of his most humiliating vices, we may move physically closer to him or even touch him lightly to maintain equal contact. (p. 25)

Couples often subtly shift the position of their chairs away from each other, which makes partner–partner dialogue difficult. The therapist should either ask them to reorient their positions to facilitate their eye contact and mutual dialogue, or comment on their increasing distance from one another. Otherwise the couple will speak to each other through the therapist.

Second, therapists should preferably try to achieve 'temporal symmetry' so that each partner has an equal opportunity to speak. To ensure that each person uses this opportunity, Broderick (1983) advocates that 'one partner should never be given the floor uninterrupted for more than a very few minutes' (p. 25). Actualizing this principle helps the therapist to show each partner that 'their interests are being served and appreciated as well as their spouse's' (ibid., p. 26).

Preserving 'temporal symmetry' also helps the therapist to achieve 'moral symmetry'. It is easy in marital therapy for clients to place the burden of blame for the marital distress on the shoulders of their spouse. As Broderick (1983) notes for many couples, the issue of who is the most virtuous is on the agenda from the first minutes of the first session. The therapist has to find non-offensive means for achieving 'moral symmetry' and Broderick advocates a primary rule in this regard: 'focus on the pain each feels rather than the pain each causes' (p. 28).

In summary, the marital therapist has to develop productive bonds with the wife as an individual, with the husband as an individual and with the marital couple system. McDonald (1975), noting the tendency of the triads to divide into a coalition of two members against the third, advocates that 'the therapist should ideally relate to the marital unit not within the marital unit. The therapist is warned to maintain his objectivity and neutrality throughout the therapeutic process by not forming coalitions or aligning himself with either one of the marital pair' (p. 144). While we concur with this view, this should not be at the expense of the therapist–wife/therapist–husband alliances.

Threats to the development and maintenance of triangular rapport come from several sources. First, the couple's relationship with each other may preclude effective triangular therapy. Some couples are so angry toward or withdrawn from each other that their joint presence in the therapeutic setting severely threatens the other alliances. In these situations the therapist should consider the possibility of employing therapeutic arenas other than conjoint marital (triangular) therapy. Second, the therapist may develop countertransference reactions to one or both partners which, if unchecked, may lead to the emergence of unproductive coalitions within the triad. Third, partners may develop transference feelings toward the therapist. Hunt (1985) noted that it was the very early manifestation of negative transference reactions towards the therapist that prevented the establishment of productive alliances in MG counselling. Some of the clients in her study used words to describe their counsellor and his attitude in ways which were similar to how they described their spouse and other people in their lives. Hunt experienced a powerful reminder of how such transference feelings even interfered with the alliance she attempted to form with her interviewees in the context of the research interview. One male client in her study reacted quite aggressively to her first question: 'How did you come to know about Marriage Guidance?' He responded as if he experienced it as a belittling question. His reply was: 'Who nowadays hasn't heard of MG? ... I am aware of what's going on you know. I am not locked up in an attic all the time.' It emerged that this man also felt that his wife was continually criticizing and denigrating him and that he had felt put down by his counsellor. As a result he had not established enough rapport with the counsellor to sustain an on-going therapeutic relationship.

The establishment of effective triangular bonds facilitates the later work of marital therapy but is probably neither necessary nor sufficient for a positive outcome. Writing about marital therapy, Barker (1984) has put this well: 'One of the most common mistakes therapists make ... is to attempt an intrusive intervention without having first established rapport. On the other hand establishing rapport alone is not enough' (p. 18).

Goals

Therapeutic goals represent what the partners wish to achieve from marital therapy. A number of issues emerge when goals are considered. First, it is more accurate to refer to a matrix of therapeutic goals. Each partner has their own goals for themselves, their partner and the relationship. Furthermore each partner has perceptions of what the other's goals are in these three areas and what these goals should be. Then there are goals that represent a consensus between the partners. Finally the therapist's goals for each individual and the couple need to be considered and added to the matrix. Alliance theory would posit that effective marital therapy is best facilitated when the participants agree on goals chosen by *the couple* and when these goals are likely to enhance the quality of life for the couple *and* each partner.

Second, the marital therapist needs to adopt an active role in helping the couple to set goals. Barker (1984, pp. 48–51) has noted that goal setting cannot be left entirely to the couple because:

1) they often are not sure of or cannot easily articulate what they want;
2) the objectives of husband and wife are likely to conflict;
3) goals are usually interrelated and cannot easily be divided into desirable and undesirable parts;
4) each marital partner has mixed and changing feelings about what is wanted. Thus a negotiating procedure for changing goals after therapy is underway needs to be established;
5) as noted above, the marital partners and the therapist might have different views of what the goals are and should preferably be.

Third, goals can be viewed along several dimensions. Goals can, for example, be placed on a specificity continuum from highly general to highly specific. Different therapeutic approaches are likely to help couples to set goals at different points on this continuum. Thus, behavioural marital therapists may be more likely to help couples to set more specific goals than psychodynamically oriented marital therapists. Goals can also be placed on an explicitness continuum. While successful marital therapy can occur without partners' goals having been made explicit, in such a circumstance therapist and clients do have a shared implicit understanding of what the partners wish to achieve. However, the problem of keeping partners' goals at an implicit level is that these goals may be more likely to be misunderstood by both the partners and the therapist than if they had been made explicit. Since goals change throughout the therapeutic process it is perhaps easier for all participants to keep a check on current goals if these have been made explicit. Some marital therapists prefer not to make goals explicit, fearing that the therapeutic process may become ossified. While this is a danger, it is less likely to happen when the therapist has managed to establish and keep open the negotiation/renegotiation communication channel discussed earlier. The danger of setting goals at the outset of marital therapy is that they are more likely to be based on current states of disturbance and conflict than goals negotiated later in the process. However, the danger of not setting goals at the outset is that the couple do not know where they are heading and may become more rather than less confused. Marital therapists need to tread carefully in this veritable minefield.

Fourth, marital therapists often have to deal with different types of goals. The achievement of a couple's ultimate outcome goals (i.e. what they ultimately wish to achieve as a result of therapy) may depend on them successfully reaching a set of mediating outcome goals. Marital therapists, for example, are often faced with couples who wish to experience a more satisfying sexual relationship (ultimate outcome goal). However, it often transpires (particularly where no specific sexual dysfunction is apparent) that the couple are unable to achieve this because they are experiencing a lot of conflict in the non-sexual aspects of their relationship. In this case the therapist has to help the couple see that their outcome goal depends on the successful attainment of mediating outcome goals (i.e. improvements in the relevant non-sexual areas of their relationship). If the therapist does not help the couple to understand these different goals and how they are linked with one another, then the alliances may be threatened because the couple may be puzzled as to why the therapist is focusing on their non-sexual relationship when their priority is in the area of sex.

Another important distinction that needs to be made is between outcome and process goals. As employed here outcome goals refer to goals that the couple are striving to achieve *outside* the context of the therapy room whereas process goals are those that are achievable *within* the therapy room. Again the therapist should preferably help the couple make these distinctions and see the link between process and outcome goals. Taking the above example of the couple who wish to improve their sexual relationship, the therapist has two tasks in the realm of goals. As mentioned before, the therapist first has to help the couple see that the achievement of their sex-related goals depend on the attainment of non-sex-related goals (e.g. they will be more likely to experience more satisfactory sex when they have learned to become more open about their differences about childrearing). Then the therapist has to help the couple see that the achievement of this latter goal outside the therapy room depends in part upon them doing this successfully inside the room. The process–outcome distinction becomes particularly relevant for therapists who see couples who are able to achieve their process goals but do not transfer these successes outside the immediate context of the therapy session.

Finally, distinction needs to be made between realistic and unrealistic goals. A couple may agree on a set of goals which, given the nature of their relationship, may be quite unrealistic. Rather than challenge them at the outset, the therapist might assume the 'let us see' approach described earlier and help the couple set shorter-term objectives the attainment of which may be more realistic. It may be more helpful for the couple to discover how far they can ascend the hierarchy of their goals than for the therapist to express doubts about these goals at the outset.

There are a number of studies that are relevant to alliance theory in the goal domain although much of this research does not focus on marital therapy. Willer and Miller (1976) found that of clients who were admitted to a psychiatric hospital those who were involved in the goal-setting process were more satisfied with and attained more from their treatment than clients who were not so involved. Client satisfaction and goal attainment were measured in this study by both clients and therapists. Galano (1977) found that treatment at a community mental health clinic was moderately more effective when collaborative goal setting was added to goal-oriented psychotherapy than when goals were set for clients without their collaboration. Raschella (1975) found that, in individual therapy, the greater the level of congruence which was established initially between client and therapist in two areas – the content of treatment goals and the priority ranking of these goals – the longer these clients remained in therapy. Here, goal congruence helped to prevent premature termination of therapy. The only marital therapy study on goals was carried out by Pearlman (1977), already discussed. To reiterate, continuance in therapy was correlated with goal congruence between therapists and couples. This only held true at the fourth session and not at the end of the initial session. As already mentioned, goal convergence was much more likely to be produced by the willingness and/or ability of the clients to alter or modify their goals than by therapists adjusting their perception of the goals of counselling. Further research on goals in marital therapy is needed, particularly in the area where goals are related to therapeutic tasks designed to implement them.

Tasks

Therapeutic tasks represent the means of helping couples reach their goals. All approaches to marital therapy require both the therapist and the couple to involve themselves in the tasks that these approaches deem to be instrumental to successful marital therapy. It is the responsibility of the therapist to implement those therapeutic strategies and techniques that are considered thus instrumental in as skilful a manner as possible. It is also the therapist's job to help the partners to (a) acknowledge the relevance of the therapist's tasks, (b) see how their tasks are related to the therapist's tasks, (c) understand how implementing their tasks will help them achieve their goals, and (d) help them execute their tasks as efficiently as possible. A number of studies have been carried out on the task domain in marital or relationship-oriented therapy. In particular, these have focused on the tasks of 'talking' and exploring in the person-centred and psychodynamic therapeutic approaches. Maluccio (1979) found that therapists in his study usually gave clients little explanation of the value of talk as a medium for change. Silverman (1970) in a study of dropouts from social work treatment also found that therapists did not explain the role of talking in the therapeutic process and how this was related to goal achievement. She further noted that clients made a distinction between 'talking' and 'being helped'. They thus waited for the talking to end and the helping to begin and dropped out of treatment when it became apparent that 'help' would not be forthcoming. Mayer and Timms (1970) also discovered that clients found the task behaviour of their non-directive, psychodynamically oriented therapists puzzling, and that these 'helpers' did little to provide a rationale for their own task behaviour and little to educate their clients how best to use the therapeutic process.

In complementary fashion, marital partners have to carry out therapeutic tasks if they are to reach their goals. However, two questions need to be answered in the affirmative before clients can be expected to involve themselves in the tasks of the particular approach to marital therapy that they have been offered. First, can they meet these task demands? We showed in the previous chapter that men, in general, experience greater difficulty involving themselves in the tasks of self-disclosure and self-exploration inherent in the house-style of MG counselling than do women (Brannen and Collard 1982; Hunt 1985). Second, can clients see the relevance of carrying out these tasks? Again, men are less likely to see the relevance of the tasks of self-disclosure and self-exploration to the solutions of their problems than women (Brannen and Collard 1982). Whether men find the execution of such tasks difficult because they fail to see their relevance or vice versa remains an open question worthy of further study.

One therapeutic task that needs to be considered here is 'advice' since a large minority of couples seeking marital therapy come with the expressed purpose of getting advice (Ambrose et al. 1983; Brannen and Collard 1982). And yet most marital therapists (certainly those working within MGCs) view advice giving as anathema to their perceived role. However, the research on the role of advice in therapy suggests that it can be an important ingredient in the change process. Reid and Shapiro (1969) distinguished among three types of advice: (1) *interrogative–* suggestions made in the form of questions (e.g. 'Have you tried calling a truce when things look as if they are getting out of control?'); (2) *declarative–* suggestions based on the professional opinion of the worker or on the research literature (e.g. 'If you want to stop physically abusing your wife, studies have shown that it is very important to significantly reduce your drinking.'); and (3) *imperative–* directive statements (e.g. If you want your husband to be home at a certain time you should let him know your opinion and not expect him to be able to read your mind.'). Ewalt and Kutz (1976) found that receptiveness to advice was positively correlated with clients' convictions that their therapists were 'sensitive to their feelings, helped them to understand their problem, listened to them often and supported their own ideas and actions' (p. 17). Thus, far from being destructive, advice, based on strong therapeutic bonds, can be facilitative. Indeed Murphy et al. (1984) found that 'talking to someone who understands' and 'advice' were the two most beneficial 'curative' factors mentioned by clients who received individual cognitive-behaviour therapy for their problems. Reid and Shapiro (1969) found that even when advice was not followed its provision stimulated clients to think about dealing with their problems in different ways and to act on these newly discovered solutions, thus dispelling the widely held belief that advice giving inhibits clients from thinking independently. Interestingly, Ewalt and Kutz (1976) found that clients in the upper socioeconomic range preferred interrogative advice while those in the lower range preferred declarative advice. It is perhaps time that the role of advice in marital therapy was subjected to more objective scrutiny.

When the two marital partners value different task activities, this makes marital therapy a more difficult enterprise than individual therapy. In such cases it is important for the marital therapist to address these differences. For example, when the wife can see the relevance of verbal exploration while her husband prefers action-oriented methods, the therapist may help the couple to see that both these tasks are valuable and may lead to shared goals. The husband may be encouraged to see that action is more profitably conducted on a firm base of understanding while the wife is shown that exploration needs to be translated into action. In so doing the therapist can then ensure that both sets of expectations may be met but at different times in the process. In showing the couple that each partner's method of solving problems is legitimate and can in fact be enhanced by the utilization of the other person's preferred style, the therapist is indirectly helping them to achieve a greater tolerance (and hopefully greater respect) for their differences. Furthermore they can be mutually helpful by sharing their strengths with each other.

Finally, it should be noted that both therapists and couples have different tasks to perform at different times in the therapeutic process (Egan 1982). This is especially true if the therapist adopts an eclectic approach to marital work. At one point he may execute tasks designed to facilitate the couple's interpersonal dialogue while at another he may perform tasks of mediation.

It probably helps strengthen the task-related alliances if the therapist provides adequate rationales for these different tasks. The couples can also be helped to see that they have different tasks to perform at different times thoughout therapy, and again the relevance of these tasks for goal achievement requires emphasis.

Management of therapeutic alliances throughout the marital therapy process

In this section we will consider issues that emerge from adopting a temporal perspective on the marital therapy process. Since it is likely that different alliances become salient at different times, we shall consider the development of these alliances in the initial phase of marital therapy, their maintenance in the middle phase and their dissolution in the end phase.

The development of therapeutic alliances in the initial phase of marital therapy

Garvin and Seabury (1984) argue that when couples first approach helping agencies they have not necessarily made any commitment to work on their problems with the agency's help. Until the couple make this commitment and it is reciprocated by the therapist and the agency, it is best to consider them as *applicants* rather than clients. As Garvin and Seabury note, at this point 'the only obligation on the part of the applicant is to explore whether or not the service is of potential use and whether he or she wishes to use it' (p. 89). Assuming that the couple's first contact is with their assigned therapist rather than an intake worker the therapist 'has no right to begin any process of change of the applicant or the applicant's situation until the applicant becomes a client' (ibid.). The tasks of therapists at this time are (a) to help the applicant come to an informed decision as to whether the service being offered is appropriate and (b) to make their own decision concerning whether or not they are the best people to help the applicant. This should of course be explained to couples at the outset. It is likely that therapists will have different ideas concerning how detailed this negotiated process will be at this stage. Some therapists will prefer to initiate a brief exchange of facts, a curtailed focus on problem material and a general exploration of mutual expectations, while others will prefer a more comprehensive and detailed pretherapy exchange.

Once a therapist and couple have agreed to work together a number of alliance issues become salient. In the case described above, where the couple have had an initial pretherapy interview with their assigned therapist, it is likely that the couple have already made preliminary judgements about their bonds with the worker. Gaunt (1981) found that while applicants for MG counselling remembered very little about what their reception interviewer said about counselling, they remembered quite detailed personal information about their interviewers. Nonetheless, an important task of the therapist in this initial phase of therapy is to develop and strengthen 'triangular rapport' (Broderick 1983). The therapist needs to join each client's own reality (Guldner 1981) and to communicate empathic understanding of each partner's phenomenal world. Here the alliances between the therapist and each marital partner receive attention. Concurrently the therapist–couple system alliance needs attention. The therapist needs to communicate understanding of the couple's unique problems, dysfunctional behavioural patterns and implicit agreements without siding with either partner. As Gurman (1981) has said, 'the therapist must learn to speak to both spouses at the same time' (p. 85). Finally the alliance between the spouses needs early attention. Some therapists (e.g. Barker 1984) prefer to focus on couples' strengths or goals before considering their problems. This is to strengthen the partner–partner alliance to enable it to be sustained during problem-focused exploration.

While the early alliance focus is likely to be in the bond domain there is some evidence to suggest that to neglect an early exploration of a couple's expectations in the task domain is to threaten this particular alliance. This may lead to early client drop-out or continued client frustration during the therapy process. Brannen and Collard's (1982) and Hunt's (1985) findings that men are more likely to drop out from MG counselling because their task preferences are not being met or fully discussed is relevant here and has already been noted. Thus, if expectations (preferences and anticipations) have not been made explicit during the pretherapy phase, they require early attention in therapy. The therapist's task here is a complex one. He has to correct misconceptions and induce realistic attitudes towards and expectations for therapy, while instilling a sense of hope in *both* partners. Without this accompanying task of instilling hope any attempt to correct misconceptions and make explicit the nature of the help being offered may in fact have the reverse effect of enhancing despair. The therapist needs to take care to provide a positive and credible alternative while correcting clients' help-seeking misconceptions. As has already been mentioned, the more the therapist can use the couple's own data in the structuring process the more effective this process is likely to be in helping the couple to become actively involved in therapy. Finally, by promoting an open three-way exchange of views about the nature of marital therapy, the therapist has initiated the processes of negotiation/renegotiation deemed by alliance theory to be instrumental in promoting effective therapy.

The structuring process will also be facilitated if the therapist has some idea concerning the couple's goals. Notwithstanding the fact that goals change throughout therapy, goal-directed work helps all participants know where they are in the therapeutic process. This is particularly important for many couples in the initial phase of marital therapy, although at this stage their specified goals do not need to be too concrete.

Goals also help both the therapist and the couple maintain a focus for their work. There is some American evidence (Noonan 1973) to suggest that marital therapy clients expect short-term intervention and are looking for quick results. Statistics from the NMGC corroborate the view that marital therapy is often quite brief (90 percent of cases are seen for between one and ten sessions – Heisler 1984). Given the short-term nature of much marital work, it is likely that a focus helps the participants make the best use of limited time. There is indeed some evidence to show that such a focus helps to prevent early drop-out from marital therapy (Pearlman 1977).

Alliance theory would posit that the creation of a focus should preferably be a shared one. Mayer and Timms (1970) in their research on clients' reactions to relationship-oriented social work have referred to the unreal quality of the counselling process when clients and counsellors do not have a shared focus to their work:

> There is almost a Kafkaesque quality about these worker/client interactions. To exaggerate only slightly, each of the partners assumed that the other shared certain of his underlying conceptions about behaviour and the ways it might be altered. (p. 77).

Hunt (1985) describes the situation where therapist and couple do not have a shared focus to their work as 'parallel tracking'. Here one or more of the participants are working on different issues and/or towards different goals than the others. To prevent the development of 'parallel tracking' an increasing number of marital therapists are advocating the use of contracts in marital work (e.g. Barker 1984; Garvin and Seabury 1984).

Drawing upon the work of Maluccio and Marlow (1974), a contract is defined here as: 'an explicit agreement between the therapist and the clients concerning the latter's target problems, their goals for change and the therapeutic strategies and techniques that will be employed to help goal attainment. In addition, a working consensus will be reached concerning the roles and tasks of all participants.' It is important to note that contracts should preferably be used flexibly and are subject to revision throughout the therapeutic process. While some marital therapists prefer to draw up written contracts signed by all participants, others prefer mutually agreed verbal contracts. A number of important issues relating to the use of contracts in marital therapy will now be discussed.

Who is the contract with?   It is apparent that if only one partner in the marriage comes for counselling, the contract is with that particular partner. However, as Bennun (1984) has noted, even in this situation both therapist and client need to consider the fact that the person is in a marital relationship and that the contract should reflect this (see also Volume 2, Chapter 1). When a contract is to be made with two persons an important question which needs to be answered is this: 'Is the contract with the two individuals in the relationship or with "the relationship"?' Different workers will have different views on this point. Our viewpoint is that the greater the number of alliances covered by the contract, the more effective the contract will be.

Timing of contracts   It is important that contracts are discussed and developed when both partners are fully involved in the contract-making process. When clients are particularly distressed or preoccupied with pressing issues it would be foolhardy of the therapist to try to involve them in the process of contract development since they may not even be able to hear what the therapist is saying.

Difficulties in developing contracts   Maluccio (1979) notes that, despite the fact that therapists see the value of negotiating contracts, there remains the question as to how frequently or systematically these are employed in practice. Hunt (1985) indicated that explicit contracts between MG counsellors and their clients were not frequently made. This was so despite the fact that the formation of explicit contracts between workers and their clients is advocated and taught during MG counsellor training. There are a number of possible explanations for the difficulties commonly experienced by both clients and MG counsellors when they try to develop contracts.

(1)   Counsellors may not have sufficient skills and experience to make a valid assessment of the couple's problems in the initial interview(s) and

are therefore unable to formulate treatment goals and to make some prediction about the length of time which will be required to achieve those goals.

(2) Clients may still be so preoccupied with their uncertain feelings about whether MG is the right place for them that they are unwilling to commit themselves to counselling.

(3) Many counsellors continue to operate in a Rogerian non-directive manner, mainly establishing a warm relationship and facilitating the exploration of the problem, and are therefore somewhat unskilled at setting specific goals and limits. The notion that the counsellor follows 'the client' bolsters their belief that arriving at an open-ended agreement with the client is more client-centred.

(4) Setting limits is often regarded as conflicting with the notion of being an all-nurturing, all-accepting, facilitating 'mother' (Temperley 1979). Temperley comments that while current thinking in many fields has become free of the 'punitive, autocratic father' of the past and replaced him with the ideal of the 'nurturing, accepting, facilitating mother', education, childrearing, psychotherapy and social work have all suffered from the idea that the 'facilitating mother' is sufficient. She says that such attitudes underestimate the inevitability of conflict and frustration and the desirability of struggle and discipline, all of which are necessary if real achievement is to occur. She suggests that there is a need to rehabilitate the limit-setting, reality-facing aspects of the 'father' in the work with clients. Counsellors commonly see their role as being a care giver and clients can seduce counsellors into this role. In such a climate, some counsellors may have difficulty in using their authority to set limits with regard to the work and to what is relevant to work on.

(5) As shown in the previous chapter, clients may enter marital therapy with a variety of motivations that make the successful negotiation of effective contracts extremely difficult.

While we have focused on how to develop productive initial alliances, there is some evidence, from research on brief individual therapy, to suggest that the practitioner's initial major concern is to avoid the development of poor alliances rather than to promote the development of sound ones (Hartley and Strupp 1983). Similarly, Bordin (1983) has noted that the strength of alliances in the initial phase of therapy does not have to be strong, but 'it must be strong enough to endure the strains of hard work in the partnership. The harder the work to be engaged in, the stronger this elementary alliance will need to be' (pp. 8–9). Further research is needed to determine the applicability of this finding to marital therapy.

The maintenance of therapeutic alliances in the middle phase of marital therapy

Given the establishment of well-bonded alliances in the therapeutic triangle, the middle phase of marital therapy is characterized by a number of features. First, the task domain of the alliances is likely to come more into prominence. If an effective focus has been contractually negotiated, the therapeutic work is devoted primarily to the execution of tasks deemed by the participants to lead to the couple's goals. While in some approaches to marital therapy the burden of change falls upon the successful execution of intherapy tasks, other approaches place more emphasis on the couple carrying out a set of extratherapy tasks (known as homework assignments). Once again it is important that (a) the participants understand what their tasks are, (b) they are able to execute them, and (c) they can see how the completion of these tasks can lead to the attainment of therapeutic goals. Bordin (1983) notes that the work of the partnership in the middle phase of therapy leads to strengthening of the therapeutic bonds, given that progress occurs and that the therapist is skilful.

Second, the middle phase of marital therapy is characterized by modification of the couple's initial goals. This is one reason why the early establishment of the processes of negotiation/renegotiation is so important in marital therapy. If the participants are not able to talk to one another about the therapeutic situation, goals which have become inappropriate may not be subject to change. The changing nature of goals throughout the process of marital therapy has an effect on task-related alliances in that the employment of a variety of therapeutic tasks may have to be tolerated by the participants. Different therapeutic tasks may be best suited to effecting different therapeutic ends and marital therapy may falter if (a) the therapist employs a restricted repertoire of tasks, (b) the partners are unwilling or unable to employ different tasks, or (c) the partners cannot tolerate the expanded task repertoire of their therapist. Barker (1984) has underscored the fact that it is in the middle phase of therapy that the therapist assumes different roles to help the couple achieve different goals.

Third, client resistance to change can be a feature of the middle phase of marital therapy. Indeed therapists would do well to forewarn couples that change will rarely take place in a linear fashion and that when couples do not execute tasks (either intherapy or extratherapy activities), this needs to be understood by all concerned. In short, the therapist and couple employ the 'let us see if we can understand...' approach outlined in the section on negotiation/renegotiation. Marital therapists who adopt alliance theory as a way of understanding the process of marital therapy will help their clients to consider a wide range of factors while striving to understand the nature of the resistance. They will ask whether this resistance can be attributed to bond alliances, goal alliances and/or task alliances. Are therapist factors mainly responsible (e.g. poor timing of intrusive interventions, failure to present a clear rationale), or client factors (e.g. one partner wishes to maintain the status quo despite overtly agreeing to pursue a particular goal)? Finally, does the reason lie somewhere in the matrix of factors within the therapist—client interaction? Thus alliance-oriented marital therapists will be loathe to reach the frequently heard conclusion 'this couple is not motivated' without having undertaken with the couple an extensive investigation into the nature of the resistance.

If marital therapists are sensitive to alliance-related issues, they are unlikely to become bogged down with a couple in an interminable therapy relationship which seems to be without direction and purpose. Also such therapists are less likely to have clients who remain in therapy but do so with frustration. Maluccio (1979) found that clients in a type of therapy (maritally oriented social work) not characterized by negotiation between therapists and clients either dropped out early in treatment or continued disillusioned and frustrated. This pattern was not found in therapy relationships where on-going negotiation and renegotiation was a major feature of the interaction.

While a lot more work on the maintenance of therapeutic alliances needs to be done in the middle phases of marital therapy, some interesting suggestions come from the work of Bordin (1983). Writing primarily about individual therapy, Bordin's view is that the strength of the alliance increases in the middle phase of therapy given the skill of the therapist, and that the repair of momentary breaks in the alliances can of itself be extremely facilitative. In marital therapy, however, there are several alliances and thus the strength of each individual alliance may not develop to the capacity as it does in individual work. Nevertheless, Bordin's view has an interesting parallel in marital work. It may be that the strength of the alliance *between* marital partners is enhanced when *they* succeed in repairing the 'breaks' in their relationship. The more they succeed in doing so using their own resources, the stronger their alliance with one another will become. Conversely, the more the therapist assumes major responsibility for this 'repair' work, the weaker the partners' joint alliance will be. Hence the preference, echoed by marital therapists of all persuasions, for couples to do most of their own work. Yet the skill of the therapist is to enable them to do so.

The dissolution of therapeutic alliances in the end phase of marital therapy

One of the prime tasks of the marital therapist in the middle phase of treatment, then, is to help the couple strengthen their own working alliance. If the work goes well and progress begins to be maintained, the task of the therapist is to dissolve the alliances between himself and the couple system without weakening the partner–partner alliance. It is not sufficient for the therapist just to help the couple achieve their goals and then withdraw, but rather he needs to help the couple become their own change agents. The ultimate goal of marital therapy, when the partners decide to remain married, is to help the couple utilize and internalize methods for solving future problems and to discourage the couple from returning for help as soon as problems materialize in their relationship. Thus, when marital therapy has gone well, the therapist's goal is to encourage the couple to view themselves as their own therapeutic change agents. This can best be done by reviewing the course of therapy with the couple, emphasizing the methods that the couple have employed to overcome their problems, and discussing how these methods might be employed in the future.

When the course of marital therapy has run smoothly, termination of the triangular relationship tends to occur as a natural culminating stage of all that has gone before. In such cases, the couple may find it difficult to bring up issues for discussion or the session tends to be characterized by social as opposed to therapeutic discourse. There are different ways of dissolving the triangular alliances. Some therapists prefer to increase the length of time between sessions (i.e. gradual disengagement), while others prefer to set the date of the final session at the outset of the end phase. According to alliance theory, therapists should preferably be guided by the unique wishes of the couple when deciding upon a mode of dissolving triangular alliances. What is important, however, is that termination should best be employed as a way of stabilizing therapy outcome (and hopefully enhancing future growth). This dictates that the couple's goals should have been attained fairly well in advance of the final session (Barker 1984).

In successful cases of marital therapy, dissolution of the triangular alliances is less difficult than disengagement in individual therapy. 'The one-to-one relationship between therapist and individual client accentuates an intense interpersonal connectedness, mutual empathy, transference and countertransference, and strong reluctance to give it up' (ibid., p. 97); whereas, when marital therapy has produced a positive outcome, the intensity of this 'interpersonal connectedness' is greatest between the partners themselves. Yet, despite the fact that the marital therapist seeks to adopt a lower profile in the latter stages of the work, there is bound to be some ambivalence on the part of the couple in disengaging from someone who has been helpful. It is constructive if all parties can acknowledge the mixed feelings of positive optimism and sadness that usually accompany a healthy life transition with all its gains and losses.

However, the dissolution of triangular alliances can frequently be fraught with problems. Obviously marital therapy can be terminated prematurely, i.e. before the couple has achieved and stabilized their goals, and this is frequently a sign that triangular alliances have not been adequately formed or are not strong enough to sustain the participants through the task demands of the therapy. In this regard, Broderick (1983) has argued that 'when the triangular relationship aborts early it is because the therapist was not able to establish symmetrical rapport with the couple' (p. 159).

Maluccio (1979) prefers to distinguish between planned and unplanned termination rather than refer to premature termination. He found that in some cases when termination was unplanned the clients felt they had achieved their goals but their therapists felt that there was still more work to be done – hence unplanned termination. In these cases 'the clients were satisfied with having obtained help in relation to specific "problems in living", while workers were concerned with overall "cures" or broad changes in an individual's situation or personality structure' (p. 182). The therapists of these satisfied clients seemed to disregard the importance of clients' goals and overestimated the importance of the therapeutic bonds as catalysts for change. Their clients, however, reported that therapy had had a triggering effect in that it helped them to utilize better the external resources in their community, that is it enabled clients to form more productive alliances with outside helping agents.

Maluccio's second group of unplanned terminators were indeed dissatisfied with the service offered and there were clear *early* signs of unformed or weakly formed therapeutic alliances.

> Clients and workers in these cases had a vague sense of what could be happening in treatment, were unable to establish an emotional connection between them, did not actively engage in contract negotiation, and ended the first session with marked vagueness and uncertainty about future plans. (ibid., p. 181)

In Hunt's (1985) study of clients' reactions to MG counselling over half of her client sample ended counselling by default either by cancelling or failing to attend appointments. She concluded that negotiation of therapeutic contracts may have minimized the incidence of unplanned endings. Furthermore, Hunt found in interviewing this group that many were left with unresolved feelings about their counselling experience and tried, in her view, to use the research interview as a way of reaching a more satisfactory conclusion to their contact with MG.

Hunt also found that unplanned termination was due in part to the failure of the participants to renegotiate a different kind of contract, particularly when couples decided to separate or divorce. This may be due to (a) clients' perception of MG as a 'marriage mending' agency and therefore not an appropriate service for dealing with 'marriage ending' matters, or to (b) counsellors' difficulties in renegotiating therapy contracts. Further research is indicated here.

Major problems can occur when termination is avoided as an issue. Sometimes marital therapists and couples get hopelessly bogged down in therapy, when it might be better to terminate the particular therapeutic relationship with a possible referral to a more appropriate helper. Therapy relationships get bogged down for many reasons but one identifying characteristic of such partnerships is failure to establish and maintain the negotiation/renegotiation process. As a result there develops a kind of collusive norm between the participants which inhibits the discussion of metatherapy issues (i.e. issues about the therapy). Supervision could be instrumental in helping the marital therapist to understand the relevant factors here (often pertaining to the therapist–couple interaction or to the existence of partner 'secrets') and thence to intervene differently – if indeed the worker is prepared to bring the case to supervision!

Broderick (1983) has noted that overdependency is another characteristic of therapies where the issue of termination is avoided.

> On the couple's side they may come to view the therapist as a powerful stabilizing influence on the runaway destructiveness of their relationship. Like the one-eyed man in the land of the blind the therapist may become, not king, but captive – too valuable to be allowed to escape. (p. 166)

This couple dynamic can complement the therapist's *need* to be helpful and/or needed and the therapeutic relationship continues until one or both parties challenge their neurotic needs.

The therapist's contribution to 'interminable' marital work often centres on two issues as noted by Broderick:

> . . . the therapist may fall into the role of warm, supportive parent to a couple

who never had one in either of their growing-up experience... or the therapist may become seduced into an enmeshed relationship because of his own unfinished business with his own parents or siblings or children (ibid., pp. 166–167).

Overdependency in the bond alliances thus interferes with the establishment of 'mature' bonds where the therapist is a temporary member of the triangle striving to help the couple to ally themselves with each other. Under these conditions the task of dissolving the therapeutic alliances cannot be successfully attempted.

Finally, many marital therapists offer couples follow-up session(s) to monitor the stability of change. Barker (1984) urges therapists 'to individualize the follow-up to suit the unique needs and circumstances of each couple who successfully terminate treatment' (p. 99). Research on the impact of follow-up sessions on triangular alliances would be fruitful in that the status of such sessions is somewhat ambiguous. They are not a part of the therapy and yet they are experiences shared by the members of the dissolved therapy relationship.

Summary

In this chapter, the focus was on the therapeutic alliances as they develop throughout marital therapy. Negotiation and renegotiation processes have to be initiated and sustained throughout the work if alliance issues are to be openly and constructively discussed by therapists and couples. These issues centre on the bonds that develop in the triangular relationship, the goals of the couple and the tasks which are executed by all participants in the service of these goals. Finally, a temporal analysis of marital therapy alliances was presented as these occur in the initial, middle and end phases of marital therapy.

References

Ambrose, P., Harper, J. and Pemberton, R. (1983) *Surviving divorce: men beyond marriage*. Brighton: Wheatsheaf Books.

Barker, R. L. (1984) *Treating couples in crisis*. New York: Free Press.

Bennun, I. (1984) Evaluating marital therapy: a hospital and community study *British Journal of Guidance and Counselling*, *12(1)*, 84–91.

Bordin, E. S. (1983) Myths, realities, and alternatives to clinical trials. Paper delivered at the International Conference on Psychotherapy, Bogota, Colombia.

Brannen, J. and Collard, J. (1982) *Marriages in trouble: the process of seeking help.* London: Tavistock.

Broderick, C. B. (1983) *The therapeutic triangle: a sourcebook on marital therapy.* Beverley Hills, California: Sage.

Egan, G. (2nd edn 1982) *The skilled helper: model, skills, and methods for effective helping.* Monterey, California: Brooks/Cole.

Elton, A. (1982) Maintaining family motivation during treatment. *In* A. Bentovim, G. Gorell Barnes and A. Cooklin (eds) *Family therapy: complementary frameworks of theory and practice,* Volume 1. London: Academic Press.

Ewalt, P. L. and Kutz, J. (1976) An examination of advice giving as a therapeutic intervention. *Smith College Studies in Social Work, 47,* 3–19.

Galano, J. (1977) Increased treatment effectiveness as a function of increased client involvement in therapy. Unpublished PhD dissertation, Bowling Green State University.

Garfield, S. L. and Bergin, A. E. (eds) (2nd edn 1978) *Handbook of psychotherapy and behavior change.* New York: Wiley.

Garvin, C. D. and Seabury, B. A. (1984) *Interpersonal practice in social work: processes and procedures.* Englewood Cliffs, New Jersey: Prentice-Hall.

Gaunt, S. (1981) The Birmingham Marriage Guidance Council reception interview scheme. Unpublished report, Birmingham: BMGC.

Guldner, C. A. (1981) Premature termination in marital and family therapy *In* A. S. Gurman, (ed.) *Questions and answers in the practice of family therapy.* New York: Brunner/Mazel.

Gurman, A. S. (1981) Creating a therapeutic alliance in marital therapy. *American Journal of Family Therapy, 9(3),* 84–87.

Gurman, A. S. and Kniskern, D. P. (1981) Family therapy outcome research: knowns and unknowns. *In* A. S. Gurman and D. P. Kniskern (eds) *Handbook of family therapy.* New York: Brunner/Mazel.

Hartley, D. E. and Strupp, H. H. (1983) The therapeutic alliance: its relationship to outcome in brief psychotherapy. *In* J. Masling, (ed.) *Empirical studies of psychoanalytic theories.* Hillsdale, New Jersey: The Analytic Press.

Heisler, J. (1984): *The National Marriage Guidance Council Client 1982.* Rugby: NMGC.

Hunt, P. (1985) Clients' responses to marriage counselling. Unpublished PhD thesis, University of Aston in Birmingham.

Maluccio, A. N. (1979) *Learning from clients: interpersonal helping as viewed by clients and social workers.* New York: Free Press.

Maluccio, A. N. and Marlow, W. D. (1974) The case for the contract. *Social Work, 19,* 28–36.

Mattinson, J. and Sinclair, I. (1979) *Mate and stalemate: working with marital problems in a social services department.* Oxford: Blackwell.

Mayer, J. E. and Timms, N. (1970) *The client speaks.* London: Routledge and Kegan Paul.

McDonald, G. W. (1975) Coalition formation in marital therapy triads. *Family Therapy, 2,* 141–148.

Murphy, P. M., Cramer, D. and Lillie, F. J. (1984) The relationship between curative factors perceived by patients in their psychotherapy and treatment outcome: an exploratory study. *British Journal of Medical Psychology, 57,* 187–192.

Noonan, J. R. (1973) A follow-up of pretherapy dropouts. *Journal of Community psychology*, *1*, 43–45.

Pearlman, S. (1977) Convergence of therapist and client goals in the initial stage of marital counseling and its relationship to continuance in treatment. Unpublished PhD dissertation, University of Toronto.

Raschella, G. F. (1975) An evaluation of the effect of goal congruence between client and therapist on premature client dropout from therapy. Unpublished PhD dissertation, University of Pittsburgh.

Reid, W. J. and Shapiro, B. L. (1969) Client reactions to advice. *Social Science Review*, *43*, 165–173.

Silverman, P. R. (1970) A re-examination of the intake procedure. *Social Casework*, *51*, 625–634.

Smail, D. J. (1978) *Psychotherapy: a personal approach*. London: Dent.

Strong, S. R. (2nd edn 1978) Social psychological approach to psychotherapy research. *In* S. L. Garfield and A. E. Bergin (eds) *Handbook of psychotherapy and behavior change*. New York: Wiley.

Temperley, J. (1979) The implications for social work practice of recent psychoanalytical developments. Paper presented at a conference on 'Change and renewal in psychodynamic social work', Oxford.

Willer, B. and Miller, G. H. (1976): Client involvement in goal setting and its relationship to therapeutic outcome. *Journal of Clinical Psychology*, *32*, 687–690.

CHAPTER EIGHT Marital Therapy
The Psychodynamic Approach
Diana Daniell

Introduction

British historical context

In England in the late 1940s there was growing public concern about the rising divorce rate. The Denning Report on Procedure in Matrimonial Causes (1947) recommended that the State should give every encouragement and, where appropriate, financial assistance to marriage guidance as a form of social service. At the same time there was an increasing recognition by mental health professionals that many of the social and medical problems they were confronting were manifestations of emotional conflict in marriage and family life.

Concurrent with these developments, a small body of caseworkers in the Family Welfare Association realized they could not understand at a rational level many of the marital problems which were presented to them. In order to intervene effectively, they found they had to explore the underlying and often irrational elements in the disturbed relationship. This work led to the birth of the Family Discussion Bureau, a pioneering group of marital caseworkers, which was set up in 1948 by the Family Welfare Association in London with Mrs Enid Balint as its first director. It soon established close working links with the Tavistock Clinic and Tavistock Institute of Human Relations. In 1956 the Bureau transferred from the Family Welfare Association to the Tavistock Institute of Human Relations and in 1969 adopted the title, the Institute of Marital Studies (IMS), the name it bears today.

A first description of the work of the IMS, then still known as the Family Discussion Bureau, was published in 1955 (Bannister et al). This was followed by the book *Marriage: Studies in Emotional Conflict and Growth* (Pincus 1960, now in its fourth reprint) which outlined an approach to marital therapy based on a psychoanalytic theory of personality development and human relationships. This approach took into account the unconscious processes which influence the individual's choice of partner and the nature of marital interaction. It also described what took place in the complex therapeutic relationship which developed during the process of marital therapy between the marital partners and their caseworkers.

As Pincus later (1968) observed,

It came as a surprise that marital therapy appears to be of special value with disturbed people who often have a great need for, and dependence upon, their family relationships, yet are in constant danger of destroying them by their demands and destructiveness. Our acceptance of them as husbands and fathers, wives and mothers, rather than as sick and isolated individuals, seems to strengthen their often precarious sense of reality. The fact that in our work both partners are seen implies that the rejected or feared aspects of the self, which have been projected into the partner, are acceptable and may be controlled, and that even destructiveness and 'madness' may be *contained* in the marriage. (p. 1)

While not all marriages can be made into wholly satisfying relationships, it seemed that there was the potential for growth in many and that work focused on the marriage afforded a good 'therapeutic wicket'.

During this time there was a parallel development of thought in the Tavistock Clinic which culminated in Dr Henry Dicks' classic book on marital problems *Marital Tensions* (1967). In this book he described how during the previous sixteen years the application of concepts derived from both classical psychoanalysis and object-relations theory had been applied to the elucidation of marital interaction in the treatment of marital disturbance in a National Health Service clinic.

Developments

Since the 1960s there has been at the Tavistock Centre a steady development of training in the psychodynamic approach to marital therapy. This has included postprofessional training for mental health professionals who intend to specialize in marital psychotherapy, and a variety of training opportunities aimed to develop the psychodynamic skills of practitioners who wish to apply this approach to understanding marital disturbance in ways appropriate to their own professional settings, for example social work, probation, psychiatry, marriage guidance and general practice.

While marital psychotherapy as described here had its early beginnings at the Tavistock Centre, marital work informed by psychodynamic understanding is now practised in a variety of settings by therapists from different disciplines, sometimes using this understanding in conjunction with other treatment methods.

The nature of marital disturbance – how marital disturbance develops and is maintained

The aetiology of marital relationships and marital disturbance is complex. Many psychological factors operate at different levels while social, cultural and economic influences all play an important part. As Geoffrey Thompson (1960) has observed,

> There are wide differences between individuals and between individual marriages in their response to social pressures and opportunities. In some marriages a given set of circumstances constitute a threat which brings about deterioration in the relationship, while in others it calls forth a positive response and a strengthening of the ties between the couple. (p. 1)

It is the inner world of the partners and the nature of their interaction which determines their response to changing circumstances.

Mattinson (1981) has discussed this in relation to childlessness:

> Some understanding of the social climate within which a couple planning to have their first child discover their inability to do so (and very few of the sterile have knowledge of their condition prior to their attempt to conceive) is important in attempting to understand the psychological consequences of the diagnosis for an individual couple. It seems that most people are most confirmed in themselves when their outer world synchronises with, and helps them to realise, their inner world of fantasy; that they will be at their most satisfied when the outer world confirms the brightest and best of fantasies, and in dire distress when it confirms their worst fears about themselves. For example, social support for parenthood and despisal of childlessness will aggravate the psychological problems of a person who consciously or unconsciously believes he is beset by the sins of the fathers or that she is too bad or too worthless to be allowed the gift of a child. (p. 2)

From clinical experience of couples seen in the IMS, certain concepts have emerged as central to understanding processes of marital interaction. First is the recognition that many of the problems of adulthood and many of the patterns of longings, fears and fantasies in marriage relationships stem from each partner's infantile and childhood experiences. Second, the motivations which underlie the choice of marital partner, sustain the relationship and give it a particular quality are as related to unconscious factors as to conscious ones. Third, there is a system of shared fantasies and shared defences which operate in a marital relationship. This leads to an unconscious as well as a conscious marriage contract in terms of what each spouse expects of the other. The overall crucial finding which emerges from an understanding of these mechanisms is that marriage has to be viewed as a psychic entity in itself – a system greater than the sum of the personalities of the two partners.

These same mechanisms are involved in all marriages, but what distinguishes unsatisfactory marriages from satisfactory ones, as Thompson (1960) has suggested, is not a fundamental difference of kind but rather the balance of the different factors involved, their relative intensity and the characteristic ways in which they play into one another in the endless and shifting complexities of the relationship.

Effect of early development on the marital relationship

In considering how marital disturbance develops and is maintained, it is important to understand the family context in which each spouse has grown up and the models of partnership and parenting they have internalized from their parents.

The development of the personality is a complex process which takes place through a sequence of phases. The changes by which immaturity gives place to maturity in terms of the progression of the individual's instinctual life has been charted by classic Freudian theory which emphasizes the growth of personality through the oral, anal, phallic and genital stages of psycho-sexual development. It is from this psychoanalytic framework that later developments in psychodynamic theory and practice have derived.

However, marital psychotherapists have reservations about the usefulness of classic psychoanalytic theory as the mainstay for the interpretations of *interpersonal* relations. It is the later developments of psychoanalytic thinking of Melanie Klein and the English object-relations theorists (Fairbairn, Winnicott, Balint) that many practitioners now use in their understanding of interactive processes. More recently the IMS has drawn on Bowlby's theory of attachment and loss (Mattinson and Sinclair 1979).

Fairbairn (1952) viewed the individual's ego development as furthered by the secure passage through a succession of positions of ambivalence towards objects (i.e. parents or parental figures). Beginning with the early perceptions of 'good' and gratifying, or 'bad' and frustrating objects first proposed by Melanie Klein, he described how the infant advances through a gradual lessening of these absolute contrasts and becomes more able to tolerate ambivalence in self and others without splitting the antithetical components one from the other. Dicks (1967) observed that individuals have strongly 'built-in' role-models for their own and the spouse's behaviour which are based on ambivalent relations to earlier love objects. He suggests how within the intimacy of the marital relationship there is an unconscious reality testing of these patterns of early object-relations.

Bowlby (1979) also draws attention to the fact that an infant's experiences of how his parents maintain or fail to maintain their relationship with him plays a vital part in the way he will later organize his own relationships. He writes of two sets of influences:

> The first, concerns the presence or absence, partial or total, of a trustworthy figure willing and able to provide the kind of *secure base* required at each phase of the life-cycle. These constitute the external, or environmental, influences. The second set concerns the relative ability or inability of an individual, first, to recognise when another person is both trustworthy and willing to provide a base and, second, when recognised, to collaborate with that person in such a way that a mutually rewarding relationship is initiated and maintained. These constitute the internal, or organismic, influences.
> Throughout life the two sets of influences interact in complex and circular ways. In one direction the kinds of experience a person has, especially during childhood, greatly affect both whether he expects later to find a secure personal base, or not, and also the degree of competence he has to initiate and maintain a mutually rewarding relationship when opportunity offers. In the reverse direction the nature of the expectations a person has, and the degree of competence he brings, plays a large part in determining both the kinds of person with whom he associates and how they treat him. Because of these interactions, whatever pattern is first established tends to persist. (p. 104)

Bowlby has reformulated what, in traditional theory, is termed a 'good object' as an attachment figure who is conceived as accessible, trustworthy and ready to help when called upon; similarly, what, in traditional theory, is termed a 'bad object' he reformulates as an attachment figure who is conceived as often inaccessible, unhelpful and at times even hostile.

Unconscious factors in choice of marital partner

While there is often a wish to start afresh in marriage and to escape the disappointments of unsatisfactory early relationships with parents or other significant persons, strong unconscious ties to these first-loved objects often help to determine the choice of a partner with whom earlier experiences can be compulsively reenacted.

Although partners may consciously choose each other for their 'good' qualities, they frequently unconsciously choose a shared level of immaturity. Many people seen in the IMS seem to choose a partner who embodies their own 'problem' (i.e. difficulties stemming from the same stage of arrested emotional development). This can, however, prove helpful if the marriage provides a container in which the partners give each other enough time, space and trust to enable them to work through their shared area of disturbance.

In therapy with couples it frequently emerges that what first attracts individuals to one another and what later on both partners complain of in the other is a projection of an unwanted and repudiated bit of themselves. It might be thought that an easier solution in trying to deal with unwanted parts of the self would be to project these outside the marriage. This is common enough, but, as Sutherland (1962) suggests, the projection within the marriage appears to have an unconscious 'wisdom' if looked at as an attempt by both partners to try to get these unwanted parts integrated within themselves.

To give one example: Mr Brooks, a very controlled, passive young man, had never been able to express his anger to his 'ill' mother, whom he loved but also deeply resented. He met an emotionally volatile girl and was attracted to her because of her capacity to be spontaneous and show her aggression. After their marriage, while he complained about his wife's irrational outbursts of rage against his parents, he unconsciously encouraged her to express for him the anger which he felt was too dangerous to acknowledge himself. In view of Mrs Brooks's experience in her own family of having to be aggressive in order to be heard, she was a willing recipient of his projections. Mrs Brooks, who initially had been drawn to her husband because of his quietness and self-control, subsequently complained about his passive and inflexible behaviour. However, she needed him to hold for her the quieter, more controlled and rational parts of herself which she had repudiated. Now in therapy, each partner is slowly attempting to reintegrate these disowned bits of themselves which have been projected into the other. Mr Brooks is becoming more assertive and feels less anxious about expressing his anger. His wife, who no longer has to express a 'double dose' of the feelings, is starting to feel more in touch with the controlled and rational aspects of herself.

Sutherland (1962) goes on to say:

> To...those familiar with the work of Melanie Klein, it will be clear that this view gives a basic role in interaction to the mechanism of 'projective identification'. To put unwanted aspects of the self into others is a flexible defence which permits a number of developments to take place. For instance, to find that the actual behaviour of the other does not confirm the degree of badness felt, can lead to a taking in again of this part, a reintrojection, as something less frightening. Hence, with less need to disown it, assimilation and learning can take place with an enrichment of the self and a greater capacity for deeper relationships. Unfortunately the process of taking unwanted parts back again is a highly precarious one. Anxious testing out is common and all too often the actual behaviour of the partner confirms the feared badness, thus setting the whole process back with the negative rejecting

feelings stirred up anew. Hence, too, the resistances and stress during any period when a change is attempted. (p. 9)

Shared fantasy and shared defence

Individuals adopt various defensive mechanisms in order to control what they feel to be unacceptable impulses or to avoid psychic pain. In marriages there is frequently a collusion – an unconscious agreement – between the partners to maintain mutual or complementary defences. This arises from a shared fantasy about the catastrophe which will result if the feared or unacceptable impulses in the self and in the partner emerge. In marital disturbance these distorted preceptions, arising from each partner's past experiences, can frequently be rigidly held and not mediated in the light of present circumstances and experience.

To give an illustration of this: both partners in one marriage (who had been brought up in one-parent families, by the parent of the opposite sex) experienced great anxiety about their sexual feelings for each other. Their shared unconscious fantasy was that these feelings were incestuous, love and sex had to be kept separate and passionate feelings between them avoided, or a catastrophe would occur. As a defence against these fears, sexual intercourse rarely occurred. When one partner desired it, the other could be relied on not to respond, and vice versa. Each of them could be a 'friend' or a 'parent' to the other, but not a husband or wife. Transitory, passionate sexual relations had to take place with others outside the marriage.

Marriages based on a mutually defensive system can work initially but may become disturbed when, either by choice or force of circumstances, a major change in life-style takes place (Daniell 1981, 1985). Requests for marital therapy often anticipate, or follow on from, critical events or natural transitions in the family life-cycle. A common illustration of this is the number of young couples who link the onset of their marital difficulties to the arrival of their first baby and their failure in adapting to becoming parents as well as being married partners – the move from a twosome to a threesome (Clulow 1982). At the other end of the time-scale are many longer-standing marriages which become disturbed when children finally leave home.

Many of these transitions are set in motion by a cluster of events; others may involve just one particular change which is perceived as significant. However, whether the change is seen initially as a gain (e.g. having a baby) or as a loss (e.g. the death of one of the spouse's parents), what these events appear to have in common is that they require the partners to define themselves and each other in a *new* way, that is to make changes in their assumptive world.

Therapy

Contextual considerations
Working with one or both partners

As *marital* therapy implies working with the interaction between spouses, it is difficult to visualize when one partner is seen on his or her own. Individual help can enable a spouse to leave an unsatisfactory marriage or it can lead to the individual's growth. However, if changes which occur in the spouse who attends are not matched by changes in the partner who has been left out, the marital disturbance may not be alleviated. Indeed, it may be exacerbated. This work is better described as individual rather than marital therapy. The policy at the IMS is to treat marriages only when both partners are willing to engage in the therapy.

In situations where a spouse applies for marital therapy without the partner, it is important to understand the exclusion and why the therapist is denied access to the 'other half' of the marriage. For example, as Pincus (1962) has observed, working with the marriage relationship does not mean accepting the complaints of the one who appears to be the victim, or trying to 'change' the other (p. 18). It means trying to understand why the partners chose each other in the first place, what each partner contributes to the conflict and what is being unconsciously expressed for one by the other. It is important to be looking for the unseen and unexpressed aspects of the personality of the presenter of the problem which will be revealed in the description of the partner and in the relationship with the therapist. An assessment of the problem, based on this type of understanding, is, however, more easily achieved with the couple.

Single/co-therapists

Work with couples can be undertaken by one therapist, or, as favoured in the IMS, by two. Spouses can be seen together or in individual sessions.

The four-person format, the marital couple and two therapists, provides a framework within which the processes of transference and countertransference are highlighted. The way the marital partners react to the therapist pair – i.e. the transference – and the way the therapists are made to feel by the marital couple – i.e. the countertransference – provide insights into the dynamics of the marital interaction. Particular use is made of the co-therapists' involvement, accepting and experiencing the couple's projections and unconsciously reflecting in their interaction with one another in the session, or in their subsequent discussion, some aspects of the struggle between the marital pair which they cannot get into conscious awareness. As is often said in the IMS, only when the therapists have solved their 'quarrel' can the clients start to solve theirs.

Successful co-therapy requires mutual respect and a trusting continuing relationship between the therapists. Sufficient similarity of theoretical approach is essential, as is that of experience, except where this model is being used for training purposes when the therapists' different levels of experience have to be taken into account.

The experience of the four-person model provides a unique experience for teaching purposes. In the training of marital therapists, the safe path is that of gradual progression, from working with a co-therapist whether in conjoint four-person sessions or concurrent single sessions to the single therapist model which, when technically appropriate, is better suited to the more experienced worker (Dicks 1967).However, the way therapy is structured needs to be determined by the primary task of any given agency. Some practitioners may be doing some marital work in an agency which has other main functions; economics of staff resources in some settings may preclude co-therapy. In these situations, regular supervision and case discussion groups are of critical importance in supporting the work of the solo therapist.

There are four main issues for therapists working on their own. First, they may have to carry a more problematic transference than two therapists would have to do, because the couple are unable to split their mixed feelings between two people. The partners may unite and project all the negative feelings onto the therapist who then becomes 'all bad'. Or, if there is a need to maintain the therapist as an 'ideal object', the couple may need to have a 'bad object' outside the therapy in the person of a previous helper who has to be kept useless; the 'reward' of being the idealized object may prove difficult to resist.

Second, a single therapist can be drawn into an alliance with one partner to treat the other as the 'patient'. Third, for spouses who have a problem of excessive sibling rivalry, the difficulty in sharing a therapist may lead to individual sessions being offered when with a co-therapist other technical considerations would have indicated joint work. Fourth, separate sessions for each partner with the same therapist can pose problems of confidentiality; the therapist runs the risk of disclosing what each partner has said in the privacy of the individual session. However, not to bring in material relating to the other partner's feelings and fantasies leaves the therapist without the evidence on which to base interpretations of the marital *interaction*. As Dicks (1967) observed, 'It is as if a pianist was forced to perform the scores for the Right and Left hand in succession instead of synchronised' (p. 235).

Work with only one therapist is not indicated when it seems important for the marital couple to have the experience of a heterosexual pair of therapists interacting with each other – when, for example, either or both spouses have been brought up in a one-parent family and may have no internalized model of a cooperating parental couple.

Criteria for seeing partners conjointly/separately

While marital psychotherapists differ on the contraindications for conjoint therapy, most agree that the joint interview should form part of the initial assessment. Seeing the couple together at the outset emphasizes that the focus in marital therapy is on the marital relationship and the contribution of each individual, rather than the problems of one partner, and that *both* share responsibility for the present conflict (Teruel 1966).

The joint assessment interview also enables the therapist to observe the unconscious collusive interaction of the partners and allows for the emergence of the conflict, shared fantasies and shared defences. In work involving two therapists which subsequently moves into individual sessions the joint assessment interview provides each spouse with the real image of the other's therapist. Dicks (1967) observed that if treatment is in individual sessions (i.e. each spouse with their own therapist), the other's therapist is only seen through the spouse's perception and the individual's own fantasies. While he suggested this could be a valuable source of material, an initial conjoint assessment session does give each spouse some experience of the actual personality of the other's therapist. This provides both the scope for fantasies of an infantile character to enter the subsequent therapy, and a readier correction by reality testing.

Skynner (1976) has related the functioning of individuals and families to Klein's 'paranoid schizoid' and 'depressive' positions as criteria for assessing their suitability for individual or group treatment. Many marital therapists agree with Skynner about the usefulness of conjoint therapy for those who make extensive use of 'paranoid schizoid' processes (i.e. who function at a basically part-object or undifferentiated level with the extensive use of denial and splitting, whereby parts of the self are projected into the other, and thus, as Skynner observes, are not true individuals with separate identities and boundaries). People operating at this level of development often appear out of touch with reality and have distorted and paranoid perceptions. As Guthrie and Mattinson (1971) found, it is difficult with this type of couple for the therapists to keep their own sense of reality and to reconcile the two opposing perceptions of one situation when the spouses are seen separately.

However, Pincus (1968) has suggested that joint sessions may not always be very effective initially with some of these spouses who have not yet discovered themselves as separate individuals. She says, 'they are like small children, who have to be understood by mother before they can be free to reveal themselves in a group. Ordinary adult language may not reach such couples' (pp. 2–3). If their problems originated at a preverbal level, the reliability, warmth, smile and tone of the therapist may be more important than any carefully chosen words or joint interpretive work in the early phase of treatment.

One characteristic of spouses operating at the paranoid schizoid level is that they are unable to feel guilt about what each is doing to the other. However, as Lyons (1973) has described, clinical observations by staff at the IMS suggest that when marital partners have begun to perceive each other as separate individuals with needs of their own and to feel sadness and concern about the effect of their behaviour on the other, they may then need some individual sessions to help them bear the painful guilt. Spouses who are starting to reach this level of development, which corresponds to the early phases of Klein's 'depressive position', are beginning to develop some capacity to contain negative feelings without projecting them, to integrate love and hate, and to tolerate the ambivalence and depressive anxiety which results. As Skynner (1976) has observed, for these individuals the capacity to keep the image of the loved one present and intact is still precarious and easily threatened through rejection or absence. Thus the emergence of hostile feelings, or even the awareness of differences, in the course of joint work can be experienced as abandonment and can lead to a premature ending of therapy.

Later, when individuals can face their ambivalent feelings about one another and be more comfortably aware of their separateness, they can use either joint or individual sessions, although in marital therapy joint sessions are more appropriate.

This framework can only act as a guide and those not familiar with Kleinian developmental concepts use other terms to describe similar characteristics. While in the IMS there is an increasing tendency towards the use of joint sessions for much of the work, the debate between members of staff as to the efficacy of the two styles of work continues.

Developing and maintaining a therapeutic alliance – the nature of the therapeutic contract

In the IMS the initial exploration with a couple seeking help usually consists in the marital couple meeting a co-therapist pair, followed by individual sessions with each partner assigned their own therapist. These initial consultations give the therapists the opportunity to learn something about each of the partners, their marital conflict and expectations, and the hopes and fears which each brings to the therapeutic encounter. Both spouses need to be given some experience of being understood.

The therapists' attitude is receptive, encouraging the partners to talk in their own ways about their reasons for seeking help, asking for clarification or eliciting material when appropriate, and sharing with the couple the therapists' initial understanding of the marital conflict. This understanding is based on attentive listening to what is said, on observing the non-verbal communications between the partners, and between the partners and the therapists, and on using the feelings and behaviour which are invoked in the therapists by the couple as important clues to the nature of their inner world and marriage. These first interviews give an opportunity for the couple to experience something of the way the therapists work and for the therapists to assess the couple's motivation and capacity to enter into a therapeutic alliance.

Greenson (1965) defined the working alliance in the psychoanalytic setting as 'the relatively non-neurotic, rational relationship between the patient and the analyst which makes it possible for the patient to work purposefully in the analytic situation' (p. 157). Inherent in this notion of a working alliance is what Erikson calls 'basic trust' on the part of the patient. The extent to which the spouses can recognize the therapists as trustworthy and potentially helpful will be influenced by their early experiences of significant figures. Those individuals whose sense of basic trust is fragile will transfer to the therapists their feelings of mistrust. However, in order for the couple to be able to co-operate it is necessary that in addition to these transference reactions they are able to ally themselves to some extent with the rational and caring parts of the therapists. In marital therapy with co-therapists the situation is complex as partners have to establish and maintain a working alliance with both therapists.

Before a therapeutic contract can be made, the therapists give practical information about what can be offered and what will be required of the clients in terms of commitment, frequency of sessions, and fees, if any, should they decide to accept an offer of therapy. It is important to look at discrepancies between what the therapists can offer and how the couple see their problem and their expectations of treatment. Spouses will have unconscious as well as conscious perceptions and expectations of therapy and frequently differ between themselves as to what constitutes the problem and what is required for its resolution.

For example, in a couple seen recently, the husband, Mr Green, initially saw the problem as his wife's lack of interest in sex for which he was bringing *her* for treatment. However, Mrs Green saw the problem as her husband's over-investment in work and uninterest in spending any time with her. In the initial exploration, it emerged that both Mr and Mrs Green had anxieties about intimacy stemming from their earlier experiences. Mr Green managed his anxiety by driving himself relentlessly at work, where he was constantly under pressure but where he felt needed. This served the purpose of giving him little opportunity to develop the closer emotional attachment to his wife which he feared. Without this closeness, Mrs Green felt she could not be responsive sexually; his behaviour reinvoked in her a long-standing anxiety of being exploited and 'used' if she risked a close attachment; so she, too, increasingly kept at a distance from him. The 'problem' had to be redefined as a *shared* one to which both contributed before a proper therapeutic contract could be made.

By applying to a *marital* agency, however, a couple can indicate that, even though consciously they locate the 'illness' in one of them, unconsciously there is an awareness of a shared problem. Still, a working alliance is not possible if one partner continues to assert over time that it is only the spouse who needs to change and remains unmotivated to look at his or her own part in the difficulties. In some instances partners carry for one another the opposite sides of their own ambivalence. For example, if a couple are both undecided whether to stay together or to separate, one may hold on to the hope of the marriage continuing while the other carries all the despair. A therapeutic contract is not possible, however, in those cases where, while outwardly seeking marital help, one spouse, for example the husband, has already made the decision to leave the marriage for another partner and is in fact only attending in order that the therapists can look after the wife.

Once treatment has started, the therapists continue to prepare the ground for the growth of a trusting relationship by providing a consistent and reliable environment. This is demonstrated, on the one hand, by offering regular sessions, keeping boundaries, and preparing the couple well in advance for any alterations in the therapeutic arrangements such as holiday breaks; on the other hand, by the emphasis on the attempt to understand, and by holding and containing anxiety. This provides a secure base which, as Lyons (1973) has described, allows the couple a 'breathing space' in which to explore their personal and shared experience and to risk relinquishing the unsatisfactory, although familiar, aspects of their relationship.

Major treatment techniques

Marital therapy as practised in the IMS is based on an attempt to understand a process of interaction, rather than on applying a set of techniques. The therapists try not to avoid the client's pain and anger by giving premature reassurance or responding to pressure to take charge, provide easy answers or give advice. As Jung is reputed to have said (Storr 1979), 'Good advice is often a doubtful remedy, but generally not dangerous since it has so little effect' (p. 27).

The overall aim of the treatment is to provide a safe enough environment whereby the partners can increasingly give expression to their feelings and perceptions. Reflections by the partners and the therapists on the feelings between them (transference and countertransference feelings) and on what is being communicated and experienced in the sessions enables unconscious conflicts to be brought into awareness, perceptions to be altered and projections to be gradually withdrawn. The partners are encouraged to take responsibility for their part in the conflict and to make decisions and choices by now based on less distorted perceptions and, therefore, more appropriate than those they made previously.

The therapists do not structure the sessions, but deal with what the couple bring for discussion on the assumption that, first, the couple know where they are at that particular point in time (what has happened to them during the week, what has left them troubled, what has made them feel better, how they have been able to use the previous session), and, second, what they choose to talk about has an important unconscious purpose in respect of their developing relationship with the therapists. Attention is paid to both the manifest content of the discussion and its symbolic meaning. Dicks (1967) describes the process of treatment as a symphony: 'the chief themes are stated early; the rest of the movement is occupied with their development and working out, ending with a restatement' (p. 268).

Within this broad framework, therapists exercise their own individual style, but remain prepared to become involved in the transaction the couple provoke. Trained to become aware of their own norm, they pay particular attention to times when they behave out of character. For example, in the early stages of treatment, Mr and Mrs Phillips had difficulty in describing the events of the previous weekend which had left them feeling particularly frustrated. A male co-therapist and I found ourselves behaving in a manner very different from our usual stance. I gradually became aware that I was being unusually active. I found it difficult to relinquish the powerful role Mr and Mrs Phillips seemed to have thrust upon me. At the same time, I started to feel irritated with my colleague for leaving me to do all the work despite my having indicated that I needed his contributions. In contrast, he increasingly experienced himself as being ignored and left out of the session. Any observations he made were attributed by Mrs Phillips to me, as if he had not spoken. After what he felt was a fruitless struggle to get back into the session, he felt quite impotent and ready to abdicate from the work. The anger that he then felt surprised him by its intensity.

Towards the end of the session, when we shared with the couple what had been happening between us (and in our subsequent discussion on our own), we gradually started to make sense of our experience in the light of what the couple had told us about their present relationship and previous family experiences. Mrs Phillips carried all the responsibility in their home; she complained that Mr Phillips did not support her; but she was out of touch with the part of herself which helped to perpetuate this pattern of behaviour. It gradually emerged that she was petrified of losing control; her fear was that if she gave up some of her conscientious efficiency she would regress to a state of complete infantile dependency. She was, apparently, overusing her efficiency as a defence against what were to her dangerous infantile longings, and had projected these into her husband.

We knew from what they had previously told us that they both had 'absent' fathers. Mrs Phillips's father died a few months after she was born. As she grew up, she felt she had to try to be a 'parent' to her depressed mother. Mr Phillips's father had long absences from home and, when he was there, was unable to 'stand up' to his dominant wife.

Our feelings and behaviour in the session enabled us to experience the strength of the projections that men were either not there or, if there, completely ineffectual, and that in their physical or emotional absence it was left to the women to take control – a system of interaction perpetuated by Mr and Mrs Phillips because of mutual dangerous fantasies relating back to earlier experiences in their families of origin. We used the historical background as an explanatory clause which gave meaning to the present behaviour, thereby lessening any feeling of being criticized or attacked when by an interpretation we drew their attention to what was going on between them and between them and us. Could they let the present be less ruled by the past? What was the worst that could happen if Mrs Phillips gave up some of the control and let her husband take over? Was the fantasy that he would die or disappear, leaving her as abandoned as she had felt as a child? Now, understanding a little more about their behaviour, could they risk trying something different?

We, by now conscious of our uncharacteristic behaviour as we got drawn into their unconscious fantasies and projections, were able to modify it. I was able to give up the control and my colleague was able to take a firmer and more appropriate stance. In doing this, we offered a model of change and gave Mr and Mrs Phillips renewed hope that this type of change could happen without the feared disastrous consequences.

Problems encountered in marital therapy

With many couples, the problems of maintaining a therapeutic alliance are now fully encountered during the course of treatment. At the assessment phase, the partners may have agreed in principle that the focus of work should be on their interaction, rather than on the illness of one partner. Once in treatment, however, this redefinition, implying, as it does, a major shift in perception, may consciously or unconsciously be resisted.

This type of change is frightening, and resistance occurs in any therapy at one time or another. If the anxiety about change which is constantly being aroused is not sufficiently understood within the current context, contained and clearly related to, a premature ending of treatment may suddenly occur. Certain marriages appear to be particularly resistant to change. There are some that are based on a total and inflexible defence against any anxiety inherent in a struggle towards maturation. The rigidity of the defensive system proves immovable. There are other couples who marry to escape from unhappy situations in their parents' home, but without any real feeling for each other. Similarly, there are couples with very low self-esteem, who marry each other for fear of never being able to find someone whom they could love. With these couples who have never been in love, there is nothing to recover and little motivation or foundation with which to work. If they can engage in the therapy, they may be helped to separate and face a less certain future with more creative possibilities. There are also couples who find it virtually impossible to give up old grudges of many years' standing. It is as if the repeated grudge and the feelings associated with it fill up either a void which would otherwise be too frightening to experience – an emptyness, a nothingness, a non-aliveness – or a similarly frightening inner chaos filled with madness and persecutors.

And then there are some marriages in which one or both partners operate on what Winnicott termed a 'false self' (1960). They seem cooperative, articulate and adult, but it soon becomes apparent that the well-chosen words and intellectual discussion are used to keep the partner and the therapists at bay. 'What looks like a therapeutic alliance turns out to be inimical to a real alliance and ... what is termed understanding is actually anti-understanding ... One begins to feel that one is talking to this ally *about* a patient, but never talking *to* the patient' (Joseph 1975, p. 206).

Finally, there are those couples in a seemingly endless search for the 'ideal therapist'. The current therapist is just one more person in the line providing further proof of how useless the so-called 'helpers' are. Unless they can be helped to understand the projection of their denied feelings about their own uselessness, they soon drop out and continue their ambivalent and self-defeating search.

The change process in therapy

Change in behaviour and in the interactive system between married partners can occur at several levels, conscious and unconscious. As the couple start to feel safer in the therapeutic situation, the anxiety level falls, and this enables them to communicate and respond more effectively to each other both within and outside the sessions. More effective communication, coupled with some small insights into why they have been behaving in a particular way (especially when it has been acquired from a clear enactment with the therapists), enables them to give up some compulsive and repetitive patterns of behaviour and withdraw some projections. Decisions can then be made from a larger basis of conscious awareness which can take account of new-found strengths and knowledge of underlying needs, sometimes previously denied. Sometimes a conscious decision is made to risk trying some new form of behaviour. At other times, the behaviour changes less perceptibly and only with hindsight do the couple realize how differently they handled a situation compared with a few months previously. Neither they nor the therapists may be able to define the exact process or date a particular session which enabled this shift to take place. Interactive processes, and therefore influence, occur at various levels of consciousness.

The extent to which these types of changes occur depends not so much on the severity of the problem as on the conscious and unconscious motivation of both partners and therapists to allow it to happen. Or one could say, it depends on their courage.

The specific criteria for change in respect of a couple obviously relate to the manifest problem which was initially presented, symptom relief, the therapists' assessment of the problem, overall psychological development and specific goals determined by the couple and therapists. For example, one couple presented a seemingly harmonious marriage, but complained of extreme problems with their respective parents-in-law which totally preoccupied them. Neither of them had been able to achieve emotional separation from their parents. The therapists saw their task as helping them to grow up and 'get married', despite the fact they had been legally married for five years. Change occurred for this couple; they were gradually able to relinquish their anxious and hostile attachment to their parents; they then discovered the previously denied difficulties between themselves on which they subsequently worked to good effect.

Another couple complained they were unable to live together happily or to separate. The treatment goal in this instance was that, whether they eventually decided to separate or to remain together, they did so with appropriate conviction, allowing themselves and the other to flourish as differentiated individuals.

Rarely does a process of change and development occur in a straightforward and steady progression. Plateaux are reached and rested upon, regressions occur, particularly when a break in the therapy is coming up or has happened, and disappointments and failures are felt more keenly after some previous progress. Sometimes it feels like one step forward only to take two steps back. Themes are repeated and worked with once more as they emerge in different aspects of the couple's life (Dicks's symphony).

There is often a panic at the first sign of a major change occurring, as, for example, when the partners start to withdraw a projection; a previously 'optimistic' partner who projected all his sadness into his partner starts to feel his own depression. This can be as frightening to the previously 'ill', depressed partner, as to the newly sad one. Loss of a familiar response can cause extreme unease and there can be a flight back into the old pattern in the fear that *a* loss means total loss of attachment. 'Therapy is making things worse' might well be said at this point.

Once an ending date for the therapy has been set, there is sometimes a re-enactment of the initial presenting problem, although without the original pressure behind it. It seems that the couple are reminding the therapists that not all their problems are solved, although, if the therapy has been effective, they have greater resources to deal with them. The safety of the therapy and attachment to the therapists has to be relinquished as do ideas of 'ideal' solutions and answers.

If the therapy has succeeded in freeing growth points within the partners, and a developmental process has been set in motion, there is a good prospect that the couple will continue to mature on their own, having learnt in the therapy that emotional conflict can never be fully resolved; it is a vital part of change and growth throughout the various stages of life.

The personal qualities of effective marital therapists

The gap between the qualities that *ideal* therapists should have and those that most of them do have has to be lived with, bearing in mind that the prime requisite is the creative capacity to continue to grow and learn from experience and mistakes. (It is useful for patients to learn that mistakes need not be disastrous and recovery can be made.)

Therapists using a psychodynamic approach come from a variety of disciplines and backgrounds. They may be married, unmarried, cohabiting, divorced or widowed. However, probably the most important quality that furthers effective marital therapy is the capacity to be both receptive and penetrating; that is to have accepted and be able to use both the feminine and masculine parts of themselves and to have got their own masculinity and femininity well 'married' inside themselves.

In the type of work described in this chapter they need to be able to expose their own style to co-therapists and to other colleagues, and to be able to bear difference and conflict, uncertainty and even muddle. They need to know what they have to offer and at the same time resist any feelings of omnipotence or of knowing 'what is best' for other people. Besides an openness to their own feelings, they need to be staunch enough to share and bear some of the pain of their patients; within a context of warmth and empathy it is necessary for them to be able to take in, hold, and attempt to make sense of the psychic pain of others, so that it can then be offered back in a more tolerable form.

The work can be stressful and it is important for therapists to recognize when they themselves need help either professionally or personally, and to have the strength and humility to ask for this for themselves. Most therapists coming into marital work will have reached a level of understanding about their own life experiences. The work offers them an opportunity for further growth if they can listen to and learn from their patients.

Case example

Referral of clients

Mr and Mrs Grey were referred to the IMS by their General Practitioner whom they had both consulted for 'stress' symptoms. The GP informed us that they had married a few months previously after having lived together for several years. Mr Grey had had a transitory affair just before the marriage, had been unsure about getting married, and had been in 'quite a state' since it happened. Mrs Grey felt increasingly insecure about his attachment to her.

A male colleague and I saw Mr and Mrs Grey for an initial exploration, offered them therapy, and have now seen them in once-weekly sessions over a period of ten months. It is still uncertain when the treatment will end.

Problems presented

Mr and Mrs Grey are both 29 years old and are graduates. When we first met them, Mr Grey, a short, stocky man, looked several years younger than his age; by contrast, Mrs Grey, a tall, thin woman, seemed prematurely 'middle-aged'. She was the most regular breadwinner and had a steady job in an insurance company. Mr Grey was in and out of what they both defined as 'off-beat', temporary jobs well below his capacity. He was currently employed emptying the cash from 'space-invader' machines.

Mrs Grey saw their difficulties starting since her husband's affair and their subsequent marriage. Since then sexual intercourse had been very infrequent due to his lack of desire for her. She felt rejected and complained about his inability to get a 'proper' job because she now wanted to start a family. They had difficulty in communicating with each other; there were either rows or silences.

Mr Grey saw their problems as stemming from their incompatibility of interests and his and his wife's contrasting views about what they wanted from life. He had lost his sexual desire for his wife since she had started wanting to have a baby. He thought the present situation was intolerable, but they could not part. When one suggested separation, the other could be relied upon to veto the idea.

Relationships in family of origin

Both Mr and Mrs Grey came from working-class families and were the only member of their respective families to have a higher education.

Mrs Grey   Mrs Grey, the eldest of five children, had a younger brother who was (congenitally) physically handicapped. She described a home which was impoverished both physically and emotionally with not enough resources to go round. Her handicapped brother took most of her mother's attention and Mrs Grey always felt she had to 'fit in' and was never able to make demands of her own. She perceived her parents as unsupportive to one another and offering her contradictory views as to what life was about: her mother, the dominant parent, was often critical, but very ambitious for her; her father, a passive and unadventurous man, denigrated by his wife, told her it was dangerous to have ideas 'above your station'.

She had been caught in a 'double bind' between these conflicting attitudes. She struggled hard to fulfil her mother's expectations, feeling she was the one who had to carry the hope of achievement for the whole family; but, however hard she tried, she never felt she did well enough to earn her mother's love. She feared failure, equating this with reproach and abandonment. Yet, as she later came to understand for herself, she also feared success, an uncomfortable triumph over her sisters and brothers, courting their envy and earning only her father's disapproval.

Mr Grey   Mr Grey was an only child. Both his parents urged him to achieve and, like Mrs Grey, all hopes were pinned on him. His parents went their separate ways, but each invested attention and indulgence on him. His mother mainly showed her love by overstuffing him with food, so that as a child and adolescent he was grossly overweight. He felt smothered and overwhelmed and with no space in which to be himself. He had few friends of his own and spent much of his time playing darts with his father and his father's friends.

He did well at school. At college he came to resent that he was there only because of his parent's aspirations. He studied little and only just scraped through his examinations. Subsequently he recognized that the competition had been much harder than at school and it was safer to be a failure who had not tried than one who had; disappointment was a feeling he could neither acknowledge nor encompass. Because of their disappointment with his poor results, his parents broke off contact with him for over a year.

Choice of partner

Mr and Mrs Grey met at college; she was serious and conscientious, working hard to get herself valued; he was busy rebelling, antiwork and mixing with 'dropouts'. Both of them, lonely and without any sense of their own worth, clung to each other. Consciously, they were drawn to each other by what they felt were their opposite characteristics, she attracted by the rebel and his casual attitude to work, he attracted by her conformity and reliability. Thus, they very clearly saw in each other those aspects of themselves which they had repudiated.

Shared fantasies and defences Less consciously, they shared fears that success was only for another's gratification and a means of getting love from a mother; and that failure and disappointment only killed love and affection. They shared an anxiety about getting themselves loved for who and what they were, rebel or otherwise, and not what another person expected them to be.

But they did expect of each other. They expected a different sort of space from what they had experienced as children – a space in which they could succeed (or fail) for themselves without loss of love. At a rational level, they had chosen a partner who was unlikely to give them what they wanted. At a less conscious level, they had kept in touch with their own and shared problem. By the sharing they had kept the problem firmly alive, externalizing it between them. They offered each other the hope and chance of solving something fairly fundamental in their struggle towards greater psychological wholeness and maturity. If they succeeded against these odds, they would certainly have proved their ability to get loved.

Yet, they feared what they most wanted. He feared that, along with her much needed reliability, she would take him over and stuff him up with her aspirations as his mother had done (and the actual marriage and prospect of parenthood had obviously heightened this fear). She feared that if she expressed the more needy and dependent part of herself, he would find her unlovable and finally abandon her as she felt her mother had done when all those other children kept her so busy. Could they dare to try to succeed for themselves, or might the disappointment if they failed be too unbearable? In their early and mid-20s, their mutual defences against these fears operated adequately enough to keep them together. They relied on their differences to accentuate who they were and to prevent a closer type of partnership. A satisfying sexual relationship kept alive the hope of a further abatement of their fears, despite a continual disappointment in each other. In their late 20s, when social pressures exerted themselves with their friends marrying and having children (and, as we believe in the IMS, an inherent struggle for growth), the fears increased and the defences worked less well. A baby meant that she would need to be more dependent on him, and he would have less space for his rebellion. Both of them were petrified, but the contrary feelings of wanting a baby and being frightened of having one were split between them: he expressed all the caution and reserve; she expressed the wish and the drive. Both of them could rely on the other to keep up the conflict, but as their own unconscious conflict increased they fell back into patterns of behaviour learned many years earlier, each projecting into the other the image of a critical, demanding mother. Nothing they said or did could please.

The therapy

The early sessions gave Mr and Mrs Grey some hope of resolving the problem. They expressed enough confidence in their continuing relationship to start redecorating their home. The description of the enterprise, however, threw into stark relief the defensive system; they could not share any of the tasks, agree what needed doing nor the choice of colour; they could effect no compromise. Mrs Grey worked hard on her own, only to feel her efforts were severely criticized, as they were. He thought his efforts were not even noticed. And, it seemed, they were not.

The same pattern of interaction was displayed in discussions about outings, getting up in the mornings, having a baby, his getting another job. What they described happening at home also happened in the sessions. Mrs Grey always took the lead and did most of the talking, but then complained that she was the only one who did any work; he was just a passenger. Mr Grey complained about being filled up with all her feelings and 'introspection' about their relationship. He always took the opposite view from her (and from us), but, whenever she acknowledged her agreement, he felt taken over and altered his position. The first months were dominated by what they termed this 'push-me-pull-you' act. When one wanted sex, the other did not.

My colleague and I focused on the interaction between them, and between them and us, using what they had told us of their past experience to clarify why some things could still feel so painful or so muddled. Some of our comments elicited further details and experiences which they then started to think about and appraise in a different way. We attempted to relate to their fears about letting things change. Our points were made more clearly when we were drawn into the projections and then understood what had happened. At times it was difficult not to sound critical – in the early sessions we 'bent over backwards' not to be so, but even our mildest comments were heard in this light. Mr Grey, particularly, left us feeling we should challenge some of his statements (taking him seriously), and at the same time it was extremely important to accept his stance as having value (equally taking him seriously). It was as difficult for them and us to put their point and our point together and create something new as it was for them to do this together at home. Mrs Grey was trying to do well as a patient, yet afraid of succeeding, which made us cautious and fearful of over-working. The more they differed, the more unified we felt, silently praising each other for our efforts and backing up each other's remarks. As this was contrary to our basically different styles, we felt all of the 'togetherness' had been projected into us.

A set-back occurred when Mr Grey had to be away for three weeks. Mrs Grey was offered the opportunity of coming on her own – i.e. something just for her. She refused on the basis that it would be unfair to him as she would get more than her share. But things deteriorated between them over the weekends. She was unable to let us know that she had changed her mind. Subsequently they talked of breaking off the treatment, and we learnt that she had felt let down by our not knowing (without being told) what she wanted.

When things became easier between them, criticisms less made and less felt, and with some better shared experiences, including sexual intercourse, but still finding it difficult to express the previously denied loving feelings, Mrs Grey expressed the fear that if they admitted that things were improving between them we would 'send them packing' – i.e. force them and their marriage to grow up too quickly and before they had time to consolidate these changes.

Since then, other changes have occurred: Mrs Grey allowing more space for Mr Grey's feelings, and experiencing herself as 'less dragged down' by his lack of ambition; Mr Grey feeling less stuffed up with her feelings and aspirations, more in touch with his own, and, therefore, much less detached from her; both of them more able to own their own mixed feelings and with less need to rely on their 'incompatibility'; a greater willingness to listen to each other empathically; and the start of their being able to 'play' together in the more imaginative use of ideas. These changes are reflected in their appearance. Mr Grey is slimmer and dresses more in accordance with his age. Mrs Grey looks prettier, and some very drab trousers have been replaced by more feminine outfits. During this time, I and my colleague have become less united and are able to be less cautious in the sessions, more able to risk some displeasure or difference of view.

There is still a long way for Mr and Mrs Grey to go, if they are prepared to risk possible disappointments and failures en route. They agree now that they are not yet ready to have a child, and he, although more motivated to exercise his basic capability in a more responsible job, has not yet been able to get himself into one. It remains open what they will choose to settle for – what is enough and which limitations in their relationship they have to accept – or what is worth struggling to change. We are prepared to stay with them through the struggle, continuing to try to understand the underlying conflicts and fears, but only if that is their wish.

References

Bannister, K., Lyons, A., Pincus, L., Robb, J., Shotter, A. and Stephens, J. (1955) *Social casework in marital problems*. London: Tavistock Publications.

Bannister, K. and Pincus, L. (1965) *Shared phantasy in marital problems*. London: Institute of Marital Studies.

Bowlby, J. (1979) *The making and breaking of affectional bonds*. London: Tavistock Publications.

Clulow, C. (1982) *To have and to hold*. Aberdeen: Aberdeen University Press.

Clulow, C. (1985) *Marital Therapy: an inside view*. Aberdeen University Press.

Daniell, D. (1981) *Early transitions in the family life cycle*. Paper given to Day Meeting of Tavistock Social Work Continuation Group, Tavistock Pamphlet.

Daniell, D. (1985) Love and Work: complementary aspects of personal identity. *International Journal of Social Economics* (1985) *12*, 2, pp. 48–55.

Denning Report of the Committee on Procedure in Matrimonial Causes (1947). London: HMSO.

Dicks, H. V. (1963) Object relations theory and marital studies. *British Journal of Medical Psychology, 36*, 125–129

Dicks, H. V. (1967) *Marital tensions*. London: Routledge and Kegan Paul.

Erikson, E. (1950, rev. 1965) *Childhood and society*. Harmondworth: Penguin Books. (First published in the USA.)

Fairbairn, W. R. D. (1952) Psychoanalytic studies of the personality. London: Tavistock Publications.

Freud, S. (1953) Three essays on sexuality. The standard edition of the complete psychological works, Volume 7. London: Hogarth Press.

Gill, H. and Temperley, J. (1972) Treatment of the marital dyad in a foursome. Postgraduate Medical Journal. 48, 550–560.

Greenson, R. R. (1965) The working alliance and the transference neurosis. The Psychoanalytic Quarterly, 34, 155–181.

Greenson, R. R. (1967) The techniques and practice of psycho-analysis. London: The Hogarth Press and the Institute of Psycho-Analysis.

Guthrie, L. and Mattinson, J. (1971) Brief casework with a marital problem London: Institute of Marital Studies.

Joseph, B. (1975) The patient who is difficult to reach. In P. Giovacchini (ed.) Tactics and techniques in psychoanalytic therapy, II. New York: Aronson.

Lyons, A. (1973) Therapeutic intervention in relation to the institution of marriage. In R. G. Gosling (ed.) Support, innovation and autonomy. London: Tavistock Publications.

Mattinson, J. (1981) Childlessness. Paper given to London Medical Group.

Mattinson, J. and Sinclair, I. (1979) Mate and stalemate. Oxford: Blackwell.

Pincus, L. (ed.) (1960) Marriage: studies in emotional conflict and growth. London: Institute of Marital Studies.

Pincus, L. (ed.) (1962) The marital relationship as a focus for casework. London: Institute of Marital Studies.

Pincus, L. (1968) Marriage. Unpublished paper.

Segal, H. (1973) Introduction to the work of Melanie Klein. London: Hogarth Press.

Skynner, A. C. R. (1976) One flesh, separate persons. London: Constable.

Storr, A. (1979) The art of psychotherapy. London: Secker and Warburg and William Heinemann Medical Books.

Sutherland, J. D. (1962) Introduction. In L. Pincus (ed.) The marital relationship as a focus for casework. London: Institute of Marital Studies.

Teruel, G. (1966) Considerations for a diagnosis in marital psychotherapy. British Journal of Medical Psychology, 39, 231–236.

Thompson, A. G. (1960) Introduction. In L. Pincus (ed.) Marriage: studies in emotional conflict and growth. London: Institute of Marital Studies.

Winnicott, D. W. (1960) Ego distortion in terms of true or false self. In The maturational process and the facilitating environment. London: The Hogarth Press and The Institute of Psycho-Analysis.

CHAPTER NINE Marital Therapy
The Rational-Emotive Approach
Windy Dryden

Introduction

Rational-emotive therapy (RET) was established in 1955 by Albert Ellis, an American clinical psychologist who began his career in the helping professions as a sex, marital and family counsellor in the early 1940s. As a result of his experiences as a marital counsellor, Ellis (1962) concluded that '. . . in most instances disturbed marriages (or pre-marital relationships) were a product of disturbed spouses; and that if people were truly to be helped to live happily with each other they would first have to be shown how they could live peacefully with themselves' (p. 3). This conclusion led Ellis to embark on intensive psychoanalytic training, believing then that psychoanalysis was the preferred mode of treatment for such disturbances. In the early 1950s, Ellis became increasingly disillusioned with both the theoretical validity and clinical effectiveness of psychoanalytic treatment and began to see more clearly that human disturbance had profound ideological roots. Drawing upon the work of early Stoic philosophers (e.g. Marcus Aurelius and Epictetus) who stressed that people are disturbed not by events but by their views of these events, Ellis began to develop a therapeutic approach[1] based upon a perspective of human disturbance that stressed philosophic determinants and deemphasized psychoanalytic psychodynamic ones.

The development of rational-emotive therapy over the last thirty years is marked by its application to a very broad range of clinical problems. As a result rational-emotive theorists, practitioners and researchers have not carried out much extensive in-depth work on the application of RET to specific clinical syndromes. In this way, the development of RET differs from that of Aaron Beck's cognitive therapy, which has been applied primarily to the fields of depression and, latterly, anxiety (Dryden 1984a).

It is thus not surprising that rational-emotive marital therapy (REMT) has not developed in a logical, stepwise direction. Up to the time of writing, there are no professional books or treatment manuals devoted to the application of RET to marital discord. However, Ellis and others have maintained an active interest in the field of REMT and there are a number of events that can be regarded as important in the history of its growth.

An early important development was the publication of Ellis's first book on RET: *How to live with a neurotic: at home and at work* (1957). In this book Ellis advanced the thesis that spouses could alleviate marital discord, first, by working to remain undisturbed about their partners' neurotic problems, and then, by experimenting with various solutions to help their partners get over their neurotic difficulties. In a later text written with Robert Harper, entitled *A guide to successful marriage* (1961), Ellis developed this thesis and also made an important distinction between marital disturbance and marital dissatisfaction (see below) which has remained a cornerstone of REMT ever since. In the same book Ellis and Harper also wrote on the important role that unrealistic expectations about marriage play in the development and maintenance of both marital dissatisfaction and disturbance. While the term 'expectation' in psychotherapy is problematic in that it does not clearly differentiate between 'hopes', 'assumptions', 'predictions' of varying certitude and absolutistic demands, Ellis and Harper made the valid point that there is often a large discrepancy between what actually happens in marriage and what one or both partners assume or predict will happen. Thus, unrealistic expectations are often the breeding ground for the later development of marital problems.

In 1962, Ellis's seminal book *Reason and emotion in psychotherapy* was published. This contained a chapter entitled 'A rational approach to marital problems' which was adapted and expanded from two earlier articles (Ellis 1958, 1960). Here Ellis clearly outlined that one of the major tasks of the marriage counsellor was to 'tackle not the problem of the marriage, nor the neurotic interaction that exists between the marital partners, but the irrational ideas or beliefs that cause this neurosis à deux' (1962, p. 210).

As will be developed later in this chapter another cornerstone of REMT is its position on the role and treatment of angry and hostile reactions in marriage. Ellis has published an important paper on this topic (1976), in which he clearly outlines both the rational-emotive position on anger – namely that it is a dysfunctional emotion which severely interferes with marital harmony – and its management in therapy.

Ellis's recent writings on family therapy (1978a, 1978b, 1979a, 1982) can also be considered an important development in the history of REMT in that the strategies and techniques employed in REMT and REFT (rational-emotive family therapy) are very similar.

Apart from Ellis, a number of other rational-emotive therapists have made important contributions to the field of REMT. Amongst others, the writings of Church (1974) on the application of RET to divorce, McClellan and Stieper (1973) on a structured rational-emotive approach to group marital counselling, and Hauck on (a) the reciprocity theory of love and business theory of marriage (1981c, 1983a) and (b) parenting styles (1977, 1983a) are particularly noteworthy. Special mention should be made of Walen, Di Giuseppe and Wessler's chapter entitled 'A rational approach to marriage and divorce counseling' in their book *A practitioner's guide to rational-emotive therapy* (1980). This chapter is unique in that it provides a clear set of procedural and technical guidelines for the practice of REMT. Despite this, there still appears to be an important place for a text which provides a comprehensive exposition of the theory and practice of REMT.

As Dryden (1984b) has observed, rational-emotive therapy has not attracted a large following in Britain. To date, only the author has had extensive experience of employing REMT in this country, using it primarily in both general practice and marriage guidance counselling settings. Indeed, one of the purposes of this chapter is to show how RET can be applied in the arena of marital therapy. Despite the fact that REMT is not widely practised in Britain, it should be noted that the publication of Paul Hauck's books in Sheldon Press's popular 'Overcoming Common Problems' series can be regarded as an important development, in that rational-emotive viewpoints on and approaches to the problems of depression, anger, anxiety, assertion, marriage, procrastination, jealousy, childrearing and love relationships are now widely available in Britain (Hauck 1979, 1980, 1981a, 1981b, 1981c, 1982a, 1982b, 1982c, 1983b). To what extent these books are actually influencing the thinking and practices of marital therapists in Britain is as yet unknown.

The nature of marital disturbance

Rational-emotive marital therapists clearly distinguish between marital dissatisfaction and marital disturbance. Marital dissatisfaction occurs when one or both partners are not getting enough of what they *want* from their spouse and/or from being married. Marital disturbance arises when one or both partners become emotionally disturbed about these dissatisfactions. Thus, they may become anxious, angry, hostile, hurt, depressed, ashamed, guilty and jealous – emotions that usually interfere with constructive communication, problem-solving and negotiation processes that aid the solution of marital dissatisfaction problems. In addition, when one or both partners are emotionally disturbed they generally act in a self- and relationship-defeating manner, thus perpetuating marital disturbance. REMT theory states that, assuming they have the necessary constructive communication, problem-solving and negotiation skills, couples are likely to solve their marital dissatisfaction problems on their own. Where they are deficient in such skills, the focus of marital therapy is on training them to develop and use these skills. However, once couples are in the stage of marital disturbance, unless their emotional problems are dealt with, marital problems usually remain, no matter how skilful one or both partners are in communicating, solving problems and negotiating workable compromises. Couples, interestingly enough, often misdiagnose their own problems. They often conclude that their marital problems are due to deficits in communication skills, while, in reality, they find it difficult to talk to one another when one or both are hurt, angry, depressed, anxious, etc.

Marital disturbance

Emotional disturbance, C according to RET's ABC theory, stems not from events (actual or perceived) at A, but mainly from a certain type of evaluative thinking or belief at B. This type of thinking which is absolutistic, devout and grossly exaggerated in nature, is called 'irrational' in RET theory, mainly to denote that it hinders people from actualizing their basic goals and purposes. Thus, irrational beliefs that lead to such disturbed emotions as anxiety, anger/hostility, hurt, depression, shame and embarrassment, guilt and jealousy, stem according to RET theory from a thinking process known as MUSTURBATION. In the marital context, this process is characterized by a spouse making *absolute* demands and commands on self, partner and/or the marital situation.

Ellis (1984) notes that, in the main, three further irrational (i.e. self-defeating) and grossly exaggerated thinking processes tend to stem from musturbation. Once humans absolutistically demand that something, for example, 'MUST' not occur, they tend, if that event occurs, to conclude: that the event is 'awful', 'horrible' or 'terrible'; that they 'can't stand it' or 'can't bear it'; and that the perpetrator of the event that 'must' not have occurred is 'no good', 'worthless' (or 'less worthy') or 'bad', whether the perpetrator is self, another person or life conditions in general. Ellis has recently noted (1983) that these four thinking processes, known colloquially in RET literature as: (1) MUSTURBATION; (2) AWFULIZING; (3) I-CAN'T-STAND-IT-ITIS; and (4) DAMNING, represent a philosophy of religiosity or devout belief where the person adopts a God-like position and *insists* (not just desires or prefers) that the world (and the people in it) be as he or she wants it (or them) to be.

The rational (or self-enhancing) alternatives to these absolutistic beliefs are framed within a non-demanding, non-absolute philosophy of desire. Here, in the marital context, it is acknowledged that marital partners do have desires, are probably happier when these are met, and become dissatisfied when these remain unfulfilled. However, as has been stressed above, marital dissatisfaction is not synonymous with marital disturbance and the latter only develops if one or both partners escalate their non-absolute desires into absolute demands. Marital dissatisfaction occurs when one or both partners' important desires are not being fulfilled (and neither is insisting that they get what they want). Marital disturbance occurs when one or both partners demand that their desires must be met. Parenthetically, marital therapy is normally more difficult when both partners are emotionally disturbed about the marriage than when only one partner is thus disturbed.

The rational versions of the four irrational thinking processes are as follows:

(1) DESIRING (vs musturbation). Here the spouse acknowledges his or her desires, does not insist that they be met, but is dissatisfied when they are not. Such dissatisfaction often serves to stimulate constructive attempts at problem solving which have a better chance to succeed with a spouse who is also not musturbating.

   Rational thinking processes 2, 3, and 4 tend to follow from non-demanding desiring just as irrational thinking processes 2, 3 and 4 follow from musturbation.

(2) DEFINING AS BAD (vs awfulizing). Ellis has often stated that 'awful' really means more than 100 percent bad since such a definition stems from the belief: 'This *must* not be as bad as it is'. Thus 'awful' is seen to be on a different continuum from 'bad'. If a spouse is not getting what he or she really wants, but is not insisting upon it, this spouse will tend to define the deprivation as 'bad' but not 'awful'. The general principle is that the more important the unfulfilled desire, the more 'bad' the definition of the deprivation is likely to be. It is, thus, only under very unusual conditions that an event can be legitimately rated as 100 percent bad. Non-absolutistically defining something as 'bad' but not 'awful' tends to lead the spouse to try to ameliorate the 'bad' situation.

(3) TOLERATING (vs I-can't-stand-it-itis).'I can't stand it' literally means, as Ellis had observed, disintegrating or dying on the spot. It more often seems to mean not being able to have any happiness whatsoever

under any conditions, rather than actually dying. However, tolerating something means (a) acknowledging that some unwanted event has occurred and believing that there is no law that says it must not occur, (b) defining it as 'bad' but not 'awful', and (c) determining whether change is possible. If it is possible, constructive attempts are made to produce the desired change, while if change is not possible, the person accepts, but definitely dislikes, this 'grim' reality. When spouses are thinking rationally, they are likely to see that, while they can tolerate a bad marriage, there is no reason why they have to. Tolerating adverse conditions is an attitude conducive to constructive change attempts while I-can't-stand-it-itis leads to destructive manipulative strategies.

(4) ACCEPTING (vs damning). This attitude can be applied to self, others and the world. When a woman, for example, unconditionally accepts herself in this way, she recognises that she is a fallible human being who has an 'incurable error-making tendency' (Maultsby 1984), meaning that she can and will make mistakes. If she is able to accept herself as such, she will more likely be able to acknowledge these errors, regard them as bad if they impede her goals, and take responsibility for committing them. Moreover, if she does not *insist* that her partner act well, she will more likely be able to accept him as fallible, dislike the fact that he is acting badly and initiate constructive negotiations for future improvement. Finally, if she does not *insist* that marriage be the way she wants it to be, she will tend to see it as a fallible institution with good and bad components which can only be improved but not perfected.

As Young (1975) has shown, rational thinking can and does (especially in the arena of marriage) lead to strong negative emotions, such as concern, annoyance, sadness, disappointment, regret and dislike. However, these emotions tend to motivate marital partners to take constructive steps to improve matters if their shared goal is to remain married.

Marital dissatisfaction

REMT theory notes that there are two major contributing factors to marital dissatisfaction - marital myths and important incompatibilities.

Marital dissatisfaction may occur if partners adhere to one or more marital myths (Ellis and Harper 1961; Lederer and Jackson 1968). Such myths tend to be unrealistic in that they idealize the state of marriage and encourage spouses to overestimate what they can realistically expect to derive from being married. Some examples of commonly held marital myths[2] that are often implicated in marital dissatisfaction include the following: love equals good sex; romantic love will endure throughout marriage; my spouse will be able to know what I want without me having to communicate my desires; good sex will always be spontaneous; I will not suffer any deprivations or penalties as a result of being married; my spouse will help me get over my feelings of unworthiness; my spouse will make up for my past frustrations; my mate will make allowances for my bad behaviour; my spouse will always be on my side, always be loyal and always love me (no matter how badly I behave). If spouses do not modify these myths in line with their experiences, they will tend to become dissatisfied, as reality proves to be discrepant from their assumptions of what is expected to happen in marriage. Furthermore, it can be easily seen how such myths can further lead to marital disturbance when linked to a philosophy of musturbation.

Marital dissatisfaction may also occur when partners are revealed to be incompatible in one or more areas of marriage. Generally, the more important the area, the greater the dissatisfaction, especially if negotiations for compromise fail to resolve the issues.

Marital incompatibility may stem from naive and superficial mate selection where partners do not really get to know one another, or may occur as a result of changes in outlook on the part of one or both spouses. A commonly encountered example of emergent incompatibility occurs when a wife seeks to develop a more independent life-style. If this exceeds the role expectations of her husband, then neither are likely to get what they want in a significant area of their marriage. If she does not act on her newly discovered desire, she is likely to become dissatisfied and act less responsively toward him so that he becomes dissatisfied. However, if she spends less time in the house, he becomes dissatisfied, since his desires for a well-kept house are not being met and, if he begins to nag her, she becomes dissatisfied because her desires for support are not met. Dissatisfaction based on emergent incompatibility can often be a stimulus for constructive renegotiation of roles and responsibilities, but equally often, especially if the incompatibility occurs in a centrally important area for one or both partners, it may lead to marital breakdown even if marital disturbance is not involved. In such a case, one or both partners conclude that the marriage no longer meets an important desire and is not likely to in the future. If the incompatibility is in another less important area, it may lead to less intrusive dissatisfaction and may hardly affect the marriage, especially if the partners can find expression for the desire elsewhere and this is accepted by the other.

The development and perpetuation of marital disturbance

REMT theory holds that marital disturbance can develop and be perpetuated in a number of different ways. Conflict may occur soon after marriage (and often before marriage) if one or both partners are quite disturbed as individuals, Similarly, conflict might develop at various stages of an on-going marriage when change occurs in the marital system. This change becomes a stimulus for one or both partners to bring their philosophy of musturbation to the new situation. Thus, a dissatisfaction can quickly become a disturbance if, for example, the husband demands that his wife *must* not ask to see his pay packet or if the wife insists that her husband *must* telephone to tell her that he will be staying late at the office. Here spouses give themselves an emotional problem about the problem of dissatisfaction. In addition, as Ellis (1984) notes, spouses may give themselves secondary emotional problems about their newly developed primary emotional problems. Thus, a man may get angry with his wife because he is demanding that she *must* not act in a certain manner; he may then notice his angry reaction and condemn himself for reacting in such a *terrible* manner. He thus becomes guilty for reacting angrily. It is unlikely that constructive communication or problem solving could ensue while he is experiencing anger alone, and doubly unlikely if he adds guilt to his emotional menu.

Ellis (1976) notes that irrational anger, stemming from the absolutistic demand that you, my spouse, must not act this way either because it is 'wrong' or because it is a threat to my 'self-esteem', is probably the most prominent reason why marital disturbance is perpetuated. Indeed, when both partners are damning each other, marital disturbance could be perpetuated indefinitely with little chance of a constructive solution being found. Another core reason why marital disturbance is perpetuated is anxiety over confronting basic issues. One or both partners may be scared that if they shared their feelings of dissatisfaction with one another that something 'awful' would ensue. They thus withdraw from one another and feel lonely, guilty and depressed about the growing distance between them.

Spouses with emotional disturbances tend to act in dysfunctional ways. These actions are considered to be behavioural Cs in the ABC framework, but also serve as an activating event (A) for the other partner. Vicious circles of disturbed marital interaction result when a dysfunctional behaviour (C) on the part of one spouse serves as the trigger (A_2) for an irrational belief (B_2) of the other spouse which in turn leads to disturbed feelings and behaviour (C_2). This serves as a new trigger (A_3) for the first spouse ... and so on. An example of such a vicious circle is shown in Figure 9.1. As this interaction pattern demonstrates, spouses make interpretations of each other's behaviour and these have been included under A, which (as mentioned earlier) stands for the event or the *interpretation* of the event. Such interpretations may be correct but, especially in the phase of marital

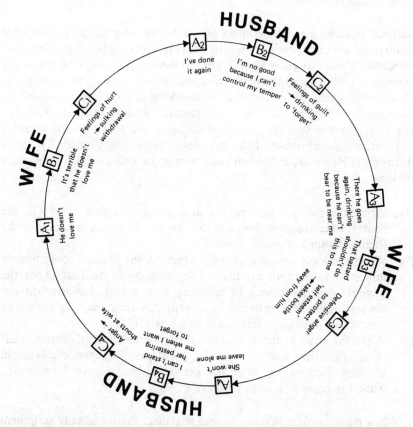

Figure 9.1 The ABCs of dysfunctional marital interaction

disturbance, are likely to be faulty, coloured as they often are by the irrational, evaluative thinking properly indexed under B of the ABC model. Nevertheless, rational-emotive marital therapists do draw on Beck's (1976) work on 'cognitive distortions' and note that partners often make errors in processing interpersonal information and that these errors often serve to perpetuate marital disturbance.

Practice

Contextual considerations

Rational-emotive marital therapists are guided by the principle of flexibility throughout the therapeutic process in working with couples. Thus, there are no absolute rules to guide REMT practitioners concerning whether to see partners conjointly, concurrently or consecutively in individual sessions. Therapeutic decisions concerning the working context are suggested by therapeutic exigencies. Ellis (personal communication) and Bard (1980), for example, consider that the decision whether to see both partners together or separately at the outset of therapy should preferably be made by clients themselves. However, individual sessions may be indicated for three main reasons:

(1) When the two partners persist in arguing non-productively in the context of conjoint sessions and thus negate the potential benefit of the therapist's interventions.

(2) When the joint presence of the partners in the therapy room unduly inhibits one or both of them. They may be *so* anxious about the possible negative effects of speaking their minds that they do not disclose significant material in therapy. In such cases, a period of concurrent individual sessions is often helpful.

(3) When the goals of the individual partners are sufficiently incongruent to preclude the establishment of a productive therapeutic alliance in conjoint therapy, e.g. when one person wishes to leave the marriage while the other wishes to preserve it.

When both partners wish to be seen together, share basically congruent goals, are not inhibited by their joint presence in therapy and can contain their strong angry feelings, then conjoint marital therapy is usually the most beneficial context for productive work.

Some REMT practitioners prefer to work concurrently with the partners in individual sessions in the 'overcoming marital disturbance' phase of treatment. They hypothesize that spouses are more likely to disclose their genuinely held 'deep' feelings (e.g. of hurt, jealousy, anger and fear) if they see the therapist alone. Spouses can thus give their full attention to the therapeutic process, while the therapist helps them to see the connections between their dysfunctional emotions/behavioural patterns and irrational beliefs and helps them to dispute and change these ideas. Since REMT is by nature an educational process, its practitioners are mindful of choosing environments that best facilitate learning. Ellis (personal communication), however, has noted that partners can learn the ABCs of REMT in the context of conjoint therapy in the 'disturbance' phase. His experience has taught him that while the therapist works with one spouse, helping him/her to identify, challenge and change their irrational beliefs, the 'listening' partner often learns the ABC framework of emotional/behavioural disturbance better than the 'working' partner.[3]

While REMT practitioners differ concerning their views about the supremacy of conjoint versus concurrent therapy in the 'overcoming marital disturbance' phase of treatment, they, generally, agree that the presence of both partners is highly desirable in the 'enhancing marital satisfaction' phase. In this phase, both partners have, ideally, made some progress overcoming their emotional disturbance about their marital differences and are ready to explore possible ways of improving their marriage, if they have decided to stay together. Rational-emotive marital therapists use a variety of methods to facilitate such exploration. Communication, problem solving and negotiation training are used in this phase, and the presence of both partners is highly desirable to enable the therapist to instruct them *both* to communicate more effectively, solve problems and negotiate more constructively so that they can improve the quality of married life.

Conjoint REMT is usually conducted with a single therapist, although there are occasions when a cotherapy arrangement would be desirable, particularly if, say, a wife feels unduly affected by the presence of a male therapist. Here a female cotherapist would be helpful to strengthen the therapeutic alliance, and such a four-person arrangement might be particularly desirable in sex therapy.

In conclusion, the conduct of REMT is not bound by strict rules of procedure: flexibility is encouraged and changes in context may occur throughout the therapeutic process. Such changes are made for therapeutic purposes which are generally made clear and agreed to by clients. It is in keeping with rational-emotive philosophy that REMT practitioners are against *insisting* that therapy must be practised in any predetermined context.

Developing and maintaining a therapeutic alliance

It is important to note, at the outset, that REMT practitioners consider that their therapeutic contract is with the individuals in the marriage and not with the marital system (Harper 1981; Walen et al. 1980). As Harper argues, the marital system is an abstraction, and, as such, REMT therapists have great difficulty seeing how a therapeutic alliance can be made with it. They prefer, whenever possible, to develop alliances with each of the involved partners. It is preferable if this is made clear to both spouses at the outset of marital therapy so that they can see that the therapist is not interested in trying to preserve, or indeed destroy, the marriage. As has already been stressed, a primary objective of REMT therapists is to help both partners over their emotional disturbance about the marital situation and then help them work on forging a more mutually satisfying marital relationship, if this is their goal. However, partners often come into marital therapy with overt *and* hidden agendas, and it is often helpful to have separate interviews with each of the partners early in the process, to determine whether the goals of each partner are sufficiently concordant to make conjoint marital therapy – which is the best working forum for partners who have similar objectives – feasible. Since the therapeutic alliance is with the individuals and not with 'the marriage', the most appropriate therapeutic arena is sought to help the individuals actualize their goals.

Since therapeutic goals can be based on irrational as well as rational thinking, it is the author's practice to explain to both partners that they are more likely to make productive decisions about whether to stay married (and, if so, what marital improvements are desired) or to separate, when they are not emotionally disturbed about what is presently happening in the marriage. Thus, I personally, like to set goals appropriate to the phase of marital therapy. If the partners are disturbed, I attempt to have them identify and set goals which involve minimizing such disturbance, and if they are dissatisfied, I attempt to work on marital enhancement goals after a decision has been made by both that they wish to stay married. Too often I have seen non-REMT therapy founder because the therapist is working on marital enhancement goals when one or both partners are emotionally disturbed, with the result that goal sabotaging needlessly occurs.

Another common error made by non-REMT practitioners occurs when the therapist is only prepared to see the partners in conjoint therapy. Thus if one partner wishes to preserve the marriage while the other has a hidden agenda to leave it, but will not declare this openly in the therapeutic triangle, such therapy is either terminated by the latter soon after its inception or is marked by little or no improvement, to the detriment of both partners. REMT therapists would be more likely to identify such a situation earlier in individual assessment interviews.

In the 'overcoming emotional disturbance' phase of REMT, it is important for the therapist to work with each partner individually either in conjoint therapy or in separate interviews. In conjoint therapy, the therapist gives each partner roughly equal amounts of time in order to maintain a productive alliance in the three-person situation – a social system which can easily be destabilized if the therapist, for example, excludes one partner for lengthy periods of time. The therapist explains at the outset of this phase that the goal is to help each of the partners overcome his or her own disturbance (intrapersonal focus) so that they can more productively work on their disagreements later (interpersonal focus). Productive REMT occurs when both partners clearly understand and agree to this modus operandi. In my experience, highly skilled REMT therapists who can present a convincing rationale concerning this important point are usually, but not always, successful at developing a good therapeutic alliance with both partners when such an alliance is based on this principle. Failure to form a productive alliance with both partners at the outset of therapy usually leads to problems later in the therapeutic process and does not bode well for successful outcome. Such failure is due to either (a) poor therapist skills, or (b) various partner factors which include: severe emotional disturbance; rigid adherence to the belief that the other person is totally responsible for the marital problems; or various hidden agendas. In such instances, the therapist is advised to consider changing the therapeutic context or to consider various systems – inspired interventions which are designed to change A factors in the ABC schema.

If the therapist can successfully manage the 'overcoming emotional disturbance' alliance, then the alliance necessary to effect productive change in the 'enhancing marital satisfaction' phase is much easier to manage, since both partners are in a position to make sound decisions about goals and are sufficiently free from emotional disturbance to work towards goal achievement.

Major treatment techniques

REMT is a multimodal form of therapy in that it employs a variety of cognitive (verbal and imagery), emotive and behavioural techniques to help partners overcome their emotional disturbances and marital dissatisfactions.

'Overcoming marital disturbance' phase The goal of the REMT practitioner in this phase of marital therapy is to help each partner become relatively undisturbed about their marital problems so that they can constructively work, if they wish, to improve their level of marital satisfaction. The therapist helps both partners to think rationally about themselves, their spouse and their marriage, which means feeling appropriately frustrated, sorry, annoyed and sad about their predicament when their desires are not met – emotions which will motivate them to work to improve their marriage or separate without needless emotional pain.

In this phase, the REMT practitioner helps both partners to see how they are needlessly upsetting themselves about their marital problems and often adopts a 'let's assume' approach with both of them.Both partners are encouraged to assume that their perceptions about, for example, their spouse, are correct, for the time being, to offset unproductive arguments about what actually occurred at A in the ABC framework. In this way, the therapist helps each partner to identify his or her underlying irrational beliefs and replace them with their rational alternatives, The therapist needs to persistently encourage both partners to focus on their own upset if the goals of this phase of treatment are to be achieved. A variety of *cognitive* methods are used at this stage. Partners are shown how to use the logico-empirical methods of science to dispute their irrational beliefs. They are taught to ask themselves such questions as: 'Where is the law of the universe that states that my wife *must* do the housework perfectly well?'; 'How does it follow that she is *bad* for doing badly?'; 'Is it true that I *cannot stand* her behaviour?' etc. They are subsequently helped to see that there is no evidence for such absolute statements, only evidence for their 'preferential' form. A number of clients appear less able to perform this kind of socratic questioning and here the therapist would help them to develop and employ rational coping statements such as: 'I don't like my wife's behaviour but she has a right to act badly.'; 'She is a fallible human being who is doing the wrong thing.'; 'I can stand her behaviour although I may never like it.' These statements can be further written down on index cards and rehearsed between sessions.

Some couples can be shown, similarly, how to dispute each other's irrational beliefs and thus serve as therapists for each other between formal therapy sessions. Other cognitive techniques employed in this phase of REMT include the use of: (a) general semantics methods (Korzybski 1933); (b) rational self-help forms (Dryden 1984b); (c) audiotape recordings (of the couple's therapy sessions or recorded lectures on rational themes); (d) bibliotherapy, especially the use of books which present the rational–emotive perspective on how to overcome emotional and behavioural disturbance; and (e) a variety of imagery techniques (Lazarus 1978).

Emotively, the therapist can employ several evocative and vivid methods of RET to help change the couple's irrational philosophies (Dryden 1984a). Such methods include the use of: (a) rational-emotive imagery (Maultsby and Ellis 1974) – where the partners deliberately imagine 'upsetting events' at A, and practise making themselves feel appropriately sad, annoyed, frustrated about those at C, which is achieved by spontaneously thinking more rationally at B; (b) vigorous and forceful repetition of rational statements (Ellis 1979b); (c) role playing – to uncover hidden feelings which can then be traced back to the relevant irrational beliefs and disputed; (d) shame-attacking exercises – where couples deliberately seek out various 'shameful' experiences and practise accepting themselves for acting 'shamefully'; and (e) therapist self-disclosure and humour to help couples not take themselves and their partners too seriously.

Behaviourally, in this phase, partners are encouraged to face and not avoid potential problems so that they may have real-life opportunity to 'stay in' these situations until they have made themselves undisturbed about them (Grieger and Boyd 1980).

'Enhancing marital satisfaction' phase   Once both partners have made some progress at helping themselves and their spouse overcome their emotional disturbances about their marital dissatisfaction, they are in a position to constructively look at ways of enhancing their degree of marital satisfaction or to be helped to amicably separate. Assuming that they wish to stay married, there are a number of well-established methods that can be used to help them to live more happily together. These include communication training (Crawford 1982; Guerney 1977), negotiation training (Stuart 1980) and a variety of behavioural techniques designed to help them to (1) develop appropriate marital and sexual skills and (2) get more of what they want from each other (see Chapter 10). Bibliotherapy is often used in conjunction with these methods.

A hallmark of REMT is that homework assignments are negotiated to encourage couples to put into practice what they have learned in therapy. Assuming that such assignments are carefully designed by the therapist and agreed to by both partners, failure to execute them often reveals further emotional disturbance – particularly that which stems from a philosophy of low frustration tolerance (LFT). REMT practitioners are alert to such possibilities and strive to help both partners, if appropriate, overcome their LFT so that they can follow through on the difficult task of changing the nature of their relationship.

A final task for REMT practitioners in this stage is to address the topic of marital myths (see the section 'Marital dissatisfaction' above) and help partners develop more realistic perspectives concerning what they can legitimately expect from marriage.

Problems encountered in REMT and their solution

The conduct of marital therapy is fraught with potential problems, no matter which approach the practitioner adopts, The more flexible the practitioner can be, the better, and in general it is highly desirable for REMT therapists to dispute their own irrational beliefs concerning how therapy *should* proceed, how clients *should* behave and what harmonious relationships *should* be like. Practitioners had better not be invested in either preserving or destroying marriages, if they are to truly help couples negotiate what is in their best interests. Apart from therapist-derived problems the following problems are often encountered in REMT.

Secrets Because REMT therapists conceive their basic task to be one of helping individual partners, rather than the marriage, they will frequently see the partners alone in individual sessions particularly at the beginning of therapy. Consequently, they will sometimes be called upon to keep 'secrets'. They are prepared to do this and, in order to help both partners disclose what is really on their mind, they will tell clients in individual sessions of their willingness to do so. This tactic also helps therapists to quickly uncover 'hidden agendas'. Consequently, they had better be mindful of what information is confidential to a particular partner and keep a mental note not to disclose this in front of the other. It should again be noted that this is done in order to develop productive contracts with both partners. Some REMT therapists stress to both partners that whatever is discussed in individual sessions is confidential to each partner concerned, so that if directly asked about what occurred in an individual session with the other partner, they can refer to this principle. Moreover, partners are advised to only talk about their individual sessions in general terms rather than in detail. It is appreciated, however, that other marital therapists prefer not to be burdened by secrets.

Persistent other-blaming   It sometimes happens that one or both partners refuse to acknowledge that they make themselves disturbed about their spouse's behaviour and cling rigidly to the assertion that their spouse is the cause of their upset. In certain of these cases, it transpires that they are anxious that if they admit that they make themselves upset, their partner will not be motivated to change. In other cases, such 'defensiveness' is motivated by fear of self-criticism: 'If I admit that I make myself disturbed, as I *must* not do, then I will condemn myself.' In these two instances, good REMT practitioners will test out such hypotheses rather than assuming that their hunches are correct. Such 'defensiveness' can also be, in certain instances, a sign that the partner is profoundly disturbed. One technique that sometimes helps such clients is to stress that if they want their spouse to change, then one of the most effective ways of achieving this is to change their own behaviour first.

When disputing fails   In certain cases, REMT therapists will fail to encourage one or both partners to identify, challenge and change their irrational beliefs which mediate their disturbance. When this occurs, the practitioner can use some of the methods which are ideally intended for use in the 'enhancing marital satisfaction' phase. In the case where one partner is overcoming their emotional disturbance and the other is not, the therapist may focus his efforts on encouraging the former to be unusually nice to the disturbed partner to encourage that partner to change. Ellis originally advocated this tactic in his book *How to live with a neurotic* (1957), and it is one that sometimes proves successful. When both partners remain disturbed, after disputing fails, REMT practitioners may use a number of systems-theory-inspired interventions which are designed to change A (see Chapter 11). Thus, for example, reframing and various paradoxical procedures can be employed to help the couple extricate themselves from a vicious circle of negative interactions. If this is successful, it occasionally provides the stimulus for one or both partners to *then* focus on their disturbance-creating beliefs. However, although such interventions may be successful in the short term, if both partners remain emotionally disturbed they might, as a result, experience more problems later, since unresolved emotional disturbance is the driving force behind the development and maintenance of disturbed interactions.

Extremely hostile interchanges These are difficult to manage when they occur in marital therapy sessions, and when they become a regular occurrence it is advisable to see the partners individually. However, in dealing with such a situation at a given time, I have found it helpful to do something unusual to gain the couple's attention. Thus, I have, in the midst of a heated interchange, got up and commenced speaking to a picture on the wall, or tried to catch an imaginary mouse. These attention-getting techniques are, in my experience, generally more effective in defusing the situation than trying to shout the couple down which tends to increase the heat in an overly hot kitchen.

The change process

In the same way as a good navigator plots his favoured course but plans several different alternative routes, should they be needed, so do effective REMT therapists have their preferred and alternative game-plans. Since couples differ markedly, the REMT therapist who adheres rigidly to a single game-plan is likely to fail with a number of couple clients.

When therapy goes smoothly, REMT practitioners are able to keep to their preferred game-plan. In cases where this applies, they help both partners see that they have two different kinds of problems: those related to marital disturbance, and those related to marital dissatisfaction. They succeed in (1) showing the couple that they had better work on marital disturbance issues first; (2) explaining that their disturbance is due in the main to their irrational beliefs about their marital dissatisfaction; (3) inducing them to work at disputing and changing these irrational beliefs and replacing them with their rational alternatives; (4) inducing them to work at identifying whether their differences can be reconciled and, if so, (5) helping them to negotiate more satisfying marital arrangements; and (6) encouraging them to work to actualize these desired alternatives. When both partners are only dissatisfied and not disturbed, only stages 4, 5 and 6 apply.

Problems still tend to occur even in this smooth change process, and can be generally attributed to one or both partners believing that change *should* be easier than it is (LFT) or to one or both partners testing the solidity of change (Stuart 1980). Here, the therapist (1) helps the couple to tolerate the discomfort that change almost inevitably brings and to see that change is rarely easily achieved, and (2) explains to the couple (preferably in advance) that 'testing' behaviour is also a common occurrence in the change process – that one or both partners sometimes test out the solidity of change by returning to dysfunctional patterns. When partners are prepared for this eventuality they are less likely to disturb themselves about it. The therapist also explains that change is rarely a linear process since humans easily return to well-ingrained but dysfunctional patterns of behaviour, thought and emotion.

When both partners are disturbed at the inception of therapy and only one changes for the better in this respect, the therapist will often, as noted above, encourage that partner to make an extra effort for their own sake and for the sake of determining the future prospects of the marriage. This involves being unusually understanding and tolerant of the still disturbed partner, a tactic which often serves as the fulcrum and lever which encourages them to begin to change, for it sometimes happens that they need to see that their partner has shown an extra amount of 'good faith' before beginning to work on their own disturbance. If such a tactic fails to yield beneficial results for the disturbed partner, then the other partner has useful information when coming to determine the viability of the relationship.

As has also been noted above, when both partners remain disturbed even as a result of the therapist's interventions in the 'overcoming marital disturbance' phase of treatment, the therapist is prepared to use a variety of behavioural and systems-theory-inspired interventions to change A in the ABC framework even though he acknowledges that this is an inelegant approach to producing philosophic change at B (Ellis 1979c). If these interventions are successful, then the couple have been helped to see that they can extricate themselves from a negative pattern and thus may be encouraged to do so for themselves. There is always the danger, however, that if they reencounter the original problem situation they will again become disturbed and thus may need further help to change A.

It needs to be reiterated that REMT practitioners tend to be flexible in their use of different therapeutic contexts and thus may initiate changes in the therapeutic arena at various points in the process of marital therapy. Such changes are usually instigated for positive therapeutic reasons, but can also be made if the therapy has become unproductively 'stuck' in a given arena.

The personal qualities of effective REMT therapists

It is highly desirable for REMT therapists to serve as good but fallible role-models of psychological health for their clients. This means that they will tend to: (a) generally put their own interests first, with the interests of others a close second, particularly in areas that are important to them as individuals; (b) show a large measure of self-direction in their lives, but be prepared to ask for assistance from others where appropriate; (c) be tolerant of themselves, others and the world, but try to change those aspects of themselves, others and the world which they dislike; (d) display a basic acceptance of ambiguity and uncertainty; (e) be flexible and thus not *insist* on following any predetermined set of rules either in their personal lives or in therapy; (f) show a decided preference for scientific thinking; (g) have a strong commitment, backed up by action, to a number of personally defined important projects; (h) take calculated risks in their personal lives and in therapy; (i) demonstrate an accepting attitude towards reality, especially when this is grim; and (j) strive to accept themselves as fallible humans particularly when they fail to meet the above criteria of mental health (Ellis 1979d).

In the practice of marital therapy, effective REMT practitioners will be: (a) comfortable using the structure of REMT, but flexible enough to work in less structured ways when the occasions arise; (b) drawn to adopting an active-directive teaching style and credible enough to teach their client couples the principles of RET in ways appropriate to the learning abilities of the people involved; (c) 'expected to be authoritative without being authoritarian; to bring up discussions of basic values without foisting their personal values on to clients; and to push, coach, persuade, and encourage clients to think and act against their own self-sabotaging tendencies' (Ellis 1982, p. 316); and (d) prepared to reveal their own feelings and beliefs and show their clients that they are not scared to take risks in helping them over their marital difficulties. Moreover, they will tend to be philosophically inclined, scientific, empirical, multimodal and antiabsolutistic in their approach to the problems of their couples, and be drawn to REMT because it allows them to fully express these tendencies. They will be comfortable working with more than one person in therapy and raising difficult issues with both partners, particularly in the area of sexual relations.

While it is not essential for effective REMT therapists to have had first hand experience of marital or cohabiting relationships, in my opinion this is desirable for a number of reasons. First, they will be able to talk with their clients about marital difficulties from a more authoritative and credible position, particularly if they have been successful in dealing with some of their own. Second, they will tend to have a deeper understanding of the stresses of marital relationships and see the potential for growth and for harm that such relationships hold. Finally, they will be able to share *specific* examples from their own experiences to help show their clients the advantages of a rational approach to marital life. However, it is noted that some REMT practitioners are quite successful without such first hand experience.

Case example

Mr and Mrs Rogers, married with no children, were seen in the context of my work as a part-time counselling psychologist for an East Birmingham general practice. Mrs Rogers, a 35-year-old housewife, was initially referred to me for 'depression'. In an initial intake interview it transpired that she was depressed about what she described as her husband's cold attitude towards her. I decided, with her permission, to invite Mr Rogers to come and see me to determine his opinions about his wife's depression and the marital situation. In cases where one spouse is referred to me whose disturbance is rooted in an interpersonal context, I prefer to interview the significant other since this contact facilitates their later involvement in therapy if this is indicated. Mr Rogers, a 38-year-old businessman, angrily complained about his wife's 'low mood'. He also expressed concern that he could not 'get through to her'. They both stated in these initial individual interviews that they wanted to stay together, but both also stated that they would like to be seen separately at first. I saw no reason to refuse their requests.

'Overcoming marital disturbance' phase

I began by helping Mrs Rogers to see that she was *insisting* that she must have her husband's love and that she was unlovable since he did not seem to love her at present. I showed her that it was this attitude rather than the assumed lack of love on his part that determined her feelings of depression, and proceeded to help her to accept herself even if her husband did not love her. I helped her to *dispute* her irrational *need* for love, but encouraged her to keep to her rational *desire* for his love, and showed her that she would be appropriately sad but did not have to be inappropriately depressed if her assumption proved to be correct now and/or in the future.

When working with Mr Rogers I zeroed in on his demand that his wife *should* not be depressed and helped him to see that this was related to another demand that his wife *should* be supportive which in turn was related to his fear of failure at work. His wife used to help him by doing important typing and book-keeping and this helped him maintain a high standard of work performance. The fact that she was no longer assisting him in this way confronted him directly with his own anxiety, which, as often occurs, was masked by anger (Wessler 1981). I encouraged Mr Rogers to face this fear and helped him to dispute his underlying irrational beliefs, namely 'I *must* do well and continue to do well at work or I'd be inadequate'; and 'I *must* keep getting promoted or I may not be able to improve our living standards which would be terrible'. For good measure, I showed him that, while he wanted his wife to support him, there was no law in the universe that decreed that she had to. Consequently, he became more tolerant and sympathetic towards his wife when she became depressed.

At this point it would have been tempting to bring Mr and Mrs Rogers together for conjoint sessions, since she was becoming less depressed and he was less anxious and angry. However, I decided to see them separately for two more individual sessions each to help them deal more thoroughly with the worst examples of A in the ABC framework that they could imagine. This strategy, in fact, elicited Mrs Rogers's acute fear of divorce. I helped her to identify and challenge her belief that divorce would be 'awful' and helped her to see that she could lead an independent, happy life and therefore was not impelled to stay in the marriage.[4] I also helped Mr Rogers deal with his morbid fear of unemployment and showed him (a) that his value as a human was not dependent on his work status and (b) that he could become vitally absorbed in other pursuits if he ever faced unemployment.

When I felt satisfied that they had made progress in dealing with their worst fears, I arranged to see them in conjoint marital therapy, having seen them individually for six sessions each.

'Enhancing marital satisfaction' phase

This phase of treatment began with a shared review of what Mr and Mrs Rogers had both learned in individual marital therapy. They reiterated their desire to stay together and work towards increased marital satisfaction. At the outset of this phase, Mrs Rogers experienced a greater degree of dissatisfaction than her husband. Although she had made great strides in accepting herself, she stated that, in her opinion, he was still taking her for granted and expected that she would devote much of her life to helping him gain a managerial position to which he had always aspired. She said that she was no longer prepared to devote as much time to helping him in this respect and wanted more time to pursue her own emerging interests. Although Mr Rogers initially appeared to understand her desire for self-actualization, his actual behaviour in subsequent weeks belied his words.

Despite the fact that I had helped them to negotiate a more equitable allocation of time to different tasks, Mr Rogers failed to keep to his part of the bargain. At this point, Mrs Rogers decided to get tough with him. She was able to do this because she was less anxious about the prospect of being alone. When Mr Rogers realized that his wife was really serious about pursuing her own goals he was jolted into realizing the implications of continuing to act in an unsupportive way towards her.[5] At this point, he was able to articulate his fears about what living with an independent woman might mean for him. He feared that she might find another man, whereas in reality Mrs Rogers wanted not only to spend some time pursuing her own interests, but also to spend more time socially with him: 'I no longer want to be a doormat,' she said.

At this point I did some individual work with Mr Rogers in the context of conjoint marital therapy. I helped him to see that he could still accept himself even if his wife did in fact leave him for somebody else, and that he could be relatively happy if this happened. Mrs Rogers tried on several occasions to reassure him that she was not interested in other men, but I showed her and her husband that this was not the central issue and that the real point was that Mr Rogers was anxious about the prospect of this happening. As he successfully disputed his irrational beliefs about her leaving him, he calmed down and listened to his wife's desires with greater empathy. At this point, I taught them how to accurately listen and respond to each other's statements, and how to check out their hunches about the meaning of such statements rather than assume that their hunches were, indeed, facts (Guerney 1977). I further helped them to consider the implicit contracts that they had made with each other at the time of their marriage about their roles as husband and wife, and showed them that these role expectations could be renegotiated (Sager 1976). This led to a full discussion of their aspirations for themselves as individuals and as a couple, and they were able to determine for themselves how they could achieve 'I-goals' and 'We-goals'. At the end of ten conjoint sessions they decided that they had achieved enough to work on 'enhancing marital satisfaction' on their own.

Observations

This example clearly demonstrates the major features of REMT. Issues of marital disturbance were dealt with first, in this instance, in individual marital therapy sessions for both partners. Conjoint marital therapy sessions were employed to deal with issues of marital dissatisfaction. Communication, problem-solving and negotiation training procedures were all employed in this second phase. The case also shows that REMT practitioners are often called upon to deal with further disturbance issues that emerge in the 'enhancing marital satisfaction' phase. As is commonly found, emotional disturbance is often uncovered as a result of the failure of one or both partners to execute carefully negotiated homework assignments. In this case Mr Rogers' anxiety about his wife having 'affairs' was elicited as a consequence of his failure to follow through on an assignment that was negotiated on two separate occasions. He was helped to see that his 'excuses' were in fact defensive in nature and served to protect him from his own self-condemnation. Mr Rogers confirmed my own hypothesis that it was my early focus on disputing his irrational beliefs in the first phase of treatment that encouraged him to disclose this core fear. In his words, 'I feel that I was helped to acquire the skills to actually deal with this particular fear. I doubt whether I would have revealed it, if I felt unable to deal with it.'

Follow-up

I conducted a follow-up session six months after treatment was terminated. Mr and Mrs Rogers maintained the gains which they had achieved in therapy, and, according to them, were experiencing the most productive period of their marriage. They reported that they were more able to express their desires to one another and be supportive of each other's goals as well as spend more time together. Mrs Rogers had taken up voluntary work, pottery classes and yoga. She spent about an hour a day typing her husband's business correspondence as compared to the four hours daily work she used to do for him. She had not experienced any depressive episodes since treatment had ended. Mr Rogers had still not acquired his coveted managerial position. He occasionally experienced bouts of panic about this fact, but said that on these occasions he was able to identify and dispute the underlying irrational beliefs. He had come to realize that work was not the 'be-all and end-all' of his life and had started to manage a local junior football team. He seemed genuinely pleased with his wife's improvement, rarely got angry with her and she felt that he showed sincere interest in her activities. Together they had taken up ballroom dancing lessons and enjoyed regular Saturday evenings at the local palais. They reported that they were more able non-defensively to challenge one another in a constructive way when problems began to emerge and that they were able to resolve matters without undue upset.

Interestingly enough, both Mr and Mrs Rogers pointed to the gains that they had made in the first phase of treatment as the most significant feature of their therapy experiences. Mrs Rogers summed this up well when she said: 'Although it was painful, you helped me most by showing me that divorce wasn't the end of the world. I thought it was, you see. Yes, that really helped. Before, we stayed together more out of fear and obligation than anything else, but now we are together because we want to be together.' That statement beautifully encapsulates the goals and spirit of REMT!

Notes

1 This therapeutic approach was originally termed 'Rational Therapy' but later renamed 'Rational-Emotive Therapy' to stress that emotive and behavioural factors were not neglected.

2 Partners often express myths in idiosyncratic form.

3 A similar phenomenon often occurs in individual RET. When clients are given audiotape recordings of therapy sessions they often learn better the ABCs of RET after they have listened to these recordings than when they are in the therapy room. It may be that this is due to the fact that, later, they are less emotionally involved with the material and can thus listen more attentively to what the therapist is saying.

4 This procedure known as 'de-awfulizing' divorce is very helpful in reducing anxiety in partners who feel impelled to stay married out of obligation rather than out of desire.

5 I have found that it is only when wives are prepared to take drastic action in pursuing their own goals that their husbands are 'shocked' into realizing the implications of not listening to them. This 'shock' is often the motivating factor for initiating constructive change.

References

Bard, J. A. (1980) *Rational-emotive therapy in practice*. Champaign, Ill.: Research Press.

Beck, A. T. (1976) *Cognitive therapy and the emotional disorders*. New York: International Universities Press.

Church, V. A. (1974) Rational therapy in divorce practice. *Rational Living, 9(2)*, 34–38.

Crawford, T. (1982) Communication and rational-emotive therapy. Workshop presented in Los Angeles, October.

Dryden, W. (1984a) Rational-emotive therapy: fundamentals and innovations. Beckenham, Kent: Croom-Helm.

Dryden, W. (1984b) Rational-emotive therapy. In W. Dryden (ed.) Individual therapy in Britain. London: Harper and Row.

Ellis, A. (1957) How to live with a neurotic: at home and at work. New York: Crown.

Ellis, A. (1958) Neurotic interaction between marital partners. Journal of Counseling Psychology, 5, 24–28.

Ellis, A. (1960) Marriage counseling with demasculinizing wives and demasculinized husbands. Marriage and Family Living, 22, 13–21.

Ellis, A. (1962) Reason and emotion in psychotherapy. Secaucus, N.J.: Lyle Stuart.

Ellis, A. (1976) Techniques of handling anger in marriage. Journal of Marriage and Family Counseling, 2, 305–316.

Ellis, A. (1978a) Family therapy: a phenomenological and active-directive approach. Journal of Marriage and Family Counseling, 4, 43–50.

Ellis, A. (1978b) A rational-emotive approach to family therapy. Part I: Cognitive therapy. Rational Living, 13(2), 15–19.

Ellis, A. (1979a) A rational-emotive approach to family therapy. Part II: Emotive and behavioral therapy. Rational Living, 14(1), 23–27.

Ellis, A. (1979b) The issue of force and energy in behavioral change. Journal of Contemporary Psychotherapy, 10, 83–97.

Ellis, A. (1979c) Rejoinder: elegant and inelegant RET. In A. Ellis and J. M. Whiteley (eds) Theoretical and empirical foundations of rational-emotive therapy. Monterey, Calif.: Brooks/Cole.

Ellis, A. (1979d) The theory of rational-emotive therapy. In A. Ellis and J. M. Whiteley (eds) Theoretical and empirical foundations of rational-emotive therapy. Monterey, Calif.: Brooks/Cole.

Ellis, A. (1982) Rational-emotive family therapy. In A. M. Horne amd M. M. Ohlsen (eds) Family counseling and therapy. Itasca, Ill.: Peacock.

Ellis, A. (1983) The case against religiosity. New York: Institute for Rational-Emotive Therapy.

Ellis, A. (1984) Foreword. In W.Dryden, Rational-emotive therapy: fundamentals and innovations. Beckenham, Kent: Croom-Helm.

Ellis, A. and Harper, R. A. (1961) A guide to successful marriage. Hollywood, Calif.: Wilshire.

Grieger, R. and Boyd, J. (1980) Rational-emotive therapy: a skills-based approach. New York: Van Nostrand Reinhold.

Guerney, B. G. Jr. (1977) Relationship enhancement: skill-training programs for therapy, problem-prevention and enrichment. San Francisco: Jossey-Bass.

Harper, R. A. (1981) Limitations of marriage and family therapy. Rational Living, 16(2), 3–6.

Hauck, P. A. (1977) Irrational parenting styles. *In* A. Ellis and R. Grieger (eds) *Handbook of rational-emotive therapy.* New York: Springer.

Hauck, P. A. (1979) *Depression.* London: Sheldon Press.

Hauck, P. A. (1980) *Calm down.* London: Sheldon Press.

Hauck, P. A. (1981a) *Why be afraid?* London: Sheldon Press.

Hauck, P. A. (1981b) *How to stand up for yourself.* London: Sheldon Press.

Hauck, P. A. (1981c) *Making marriage work.* London: Sheldon Press.

Hauck, P. A. (1982a) *How to do what you want to do.* London: Sheldon Press.

Hauck, P. A. (1982b) *Jealousy.* London: Sheldon Press.

Hauck, P. A. (1982c) *How to bring up your child successfully.* London: Sheldon Press.

Hauck, P. A. (1983a) Working with parents. *In* A. Ellis and M. E. Bernard (eds) *Rational-emotive approaches to the problems of childhood.* New York: Plenum.

Hauck, P. A. (1983b) *How to love and be loved.* London: Sheldon Press.

Korzybski, A. (1933) *Science and sanity.* Lancaster, Penn.: Lancaster Press.

Lazarus, A. A. (1978) *In the mind's eye.* New York: Rawson.

Lederer, W. J. and Jackson, D. D. (1968) *The mirages of marriage.* New York: Norton.

Maultsby, M. C. Jr (1984) *Rational behavior therapy.* Englewood Cliffs, N.J.: Prentice-Hall.

Maultsby, M. C. Jr. and Ellis, A. (1974) *Technique for using rational-emotive imagery.* New York: Institute for Rational-Emotive Therapy.

McClellan, T. A. and Stieper, D. R. (1973) A structured approach to group marriage counseling. *Rational Living, 8(2)*, 13–18.

Sager, C. J. (1976) *Marriage contracts and marital therapy.* New York: Brunner/Mazel.

Stuart, R. B. (1980) *Helping couples change: a social learning approach to marital therapy.* New York, Guilford.

Walen, S. R., Di Giuseppe, R. A. and Wessler, R. L. (1980) *A practitioner's guide to rational-emotive therapy.* New York: Oxford University Press.

Wessler, R. A. (1981) So you are angry: now what's your problem? *Rational Living, 16(1)*, 29–31.

Young, H. S. (1975) Rational-thinkers and robots. *Rational Living, 10(2)*, 29–31.

CHAPTER TEN   **Marital Therapy**
The Behavioural Approach
Dougal Mackay

Introduction

Historical developments of the approach

Behaviour therapy was introduced by Joseph Wolpe (1958) who defined it
as 'the use of experimentally established principles of learning for the
purpose of changing unadaptive behaviour' (p. 9). In the early days, the
main task was to develop standard treatment packages, derived from the
classical and operant conditioning paradigms, for each of the major
neuroses. However in view of the limitations of psychiatric diagnosis as an
assessment tool for psychotherapy (Mackay 1975), and the inability of
learning theory to account adequately for either the causes or effective
treatment of psychological disturbance (Mackay 1983, 1984), this exercise
has been discontinued for the most part. Instead, the individual's unique
problem is now regarded as an object for scientific inquiry in its own right
and the behavioural analysis (Kanfer and Phillips 1970) has been developed
to assist with this process. Similarly, the importance of cognitions in the
genesis and maintenance of maladaptive behaviour is now recognized and
a variety of techniques for directly modifying internal events have been
incorporated into this approach.

    Another characteristic of early behaviour therapy was the tendency to
treat the designated patient on an individual basis and to ignore the marital
or family context within which these difficulties were manifesting
themselves. A good illustration of this is Lazarus's (1963) study in which
'frigid' (sic) women were desensitized without the involvement of their
husbands in therapy. Even more illuminating is Bandura's (1969) explanation of the high drop-out rate reported in this investigation:'The majority
of others, most of whom displayed intense and generalized hostile attitudes
toward men, terminated therapy after several interviews. This subgroup of
women evidently required a treatment program aimed at reducing hostile
behaviour' (p. 469). Leaving aside the obvious allegation of 'sexism', this
quotation clearly illustrates the reluctance of the pioneering behaviour
therapists to look beyond the individual when planning treatment. The

eventual realization that relationships can be in difficulty as well as individuals led to the establishment of behavioural marital therapy (BMT). Stuart (1969) is generally credited as being the first therapist to adapt the behavioural model for work with couples. Using concepts derived from operant conditioning, he proposed that a successful marriage is one in which both partners are operating on a positive reinforcement schedule. In other words they are both regularly rewarding each other for desired behaviour with the result that these responses are occurring regularly, to the satisfaction of both parties. In an unsuccessful marriage, few rewards are dispensed and the main strategy for behavioural control is the threat of punishment (aversive control). To reinstate positive reinforcement in distressed marriages, Stuart proposed a token economy system through which an individual, by meeting his partner's requests, could 'earn' plastic discs which were later exchangeable for a reward of his own choice. In a study with couples complaining of 'low-rate conversational and sexual behavior' (ibid.), husbands were awarded a single token for each hour they conversed with their wives 'at the criterion level'. When they had accumulated a sufficient number of these secondary reinforcers, they were in a position to request sex. The 'exchange rate' adopted was three tokens for 'light petting', five for 'heavy petting' and fifteen for sexual intercourse. Although he reported some success with this approach, the notion of buying favours from one's partner has since been dismissed as superficial, mechanistic, and even unethical (Knudson et al. 1978).

Nevertheless Stuart's basic principle of 'reward your partner for rewarding you' was well received in behavioural circles and led to two important developments. The first was the emergence of a more acceptable technique for increasing the exchange rate of positive reinforcers in a marital relationship, which has become known as contingency contracting. Here the therapist helps the couple to produce a written agreement which specifies positive behavioural requests from each spouse, together with the rewards to be dispensed on completion of each activity. Contingency contracting proved extremely popular with behaviourally oriented clinicians in the 1970s and became almost synonymous with BMT for a time. However, in recent years, it too has come in for its share of criticism. Jacobson and Margolin (1979) state their reservations as follows: 'Changes which would otherwise be well-received and attributed to internal factors such as the partner's "desire" to improve the relationship, or his "caring", might be attributed to the fact that the spouse was forced to change because of the contract' (p. 288). Thus it is now generally recognized that the attempt to view marital distress as a trading disagreement between business associates is unlikely to bring about a fundamental improvement in the quality of the relationship.

A more significant derivative of Stuart's pioneering work was a less structured form of BMT known as 'reciprocity counselling' (Azrin et al. 1973). Once again, the aim of treatment was to teach the couple to bargain with each other in an endeavour to make the relationship more mutually rewarding. However, this treatment approach was less concerned with establishing rigid behavioural exchanges than with instilling in both partners the more general principle of mutual positive control. The rationale here is that if they can both maintain the attitude of 'I will please you like you are trying to please me', they will be better able to enhance marital satisfaction both in the present and in the future.

With its emphasis on changing cognitions as opposed to formalizing reward schedules, this paper represents an important transition from operant conditioning to social learning theory as the rationale for contemporary BMT. According to this model (Jacobson and Margolin 1979; Stuart 1980), the prime aim of therapy should be to enable the couple to fully appreciate the interactionalist nature of their marital difficulties and to approach their problems in a spirit of collaboration. It is argued that, provided thay can learn to do this, solutions will be found without recourse to crude behavioural contracts.

Although interventions aimed at modifying dysfunctional attitudes may be sufficient to alleviate distress in moderately disturbed marriages, it is also recognized that most couples who seek help will also benefit from training in communication. In other words, there is little point in enabling a couple to see their problems in a different perspective if they are unable to engage in constructive discussions outside of therapy. Liberman et al. (1980) describe a 'personal effectiveness' treatment package they have designed to coach couples in a wide variety of interpersonal skills for improving the quality of emotional interchanges. A similar programme, devised by Jacobson and Margolin (1979), includes a problem-solving component on the grounds that rational discussions of feelings do not automatically lead to behaviour change. All authorities agree that it is essential that both partners should have reached the stage where they view their problems in interactionalist terms before techniques for improving communication are implemented.

The most recent advancement in this treatment approach has been the introduction of a cognitive intervention for modifying inappropriate beliefs and perceptions. In a sense, the importance of mediational factors in effecting behaviour change has always been recognized in BMT. Stuart's (1969) pioneering study, which purported to be based on the operant conditioning paradigm, includes references to such subjective concepts as 'negatively biased attitudes', 'impressions' and 'expectations'. The later work of Azrin et al. (1973) can be seen to be a more obvious attempt to change the way in which the couple make sense of their collective problems. However, reciprocity counselling concerns itself exclusively with global attitude change regarding the nature of marital distress and offers little to combat idiosyncratic beliefs. Another limitation of early BMT is the assumption that behavioural interventions are always the most effective techniques for bringing about change in internal processes. Following the work of Goldfried et al. (1974) and Meichenbaum (1977) in individual behaviour therapy, this view has been challenged. Cognitive restructuring involves the direct manipulation of specific maladaptive thought processes to enable clients to cope more effectively with stress. Given that no amount of communication training will improve the morale of a marriage in which one or both partners are holding on to inappropriate beliefs, this technique is now recognized as an important component of contemporary BMT.

Thus, in the last twenty-five years or so, behaviour therapy has evolved from a set of simplistic techniques for the treatment of psychiatric disorders to a comprehensive theoretical framework for understanding and reducing psychological distress in both individuals and relationships. The social learning theory model, with its emphasis on attitude change, the establishment of a collaborative set, and the acquisition of cognitive and interpersonal skills, provides a sound basis for work with troubled marriages.

Developments in Britain

Despite the fact that behaviour therapy first became established in this country, most of the advances referred to above are attributed to American researchers and clinicians. British behavioural researchers, in their endeavour to be 'scientific', remained loyal to the conditioning model long after their American counterparts had incorporated cognitions into their framework. Similarly, while BMT has been developing rapidly across the Atlantic, the scientific literature in this country has continued to focus on models and techniques related to individual therapy. Yet, despite this lack of enthusiasm for research into systems, behaviourally oriented workers from these shores have made significant contributions to conjoint therapy for psychosexual problems (see Volume 2, Chapter 4). Leaving aside the proven superiority of conjoint treatment over individual therapy in this area, this is probably due to the fact that sexual behaviour is regarded here as 'harder' data than relationship satisfaction. Nevertheless, it is unfortunate that Masters and Johnson's (1970) proposal that there is 'no such entity as an uninvolved partner' (p. 5) should be accepted by academic behaviourists in Britain as applying only to sexual inadequacy. Nevertheless, although few original contributions to this field have emanated from this country, BMT has always been popular with clinicians and is now widely practised here by practitioners from a variety of professional backgrounds.

The nature of marital disturbance

The contemporary behaviourist explanation of marital disturbance is largely derived from the social exchange model originally proposed by Thibaut and Kelley (1959). According to this model, a couple decide to marry when each expects the rewards associated with such a commitment to exceed the costs. Examples of perceived potential reinforcers for the individual are regular sexual activity, starting a family, parental approval, companionship, and social status. Anticipated negative consequences might include financial hardship, household chores, and lack of individual freedom. Difficulties will arise almost immediately if one or both partners have overvalued the rewards and underestimated the costs associated with the married state. This failure to properly appraise the situation could be one explanation for the high proportion of marriages in Britain which break up within the first two years (HMSO 1967).

Where this is not the case, the first phase of the marriage is generally characterized by a very high rate of rewarding exchanges between partners. Jacobson and Margolin (1979) suggest four reasons why this might be so:

(a) initial attraction is usually based on minimal knowledge of each other's behaviour which means that interactions tend to be confined to those areas which are pleasing for both partners;

(b) a number of potentially high-cost factors, such as children and career prospects, are not yet impinging on the relationship;

(c) the novelty of sex, communication and recreation with each other ensures that the mutually reinforcing properties of the marriage are at their peak;

(d) since many areas of the relationship have not yet been directly experienced, both partners, on the evidence to date, predict additional rewards in the future and minimize anticipated costs.

Since there is clear evidence that rates of rewards exchanged by spouses are highly correlated (Birchler et al. 1975), it follows that this situation is self-perpetuating, at least for a time.

However, since a marital relationship is continually evolving, it does not follow that a favourable perceived reward/cost ratio in the early years is a guarantee of relationship stability in the longer term. As the marriage progresses, situational factors, together with the needs of the individual, are in a constant state of flux. For example, sex may become ritualized, the arrival of children will lead to an alteration in roles, job opportunities can take priority over home life, and the desire for personal independence may increase as the novelty of constant companionship diminishes. It follows from this that no fixed arrangement can assure maximum happiness and minimal annoyance indefinitely for the couple. A successful marriage is one in which both partners are sufficiently flexible to be able to adjust their expectations and behaviour so that change does not lead to a significant decrease in their satisfactions with each other. Moreover, the happily married couple express their needs openly and continue to positively reinforce each other for pleasing behaviour. Marital disharmony, on the other hand, arises when the costs of remaining married exceed the rewards. Factors which cause and maintain this state of imbalance include the withdrawal of favours, futile attempts to force compliance, failure to communicate properly, inability to solve problems collectively, and the presence of inappropriate expectations regarding the relationship. Under these circumstances, the reward/cost ratio of the non-married state may be perceived as superior to that of the marriage.

Low level of rewards exchanged

Although the operant conditioning paradigm is an inadequate conceptual model for understanding all the complexities of human relationships, it nevertheless has some explanatory value. The fundamental principle of reinforcement theory is that the most effective procedure for maintaining or increasing the frequency of a particular response is to make a reward contingent upon its occurrence. So far as marriage is concerned, it follows that the most effective strategy for assuring reinforcers for oneself is to reinforce one's spouse for providing them. Failure to do so, according to this principle, will inevitably lead to the extinction of the desired behaviour.

Azrin et al. (1973) suggest a number of reasons why an individual may hold back positive reinforcers in a marital relationship. Where rewards received are too few in number or are confined to certain low-priority areas (e.g. sex; home decorating) the recipient may feel disinclined to show appreciation by reciprocating. Alternatively, a particular reinforcer (e.g. financial security) may not be recognized as originating from one's spouse. Finally, previous reinforcers may no longer be satisfying while emergent desires appear to be unrecognized. All of these factors can lead the individual to think that they are getting a 'bad deal' from the marriage and decide to reciprocate in kind.

There is convincing evidence (Gottman et al. 1977) that the tendency of one individual to withhold rewards, for whatever reason, will lead to negative reciprocation on the part of their partner. In view of the proven link between pleasing behaviours and marital satisfaction (Wills et al. 1974), this self-defeating pattern can be regarded as a major factor in the development and maintenance of marital distress.

Self-defeating change strategies

According to social learning theory (e.g. Liberman et al. 1980), a major causal factor underlying negative reciprocity is the tendency of unhappily married persons to use behavioural strategies, other than positive control, in order to produce a change in the relationship. Instead of requesting a particular class of responses, and rewarding any attempts made by the partner in this direction, frustrated spouses frequently implement contingency schedules based on negative reinforcement or punishment. The prime example of this is *passive aggression*, as described in the preceding section, where positive reinforcements are deliberately or unconsciously withheld. A common example is where the wife refuses to have sex with her husband because she feels he has failed to recognize her need for emotional support. Under these circumstances, there is always the risk that he will look outside the marriage for sexual gratification, thereby complicating the situation still further. Since passive aggression is known to be highly contagious, it must be regarded as the most potentially destructive of all change strategies.

Another common ploy is coercion or *aversive control*. Here the distressed partner attempts to force compliance from his spouse by issuing a threat: 'unless the house is immaculate when I come home from work, I will go down to the pub.' The drawback here is that, if the conditions are met, this will be for reasons of appeasement rather than affection. Moreover, should this intervention result in behaviour change, the protagonist has effectively modelled a change strategy which may well be imitated subsequently by his spouse. The probable end result is a marriage in which both parties act according to the philosophy 'anything for a peaceful life'.

A third self-defeating strategy is where the unhappy spouse regularly dispenses *negative emotional responses*. Liberman et al. (1980) define these as 'words, expressions, insulting remarks, crying, an angry tone of voice, hostile silence, sarcastic comments, put-downs, and ridicule' (p. 69). According to reinforcement theory, the use of punishment in this way is unlikely to lead to change unless approximations to the desired response are simultaneously 'shaped' through reward. Where this component is not included, the two most likely consequences are retaliation (the 'slanging match') or withdrawal (the 'hen-pecked' husband; the 'brow-beaten'wife).

Communication skills deficit

Marital harmony involves more than the shared belief in positive reciprocity as the underlying philosophy for the relationship. In an ideal marriage, both partners should be able to communicate their thoughts, attitudes and feelings to each other about any aspect of the relationship, and feel that these self-disclosures are accepted and understood. The fact that this rarely occurs in any kind of relationship reflects, in part, the haphazard way in which people acquire interpersonal skills. These are learned from inexpert role-models, such as parents, siblings and friends, and from feed-back received from others who are just as likely to be deficient in certain aspects of communication.

Liberman et al. (1980) have pin-pointed the following interpersonal skills which they have found to be lacking in distressed marriages:

(1) expressing warmth and affection both verbally and non-verbally (e.g. vocal tone; eye contact);
(2) acknowledging a favour in a way which is rewarding to one's partner;
(3) asking openly for a favour for oneself, rather than hinting, demanding or commanding;
(4) expressing negative feelings assertively (i.e. without blaming, accusing or criticizing);
(5) demonstrating accurate empathy following a disclosure of feelings from one's partner, as opposed to defending, justifying, retaliating or suggesting a quick practical solution;
(6) dealing with unexpected hostility and persistent bad moods in such a way as to defuse anger in one's partner;

(7) perceiving accurately the spouse's mood state and adapting one's approach accordingly to ensure a high level of congruence during an interaction.

According to the behavioural model, repeated failure on the part of one or both partners, to perceive, transmit and receive emotional messages appropriately will significantly reduce the level of mutual satisfaction within the marriage. Supportive evidence comes from a large-scale survey on family communications (Fisher and Sprenkle 1978) which found such skills as positive responding, attending and self-disclosure to be associated with strong relationships whereas such maladaptive responses as paraphrasing and premature closure were shown to be negatively correlated. The failure to overcome pronounced interpersonal skill deficits may lead to a shift from positive to negative reciprocity as the basis for all communications within the relationship and, for this reason, must be regarded as a serious threat to marital harmony.

Poor problem-solving skills

Although the interpersonal skills described above are a prerequisite for the effective resolution of conflicts, it does not necessarily follow that the ability of both partners to express feelings and listen empathically will lead to practical solutions to the various problems which arise in a marriage. This point is taken up by Jacobson and Margolin (1979):

> Other couples develop a superficial ability to 'communicate' about problems, but they spend their problem-solving time with an unproductive focusing on insight and understanding. Feelings are expressed, but needed changes are not agreed upon or implemented, solutions are not forthcoming. All of us are familiar with couples who openly and honestly communicate about their relationship, yet separate to the surprise of many. Often a scrutiny of their history reveals a lack of accommodation and change in response to conflict, despite their open communication. (p. 23)

According to these authors, marital problem solving is a tightly structured form of interaction comprising such skills as defining the problem clearly, brainstorming, generating options, and agreeing on a solution. Since this is a collaborative exercise, it is essential that both partners are willing and able to move beyond the preliminary stage of sharing feelings to the more disciplined patterns of communication necessary for the formulation of practical plans.

There is convincing evidence to support Jacobson's (1978) claim that deficits in problem-solving skills are causally related to marital distress. For example, in a well-designed longitudinal study with engaged couples, Markman (1979) found the ability to solve problems to be the single best predictor of subsequent marital satisfaction. Moreover, from his review of the empirical literature on marital satisfaction, Birchler (1979) concludes that it is not specific problems but the skills and strategies employed for problem resolution which differentiate distressed from non-distressed relationships.

Maladaptive cognitions

As is the case in rational-emotive marital therapy (see Chapter 9), behavioural marital therapists recognize the important role played by cognitions in producing relationship difficulties. It is clear that the criterion used by one partner to judge the adequacy of rewards received from the other is a function of his or her beliefs and expectations regarding matrimony. These are usually derived from childhood observations of the parental marriage, although information from teachers and religious instructors, romantic magazine stories, feature films, and reported experiences of friends can also influence attitudes. According to social learning theory (Stuart 1980), the above-mentioned causes of marital distress can be at least partially attributable to cognitive dysfunction on the part of one or both partners, Eidelson and Epstein (1982) have identified the following five irrational beliefs which are commonly associated with marital problems.

(1) 'Disagreement is destructive': According to Satir (1967), many individuals believe that disagreement represents a lack of love or even a sign that divorce is imminent. He notes that persons holding this belief tend to adopt self-defeating change strategies.

(2) 'Mindreading is expected': A common misconception is the belief that 'if he really loved me he would know how I feel'. The expectation that one's partner is an expert in telepathy is one reason why communication skills are often not employed with regard to important areas of the relationship.

(3) 'Partners cannot change': The view that one's partner is characterized by certain unattractive traits which cannot be modified is regarded by Hurvitz (1970) as a 'terminal hypothesis'. There is evidence (Doherty 1981) that those who hold such a belief will make fewer active attempts to solve problems.

(4) 'Sexual perfectionism': As Walen (1980) points out, the belief that sexual performance must always be of a very high standard acts as an impediment to sexual gratification. Consequently, holding such an attitude will significantly reduce an important potential source of rewards for both partners.

(5) 'The sexes are different': To view one's partner in terms of a particular gender stereotype is to lower awareness of his or her particular needs and desires. Furthermore, attributing marital conflict to the fixed characteristics of the opposite sex can lead to a sense of 'helplessness regarding the relationship as a whole' (Doherty 1981).

Although such beliefs can often be seen to be a primary cause of marital dissatisfaction, maladaptive change strategies and interpersonal skill deficits play an important role in maintaining dysfunctional cognitions. An important assumption of the behavioural model is that effective communication between partners will lead to a modification of the erroneous beliefs which an individual may bring to the relationship.

Therapy

Contextual considerations

Individual or marital therapy The vast majority of clients referred for behaviour therapy are individuals with specific phobias, agoraphobia, obsessional ruminations, chronic anxiety or depression. In contrast to the 'systems theory' model (see Chapter 11) the behavioural therapist does not assume that the client's difficulties reflect some kind of disequilibrium in the marital or familial situation. He does not hold any preconceived ideas concerning the factors which have led the individual to seek help, but rather regards their unique set of problems as a subject for scientific inquiry. There are four sets of conditions which could lead the therapist to include marital therapy as a component of the treatment programme, illustrated here with reference to the depressed client:

(a) the partner's behaviour is serving as a powerful cue for the individual's depressive responses (stimulus control);

(b) the client's perceptions of the partner, or the relationship, is producing a lowering of mood;

(c) the partner is reinforcing the client for being helpless, unassertive, or adopting the 'sick role';

(d) the client's depression is posing problems for the marital relationship with the result that the spouse is also in need of help.

In BMT, the relevance of relationship factors to the individual's presenting problem is an issue which should be determined through the behavioural analysis and should not be assumed by the therapist on the basis of preconceived notions or a 'clinical hunch'. Unless there is clear evidence that the client's difficulties are being at least partially maintained by the spouse's behaviour, individual therapy would be the treatment of choice.

An important point here is that, should the therapist deem it necessary to involve the spouse, he must be clear from the outset whether he intends to implement a programme of marital therapy or simply to enlist the help of the designated client's partner. This should be made explicit to both partners when the therapeutic contract is drawn up. If the right decisions are made, there is little doubt that marital therapy can augment conventional treatment packages for a wide variety of problems other than clearly recognized relationship difficulties (Cobb et al. 1980).

Marital therapy with one or both partners   The major authorities in this field argue that marital therapy should always be conducted on a conjoint basis and there is convincing empirical evidence to support this stance (Gurman and Kniskern 1978). Since the treatment goals are to heighten the 'reciprocity awareness' of the couple (Liberman et al. 1980) and to evolve more mutually satisfying patterns of interaction, it is difficult to see how this might be achieved other than through collaborative work with both partners. The only exception to this rule is during the assessment phase, when each client should be allowed the opportunity to reveal information, pertinent to the analysis, which they are unwilling to disclose to the spouse. Failure to unearth such secrets as involvement in an extramarital relationship would lead to the establishment of an 'illicit contract' (Weiss et al. 1973) between all concerned, with the result that the problem formulation would be incomplete.

Single therapist or cotherapists   Given the directive chairmanlike role envisaged for the behavioural marital therapist, most authorities maintain that cotherapy teams introduce an unnecessary complication to the therapeutic process. The only investigation into the relative effectiveness of cotherapists and single therapists in BMT failed to yield significant differences. The authors (Mehlman et al. 1983) conclude that: 'This finding is encouraging because it suggests that professional time can be used efficiently when administering BMT since only a single therapist need be employed to treat each couple' (p. 263). The exception to this rule is where the therapist, on assessing the problem, experiences difficulty in maintaining an equivalent alliance with both parties. Under such circumstances, the involvement of a colleague can facilitate the treatment alliance with the couple.

Developing and maintaining a therapeutic alliance

The initial interview   According to Jacobson and Margolin (1979), 'The most desirable goal of an initial interview is not to gather assessment information but rather to set the stage for therapeutic change by building positive expectancies and trust in the couple, and by actually providing them with some benefits' (p. 51). In his endeavour to achieve these targets, the therapist should structure the session and remain in control throughout. This prevents unproductive digressing and ensures that the session does not deteriorate into a sequence of negative emotional interchanges. In addition he should attempt to bring to the surface the positive aspects of the relationship in order that both he and the couple might obtain a balanced overview of the situation. Finally, he should convey the impression that change is possible but without making unrealistic claims concerning the effects of therapy.

The therapeutic contract   Given the need for structure in BMT, it is essential that a therapeutic contract should be established in order to clarify the expectations of all three parties with regard to goals, time allocation, therapeutic procedures and homework assignments. This should take place at the end of the assessment procedure when both the therapist and the couple are presumed to share a common conceptualization of the problems and can agree on the overall treatment plan. Whether or not this should be in writing will depend on the clinical style the therapist wishes to adopt with a particular couple, following his assessment of their problems.

Inducing a collaborative set   Most spouses, on entering into therapy, are unable to fully appreciate their particular individual contributions to marital disharmony and tend to overattribute the difficulties which have arisen to their partner's behaviour or to a variety of external factors. Before therapy proper can begin, it is important that both clients should be aware of the responsibility they each have for determining the nature of their interpersonal environment. The most effective way of inducing a 'collaborative set' is to direct the couple to engage in cooperative behaviour while holding on to their original theories. Homework tasks, involving the mutual dispensation of rewards, can give rise to satisfying consequences which, in turn, may lead to the modification of counterproductive beliefs. In the words of Jacobson and Margolin (1979), 'the encouragement of collaborative behavior here is put forth for its strategic value, as a temporary expedient whose ultimate goal is attitude change as well as behavior change' (p. 137).

Major treatment techniques

Behavioural analysis The cornerstone of contemporary behaviour therapy is the functional analysis of interactions both within the individual and between him and his external environment. The intrapsychic analysis involves an examination of the subtle ways in which the individual's cognitive, physiological and behavioural response systems interact (Hughdahl 1981). The extrinsic assessment requires a thorough examination of the differential effects of situational factors on the person's behaviour and the external factors which may be maintaining maladaptive responses (Kanfer and Phillips 1970). In certain respects, it is actually easier to assess a troubled marriage than an individual's problem since the therapist can directly observe the relevant antecedents and consequences of the target responses, during the treatment sessions, rather than rely on self-reports. Through a systematic analysis of the data, the therapist is then able to test out his various hypotheses concerning the nature of the couple's difficulties and arrive at a comprehensive formulation of the problem. The techniques he chooses to employ in therapy should follow on logically from the results of this assessment procedure. Since the behavioural analysis is an on-going process, the therapist must be prepared to modify his formulation and treatment plan according to the clients' response to these interventions.

It should be recognized that the behavioural analysis is not simply an assessment tool but an important therapeutic procedure in its own right. Since the clients are actively involved in the process of setting up and testing out the possible hypotheses, they can come to see their problems in a more objective fashion than before. Instead of dismissing the marriage as 'bad', they can be helped to recognize its strengths as well as its limitations.

Furthermore, through achieving greater understanding of the precise mechanisms which are preventing them from achieving greater satisfaction together, they are less likely to persist with their 'catastrophic' reactions.

Increasing awareness of existing rewards   In an endeavour to improve the clients' perceived reward/cost ratio with regard to the relationship, a useful way of starting is to make the couple fully aware of the frequency with which pleasing behaviours are currently being exchanged between them. Azrin et al. (1973) describe a simple 'reciprocity awareness' exercise which can dramatically improve the morale of both partners. They are each asked to write down ten 'pleases' which they regularly dispense to the other and a further ten which they receive. For this to be a useful learning experience, it is important that the therapist should ensure that the pleases are clearly specified and written in positive terms (e.g. 'Brings me a cup of tea in bed every morning').

Increasing the frequency of positive behaviours   Liberman et al. (1980) describe a simple exercise, entitled 'Catch your spouse doing something nice', which both helps the clients to give precise feedback to each other and trains them to use positive reinforcement for shaping their partner's behaviour. The couple are asked to record separately all pleases received during a particular day. Before retiring, they exchange lists and explain clearly why each item constituted a source of satisfaction for them. By exchanging this information on a daily basis, it is presumed that the regularity of feedback, together with repeated demonstrations of approval, will lead to a significant increase in desired responses. There is convincing evidence that non-contingent behaviour exchanges of this kind give rise to an increase in pleasing behaviour, at least in the short term (Jacobson 1984).

Interpersonal skills training   Since the inability of the couple to communicate effectively is considered to be an important factor in the cause and maintenance of most marital difficulties, it follows that the majority of treatment programmes will include a component concerned with the promotion of constructive interactional behaviour. On the assumption that interpersonal skills can be learned like any other specific aptitudes (Mackay 1985), the usual treatment format is (a) to demonstrate to the clients the required response (i.e. modelling), (b) to encourage them to practise it under simulated conditions (i.e. behaviour rehearsal), and (c) to provide precise and immediate knowledge of results (i.e. feedback). Liberman et al. (1980) use these procedures to coach clients in such varied skills as the appropriate expression of positive and negative feelings, empathic listening responses, verbal acknowledgements of pleasing behaviour, and tactics for defusing hostility.

Training in problem-solving skills   A possible limitation of interpersonal skills training is that, while it may give rise to more constructive exchanges of opinions and feelings, it does not automatically lead to the generation of practical solutions for the various day-to-day problems facing a couple. Jacobson and Margolin (1979) define problem-solving training as a 'structured interaction between two people designed to resolve a particular dispute between them' (p. 215). The therapist directs the couple to define the problem, generate strategic options through brainstorming, consider alternative tactics, and implement an agreed course of action. If a satisfactory end result is not achieved, the whole process is repeated. This technique should not be considered as an alternative to interpersonal skills training but as the final component of a comprehensive training programme in communication.

Contingency contracting   A contingency contract can be defined as a written agreement between husband and wife which specifies the particular rewards to be dispensed when one partner behaves in a way requested by his spouse. The therapist, in his role of mediator, is responsible for ensuring that these contracts are explicit, realistic and fair to both partners. The original version of this technique, described by Weiss et al. (1974) as the 'quid pro quo' contract, involves the direct, simultaneous exchange of behaviours. The difficulty here is that the two sets of contracts are inextricably bound up with each other with the result that one spouse's programme can be jeopardized by the failure of the other to cooperate. To get round this problem, Weiss et al. recommend the 'good faith' contract, which comprises two separate contingency schedules run in parallel. Thus, for example, the husband can claim his reward after cleaning the bathroom even though his wife has not completed her task of removing clothes from the bedroom floor. Although there is no clear evidence for the superiority of 'good faith' contracts over the 'quid pro quo' version (Jacobson 1978), most clinicians prefer the former since it is less likely to lead to stalemate.

Jacobson and Margolin (1979) are not convinced that contingency contracting adds anything to contemporary BMT. They argue that once the couple have learned to communicate and negotiate in the problem areas of their marriage, there should be no need to introduce elaborate techniques to tighten up their agreements. Moreover, a written agreement could lead a spouse to attribute partner compliance to their need to please the therapist rather than to a genuine desire to 'give ' in the marriage. This technique has declined in usage recently and its current status is that of a possible final stage in the problem-solving process.

Cognitive restructuring A controversial issue in BMT is whether the therapist should regard percepts and attitudes as dependent variables which will be modified through behaviour change, or whether techniques for directly effecting cognitive change should be incorporated into this approach. An important study by Margolin and Weiss (1978), which demonstrated clearly the importance of the cognitive restructuring component in BMT, would support the second point of view. In any event, the decision as to whether or not the main thrust of therapy with a given couple should be behavioural or cognitive is dependent on the problem formulation as derived from a comprehensive behavioural analysis of their difficulties.

A cognitive technique which can be easily adapted for marital work is *systematic rational restructuring* (Goldfried et al. 1974). The therapist begins by explaining to the couple the link between beliefs and emotional reactions and suggests that much of their distress may be due to the way in which they interpret each other's behaviour in terms of their own theories. He then encourages them to analyse past crises with a view to unearthing the irrational beliefs and erroneous interpretations which are presumed to underly such catastrophic reactions. Finally, he helps them to develop more adaptive self-instructions to enable both partners to cope more effectively with stress in the marriage. Where communication training has been included in the programme, role-play will enable both cognitive and interpersonal skills to be exercised simultaneously.

Problems encountered and their solution

The reluctant spouse Common reasons why a partner may be unwilling to attend for marital therapy include the denial of relationship difficulties, concern at being blamed for the spouse's distress, and a fear of the consequences of conjoint work. The therapist's task here is to provide appropriate reassurance while outlining the advantages to that individual of becoming involved. Devious attempts to 'hook' the client by establishing a secret alliance (e.g. 'We both know it's really his fault') or by attempting to merge the assessment phase with treatment proper are both unethical and unproductive and should be avoided at all costs (Ables and Brandsma 1977).

Resistance to behaviour rehearsal   While accepting the rationale for this treatment approach, many clients express an unwillingness to engage in role-playing for reasons of embarrassment or because they consider such an exercise to be artificial. Given that coaching in communication skills is a major component of this form of treatment, it is important that the therapist should develop some strategies for overcoming such resistance. An effective ploy is for the therapist to take over the role of the reluctant client in order to demonstrate not only that one does not appear foolish when trying out skills but that this technique can be very effective in bringing real feelings to the surface. Where both partners are disinclined to participate, a colleague can be brought in to enact a scene with the therapist, while the clients are invited to assist as 'auxiliary egos' (Liberman et al. 1980). If the resistance persists despite these efforts, it will be necessary to review the therapeutic contract with the clients and the possibility of discontinuing this form of therapy will have to be discussed.

Failure to carry out homework assignments   The author disagrees with those authorities who advocate punishing the uncooperative couple by withholding a portion of the money they have deposited as 'collateral' for compliance, or who propose that secretaries should cajole the couple by telephone (Liberman et al. 1980). Such strategies run counter to the principle of positive control which is an essential part of the whole treatment philosophy underlying BMT. Instead, the failure to execute an agreed assignment should be viewed as evidence of an incomplete behavioural analysis or an indication that one or both partners have not fully accepted the treatment contract. Thus, rather than regard non-compliance as an irritant, the therapist should treat this information as important clinical material in its own right.

The change process in therapy

Bandura (1978) has introduced the term 'reciprocal determinism' to refer to the bidirectional interactions which take place between the individual and his interpersonal environment. When two persons are engaged in a social encounter, one individual's response serves as a stimulus for the other, and so on, with the result that a particular S-R-S-R sequence develops. Thus each individual can be seen to be exerting control over the other's behaviour. In marriage, such patterns of interaction become well established, with both partners being equally responsible for determining the degree to which these lead to satisfying outcomes. However, where the relationship is not perceived as rewarding, the two partners tend to attribute the cause to deficiencies in the other while failing to acknowledge the part that they play in this process. The belief that the other person is 'to blame' increases the probability that such negative sequences will recur, with the result that these maladaptive cognitions will be further reinforced.

The rationale underlying BMT is that, through acquiring more adaptive skills for communicating, negotiating and problem solving, the couple shift from a relationship based on negative reciprocity to one in which the willing exchange of rewards for desired responses becomes the norm. An assumption of this model is that, through implementing behavioural techniques to disrupt the self-defeating patterns of interaction, the therapist is enabling the couple to fully recognize the interactionalist nature of their difficulties. Where such interventions fail to lead to attitudinal change in one or both partners, cognitive change methods are employed to assist in this reattribution process. Whichever techniques are used, the primary aim of therapy is to enable the couple to regard both the present and the future of their relationship as a subject for collaborative enterprise.

There is an additional theoretical concept, currently in vogue with regard to individual behaviour therapy, which may well have some relevance to a full appreciation of the active ingredients of marital work. Bandura (1977) has introduced the term 'self-efficacy' to refer to an individual's conviction that he can successfully execute the appropriate responses in a particular situation in order to produce a desired outcome. According to this theory, the person's expectations regarding his performance will determine whether or not he will attempt to overcome a particular set of obstacles and, should he choose to, the amount of time and energy he will expend when attempting to achieve his goal. Social learning theorists maintain that perceived self-efficacy is one of the most powerful predictors of behaviour. Moreover Bandura claims that much of the success of early behaviour therapy work can be attributed to the fact that the experience of mastery led these clients to enhance their expectations of personal efficacy. The degree to which specific behavioural interventions lead to generalized improvements in the client's functioning (McPherson et al. 1980) is certainly consistent with such a hypothesis.

Using this conceptual framework, it is possible to view the low morale of couples attending for marital therapy as indicative of low perceived self-efficacy on the part of one or both partners regarding the achievement of marital satisfaction. The very fact of attending for therapy is a sign that they believe this particular outcome to be beyond their control. By using structured exercises to demonstrate that specific goals can be obtained, the marital therapist is essentially raising their individual and collective expectations concerning their ability to achieve happiness within the relationship.

The personal qualities of effective marital therapists

According to Stuart (1980) the behavioural marital therapist should be prepared to act as a *mediator* when conflicts arise, a *reeducator* where the causes of the problems are being wrongly attributed, a *director* when exercises are to be carried out, a *model* of good communication skills, an occasional *side-taker* when therapy gets 'stuck', and a *celebrant* when success is achieved. Given the nature and number of these therapeutic roles, it is clear that certain individuals will find BMT an easier approach to adopt than others. It is therefore surprising that there are no reports in the behavioural literature of any attempts to systematically tease out the characteristics of effective therapists engaging specifically in marital work. However, it is likely that the following therapist variables, which have been shown to be significant determinants of outcome in individual behaviour therapy, are of relevance here:

(1) the therapist's *confidence* in his approach and his ability to communicate this to his clients (Ryan and Gizynski 1971);
(2) his *flexibility* in terms of adapting his style to suit the particular needs of his clients (Ford and Kendall 1979);
(3) the extent to which he is perceived as *warm* and *empathic* by his clients (Morris and Suckerman 1974), though a cautionary note is warranted here. Since an overly warm approach can be perceived as aversive by certain clients, the optimal social distance for a particular couple should be determined during the assessment stage (Turkat and Brantley 1981) and not assumed in advance by the therapist.

Case example

The clients

Nicholas, an ex-solicitor aged 50, had become depressed within months of taking early retirement. For several years he had been finding it increasingly difficult to cope with the pressures of work and felt that this source of stress was interfering with his ability to meet his wife's emotional needs. He made the decision to retire when it was clear that Veronica, also aged 50, was seriously contemplating divorce. Since they both attributed their marital problems to the demands of his job, it was assumed by them that the domestic situation would improve once he had left it. In fact it deteriorated rapidly after this, with Veronica becoming increasingly frustrated while Nicholas was becoming more and more withdrawn. At this point they were referred by their general practitioner for BMT.

The initial interview

Veronica failed to keep the first appointment and, in a letter to the therapist, explained that she would not agree to come along until there had been 'a marked change in his attitude'. The therapist, in his reply to her, made the point that it would be difficult for him to assess the situation properly in her absence and invited her to attend the next session. She kept this appointment but it immediately became clear that her primary reason for attending was to put the blame on Nicholas for their marital problems. The therapist, in his endeavour to structure the situation and establish a degree of balance, assumed the role of mediator while directing them both to communicate only 'through the chair'. When the level of emotional intensity had dropped sufficiently, he proposed that they focused their energies on evolving a plan for improving one aspect of the marriage forthwith. After voicing her scepticism at such a suggestion, Veronica suggested that they might attempt to sort out their current financial crisis as Nicholas was apparently unwilling to enter into discussions about money. He contradicted this supposition but maintained that this proposal would only be constructive if they could concentrate exclusively on factual matters. In his endeavour to help them engage in a successful collaborative enterprise, the therapist suggested that they held a time-limited meeting, during which Nicholas would present a clear statement of their financial position with Veronica's contributions being restricted to questions of detail.

Behavioural analysis

At the next session, both partners expressed surprise that they had succeeded in accomplishing the task successfully, and reported a significant increase in their morale. Since Veronica expressed a willingness to enter treatment, the therapist began a thorough assessment of their difficulties. From an analysis of recent crises, the following pattern emerged.

Such external factors as an unexpected expense or a 'distress call' from their daughter at university would typically trigger off 'catastrophic' thought processes in Nicholas. The main theme was that he was totally inadequate as a husband, parent and provider and therefore not 'worthy' of Veronica's affection. At the overt behavioural level, his response was to withdraw from her. His silence would lead Veronica to become extremely agitated because of her long-standing inability to tolerate ambiguity in emotional relationships. If he continued to be uncommunicative, she would attribute this to passive aggression on his part and would start to engage in negative emotional discharges. Nicholas would then interpret these criticisms and accusations as confirmatory evidence of his failures and would withdraw still further from her. When eventually Veronica began to threaten divorce, he would plead with her to stay and, with this emotional disclosure, the sequence would come to an end. An important fact to emerge from the analysis was that, in the prolonged absence of the relevant triggers, they were capable of enjoying a mutually satisfying relationship.

Both partners were actively involved in the three assessment sessions and a number of therapeutic gains were achieved at this stage. Instead of seeing Nicholas as entirely to blame for their marital problems, Veronica came to appreciate that her misattribution of his uncommunicative behaviour was causing a difficult situation to deteriorate still further. Nicholas began to see her verbal attacks on him as manifestations of her frustration rather than as evidence of his incompetence. Finally, on being reminded of the positive times they had spent together, they both came to accept that it was not so much a 'bad' marriage as a potentially rewarding relationship which was insufficiently robust to deal with adverse circumstances. Once the therapist and both clients could agree on the formulation of the problem, a treatment contract was drawn up. The primary goal was to enable them to work together to prevent minor set-backs from becoming major crises. It was made explicit that, in order to achieve this, they would be required to attend regularly and carry out a number of homework assignments.

Treatment techniques

Given that they were capable of communicating effectively in the absence of external pressures, the therapist began by tackling the erroneous interpretations which led to uncooperative behaviour on the part of both partners when problems arose. Consequently *cognitive restructuring* was introduced in an endeavour to evolve adaptive self-instructions for coping with stress.

Veronica produced the following message to herself:

'Oh no! He's gone all silent again. I wonder what's going on. Now don't panic. Remember he only goes like this when he's worried about something and feels he's to blame. He's not trying to punish you so don't retaliate. He's taking it out on himself and needs your help to get out of the tangle he's in. Now I wonder what the matter is this time. Ask him gently and be sure to let him know you understand how he feels.'

Nicholas felt unable, at this stage, to develop an effective strategy for countering the feelings of inadequacy brought on by set-backs outside the relationship. However, he was motivated to develop a self-statement to help him to relabel Veronica's negative emotional discharges:

'So she's started attacking me again. Well that's what I deserve, isn't it? Now hold on, remember what she told you. She's only having a go at you because she hates not knowing what's going on. And, let's face it, you have been a bit quiet during the last few days. Why make things even worse for her? I'll tell her what's happened and how that makes me feel.'

The next step was to combine this cognitive intervention with *interpersonal skills training,* by role-playing crises which had been handled badly in the past. Nicholas was helped to disclose negative feelings in an appropriate manner while Veronica was trained to reflect back the emotional content of his statements. Whenever they showed signs of returning to their former patterns of communication, the role-play was interrupted and they were both requested to rehearse their newly acquired self-instructions.

Once they were able to satisfactorily demonstrate their cognitive and interpersonal skills in the treatment context, they were set a series of homework tasks to facilitate generalization to the home situation. They were encouraged to engage in time-limited, structured interactions on a topic chosen by the partner who chose to call the particular meeting. Written instructions were provided, similar to the guidelines for 'executive sessions' (Liberman et al. 1980), to ensure that these emotional interchanges would prove constructive.

Finally, in view of their inability to evolve practical solutions to dealing with finance and family concerns, the couple were given training in *problem solving.* The therapist arranged to hold two 'committee meetings' and invited both partners to submit agenda items which they would be prepared to discuss. Since all the chosen topics had previously been the subject of 'executive sessions', the therapist insisted that the task should be to decide on specific courses of action rather than to continue to ventilate feelings. Once decisions had been taken and implemented, the therapist encouraged them to hold regular 'business meetings' at home to review progress and modify plans where appropriate.

Although treatment proper was terminated after twelve weekly sessions, two follow-up appointments were arranged before they were finally discharged. At the final appointment, both clients maintained not only that the treatment goals had been achieved, but that the quality of their marriage during non-stressful periods had improved significantly as well. The only reservation expressed was that, although they were now better able to deal together with crises, Nicholas was continuing to react inappropriately to minor set-backs. He was given the opportunity to pursue this problem through individual cognitive behaviour therapy, but he declined this offer on the grounds that it was no longer seriously interfering with his life.

The change process

Given Veronica's initial reluctance to enter into conjoint treatment, the therapist was required to impose a tight structure during the initial session, and follow this up with an attainable homework task, in his endeavour to induce a collaborative set. The success of this exercise led to a sudden increase in perceived self-efficacy, on the part of both clients, which increased their motivation to work on the marriage. Although involvement in the behavioural analysis led to a significant cognitive shift, it was apparent that this would only be temporary unless they were provided with more durable and tangible coping strategies. It was also recognized that more adaptive self-instructions were unlikely to be effective so long as their emotional interchanges, in times of crisis, continued to be so non-productive. Consequently it was considered necessary to train them in cognitive and interpersonal skills simultaneously. The problem-solving component was added to encourage Nicholas to approach rather than avoid difficulties, and to reduce the frequency and intensity of future crises by enabling them to plan ahead together.

The behavioural analysis enabled the therapist to take account of internal processes and interactional factors when formulating the problem and deciding on treatment goals and subgoals. Moreover it gave rise to a multi-component treatment programme, with each technique following on logically from its predecessor. Given Veronica's intolerance of ambiguity and her uncertain motivation, it could be argued that the establishment of this structured treatment plan, with its clear underlying rationale, proved to be the factor most responsible for the successful outcome achieved in this case.

References

Ables, B. S. and Brandsma, J. M. (1977) *Therapy for couples.* San Francisco: Jossey-Bass.

Azrin, N. H., Naster, B. J. and Jones, R. (1973) Reciprocity counseling: a rapid learning-based procedure for marital counseling. *Behaviour Research and Therapy, 11,* 365–382.

Bandura, A. (1969) *Principles of behaviour modification.* New York: Holt, Rinehart and Winston.

Bandura, A. (1977) Self-efficacy: toward a unifying theory of behavioural change. *Psychological Review, 84,* 191–215

Bandura, A. (1978) The self system in reciprocal determinism. *American Psychologist, 33,* 344–358.

Birchler, G. (1979) Communication skills in married couples. *In* A. Bellack and M. Hersen (eds) *Research and practice in social skills training.* New York: Plenum.

Birchler, G., Weiss R. L. and Vincent J. P. (1975) A multi method analysis of social reinforcement exchange between mentally distressed and non-distressed spouse and stranger dyads. *Journal of Personality and Social Psychology, 31,* 349–360.

Cobb, J., McDonald, R., Marks, I. and Stern, R. (1980) Marital versus exposure therapy: psychological treatments of co-existing marital and phobic-obsessive problems. *European Journal of Behavioural Analysis and Modification, 4,* 3–17.

Doherty, W. J. (1981) Cognitive processes in intimate conflict: II. Efficacy and learned helplessness. *American Journal of Family Therapy, 9,* 35–44.

Eidelson, R. J. and Epstein, N. (1982) Cognition and relationship maladjustment: development of a measure of dysfunctional relationship beliefs. *Journal of Consulting and Clinical Psychology, 50,* 715–720.

Fisher, B. L. and Sprenkle, D. H. (1978) Therapists' perceptions of healthy family functioning. *International Journal of Family Counseling, 6,* 9–18.

Ford, J. D. and Kendall, P. C. (1979) Behaviour therapists' professional behaviours: converging evidence of a gap between theory and practice. *The Behavior Therapist, 2,* 37–38.

Goldfried, M. R., Decenteceo, E. T. and Weinberg, L. (1974) Systematic rational restructuring as a self-control technique. *Behavior Therapy, 5,* 247–254.

Gottman, J., Markman, H. and Notarius, C. (1977) The topography of marital con-

For those interested in acquiring or developing skills in BMT, training courses are organized regularly by the British Association for Behavioural Psychotherapy and Psychotherapy Workshops.

flict: a sequential analysis of verbal and nonverbal behavior. *Journal of Marriage and the Family, 39,* 461–477.

Gurman, A. S. and Kniskern, D. P. (1978) Behavioral marriage therapy: II. Empirical perspective. *Family Process, 17,* 139–148.

HMSO *Figures produced by the Registrar General for 'The Committee on the Age of Majority'* (1967) Appendix 8, Cmnd 3342.

Hughdahl, K. (1981) The three-systems model of fear and emotion – a critical examination. *Behaviour Research and Therapy, 19,* 75–86.

Hurvitz, N. (1970) Interaction hypothesis in marriage counseling. *The Family Coordinator, 19,* 64–75.

Jacobson, N. S. (1978) A review of the research on the effectiveness of marital therapy. *In* T. J. Paolino and B. S. McCrady (eds) *Marriage and marital therapy: psychoanalytic, behavioral and systems theory perspectives.* New York: Brunner/Mazel.

Jacobson, N. S. (1984) A component analysis of behavioral marital therapy: the relative effectiveness of behavior exchange and communication/problem-solving training. *Journal of Consulting and Clinical Psychology, 52,* 295–305.

Jacobson, N. S. and Margolin, G. (1979) *Marital therapy: strategies based on social learning and behavior exchange principles.* New York: Brunner/Mazel.

Kanfer, F. H. and Phillips, J. S. (1970) *Learning foundations of behavior therapy.* New York: Wiley.

Knudson, R. M., Gurman, A. S. and Kniskern, D. P. (1978) Behavioral marriage therapy: a treatment in transition. *Family Process, 17,* 121–138.

Lazarus, A. A. (1963) The treatment of chronic frigidity by systematic desensitization. *Journal of Nervous and Mental Disease, 136,* 272–278.

Liberman, R. P., Wheeler, E. G., de Visser, L. A. J. M., Kuehnel, J. and Kuehnel, T. (1980) *Handbook of marital therapy, a positive approach to helping troubled relationships.* New York: Plenum.

Mackay, D. (1975) *Clinical psychology: theory and therapy.* London: Methuen Essential Psychology Series.

Mackay, D. (1983) Principles of learning. *In* M. Weller (ed.) *The scientific basis of psychiatry.* London: Bailliere Tindall.

Mackay, D. (1984) Behavioural psychotherapy *In* W. Dryden (ed.) *Individual therapy in Britain.* London: Harper and Row.

Mackay, D. (1985, forthcoming) Social and interpersonal difficulties. *In* H. Lettner and B. Range (eds) *Handbook of behavioural psychotherapy.* Brazil: Editora Pedagogica e Universitaria.

Margolin, G. and Weiss, R. L. (1978) Comparative evaluation of therapeutic components associated with behavioral marital treatment. *Journal of Consulting and Clinical Psychology, 46,* 1476–1486.

Markman, H. (1979) The application of a behavioral model of marriage in predicting relationship satisfaction of couples planning marriage. *Journal of Consulting and Clinical Psychology, 47,* 743–749.

Masters, W. H. and Johnson, V. E. (1970) *Human sexual inadequacy*. Boston: Little, Brown and Co.

McPherson, F. M., Brougham, L. and McLaren, L. (1980) Maintenance of improvements in agoraphobic patients treated by behavioural methods in a four year follow up. *Behaviour Research and Therapy*, *18*, 150-152.

Mehlman, S. K., Baucom, D. H. and Anderson, D. (1983) Effectiveness of cotherapists versus single therapists and immediate versus delayed treatment in behavioral marital therapy. *Journal of Consulting and Clinical Psychology*, *51*, 258-266.

Meichenbaum, D. H. (1977) *Cognitive-behavior modification*. New York: Plenum.

Morris, R. J. and Suckerman, K. R. (1974) The importance of the therapeutic relationship in systematic desensitization. *Journal of Consulting and Clinical Psychology*, *42*, 147.

Ryan, V. L. and Gizynski, M. N. (1971) Behavior therapy in retrospect: patients' feelings about their behavior therapists. *Journal of Consulting and Clinical Psychology*, *37*, 1-9.

Satir, V. (1967) *Conjoint family therapy*. Palo Alto, California: Science and Behavior Books.

Stuart, R. B. (1969) Operant interpersonal treatment for marital discord. *Journal of Consulting and Clinical Psychology*, *33*, 675-682.

Stuart, R. B. (1980) *Helping couples change: a social learning approach to marital therapy*. New York: Guilford.

Thibaut, J. W. and Kelley, H. H. (1959) *The social psychology of groups*. New York: Wiley.

Turkat, I. D. and Brantley, P. J. (1981) On the therapeutic relationship in behavior therapy. *The Behavior Therapist*, *4*, 16.

Walen, S. R. (1980) Cognitive factors in sexual behavior. *Journal of Sex and Marital Therapy*, *6*, 87-101.

Weiss, R. L., Birchler, G. R. and Vincent, J. P. (1974) Contractual models for negotiation training in marital dyads. *Journal of Marriage and the Family*, *36*, 321-331.

Weiss, R. L., Hops, H. and Patterson, G. R. (1973) A framework for conceptualizing marital conflict, a technology for altering it, some data for evaluating it. *In* L. A. Hamlynck, L. C. Handy and E. J. Nash (eds) *Behavior change: methodology, concepts, and practice*. Champaign, Illinois: Research Press.

Wills, T. A., Weiss, R. L. and Patterson, G. R. (1974) A behavioral analysis of the determinants of marital satisfaction. *Journal of Consulting and Clinical Psychology*, *42*, 802-811.

Wolpe, J. (1958) *Psychotherapy by reciprocal inhibition*. Stanford: Stanford University Press.

CHAPTER ELEVEN   Working with Marital Partners
Systems Approaches
Andy Treacher

Historical context and developments in Britain

In 1983 Jay Haley was asked to be principal speaker at the American Association for Marriage and Family Therapy's annual conference. His talk 'Marriage *or* Family Therapy' was decidedly controversial since he cast doubt on the wisdom of regarding the two as synonymous activities (Rohrbaugh 1984). Instead he was at pains to stress the historical, conceptual and professional differences between them. Haley argued that despite its forty to fifty years of existence the marriage counselling movement in America had had little influence on the development of either family therapy or the therapy field in general.

Haley assumes that this lack of influence is due to an inherent weakness in the approach adopted by marriage counsellors. Haley insists that they have typically committed the error of focusing too much attention on the marital dyad and too little attention on the wider family systems which inevitably impinge upon it (and vice versa). Haley assumes that the marital dyad is an inherently unstable social unit so any attempt to understand couples in isolation is like building castles on the sand. Haley's own position (explored, for example, in Chapter 6 of his classic book, 'Problem Solving Therapy' 1976) is founded on the belief that problems between marital partners must invariably involve coalitions with third parties – parents, children, lovers and even, in more complicated cases, therapists.

I think that most systems-oriented family therapists will tend to agree with Haley's position. For most of us, marriage is indeed a family affair. But if we are to accept this position, it becomes very difficult to undertake the writing of this chapter because, in a very fundamental sense, it is a nonsense to talk about systems approaches to marital therapy. A thoroughgoing systems therapist would be grossly inconsistent to her theoretical position if she were to focus attention solely on the behaviour of marital partners, because it is inherent and implicit in systems thinking that it is impossible to isolate the behaviour of one part of a system from the behaviour of other parts of that system. Since the marital partners inevitably come from two different families of origin which become connected to each other through the marriage, a systems theorist needs to develop ways of understanding how the behaviour of the marital partners both is contingent upon the behaviour of other parts of the wider family system, and at the same time contributes to the behaviour of the other parts of the system.

This point in turn helps to explain a very interesting fact – that with one notable exception there seems to be no extant textbook of marital therapy written by a major systems theorist (although there are a number of handbooks of marital therapy, e.g. L'Abate and McHenry 1983). The exception is Lederer and Jackson's book *The mirages of marriage* (1968). This book really requires more attention than I can give it in this chapter but its prime importance lies in its attempt to provide a classification of the basic modes of relationship that can exist between a couple. Don Jackson was, of course, a notable pioneer in the development of systems theory ideas but the book is very narrow in its vision since it fails to deal with transgenerational issues. The thrust of the book is to explore the thematic games that couples get caught up in and it is, therefore, quite similar to Berne's famous book *Games People Play* (1964). In my opinion Jackson's book ultimately fails at a theoretical level precisely because it attempts to deal with the marital system in isolation. Systems theory ideas are explored in the book but since its main emphasis is on marriage as a state involving continual bargaining and negotiating (and the main thrust of the therapeutic interventions discussed involves the use of quid pro quo techniques) it could be legitimately argued that the approach is closer to behavioural marital therapy and even educational approaches than 'genuine' systems theory approaches.

It is for these reasons that I will not attempt to explore the history of systemic approaches to marital problems – instead I will attempt to summarize some of the main systems theory ideas that family therapists have found useful in developing their work with marital partners. This policy may at first sight seem rather cavalier but it is salutary to note that there have also been no major developments of systems approaches to marital therapy in Britain.[1] Marital therapy has remained influenced mainly by psychodynamic or Rogerian ideas, although it is important to point out that there are some minor exceptions to this rule. For example, the monograph *The Melancholy Marriage* by my former colleagues, Mary Hinchcliffe, Douglas Hooper and John Roberts (1978), did attempt to develop systems-oriented ideas. The book reports on a project which explored the interpersonal dynamics of marriages in which one partner was depressed. Unfortunately the book is essentially research oriented and is not a handbook for therapists. Therapists have, therefore, probably neglected it despite its many useful insights

Systems theory perspectives and the nature of marital disturbance

As Steinglass (1978) has pointed out in his review of marriage from a systems perspective, the ideas that are normally described as 'systemic' are in fact loosely connected and it is therefore impossible to talk of systems theory as a fully integrated perspective. It is, perhaps, more appropriate to talk about systems theorizing as a style or method of thinking about complex relational processes than as a substantiative body of theory which is capable of making specific predictions about how a given system will behave.

Sue Walrond-Skinner (1976) in her very cogent introduction to systems theory ideas makes a similar point but she provides us with an important rationale for understanding the state of confusion that prevails:

> Currently the conceptual framework underpinning family therapy continues to be a matter of some confusion and considerable debate – the problem being chiefly focussed around the difficulty of evolving a theory that is both 'pure' enough to be universal and yet is capable of application to the diversity of the clinical situation. It is therefore difficult to create a synthesis out of the welter of theoretical standpoints that exist, and if one were to succeed in distilling a pure and all embracing theory of the family, such an attempt would necessarily involve a high level of abstraction. (p. 11)

Many of the originators of the family therapy movement turned to General Systems Theory (GST) as a means to solve the theoretical problems that confronted them as they attempted to broaden the focus of their attention from individuals to the families and networks in which they were inextricably caught up. GST was developed prior to the Second World War by Ludwig von Bertalanffy but it did not begin to influence therapists until the late 1940s and early 1950s. Von Bertalanffy's attempt to produce a new paradigm or method of theorizing which could explain the behaviour of all types of interactional systems had an immediate appeal to a diverse group of theorists and practitioners (including Gregory Bateson, Roy Grinker, Jay Haley, Don Jackson and John Weakland) who were attempting to escape from the impasse in practice and theory which they were experiencing at that time. Learning-theory ideas were in their infancy and had not been seriously applied to clinical problems. Psychiatry was dominated either by the medical model or by psychoanalytic ideas. Both approaches conspired (for different reasons) to prevent or impede the development of interactional frameworks that could examine behaviour patterns as they occurred, second by second, in the here and now. Von Bertalanffy's work, together with parallel work in operations research, cybernetics, gestalt psychology and mathematical GST, helped create a new intellectual mood in which theoreticians could abandon the strait-jacket of assuming that dysfunctional forms of behaviour must be the sole property of individuals rather than a resultant of the interplay between individuals and the complex social and physical environments that impinge upon them.

Von Bertalanffy attempted in his work to provide a unifying theoretical framework for both the natural sciences and the social sciences. He has been correctly criticized for being overambitious; nevertheless many of his ideas have been extremely valuable to family therapists. I will therefore attempt to briefly review the major concepts that have proved most valuable in helping family therapists understand the interactional properties of both families and couples. My discussion draws heavily on the excellent review provided by Sue Walrond-Skinner (1976).

System

A system can be defined as a 'set of objects together with the relationships between the objects and between their attributes. The objects are the component parts of the system, the attributes are the properties of the objects and the relationships tie the system together' (Hall and Fagen 1956 – cited by Walrond-Skinner 1976, p. 13).

GST has also developed a series of new terms which enable us to talk about the relationships that a system has with other systems and with its own 'interior' parts. Thus the term 'suprasystem' is used to describe the environment surrounding a system while the term 'subsystem' is used to describe a component within the system. So it would be possible, in GST language, to talk about a couple being a subsystem of a system – their nuclear family, which could include, for example, their two children. The two children are referred to as the 'sibling subsystem', while the couple can be referred to as the 'marital subsystem' or the 'parental subsystem'. The suprasystem of the family will include the families of origin of the two partners but we may wish to include neighbours and other social groups as part and parcel of this suprasystem.

Hierarchy

These three terms (suprasystem, system and subsystem) are used by systems theorists because they reflect a major feature of systems theorizing – its stress on the issue of *hierarchy*. It is assumed that most systems function in a hierarchical way with certain subsystems having an executive function in relation to others. For example, if we apply this idea to a family it is assumed, at least by a wide range of theorists including Minuchin (1974), that a well-functioning family will have an effective executive subsystem (the parents) who will be responsible for the main decision making within the family. If the siblings take over executive functioning it is assumed that the family is in trouble because children are ill-equipped and ill-prepared for the onerous tasks of parenting. (Obviously such a view is laden with value judgements but it is important to stress that GST, despite its apparently 'objective' and 'scientific' terminology, is no less value-laden than any other theory of human behaviour.)

If we talk about the parents as being the executive subsystem of the family it is confusing to retain the term suprasystem to describe the systems that impinge on the family. The simpler term 'wider' system is now more properly used to describe groupings that are not part and parcel of the family. However, this change in terminology should not distract us from understanding that the interaction between the wider system of the family and the subsystems within a family are reciprocal and not unidirectional. In other words, there may be a hierarchy of relations but at the same time, to use Koestler's description, 'the functional units on every level of the hierarchy are double-faced as it were; they act as a whole when facing downwards, as parts when facing upwards' (Walrond-Skinner 1976, p. 12).

Boundaries

The concept of a boundary has been developed in order to provide a description of how systems and subsystems interface with each other. It is the system's boundary that largely determines its identity since it is the boundary that controls the way that the system influences and is influenced by other systems and subsystems. Minuchin (1974) utilizes the concept of a boundary to enable him to discuss the different types of family system that he has encountered in the course of his work. Every family system has a set of subsystems that contribute to its overall structure. These subsystems are given various labels – parental, grandparental, spouse, sibling, parent–

child, male–female – but the functioning of the subsystems is crucially related to the nature of the boundary that demarcates them from other subsystems. Minuchin uses the term 'clear boundary' to describe a boundary which allows unimpeded two-way communication to occur across it. A 'rigid boundary' is one which involves blocked or non-existent communication, while a 'diffuse boundary' is one that has become so permeable that the two subsystems on either side in a sense coalesce.

Minuchin assumes that all families can in fact be located along a continuum which stretches from disengaged families (with rigid boundaries) at one end to enmeshed families (with diffuse boundaries) at the other, as the following table demonstrates.

Type of Boundary	Rigid	Clear	Diffuse
Type of Family	Disengaged	'Normal' Range	Enmeshed

This classification of families has some value, but it is commonplace to find families that have rigid, clear and diffuse boundaries all within the same family structure. It is therefore useful for conceptual reasons to consider that families can exist in a kind of triangular space as Figure 11.1 demonstrates.

A family located at point A would be one which contains all three types of boundary; the family at B contains predominantly rigid and diffuse boundaries; the family at C clear and rigid boundaries; D clear and enmeshed. But the families at E, F and G, are 'pure' types in which the boundaries are either diffuse or clear or rigid.

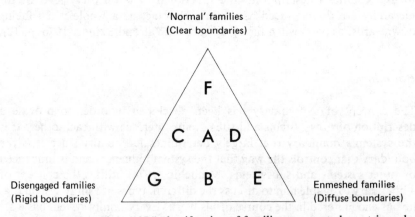

Figure 11.1 Minuchin's (1974) classification of families represented as a triangular space.

This method of conceptualizing the boundaries makes for greater flexibility in interpreting the complexity of family structures that are encountered in everyday practice. However, there is a major normative assumption implicit in Minuchin's approach. He assumes in a straightforward, no-nonsense way that clear boundaries make for effective family functioning. Clear boundaries are assumed by him to allow the overall family system to grow and differentiation to occur within and between the subsystems. Every family subsystem is assumed to have specific functions and to make specific demands on its members. However, the development of interpersonal skills that can be achieved within these subsystems is dependent on subsystem's freedom from interference from other subsystems. For example, a parent who never allows his children (aged 10 and 12) out of the house unaccompanied by an adult will effectively deskill them and prevent them from growing up.

A family therapist working with such a family could attempt to deal with such a diffuse boundary by getting the parent and the children to negotiate new rules which would regulate, for example, how and when the children could visit friends or report back when they were delayed by activities at school. If the parent can be helped to achieve a new flexibility in relation to such issues then the children can also be helped to achieve a greater degree of responsibility in coping with activities outside the home.

The concept of a boundary is also crucial in enabling us to discuss more general properties of systems. Here the terms 'open' and 'closed' systems require explanation. An open system is one which is surrounded by a 'clear' boundary which enables that system to exchange materials, energies or information with its environment. A 'closed' system is (as the word implies) one which is shut off from transactions with its environment because of the rigid boundary that surrounds it When we apply these terms to families we are alerted to the rather obvious fact that there is a continuum ranging from relatively open family systems (exemplified by families who show a high degree of reciprocity with their own kin, other families and the community at large) to relatively closed families (who show a minimal level of interchange with 'outside' groupings).

Wholeness

One of the most crucial GST concepts is *wholeness*. Crudely put this states that a system is a whole and the behaviour of its parts or components cannot be understood in isolation from that total system. A related principle, non-summativity, states that a whole is greater than the sum of its part. This idea (shared by gestalt psychology) forces us to acknowledge that analysing the behaviour of individual parts or components of a system in isolation from each other is fruitless – our theorizing needs to reflect the fact that a system can produce 'emergent' characteristics that cannot be produced by isolated elements of that system by themselves. To take a very obvious example – a car is a relatively inert system whose behaviour is highly predictable. But if we add a driver to the car (producing a new system – driver plus car) we then have a system whose behaviour is unique and cannot be predicted by the study of either the car or the driver in isolation from each other.

Homeostasis

This term literally means 'same state' – a 'same' or 'steady' state is achieved if a system has the ability to monitor and control its relationship with its environment in such a way that any changes in this relationship are counter-balanced by changes within the system itself. The classic example used by systems theorists to communicate this idea is the thermostatically controlled central heating system found in most modern houses. The thermostat is the key regulator of the system since any positive or negative deviation from the temperature at which the thermostat is set results in a deviation-reducing message being sent out by the thermostat. For instance, if the outside temperature of the house falls, the thermostat control triggers the boiler to fire; if the outside temperature rises, the thermostat inhibits the boiler from firing. (If the temperature rise was very great, an 'ideal' system would turn on an air-conditioning system which would actively lower the internal temperature of the house.)

Obviously the use of the term 'homeostatic' to describe the functioning of a family system is by no means straightforward. A central heating system is (at least in the short term) effectively a closed system which only 'trans-acts' actively with its environment through the input of fuel and through exchanges involving its temperature sensor. How can a family system be convincingly compared with such a system? A number of commentators, including Speer (1970), Dell (1982) and even von Bertalanffy (1972) himself, have wrestled with this issue, but there is now a general consensus, articu-lated by Walrond-Skinner (1976), that the application of the term to family systems requires very careful thought:

'Homeostasis' does not imply something set and immobile and stagnation. It means a condition - a condition which may vary but which is relatively constant. Clearly the healthy functional family system requires a measure of homeostasis in order to survive the 'slings and arrows of outrageous fortune' and to maintain stability and security within its physical and social environment. It is only when these mechanisms 'over-function' that the system becomes fixed and dysfunctional in its rigidity. (pp. 14–15)

So the type of homeostasis we are talking about is a state of dynamic equilibrium which may be different at different stages in the lifecycle. This point can be illustrated by again referring to Walrond-Skinner's argument. She uses an excellent example to demonstrate the complex nature of homeostatic mechanisms within a family system:

A family is faced with several external threats to its survival ... Mother has to be hospitalised ... and father has to find a new job (following unemployment). The family would need the assistance of homeostatic mechanisms to 'regulate' it in this crisis situation and might, for example, require the eldest daughter to take over some of mother's practical and emotional functions during her absence. She might need to be more 'maternal' to her younger siblings and more supportive and companionable to her father in his own insecurity. In this situation the daughter's role changes would act as useful homeostatic mechanisms. (p. 15)

Obviously a number of different scenarios could develop from this point. If mother's illness has been extensive then a real problem may arise if she attempts to take up her role of wife and mother again. Father's affection may now have been strongly pulled towards his daughter and away from his wife so that a major marital problem has now arisen. It is likely in such a situation that either the mother or the daughter will begin to develop a symptom (such as agoraphobia) which will serve to mask the underlying marital difficulties that are occurring. The family's energies may then get directed to helping the (identified) patient who now has a worrying and persistent symptom. Helping agencies may get drawn into the situation and attempt to 'cure' the agoraphobia and yet the underlying marital difficulty may be carefully concealed from them.

Walrond-Skinner's example (which I have presented in a slightly different way in order to bring out some of the theoretical possibilities implicit in it) focuses our attention once again on the weaknesses inherent in using the term 'homeostatic mechanism' to describe the complex changes occurring in this family system. Walrond-Skinner suggests that many of the difficulties can be surmounted by using Wertheim's alternative terminology. Wertheim (1973) abandons the term homeostasis as being too confusing and instead replaces it with two terms which reflect the two-sided process that is implicit in the term:

> *Consensual morphostasis* derives from approximately balanced intra-family distribution of power. The term refers to genuine stability of the family system, consensually inhibited by its members. *Forced morphostasis* is rooted in intra-family power imbalance. The term ... refers to apparent stability of the family system maintained in the absence of genuine consensual validation by its members. (Wertheim 1973 – cited by Walrond-Skinner 1976, p. 16)

Clearly the failure (in the example) of the wife/mother to reenter her normal roles when she returned to the family would be an example of forced morphostasis. This process would take place mostly outside family members' consciousness since in the mother's absence a new unspoken rule had been generated: in this family a daughter becomes a wife/mother when the wife/mother is absent and the father feels isolated and insecure.

Morphogenesis

Wertheim's attempt to replace the rather mechanistic (and deterministic) term homeostasis is valuable but, as Walrond-Skinner (1976) points out, other theorists such as Speer (1970) have attempted to challenge the use of the term at a more fundamental level. Speer has attempted to popularize the idea of morphogenesis. The term literally means 'generating changes in structure' – during a morphogenic change a system will show an increase in the degree of differentiation between its component parts so each part increases its complexity of functioning and yet the system still survives as a coherent whole.

Speer does not abandon the use of the term homeostasis entirely since he wishes to retain its use in order to reflect some features of the systems he is attempting to describe. He therefore attempts to combine his new notion of morphogenesis with the older idea of homeostasis. In doing so he introduces a third term 'viability' which is used to describe the essential character of complex social systems such as families. The term viability is in practice somewhat loosely defined, as the following quotation reveals:

> While equilibrium is the fundamental principle of organic chemical and mechanical systems; and homeostasis is the basic principle of lower and higher biological and organismic systems; *viability* with the implication of inherent capacities for growth and self-directed change is the criterion principle for social systems. (Speer 1970 – cited by Walrond-Skinner 1976, pp. 16–17)

So the term viability attempts to summarize a system's ability to maintain structure and yet change structure at the same time. A healthy and functional family is able to maintain an appropriate balance between these countervailing tendencies; but it is essential to add that wider cultural and societal forces impinge on families as they move through their life cycle (Haley 1973), so there is a constant necessity for a family to adapt and change to external forces.

Communication within and between systems

In order to discuss how systems components interact it is necessary, as Walrond-Skinner (1976) points out, to introduce ideas from communication theory. The most salient idea is that systems exchange not energy but information. But exchanges of information are essentially reciprocal and involve feedback loops. This means that components within a system are assumed to be always caught up in a process which involves them in mutually affecting each other. In GST terms, transactions are therefore viewed as circular (A affects B, B affects A which affects B) rather than straightforwardly linear (A affects B). However, feedback is characterized as being either negative or positive. Negative feedback to a system is used to trigger off homeostatic mechanisms which decrease the system's output, while positive feedback involves an information flow which upsets the normally occurring homeostatic mechanisms. At this point morphogenic mechanisms come into play which allow the system to reach a higher state of differentiation and growth. Positive feedback is therefore deviation amplifying but it does carry with it the danger of inducing a runaway situation in which the whole structure of the system may be disrupted.

Circular patterns of interaction – circular explanations of behaviour

Since GST postulates that communication patterns are of the A → B type and not the A → B type, it is axiomatic to the approach that linear (cause and effect) explanations of behaviour are abandoned. Walrond-Skinner (1976) gives us a neat example of the force of this argument by considering the case of a family which attributes its current difficulties solely to the fact that the son of the family, Johnny, has been stealing:

> [The] family may see Johnny and his delinquency as the 'cause' of their distress, forgetting that Johnny's stealing may be reactive to his mother's

emotional absence, which may be reactive to her husband's harsh handling of Johnny ... (p. 21)

GST insists that we should attempt to analyse behaviour patterns in this way – adopting this approach enables us to avoid blaming individuals while at the same time acknowledging that every participant in the family system contributes to the process which ends up with Johnny stealing. The abandonment of linear causality therefore allows us to abandon the type of pejorative blaming stances which tended to dog the early evolution of ideas within the family therapy movement. (Fromm-Reichmann's (1948) hypothesis that schizophrenia is caused by 'schizophrenogenic' mothers is an example of this type of theorizing which is best forgotten.)

Symptom formation within the framework of GST

We have already discovered that GST postulates that a symptom can arise within a family system when homeostatic mechanisms are operating in order to effectively reduce the family's ability to be flexible and increase its process of differentiation. However, this formulation is rather vague and imprecise. Communication theory ideas (which have been incorporated into GST) enable us to describe symptoms in new ways. A family that is dysfunctional and in need of help can be viewed as suffering from a breakdown in its normal self-correcting (and growth-embracing) feedback processes. Disruptions may have occurred in the way that family members transact with each other but often there is also a basic disruption in the family's transactions with its wider system.

Walrond-Skinner (1976) has succinctly summarized the types of disruption in communication that occur in such situations:

> ... communication can be either *blocked* ... [or] ... *displaced*. With the first possibility, transactions between family members or between the family and the outside world may have become reduced to the extremes of prolonged silence, withdrawal, isolation or to bizarre written communication ... The possibility of growth and change is drastically reduced by the blocking off of feedback mechanism ... Silence and withdrawal is, of course, a form of communication – but when variety is reduced to this one type communication channels have become severely blocked. A less extreme example is the family *secret* ... Family members are at pains to protect the 'secret' and collude with each other ... Any diversionary tactic is useful in maintaining the secret – a particularly effective one being the heavy scapegoating of a marginally involved family member ...
> Displacement occurs through the eruption of symptomatology – the selec-

tion of the symptom and the symptom bearer becoming highly significant means of communication between family members. The symptom becomes a displaced means of communicating an important trust about the family group ... (pp. 20–21)

Walrond-Skinner adds a third category ('damaged' communication) to her list but this category is unsatisfactory principally because she uses the example of the double bind to illustrate it. The original formulation of the double bind (Bateson et al. 1956) was based on the idea that every communicated message has two levels – a report level which deals with the information being communicated, and a command level which conveys a message about how the information being communicated is to be received and acted upon. Damaged communication arises when the two levels are not congruent. A classic example of a double bind is demonstrated by the following scenario involving the mother of a schizophrenic son – the mother asks her son for an embrace (at a verbal level) while giving postural clues that she cannot bear to be embraced by him. Her son is placed in an impossible situation since to respond to one level of communication is to fail to respond to the other. If we also postulate that the son has not got the ability to comment on the discrepancy of the two messages (because that is an essential feature of the process of 'schizophrenia induction') then we have a plausible explanation of how paralysing the process can be.

Sadly, empirical research has not been able to confirm or disconfirm this hypothesis in a definitive way (Berger 1978) but the hypothesis has undoubtedly been of great value in prompting therapists to concentrate on correcting the dysfunctional communication patterns of families and couples.

Applying systems thinking to marital relationships

The systems ideas that I have explored so far have not been specifically aimed at understanding the interactional processes which are unique to marriages and marital problems. This section of the chapter will, therefore, attempt to explore how a systems-oriented theorist would approach a marital problem. Most of the section will be based on Feldman's short paper 'Depression and marital interaction' (1976). This is an excellent example of sophisticated systems thinking but there is an additional reason why I have chosen to explore his work – Feldman is very appealing to me as a theoretician and practitioner because, unlike more dyed in-the-wool systems theorists, he is intent upon developing a sophisticated theory which integrates ideas derived from systemic, behavioural and psychodynamic frameworks. Gurman (1978) in his important article comparing contemporary marital therapies predicted that while these three basic orientations might well persist for some time there would eventually be a blending of them to produce different combinations and permutations. Feldman's work is therefore important, since it represents one of the first attempts to achieve this integration (Feldman 1976, 1979; Feldman and Pinsof 1982).

Obviously Feldman's approach is not a 'pure' systems approach of the type advocated by Palazzoli and her co-workers (Palazzoli et al. 1978) but family systems ideas are central to his formulation. This can best be discussed by considering the flow diagram which Feldman used to clarify his model (see Figure 11.2).

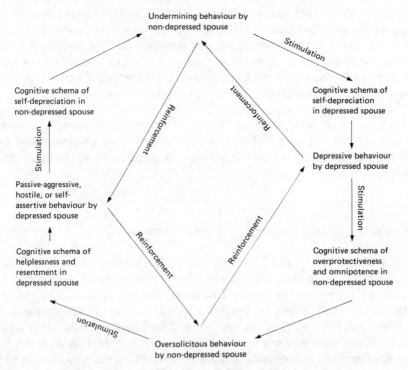

Figure 11.2 Feldman's (1976) diagram showing the interlocking behaviours of a depressed and a non-depressed spouse

This diagram shows the pattern of reciprocal stimulation and reinforcement that occur within a marital system that is permeated by depression. It is hypothesized that the depressed partner's current patterns of reciprocal interaction with his or her partner exert a powerful effect in triggering and maintaining the depression. The process is circular rather than linear since it is assumed that the causality is mutual and of the type $A \rightleftharpoons B$ rather than $A \rightarrow B$ and it is valuable in helping us understand the 'locked-in', cyclical nature of depression. Feldman makes this point by mobilizing some of the key concepts of systems theory, as the following brief quotation from his paper illustrates:

> From the point of view of family-systems theory, the depressed patient is a part of a complex and interlocking system of behaviour, cognition and affects. In any such system, the whole is more than the sum of its parts. (Lederer and Jackson, 1968). The additional dimensions are the multiple and complex relationships among the parts and between each part and the whole. The relationships are governed by implicit or explicit relationship rules(Jackson, 1965) that serve to define the structure of the relationship. The relationship rules are inferred from observable patterns of repetitive familial interaction in which family members reciprocally stimulate and reinforce each other's behaviour. Internal stability (homeostasis) is maintained by negative (deviation-counteracting) feedback, while system change (morphogenesis) is brought about by positive (deviation-amplifying) feedback (Speer, 1970). (Feldman 1976, p. 390)

Feldman's quotation is very succinct and to the point but some of the ideas it contains require some elaboration. In particular, the idea that marriage is a rule-governed phenomenon needs further expansion. Lederer and Jackson (1968) in an important section of their book initially explore the issue by considering how the interaction between a hypothetical couple can be discussed both legitimately and illegitimately:

> We cannot say, 'Mr. Jones will light a cigarette at 8.00pm Sunday evening and Mrs. Jones will give him hell because he is smoking on the Sabbath'. We *can* say that the Joneses have an interacting rule-governed system, one particular quid pro quo of which is his right to violate certain of their shared principles in return for allowing her to feel superior to him and to express that feeling in criticism. We can, then, describe rules which indicate the probable outcome of the interactions of a married pair, but not the particular acts the couple perform or the specific events or contingencies which may occur in the marriage. (p. 95)

At present there is far too little research that enables us to understand how these relationship rules are built up, but Lederer and Jackson offer us a somewhat schematic understanding of it:

At first the [newlywed] man and woman randomly exchange a wide variety of behaviour; eventually they work out mutually acceptable ways of labelling and of interrelating their behaviour, so that each individual feels he [sic] is an equal. In a workable marriage . . . the maladaptive patterns die out. If both develop a satisfactory relationship by the time the marriage is some years old they probably will have forgotten this period of probing, vacillation and behavioural juggling, and they probably will not recall the action-reaction complexities. (p. 95)

Lederer and Jackson's presentation of the 'behavioural exploration' which takes place between the couple at the beginning of a relationship is relatively straightforward but it lacks the subtlety and sophistication of the work of some other theorists. For example, Sager's well-developed therapeutic approach (Sager 1981), which hinges around a detailed exploration of the explicit and implicit contracts that are established by a couple in the course of maintaining their relationship, is far richer. However, Lederer and Jackson's contribution is valuable since it does address a crucial feature of marital interaction – typically couples do eventually establish reciprocal patterns of behaviour which are predictable and rule-governed. In order to communicate this idea, Lederer and Jackson use the heating-system analogy which I have discussed earlier in this chapter:

Weiner [who first coined the term 'cybernetics'] felt that randomly distributed objects or particles in a state of rhythmic oscillation can affect one another through interactions, these interactions between them generally consisting of a feedback of information that tends to stabilize the system. In an 'error-activated system' overdeviation is corrected by what is known as negative feedback. A good example is the thermostat of a furnace. As soon as the heat drops below, let us say, 68 degrees, an electrical impulse activates the furnace which goes on and brings the temperature of the room back to 68. Married couples may act upon each other in just such a fashion and thus keep the deviations of behaviour within their marriage to a comfortable range. (p. 95)

This quote is extremely interesting from a theoretical point of view since it serves to illustrate both the strengths and weaknesses of systems thinking. To say that a married couple act upon each other in 'the same fashion' as the parts of a heating system requires far more discussion and justification than Lederer and Jackson allow. Comparing an open system with a closed system is extremely hazardous but it is, nevertheless, worth while if the comparison enables us to understand, for example, the ways in which a couple disallow certain options open to them and hence reduce the potential freedom of action that is theoretically within their grasp. Societal and family pressures that operate in order to keep a couple married (rather than seeking the option of divorce) may mean that it becomes realistic to consider their system as a relatively closed one. This in turn enables us to understand why they begin to establish sequential patterns of behaviour which are relatively fixed and predictable.

The important theoretical contribution that Feldman (1976) makes is to correct the mechanistic failings of systems theory by insisting that the behaviour of one individual does not just trigger the behaviour of another and vice versa. Such a view ignores the crucial issue that all human behaviour is mediated by cognitive processes. He, therefore, draws heavily on the work of Beck (1967) in order to flesh out the bones of the systems theory framework that he has adopted. Referring again to his basic flow diagram, Feldman elaborates his argument as follows:

> Complementary cognitive structures (schemata) in *both* spouses are triggered in the course of their interaction and lead to repetitive patterns of reciprocal stimulation and reinforcement. In such a circular pattern of interaction, each particular behaviour is simultaneously a stimulus (of the succeeding cognitive schemata and behaviour of the other), a response (to the preceding behaviour of the other and to one's own cognitive schemata) and a reinforcer (of the preceding sequence of behaviour by self and other). (p. 390)

If I explore this rather abstract statement in relation to Feldman's diagram I find that I can discuss some of the typical loops it contains using a much richer language than before, although, as I will argue later on, I feel that Feldman's conceptualizations are at times unnecessarily linear and intrapsychic. His discussion of the loops within his diagram are very much to the point so I again quote him in some detail:

> The non-depressed spouse's undermining behaviour is generally an 'innocent' remark or act that 'just happens' to strike at a particularly sensitive spot in the depressed spouse's shaky sense of self-worth. This leads to a depressive response (e.g. sadness, dysphoria, self-depreciation, guilt), which stimulates, in the non-depressed spouse, a cognitive schema of overprotectiveness and omnipotence, leading to depression-reinforcing behaviour (e.g. attention, overconcern).
>
> At this point, an important shift occurs. Although the non-depressed spouse's attention and concern are reinforcing, they also have qualities. That part of the depressed person's personality that wishes to be autonomous and competent is repeatedly frustrated by the spouse's oversolicitousness, leading to feelings of helplessness and resentment. The depressed spouse may respond by withdrawal (passive-aggressivity), overt hostility, or by making a move toward self-assertion. Each of these potential responses triggers cognitive schemata of self-depreciation in the non-depressed spouse. This, in turn, leads to depression-inducing behaviour by the non-depressed spouse, and the cycle has come one full turn. (p. 390–391)

Feldman correctly points out that the idea that the overall process of depression induction is essentially circular enables us to understand that the starting point of a particular series of interchanges between the couple is basically arbitrary. Irrespective of which partner initiates a particular sequence, in the final analysis the depressed spouse will end up in a position of literally being 'depressed' (in self-esteem terms) by the undermining and oversolicitousness of the spouse while the latter is locked into his or her role by the reciprocal down power of his or her partner. Feldman, I feel, summarizes the crucial elements of the situation quite brilliantly:

> Cognitive schemata of self-depreciation are central to the psychological dynamics of both spouses, though they are manifested in different ways. The depressed spouse vacillates between states of acutely painful, conscious self-depreciation and periods of passive or active other-directed hostility. The non-depressed spouse, on the other hand, seldom experiences conscious self-depreciation. Instead he or she adopts the defensive self-image of protector and rescuer. When, in the response to the other's aggressive or self-aggressive behaviour, his or her own self-image is threatened, an unconscious search is triggered for a way to regenerate the cycle of depressive symptomatology so that he or she can again be the omnipotent rescuer. (p. 392)

I feel that Feldman's presentation is extremely valuable but there is one important theoretical issue that still requires futher exploration. You will, as a reader, have probably noticed that at certain points Feldman slips into using linear terms such as 'cognitive schemata' or 'that part of the depressed person's personality that wishes to . . .'. I believe that such terms need to be translated into more interactional terms since my experience has repeatedly taught me that the use of linear terms tends to create major errors as far as therapeutic interventions are concerned. Linear terms (particularly those derived from personality theories) tend to lead therapists away from making concrete analyses of the interactional processes which lie beneath the surface texture of the behaviours that their clients present to them during therapy sessions. Feldman comes very close to accepting this position but I believe that he does not fully succeed in escaping from the linear frameworks which he seeks to integrate with his systems-based ideas. This point can be discussed most easily by exploring the important triggering and reinforcing mechanisms which Feldman assumes are crucial to maintaining the circularity in which the couple is involved. Discussing a particular example from his case-load (Mr and Mrs A), Feldman develops his argument as follows:

> During the course of conjoint interviews with this couple a complex pattern

of 'triggering' and 'reinforcing' mechanisms became apparent. Mr. A. triggered depressive responses from his wife by subtly undermining any moves she made toward autonomy. For example, when Mrs. A. asked him how he would feel if she lost her job, he said 'I wouldn't think you were lazy or anything like that.' This triggered memories in Mrs. A. of the many times during childhood and adolescence when her father had given her conflicting messages about working: 'My father used to say I was lazy and didn't want to work when I would lose a job; at the same time, though, he used to tell me I didn't have to work, that I could stay home. And you say the same thing.' In fact it became quite apparent that Mr. A. was highly threatened by the prospect of Mrs. A. succeeding in her work and subtly (and unconsciously) encouraged her to fail. (p. 392)

Here Feldman is describing what I would choose to call a resonance between a here and now process (the husband putting his wife down) and a there and then process (a father seeking to block the individuation of his daughter as she negotiates the important transition from adolescence to adulthood). The overlapping nature of these two processes perhaps explains why they are felt to be so powerful and inevitable by the people who experience them. The felt experience is of being in a time-slip – of being returned to an earlier stage in one's life cycle in which the ability to be oneself and to take independent decisions was much more circumscribed.

I believe that Beck's cognitive schemata can be related to these processes. During the course of an individual's life cycle, interactional exchanges, particularly with significant others, are being continually experienced, stored and reedited in an almost endless flow. Expectancies and options about 'possible' and 'impossible' ('permissible' and 'impermissible') ways of behaving and interacting are being established. Typically the individual tends to make some moves away from the family of origin, joining circles of peers and friends, and eventually (in most cases) joining the family of procreation (through the process of courting and couple formation). But each of the two individuals that come together to form the couple is not a tabula rasa – they bring their interactional histories with them and hence the way they relate to each other is partially contingent on the previous ways that they have related to significant others. Mrs A brings to the marriage her images and expectancies that men she loves will be contradictory and ultimately insecure if she is too up-front and independent. But what of Mr A? Feldman explores his contribution to the circularity in the following terms:

Mr. A's use of the word 'lazy' is not accidental. He knew that this word had special meaning for his wife, and without consciously intending to, used it to undermine her budding self-esteem. (p. 392)

In fact Mr A had great difficulty in tolerating a wife who was up-front and independent or demonstrated anger in any way – he preferred to have a wife who was vulnerable (and whom he could cling to) because his habitual role in his family of origin was to be a protector of his 'helpless' mother who was continually exposed to verbal and physical onslaughts from his 'abusive' father.

The 'degree of fit' between this couple was therefore extremely close and this perhaps explained the precision of the circular process in which they were caught up. Feldman finishes his exploration of this circularity by pointing out Mrs A's equally active role in its maintenance:

> Mrs. A... was just as much an active part of the marital system as her husband and triggered depression-inducing and -maintaining behaviour in him. When she said she was too 'sick' to work and that she needed him to stay home and take care of her, she stimulated his need to 'hover' over her, which led to his becoming excessively clinging and overprotective. This in turn stimulated a depressive response in her, as it reinforced the part of her self-image in which she saw herself as weak and helpless. (p. 392)

I would add a rider (which Feldman neglects) that she had been given that negative image of herself through the process of interaction with her father, who could not genuinely and unconditionally affirm her as an independent woman. In other words, she had what Minuchin accurately calls 'a voice in her head' which was continually putting her down. Sadly, individuals come to 'own' these voices in their heads because the voice has an uncanny ability to establish the rule that it cannot be challenged – Mrs A actively denigrated herself but she had lost the ability to connect her self-downing with the voice of her father who had previously taken every opportunity to put her down and hence (I would guess) enhance his own self-esteem through the process of saying to himself: 'I may have my weaknesses but they are nothing compared to my incompetent daughter's.'

Feldman adds one final sophistication to his presentation – obviously behaviour patterns can also be mutually and directly reinforcing as well as triggering:

> In addition to triggering behaviour in a reciprocal manner, Mr. and Mrs. A. also reinforced each other's behaviour in consistent ways. When Mrs. A. got depressed and irritable, Mr. A. became over solicitous. Although Mrs. A. complained about this, on those rare occasions when Mr. A. exhibited anger instead of 'concern', Mrs. A. rejected him on the grounds that he was acting just like his abusive father. Since that was the last thing in the world that Mr. A. wanted (consciously, at least) he quickly returned to his usual passivity. Mrs. A. reinforced her husband's clingingness and solicitousness by periodic

demonstrations of helplessness and inadequacy. Her verbal messages ('I don't want you to hover over me') were contradicted by her behavioural messages. (pp. 392–393)

I hope that this detailed presentation of Feldman's work has communicated some of the basic ideas adopted by a therapist who wishes to adopt a systems-oriented approach. I will be dealing with methods of therapeutic intervention in the next section of this chapter but it is essential to emphasize two important points before moving on. The first point concerns symptom formation. Systems theorists argue that symptoms arise within blocked or stuck systems that cannot change and adapt as they receive new inputs from the environments that surround them. Typically family systems get stuck at transitional points in the family life cycle (as Eddy Street argues in Volume 2, Chapter 3). Because of the extent of the unfinished business that Mr and Mrs A both brought to their marriage they could not establish an egalitarian, adult-to-adult relationship which offered them not only a basic degree of connectedness but also the ability to be relatively independent and hence able to continue to individuate as adults in the major areas of their lives. The symptom of depression arose as the unwanted and unplanned-for but necessary ingredient that enabled them to stay together as a couple who were, in fact, loyal to the definitions of a 'husband' and a 'wife' which were allowed within their families of origin.

The second point (which is almost contained in the first point) concerns the importance of transgenerational issues. At the beginning of this chapter I criticized theoretical approaches that sought to concentrate solely on the marital system as a system in isolation from other systems. I hope that the richness of Feldman's case has served to confirm my position although, paradoxically, I would hasten to add that it is an open question whether therapeutic intervention needs to focus specifically on such issues in every case. Changes induced by here-and-now processes can often have remarkable knock-on effects so that a couple may be able to free themselves from their unfinished business in quite spontaneous ways which are apparently independent of any work devised by their therapist.

Therapy

Contextual considerations

Systems theorists pride themselves on being most sensitive to contextual factors which may influence the process of therapy, but in my opinion this claim does not stand up to critical examination since there is often a glaring divorcement between theory and practice. I am a member of a family therapy cooperative which has recently published a book (Treacher and Carpenter 1984, especially pp. 1–7) which is designed to deal specifically with such issues. The contextual issues surrounding marital work are not directly explored in the book since I assume that any marital work undertaken by a therapist would be part and parcel of a more general package of family therapy that he would be offering his clients. However, clients do, of course, approach a whole series of different agencies with a bewildering range of problems which mask underlying marital difficulties. It is these 'surface' problems that form the 'ticket of entry' to the agency that makes the initial contact with the clients but it requires considerable skill to move beyond the surface presentation to uncover the deeper structural difficulties within the marriage. Eddy Street (Volume 2, Chapter 3) explores this issue in relation to child-focused problems which conceal underlying marital problems so I will concentrate on other examples (although my discussion cannot, for reasons of space, be in any way comprehensive).

Obviously marriage guidance settings are specifically designed to deal with marital problems, but this does not necessarily mean that contextual issues can be ignored. Indeed it would be possible to argue, especially from a strategic point of view, that it is a mistake to label an agency so specifically. The British reluctance to openly explore emotional matters (reflected in such dictums as 'keep smiling' and 'keep a stiff upper lip') is, fortunately, at last beginning to die out, but it is nevertheless true that referral and 'agency-contacting' procedures can be extraordinarily recondite because couples so often find it extremely difficult and painful to admit that they have a marital problem. Couples that can admit to such problems may well go directly to marriage guidance counsellors but in a large percentage of cases it is the wife that makes the initial contact. In other settings, such as social services departments and psychiatric outpatient settings, marital problems may well be concealed behind other issues, but there is usually the complicating factor that it is only one of the partners (again usually the wife) who makes first contact with the agency. Obviously from a traditional systems theory standpoint it would be hazardous to commence therapy with just one member of the partnership. Some more maverick systems theorists, however, such as Bowen (1978) and Watzlawick and his colleagues at the Mental Research Institute, Palo Alto, would be happy to develop interactional work on the basis of seeing a single client. They assume that the individual who has approached the agency is the 'customer' for change so they therefore are prepared to make interactional interventions using their client as the vehicle for the intervention (Fisch et al. 1982). This approach is undoubtedly workable although it requires considerable skill.

In my opinion the advantages of successfully convening the whole of the system with which I would want to work far outweigh other considerations, so the initial thrust of my work is to ensure that both partners attend. Convening absent members of a system is a delicate and skilful art which I have explored in some detail in two previous articles (Carpenter and Treacher 1983; Treacher and Carpenter 1983), but for the purposes of the present discussion it is perhaps sufficient to stress that in my experience joint attendance of both partners is essential if a valid assessment of the interactional nature of their problems is to be established. Direct observation of the verbal and non-verbal interplay of the couple is crucial if the therapist is intent upon assessing the specific nature of the *process* between them. Heavy reliance on purely verbal techniques and the reporting of events (rather than direct observation of process material) usually leads to the therapy becoming bogged down with *content* issues. This does not, of course, mean that therapy ceases if one partner fails to attend, but it does mean that I will immediately devise a 'convening' intervention if one partner does not show up (Carpenter and Treacher 1983).

Paradoxically, although I make concerted efforts to have both partners attend and although I will also convene members of the couple's families of origin (and their current family of procreation) if the need arises, I will, nevertheless, also see each partner on their own. Our tactics must be flexible (and try to avoid dogmatic rules) because shifting a marital system requires ingenuity – often only unexpected, non-commonsensical tactics are sufficient to the task, so holding a session with one partner (after a series of conjoint sessions) may be sufficiently unbalancing to create a new climate for change when the conjoint sessions resume.

Cotherapy

The early pioneers of family therapy used a variety of cotherapy arrangements when working with families but the introduction of one-way screens has opened up alternative possibilities. Our preference is to use a therapist/consultant model. Ideally the therapist works directly with a couple in the room while the consultant provides support from behind the one-way screen using either a telephone or an earbug (Carpenter 1984; Procter and Stephens 1984). If a one-way screen is not available, I adopt the 'consultation-in-the-room' model advocated by my colleagues Donna

Smith and Phil Kingston (Smith and Kingston 1980; Kingston and Smith 1983; Carpenter 1984). The essential feature of this model is its insistence that the consultant should stay 'meta' to the therapist–couple system. This is achieved by the consultant sitting away from the therapist–couple triangle but nevertheless being able to make interventions into the process of the session through directing messages and comments to the therapist. Thus it adopts many of the features of the consultant – therapist – couple structure when a screen is being used.

This method is obviously distinctively different from traditional cotherapy which allows both partners to communicate directly with both therapists. On theoretical grounds I would argue that traditional cotherapy is more suitable for psychodynamically oriented therapists who utilize both mirroring and techniques based upon transference and countertransference. Systems therapists tend not to utilize such techniques so they can legitimately employ other forms of cotherapy or co-working.

Maintaining the therapeutic alliance

The approach to marital work that I adopt is based upon the work of Minuchin (1974) and Haley (1976). If I had to use a label to describe it I would call it 'structural-strategic family therapy'. (Stanton (1980) has described marital therapy from this viewpoint but for the theoretical reasons outlined at the beginning of this chapter I would not call myself a marital therapist.) The essence of this approach is to adopt initial tactics derived from Minuchin's structural family therapy but to be prepared to interleave strategic work when, and if, the need arises. I find strategic techniques very useful in getting therapy unstuck but find the overall framework of structural family therapy enables me to remain better oriented and more aware of the wider family systems issues that may be impinging on the couple I have in treatment.

In particular I am sympathetic to Minuchin's strong emphasis on successful joining techniques being a prerequisite for later therapeutic intervention (Minuchin and Fishman 1981). Joining techniques are mobilized during the social phase of the first interview (Haley 1976) – the therapist avoids talking about 'the problem' and instead explores the couple's current life style, the work they do, their hobbies and leisure-time activities, as well as lightly pencilling in some facts about their families of origin and how they met and courted each other. The essence of this tactic is to put the couple at ease and to communicate the basic message that the therapist's interest in them is primarily as *people* not as *people-who-have-a-problem*. The therapist uses self-disclosure to build bridges to both members of the couple in order to put over the message that she is not an invulnerable, all-knowing 'expert' but somebody who is human and struggles, like they do, to make sense of life and get the most from it.

Clearly, successful joining techniques facilitate contract making – a couple who feel liked and respected by a therapist, who has been able to put them at their ease and deal with their fears about the impact of therapy on them, will be willing and able to make a firm contract to work with their therapist. Contracts can take many forms and need to be custom-built to suit each couple but I generally adopt a procedure of negotiating an initial contract of four sessions. The fourth session is used to review progress or lack of it but it is made clear to the couple that a new contract will be negotiable at the end of the fourth session. We find this procedure motivates couples (and families for that matter) more advantageously than either session-by-session contracts or longer contracts, although with exceptionally difficult couples (who have grave reservations about their attendance at sessions) we may well choose to adopt a much more exploratory session-by-session contract.

Major treatment techniques

Since I am prepared to utilize techniques derived from both structural family therapy and strategic family therapy I have a wide range of techniques at my disposal. I cannot, therefore, adequately summarize all the possibilities of my approach in this chapter. Nevertheless, I will attempt to make some general comments which will communicate the main thrust of my work.

Adopting ideas derived from structural family therapy (and the trans-generationally oriented work of such theorists as Bowen (1978), Lieberman (1979) and Boszormenyi-Nagy (Boszormenyi-Nagy and Spark 1973) I focus a great deal of my attention on the ability of the couple to individuate from their families of origin and to act independently of each other. In terms of the process of a session this may mean that I intervene at a 'microlevel' (Street and Treacher 1980) to change the habitual styles of responding that the couple may have. For example, one member of a couple may demonstrate a persistent tendency to mind-read the state of the other (a pattern perhaps derived from a preexisting family-of-origin pattern). The type of intervention we would make in this case is well illustrated by Sluzki

(1978) in his brilliantly conceived paper on marital therapy from a systems-theory perspective. This paper consists of a discussion of eighteen or so 'theorems' (derived from systems theory) which provide a very concrete guide to the type of intervention that a therapist should be aiming to make during the course of an average session. 'Theorem 3' deals specifically with the example I have cited so I quote directly from Sluzki:

> 3. If A makes an unsubstantiated reference to B's subjective state ('Mind-reading'), then ask A what it is that A perceives, differentiating perceptions from inferences.
>
> **Example: A:** 'And she doesn't like me to say those kinds of things about us'.
>
> **Therapist:** 'Rather than checking it with you, B, let me ask you, A, how is it that you know that B doesn't like it?' (p. 195)

These types of intervention, if carried out repeatedly, effectively 'shape' the couple's behaviour so that they begin to own their own points of view more effectively and stop intruding into each other's space. As they differentiate more, they can, in fact, open up possibilities for negotiating more realistically. Typically in my sessions I stage a lot of role-plays, which are concerned with negotiating and quid pro quo techniques. I may well get the couple to enact their current ways of negotiating (or rowing or arguing) and then have them reenact the same scenario but this time inviting them to introduce new ways of behaving. Often videotape playback can be used to enhance this process – I get the couple to talk their way through a videotaped sequence. They are often able to 'see' just how they tie each other in knots precisely because they can be 'outside' the actual sequence now that it is recorded on videotape. This distancing enables them to detect the 'dance' in which they are caught up. If they are able to devise new 'steps', these can be reenacted and recorded on the videotape so they can then gain the reward of seeing themselves doing things differently and more productively.

Any gains achieved in this type of session are backed up the setting of homework tasks which enable the therapist to test out the ability of the couple to transfer the learning of new patterns of behaviour from the therapy sessions to the exacting rough and tumble of everyday life. Many different types of task can be set but it is essential to custom-design each task so that it achieves a specific goal which has been conceptualized in systems-theory terms rather than being thought up (on the spur of the moment) during the session. Typically a homework task is set after the therapist and consultant have taken a consultancy time out towards the end of a session. (Andolfi (1979) has provided a working classification of different types of tasks although his approach is not entirely consistent because some of his categories overlap. Nevertheless, it is worth consulting his book if you are interested in improving task-setting skills.)

When strategic tactics are used, the primary aim of any intervention is to disrupt the couple's current mode of responding to each other. A classic major strategic intervention would consist, for example, in advising the wife of an alcoholic husband to join him regularly at the pub. Obviously such an intervention would require considerable trust in the therapist on the part of the wife (and probably also some specific coaching about how to behave in the pub). But the effect of the intervention would be to entirely disrupt the normal sequence of events whereby the couple would quarrel, the husband would disappear to the pub to seek consolation, and his wife would fret at home only to jump on him when he returned. Getting drunk together can be an effective transitional move which opens up new possibilities for different ways of behaving. Obviously such tactics appear risky but there seems to be dialectical truth that dictates that very sclerosed systems require quite extraordinary interventions if they are to be shifted.

Problems encountered in marital therapy

Since my approach contains a basically pragmatic and problem-solving cutting edge, any problem that is encountered in the course of undertaking therapy with a couple is treated as grist to the mill. I tend to eschew any concept of resistance since I find that the concept has very little, if any, theoretical or practical value. Some of my colleagues and myself have attempted to devise a general method for overcoming 'stuckness' in therapy (Treacher and Carpenter 1982; Carpenter et al. 1983) which involves a concerted effort to identify in which dimension the stuckness is taking place. For heuristic purposes we have recognized four dimensions which we think make good theoretical sense. The first dimension (which we loosely label contextual factors) deals with all those aspects of therapy which are to do with the definition of the problem, issues of customerhood, and issues concerned with defining to whom the problem is a problem. Often therapy gets bogged down solely because the whole process of problem definition has not been adequately dealt with. The second dimension (technical factors) deals directly with issues concerning the techniques of therapy. It may be that the therapy is blocked solely because the therapist has not adopted the correct technique for circumnavigating the point of stuckness. The third dimension deals with problems concerning the loss of the therapist's manoeuvrability through becoming a homeostatic part of the family-therapist system. The fourth dimension explores an even deeper form of stuckness which involves the therapist's consultancy and support system becoming blunted and counterproductive. Each form of stuckness requires a different form of intervention but we have discovered from our work as supervisors and consultants that stuckness can occur simultaneously in several (or all) of these dimensions.

The change process in therapy

Despite many valiant attempts to understand the change process in marital family therapy, I personally feel that the whole area is very confused and underresearched. Hoffman's elegant book *Foundations of family therapy* (1981) is the most convincing theoretical account provided so far by any systems theorist. Building on the work of Watzlawick and his colleagues (Watzlawick et al. 1974), she stresses the importance of the difference between first order change and second order change, i.e. the difference between a superficial, surface type of change and a deep structural form of change which actually alters the rules which determine the functioning of a system. This makes good sense at a theoretical level but when this idea is applied to a particular concrete example of a couple or a family it is extraordinarily difficult to be sure whether first or second order change has taken place. At a purely pragmatic level I tend to assume that a basic (second order) change in functioning has occurred if a family or couple working with me take over the initiative of the therapy from me. For example, a couple who decide that they did not like the task I devised for them as homework (because it would not be very productive) but invented a better one themselves would be an example of a couple who have probably changed in a basic (probably non-reversible) sense.

Obviously only careful follow-up studies can possibly clarify these issues. I tend to carry out three-monthly or six-monthly follow-up sessions with my couples and families to establish whether the changes they reported at discharge have been maintained. I also explore in great detail what sense they have made of the therapy that was undertaken with them and whether they have absorbed the techniques I shared with them. If they have absorbed these techniques then they are usually in a position to devise new ways of tackling the new problems that inevitably face them as they move forward to the next phase of the family life cycle. Obviously strategic interventions must be excluded from this aspect of my work since they intrinsically require the presence of a third party (the therapist).

The personal qualities of effective therapists

There is very little research so far published which explores the personal qualities of effective family or marital therapists. Gurman and Kniskern (1981) in their review of outcome studies have stressed that the single factor that seems important in affecting therapy outcome is the therapist's relationship skills:

> ... [The] literature suggests that it is generally important for the martial-family therapist to be active and to provide some structure to early interviews but not to confront tenuous family defences very early in treatment. Excesses in this direction are among the main contributors to premature termination and to negative therapeutic outcomes (Gurman and Kniskern, 1978). A reasonable mastery of technical skills may be sufficient to prevent worsening or to maintain pretreatment functioning in very difficult cases, but more refined relationship skills are necessary to yield truly positive outcomes ... (p. 751)

Unfortunately I can pursue the discussion no further than this, but Gurman and Kniskern's statement does make good sense to me, particularly as it vindicates Minuchin's position concerning the importance of joining techniques – obviously there is an urgent need for more research work to be undertaken in this area.

Case illustration

Mr and Mrs Smith originally came with their four children to the Child Guidance Clinic because of worries and conflicts involving their eldest teenage daughter. A therapist/consultant team (myself and a colleague) was assigned to the family and therapy commenced using live consultancy of the type we have explored in a previous section of the chapter. Initially a family therapy contract was negotiated with the family but after completing five sessions a new contract was established since it was clear that major marital difficulties lay at the centre of the problems which this family was experiencing. The family therapy sessions had revealed that Mr and Mrs Smith were experiencing difficulties in allowing their elder children Rosemary (19) and Elizabeth (17) to grow up and leave home. Rosemary had left home but her independence was extremely shaky, particularly as she had recently conceived an illegitimate daughter. The pregnancy had been concealed by her right up until the day of delivery because she felt unable to tell her parents of her predicament. Her younger sister had also left home to live rough with her boyfriend for several months but she had then returned home with her boyfriend in tow. The boyfriend was a heavy drinker and there was considerable friction because of his presence in the home.

The initial family work was designed to help Mr and Mrs Smith regain control of their household and begin to develop an effective boundary between themselves and their children. The initial session of the marital contract refocused on these issues since the marital relationship had been neglected because a key family rule dictated that 'children must come first'.

The therapeutic interventions made during the sessions concentrated on helping the couple differentiate from each other and adopt more respectful ways of behaving towards each other. The couple tended to refer to each other in the third person and not to communicate directly, preferring to triangulate one of their children (or the therapist) by drawing them into the conversation. A series of enactments were staged in the sessions – these involved the couple holding hands with each other and making direct eye contact while they discussed problem areas or discussed plans to have trips out together.

This initial work was successful at least at some levels – the couple began to communicate better and to achieve some independence from the rest of the family. However, Mrs Smith's underlying depression deepened and she threatened to commit suicide. She phoned me up to communicate her threat but I countered the move by expressing deep sympathy for her predicament while insisting that I always respected the right of my clients to take their lives if they felt there was no alternative. The next appointment was brought forward and was treated as a crisis session which reoriented the work being undertaken with the couple. It was decided that some specific cognitive behaviour therapy work should be undertaken with Mrs Smith using Mr Smith as an adjunct therapist. As a result of gains from the earlier sessions, Mr Smith had shifted his role from being an avoider who used jokes and other distracting devices to prevent any real discussions occurring. At the same time Mrs Smith had become more direct in her approach to him and did not use the tactic of backing off or sulking.

The cognitive work was partially successful since Mrs Smith began to challenge her negative 'self-talk', but it was decided not to extend this work as the couple seemed to have considerable caring resources which they were beginning to mobilize in support of each other. Following a lengthy review which was held between sessions, my consultant and I decided to set a ritual task in order to clear away some of the unfinished business that continued to dog the couple. Despite concrete progress, they habitually reverted to bringing up old conflicts and problems and to being preoccupied with their sense of failure as parents and marital partners, although their achievements in the here-and-now gave the lie to these ideas about themselves. The ritual task designed for them was based on the elegant work of Seltzer and Seltzer (1983) who have discussed the importance of ritual tasks and their need to ring true to the cultural background of the families with which they are used. The specific details of the task are as follows.

(1)   The couple had to send their children away to stay with friends so that they could have a whole day and a night by themselves.

(2)   They were to devise a ritual meal of at least five courses, do the shopping for it together and then prepare the meal up to the point of actually beginning the cooking.

(3)   Having reached this point they were to retire to their front room to begin the 'core' part of the task – this consisted of writing down, on separate pieces of paper, all the unpleasant things they had ever done to each other during the entire course of their marriage. Each item was to be discussed and then ritually burnt (either on an open fire or in a metal paper- or waste-bin). The burning of the pieces of paper was to continue until each piece had been burnt.

(4)   When the burning ceremony was over the couple were to retire to the kitchen to prepare the meal which would then be served, tête-à-tête, with due pomp and ceremony.

This task was actually set after the sixth session, which was treated as the last of the series, although a three-month follow-up session was negotiated.

The team estimated that sufficient work had been undertaken to get the couple beyond launch point but it was also felt that the couple were becoming dependent on the clinic. They were enthusiastic attenders and the sessions were always characterized by great energy and hilarity because one of the major strengths of the couple was their ability to send themselves up. (Needless to say this could also be a major weakness too.) The couple had successfully cleared up their 9-year-old son's enuresis problem using a bell and pad provided by the clinic, and the confidence that they had gained from this seemed to permeate other aspects of family life. The original circularity in their relationship had involved Mr Smith feeding his wife's depression by not taking her attempts at self-assertion seriously. Due to his own feelings of depression, which derived from his feeling of being totally stuck in a dead-end job, he had a vested interest in undermining his wife's competence. This circularity had been broken by the interventions that had been made and the couple were now genuinely supportive.

At the follow-up the couple reported that the task had been very successful. They had been warned not to undertake the task until both of them were ready to 'put the past behind them' and it had taken them a month before they felt ready to undertake it, but they had found that the task had indeed released them from the past and their marital relationship was now much more symmetrical with both being able to reward and appreciate each other. They did report continued difficulties with their children but felt they had the confidence to deal with them. The couple were formally discharged from therapy with the proviso that a six-month follow-up would be negotiated at a later date.

This session never took place because the clinic received a crisis call about two and a half months later. Renewed problems had arisen, this time focusing on Rosemary and the youngest daughter in the family, Angela (15). They were quarrelling very tempestuously and Mrs Smith was very anxious that actual physical damage would be done. Three family therapy sessions were held – one of these proved exceptionally productive in clarifying the underlying processes that led to the explosive behaviour of the two sisters. The session was undertaken in front of a one-way screen with members of the clinic's back-up team being used to play the role of grandparents. An elaborate three-generation sculpting of the family system was undertaken – the family members played themselves with the team members joining them in order to complete the full cast of players that was needed to flesh out the family. The use of sculpting (Walrond-Skinner 1976) proved very illuminating since it revealed that much of the behaviour of the family was being influenced by the unfinished business involving Mrs Smith and her 84-year-old mother. It was clear from the sculpt that Mrs Smith had never adequately separated herself from her family of origin. She was obsessed with her own inadequacies and continually put herself down because she felt she had failed her parents who had brought her up to be 'proper' in all ways.

As a result of this session it was decided to work directly on Mrs Smith's unfinished business. Several individual sessions were devoted to preparing her for an eventual meeting with her mother which took place at the clinic two months later. The meeting was a very low-key affair in which the therapist gently explored Mrs Smith's childhood using her mother as the informant. Mrs Smith was also set (concurrently) the homework task of having to have a heart-to-heart talk with her mother. The two events combined to liberate Mrs Smith – she was able to see that she did not have to accept her mother's point of view; her own view of herself was perfectly valid and could be accepted without reservation.

This 'transgenerational' work was interleaved with specific cognitive behaviour therapy sessions which were designed to attack Mrs Smith's more general self-downing tendencies. The therapy was based on Burns's excellent self-help manual (Burns 1980) – Mrs Smith was soon able to master Beck's triple-columning techniques and once she achieved this mastery she was able to avoid slipping back into depression when new difficulties entered her life.

A final conjoint session was held with the couple to once again probe the couple relationship. This session revealed big gains both in the couple relationship and in the rest of the family. Rosemary and Angela had been out on several trips together and had resolved their difficulties, while Mrs Smith was now able to relate warmly to Rosemary for the first time in several years. The basis for this reconciliation seemed to have been established when Mrs Smith skilfully engineered a meeting between her mother, Rosemary and the great-grandson. The great-grandmother was able to rise to the occasion and accept her great-grandson (despite his being born out of wedlock – a fact which she had previously found deeply shocking).

This reconciliation had demonstrated to Mrs Smith that her mother was, in fact, far more flexible than she imagined, a point the therapist was able to reaffirm in the final session by sharing the following poem with the couple:

> What if your mother did
> Float about above you
> Big as a barrage balloon
> Blocking out the light?
> Nobody's mother can't not do nothing right.
> (Liz Lochhead)

Note

1 The Family Institute at Cardiff has made a very important contribution to the development of systems approaches to family therapy. A large number of therapists have been trained by Brian Cade and his colleagues, and in the course of this training they are exposed to systems ideas which are, of course, relevant to marital therapy. It is nevertheless true that no major publication about marital therapy has emerged from the Institute. This is understandably a pity because the creativity of the approach is undeniable.

References

Andolfi, M. (1979) *Family therapy: an interactional approach.* New York: Plenum Press.

Bateson, G., Jackson, D. D., Haley, J. and Weakland J. (1956) Towards a theory of schizophrenia. *Behavioural Science, 1,* 251–264.

Beck, A. T. (1967) *Depression: clinical, experimental and theoretical aspects.* New York: Harper and Row.

Beck, A. T. (1971) Cognition, affect and psychopathology. *Archives of General Psychiatry, 24,* 495–500.

Berger, M. (1978) *Beyond the double bind.* New York: Brunner/Mazel.

Berne, E. (1964) *Games people play.* London: Penguin.

Bertalanffy, L. von. (1972) General systems theory – a critical review. *In* I. J. Beishon and G. Peters (eds) *Systems behaviour.* London: Harper and Row.

Boszormenyi-Nagy, I. and Spark, G. (1973) *Invisible loyalties.* London: Harper and Row.

Bowen, M. (1978) *Family therapy in clinical practice.* New York: Jason Aronson.

Burns, D. (1980) *Feeling good.* New York: Morrow Book Company.

Carpenter, J. (1984) Working together: supervision, consultancy, and co-working. *In* A. Treacher and J. Carpenter (eds) *Using family therapy.* Oxford: Blackwell.

Carpenter, J. and Treacher, A. (1983) On the neglected but related arts of convening and engaging families and their wider systems. *Journal of Family Therapy, 5,* 337–358.

Carpenter, J., Treacher, A., Jenkins, H. and O'Reilly, P. (1983) An exploration of how to identify and overcome 'stuckness' in family therapy. Part 2: Stuckness in the therapeutic and supervisory systems. *Journal of Family Therapy, 5,* 81–96.

Dell, P. (1982) Beyond homeostasis: towards a concept of coherence. *Family Process, 21,* 21–42.

Feldman, L. B. (1976) Depression and marital interaction. *Family Process, 15,* 389–395.

Feldman, L. B. (1979) Marital conflict and marital intimacy: an integrative psychodynamic-behavioural-systemic model. *Family Process, 18,* 69–78.

Feldman, L. B. and Pinsof, W. M. (1982) Problem maintenance in family systems: an integrative model. *Journal of Marital and Family Therapy, 8,* 295–308.

Fisch, R., Weakland, J. H. and Segal, L. (1982) *The tactics of change – doing therapy briefly.* San Francisco: Jossey-Bass.

Fromm-Reichmann, F. (1948) Notes on the development of treatment of schizophrenics by psychoanalytic psychotherapy. *Psychiatry, 11,* 263–273.

Gurman A. S. (1978) Contemporary marital therapies: A critique and comparative analysis of psychoanalytic, behavioural and systems theory approaches. *In* Paolino T. J. and McCrady B. S. (eds) *Marriage and marital therapy: psychoanalytic, behavioural and systems theory perspectives* (1978) New York: Brunner/Mazel.

Gurman, A. S. and Kniskern, D. P. (2nd edn 1978) Research on marital and family therapy: progress, perspective and prospect. *In* S. Garfield and A. Bergin (eds) *Handbook of psychotherapy and behaviour change.* New York: Wiley.

Gurman, A. S. and Kniskern, D. P. (1981) Family therapy outcome research:

knowns and unknowns. *In* A. S. Gurman and D. P. Kniskern (eds) *Handbook of family therapy.* New York: Brunner/Mazel.

Haley, J. (1973) *Uncommon therapy.* New York: Norton.

Haley, J. (1976) *Problem solving therapy.* New York: Harper Colophon Books.

Hall, A. D. and Fagen, R. E. (1956) Definition of system. *In* L. von Bertalanffy and A. Rappoport (eds) *General Systems Yearbook 1.* Society of General Systems Research.

Hinchcliffe, M. K., Hooper, D. and Roberts, F. J. (1978) *The melancholy marriage: depression in marriage and psychosocial approaches to therapy.* New York and Chichester: Wiley.

Hoffman, L. (1981) *Foundations of family therapy – a conceptual framework for systems change.* New York: Basic Books.

Jackson, D. (1965) The study of the family. *Family Process, 4,* 1–21.

Kingston, P. and Smith, D. (1983) Preparation for live consultation and live supervision. *Journal of Family Therapy, 5,* 219–233.

L'Abate, L. and McHenry, S. (1983) *Handbook of marital interventions.* New York: Grune and Stratton.

Lederer, W. J. and Jackson, D. D. (1968) *The mirages of marriage.* New York: Norton

Lieberman, S. (1979) *Transgenerational family therapy.* London: Croom Helm.

Minuchin, S. (1974) *Families and family therapy.* London: Tavistock.

Minuchin, S. and Fishman, C. (1981) *Family therapy techniques.* Cambridge, Mass: Harvard University Press.

Palazzoli, M. S., Cecchin, G., Prata, G. and Boscole, L. (1978) *Paradox and counter paradox.* New York: Aronson.

Procter, H. and Stephens, T. (1984) Developing family therapy in the day hospital. *In* A. Treacher and J. Carpenter (eds) *Using family therapy.* Oxford: Blackwell.

Rohrbaugh, M. (1984) The 41st Annual Conference of the AAMFT. *Family Therapy Networker, 8,* 52 and 54.

Sager, C. J. (1981) Couples therapy and marriage contracts. *In* A. S. Gurman and D. P. Kniskern (eds) *Handbook of family therapy.* New York: Brunner/Mazel.

Seltzer, W. J. and Seltzer, M. R. (1983) Magic, material and myth. *Family Process, 22,* 3–14.

Sluzki, C. (1978) Marital therapy from a systems perspective. *In* T. J. Paolino and B. S. McCrady (eds) *Marriage and marital therapy: psychoanalytic, behavioral and systems theory perspectives.* New York: Brunner/Mazel.

Smith, D. and Kingston, P. (1980) Live supervision without a one-way screen. *Journal of Family Therapy, 2,* 379–387.

Speer, D. (1970) Family systems: morphostasis and morphogenesis, or is homeostasis enough? *Family Process, 9,* 259–328.

Stanton, M. D. (1980) Marital therapy from a structural/strategic viewpoint. *In* G. P. Sholevar (ed.) *Handbook of marriage and marital therapy.* Englewood Cliffs, New Jersey: Spectrum Publications.

Steinglass, P. (1978) The conceptualization of marriage from a systems theory perspective. *In* T. J. Paolino and McCrady B. S., (eds) *Marriage and marital therapy: psychoanalytic, behavioural and systems theory perspectives.* New York: Brunner/Mazel.

Street, E. and Treacher, A. (1980) Microtraining and family therapy skills – towards a possible synthesis. *Journal of Family Therapy, 2,* 243–257.

Treacher, A. T. and Carpenter, J. (1982) 'Oh no! Not the Smiths again.' An exploration of how to identify and overcome 'stuckness' in family therapy. Part 1: Stuckness involving contextual and technical aspects of therapy. *Journal of Family Therapy, 4,* 285–305.

Treacher, A. and Carpenter, J. (1983) On the failure to take convening strategies seriously – a reply to Campion. *Journal of Family Therapy, 5,* 259–262.

Treacher, A. and Carpenter, J. (1984) *Using family therapy – a guide for practitioners in different professional settings.* Oxford: Blackwell.

Walrond-Skinner, S. (1976) *Family therapy – the treatment of natural systems.* London: Routledge and Kegan Paul.

Watzlawick, P., Weakland, J. and Fisch, J. (1974) *Change: principles of problem formation and problem resolution.* New York: Norton.

Wertheim, E. S. (1973) Family unit therapy and the science and typology of family systems. *Family Process, 12,* 361–375.

CHAPTER TWELVE Approaches to Marital Therapy

Comparative Analyses
Windy Dryden, Dougal Mackay,
Thomas Schröder and Andy
Treacher

Representatives of the four approaches to marital therapy were each invited to write a comparative analysis of the approaches covered. They were given 2,500 words for this purpose and their responses are printed as received.

A PSYCHODYNAMIC PRACTITIONER'S POINT OF VIEW – THOMAS SCHRÖDER

Comparing and integrating approaches to individual therapy has been fashionable for long enough now for us to be able to assess some of the problems inherent in this enterprise which originally was a welcome move away from the often scholastic debates between the various theoretical persuasions. On the one hand it easily deteriorate into the type of eclecticism which replaces thought by action in the desire to arrive at a set of techniques that 'work'. On the other hand, reducing various approaches to what is common to all can seriously restrict the variety of thought and inhibit rather than promote development. Similarly, attempts to 'translate' from one framework to another often lead at best to some inevitable loss of meaning and at worst to a patronizing reinterpretation of what other approaches 'really' are about.

However, bearing these pitfalls in mind, the task is made somewhat easier with regard to marital therapy, given that all four of the contributors to the preceding chapters have emphasized the grounding of their particular approaches as lying in the response to practical, clinical demands rather than primarily in the application of a paradigm (though in the case of BMT this appears to be a more recent development). Consequently, although differences can be explored mainly in relation to the theoretical formulations, the practice of marital therapy seems to be broadly convergent. Distinctions between approaches are therefore more likely to be in the nature of differences of emphasis rather than principle.

Differences between therapeutic approaches

The main issue which differentiates the therapeutic approaches represented in this book is in my view the relative importance afforded to the couple as the focus for the conceptualization of marital disharmony. We can thus locate the different theoretical persuasions as lying on a continuum.

At the one end, REMT is firmly focused on the individual (especially from the 'marital disturbance' angle) and can therefore conceive of one partner resolving the disturbance him/herself, without change for the other being a necessary precondition or consequence. The key to understanding the problems of the couple is therefore in the understanding of how individuals can give themselves problems, as exemplified historically by Albert Ellis's shift from the dyad to the monad as the most useful field of investigation.

BMT, lying next on our assumed continuum, concentrates its attention on the social exchange between partners. The key to understanding marital problems is therefore in the interaction which is experienced by the spouses as unsatisfactory and unrewarding. Individual satisfaction is contingent on the partner's response, a view which distinguishes BMT clearly from REMT despite the importance which both approaches place on maladaptive cognitions.

From a psychodynamic point of view, the emphasis is on the couple as a psychic entity rather than on individuals or their interaction. Here the key to understanding marital tensions lies in the disturbance of the balance which originally accounted for the attraction between the partners. Individual personalities, although unique, contribute by virtue of their developmental histories to the 'marital fit' – especially if they are seen from an object-relations standpoint as the product of more or less complete separation and individuation from a mother–child dyad. That this dyad is reproduced in the marital relationship is central to a psychodynamic understanding of couples.

The systems approach to marital therapy represents the other endpoint of our conceptual spectrum by focusing on the family (and presumably potentially on wider social networks) as an appropriate unit for theorizing. Couples, in this view, are best understood as subsystems which behave according to the parameters set by the context in which they operate. Therefore any attempt to understand the distressed couple without reference to the wider social system is bound to be reductionistic and misleading. Consequently, marital disharmony is presented as at best a misnomer, at worst a concept which obscures reality.

It seems to me that the differences in emphasis outlined above form the matrix from which most of the theoretical and some of the practical differences (such as they are) originate. Thus, the various stages of the life cycle and their influence on the couple, for example, hardly merit a thought in REMT but are seen as potential sources of previously hidden 'expenses' in BMT and they play a more important role in psychodynamic understanding (as highlighting unresolved intrapsychic conflict) and in the systems approach (as exemplified in the homeostasis–morphogenesis argument).

Similarly, transgenerational issues do not figure in REMT and BMT with their respective individual and interactional foci. They appear in psychodynamic thinking, although still centred on the individual (as he or she 'repeats history'), and feature quite logically in the systems approach as a major parameter of current conflict.

To name one further example: the 'incompatibility' of marital partners can be understood from the individual vantage point of REMT as 'naive mate selection', from the interactional perspective of BMT as lack of a 'collaborative set', from the couple-focused psychodynamic point of view as the inevitable outcome of a shared level of immaturity, and from the systemic angle as making sense in satisfying the requirements of two family networks.

Even on a technical issue, such as the question of single therapist versus cotherapy, the theoretical attitude to the couple is pervasive as a determinant. REMT (while rigidly postulating flexibility) gives preference to the individual therapist. BMT, with its view of the therapist refereeing the couple's interaction, sees cotherapy as an unnecessary complication (although it seems surprising that an approach at least partly grounded in social learning theory would eschew the opportunity for modelling). Psychodynamic marital therapy regards the therapist couple, with its potential for mirroring, as naturally the best choice; and systems therapy aims to reproduce its theoretical view by placing the single therapist within a consultancy metasystem.

It would not be difficult to extend the range of examples for the stratification I have argued above. Suffice it to say that conceptual clarity regarding the relative importance of the individual versus the couple versus the system will help the practitioner of marital therapy towards consistency in his or her approach.

Similarities between therapeutic approaches

It has been somewhat surprising to me that a book on 'Marital Therapy in Britain' should not contain a chapter on the client-centred mode as a separate therapeutic approach, especially when considering that the philosophy of Marriage Guidance and marital counselling agencies owes a great deal to this way of thinking.* Perhaps the most convincing explanation for this omission would be that Rogerian tenets, such as the importance of empathy and unconditional positive regard, have become so widely accepted as necessary conditions for the building of therapeutic relationships (and hence as necessary preconditions for the establishment of a therapeutic alliance), that they seem hardly worth mentioning, especially now that the majority of client-centred therapists would no longer regard them as in and of themselves sufficient for therapeutic change. Nevertheless, it warrants underlining that all the approaches described in the preceding chapters pay tribute to the bonding element of the therapeutic alliance, paraphrasing the issue in terms such as 'mobilizing joining techniques', 'building positive expectancies and trust', 'giving an experience of being understood', or 'making clear to both spouses that the therapist is not interested in trying to preserve or destroy the marriage'. Differences in overt behaviour – e.g. self-disclosure of a systems therapist as contrasted with attentive listening of a psychodynamic clinician – therefore may well be understood as different ways of communicating the same internal stance. The need to establish a contract – i.e. to have (more or less explicitly) some agreement on tasks and goals – and the need to maintain that contract throughout therapy and if necessary to restate it, equally appears so universally established that it hardly merits pointing out.

Although interventions vary according to different conceptual stances, there seems to be considerable convergence in the degree to which the interaction of the couple is held to be of practical importance (as opposed to being theoretically central). Overcoming disturbances in the couple's communication and negotiation of differences therefore seems to be a common concern of most marital therapists (regardless of whether their internal framework would point them to 'skills deficits' or 'meaningful blocks'). Equally, the improvement of marital interaction might generally be regarded as a good criterion for positive outcome (no matter whether the change is seen as a cause or a consequence or both). In observing interaction, the existence of stable, often self-maintaining patterns seems generally recognized as well, and is referred to in terms such as 'games', 'shared collusive defences', 'vicious circles', or 'feedback loops'. That these patterns provide valuable information about the precise nature of the couple's problem and a useful point of therapeutic leverage appears commonly held, too,

Editor's note: However, see Chapter 5.

although in psychodynamic marital therapy much of the recognition and at least the primary intervention may well be 'by proxy' within the cotherapy dyad.

As a final thought we might do well to remember that much of the above comparisons are based on clinicians describing their respective approaches. Direct observation of various therapists in action might well yield more similarities in the practical work than their written accounts would suggest.

Enhancing my practice of marital therapy by learning from other approaches

Improving as a clinician in whatever form of therapy is, in my view, not a matter of collecting techniques or learning 'tricks', but rather a way of having one's own internal framework challenged and changed by new thoughts. Which of these thoughts will eventually be integrated into one's own view of the world does not strike me as the result of intellectual appeal but rather as a consequence of having been able to have new experiences. The following thoughts are therefore more an invitation to myself to broaden my view than the fitting together of a theoretical jigsaw.

When reflecting on a particular client couple, I may easily become stuck in a well-worn groove of giving particular psychological meanings to the problems they are bringing and I am having. The theoretical continuum, outlined in the section on 'differences' above, will help me to suspend my usual vantage point and see whether the angle of the individual, the inter-action, or the system throws fresh light on the issues I am stuck with.

The distinction between marital disturbance and marital dissatisfaction, as developed in the chapter on REMT, helped me to think afresh about a perennially troublesome issue which is also briefly discussed in Daniell's chapter: how to help a couple where both partners are so vulnerable that they do not appear to be in a position to address relationship issues, given their respective preoccupations with their own individual needs. Usually I would be inclined to recommend either some separate individual work for each partner, or alternatively a couples' group which might provide both with an opportunity of having some of their individual needs for develop-ment met without excluding the partner. However, in the light of the comments made on the 'marital dissatisfaction phase', I might be encour-aged to try and keep such a couple in conjoint therapy by attempting to support both their capacities to rationalize, which might, after all, well prove to be a more adaptive defence and afford both of them space to negotiate some couple issues, thus setting up the beginning of a 'benign cycle'. Although this might appear unsatisfactory to my therapeutic perfectionism, it could well be a very valuable 'false solution' for the couple and therefore in their best interest.

When reading through the chapter on BMT, I was reminded of the difficulties I sometimes have in pin-pointing exactly how a couple's problems are expressed in their interaction, and the various headings to the section on the nature of marital disturbance seemed to provide a checklist to help me clarify my thinking. To talk about 'self-defeating change strategies' also strikes me as a way of interpreting a defence to a couple while acknowledging at the same time their desire to have their needs met within the marital relationship.

Finally, I have found it very useful in the past to make use of the concept of paradoxical intervention from strategic systemic therapies, if the paradox coincides with a core interpretation. For instance, having become stuck with a couple who consistently confirm to each other that they would be better off without their marriage while appearing at the same time unable to separate, a paradoxical formulation, stressing the importance of the couple continuing to fight with each other as this is their way of expressing their commitment to each other, appears to me to add greatly to my understanding of their basic conflicts and might therefore enable me to become 'unstuck'.

In conclusion I would want to contend that an integration between various approaches to marital therapy is not something that can be achieved on paper, but has to be struggled for in practice. A secure internal framework, of whatever variety, seems to me a valuable and necessary basis from which to be open to new thoughts as well as to the constant supervision our client couples provide us with.

A RATIONAL-EMOTIVE THERAPIST'S POINT OF VIEW – WINDY DRYDEN

In this section I will not only draw upon the chapters by Daniell, Mackay and Treacher but will also consider other writers on psychodynamic, behavioural and systems approaches to working with couples.

Major similarities

The rational-emotive approach to marital therapy has some similarities with the other three approaches outlined in this volume. It agrees with the view posited by *the psychodynamic approach* that one or both partners who have marital problems often have 'a shared fantasy about the catastrophe which will result if the feared or unacceptable impulses in the self and in the partner emerge' (Daniell). Rational-emotive theory holds that such partners *define* these consequences as 'terrible' or 'catastrophic' and thus erect defences to prevent the emergence of these consequences. Thus, rational-emotive marital therapists would concur with psychodynamic marital therapists that an important goal of marital therapy is to help partners surrender their defences, but they differ from their psychodynamic counterparts concerning how this is best done. RET marital therapists would emphasize helping people to redefine these consequences as 'unfortunate' rather than 'terrible' and show them that they are not worthless individuals for having so-called unacceptable impulses; rather they are fallible human beings with good and bad aspects and had better accept themselves as such. Finally, both approaches focus on the contribution that each individual makes to the couple's marital problems.

The theory of rational-emotive marital therapy is similar to that of *behavioural marital therapy* in stressing that married couples are affected by reward/cost considerations. It also shares the behavioural viewpoint that couples' problems are accentuated by deficits in communication, problem-solving and negotiation skills, although these deficits are deemed by RET theory to be a feature of marital dissatisfaction rather than the cause of marital disturbance (see Chapter 9 for a full discussion of this important distinction). As Mackay, in his chapter, has shown, behavioural marital therapists now recognize that maladaptive cognitions play an important role in the development and maintenance of marital problems and thus cognitive restructuring methods are now important features of the practice of BMT. This cognitive focus has of course always been a central feature of rational-emotive marital therapy, which places more emphasis on these cognitive factors than does BMT.

REMT and BMT therapists share the view that it is important to adopt an active-directive approach to the practice of their respective therapies, although, as will be shown, they differ concerning to which features they attend at different phases of treatment. Rational-emotive marital therapists often use a large number of behavioural techniques routinely employed by BMT therapists (e.g. communication training, problem-solving and quid pro quo techniques) although they will use them generally in the latter stages of therapy when issues of marital dissatisfaction become salient.

REMT theory would agree with *systems theory* that it is important to understand marital problems in their context and that couples' interactions with other subsystems and wider systems can often serve as important contributions to their problems. In addition, recent developments in rational-emotive theory stress that contexts (A), thoughts (B), and emotions and behaviours (C) are truly interdependent processes and cannot legitimately be considered in isolation from one another. Thus, interpersonal contexts affect people's beliefs, emotions and behaviours; the way people view situations affects their feelings about and actions towards these situations and thus helps to create these situations. Similarly, the way people feel and act affects both their attitudes towards situations and the situations themselves. This view is in accordance with systems theory which holds that processes (and their interaction) at different levels of organization must be considered if accurate appraisals of marital and family problems are to be made.

In his chapter Treacher outlines one (i.e. his own) approach to the practice of *systems-oriented therapy* with couples. It is probable that Treacher focuses more on the attitudes and beliefs of family members than do other systems-oriented practitioners. However, the fact that he does focus on these 'cognitive' factors demonstrates that in some important respects some systems and REMT therapists share a similar therapeutic focus. Finally, systems and REMT practitioners are similar in adopting an active-directive approach to working with couples although again they tend to differ concerning the material to which they direct themselves.

Major differences

Rational-emotive marital therapy differs from *psychodynamic marital therapy* in a number of respects. The latter stresses that it is important to gain an understanding of the infant and childhood origins of the partners' present problems during therapy. REMT theory argues that such understanding is not important and the focus of therapy is decidedly on each partners' presently held beliefs. Furthermore, REMT pays less attention to issues of marital choice than does the psychodynamic approach other than focusing upon the various marital myths to which one or both partners adhere. However, such myths generally can be gleaned frc discussions about present disturbance/dissatisfaction rather than from iscussions about marital choice. With respect to the practice of .al therapy, rational-emotive therapists differ markedly from psychodynamic marital therapists. First, they are more active and directive in approach and more self-disclosing and less neutral in style. Second, they focus less on transference and countertransference issues and, when dealing with those phenomena, they trace them back to their current ideological roots rather than to their psychoanalytic psychodynamic origins. Third, because they focus less on transference and countertransference issues, rational-emotive marital therapists tend to work on their own with couples and rarely work in foursomes (two therapists – two clients in the same room) or concurrent singles (each partner being seen by a different therapist) which is the norm in psychodynamic marital therapy.

REMT also differs from *behavioural marital therapy* in a number of ways. First, it lays greater stress on helping partners change their basic philosophic assumptions than do BMT therapists. Although both sets of therapists do focus on partners' maladaptive cognitions, REMT therapists are primarily concerned with each person's absolutistic evaluations (i.e. musts, shoulds and oughts) particularly in the first stage of marital therapy (i.e. overcoming marital disturbance). On the other hand, BMT therapists will more likely focus on partners' distorted inferences throughout therapy, cognitions which REMT therapists are more concerned with in the later phase of therapy (i.e. overcoming marital dissatisfaction). Second, REMT therapists consider that:

> Some behavioral methods of individual and family change – such as social reinforcement and gradual desensitization of fears – not only have distinct limitations but have profound philosophic implications that may lead to anti-therapeutic results. Thus, if therapists reinforce family members' changes by giving them social approval these clients may become overdependent on the therapist and may increase rather than decrease their dire needs for approval, which are often one of the main sources of their disturbances. (Ellis 1982, p. 313)

Third, although REMT theory considers that partners' social learning experiences (as stressed by BMT) do contribute to couples' marital problems, it places distinct emphasis on the biological basis of human irrationality which determines their emotional problemss (Ellis 1976, 1984). As Ellis (1984) has noted, even if marital partners were very sanely raised in a non-devout fashion, they would still tend to take their strong desires and wants and turn them into devout musts and shoulds.

Finally, REMT therapists are likely to employ a wider range of emotive techniques than BMT therapists (see Chapter 9).

REMT differs from systems approaches to working with couples in the following ways. First, while systems therapists tend to focus on the relationships between the partners themselves and between the marital subsytem and other subsystems and suprasystems, they tend to deemphasize the serious personal problems of individual family members – i.e. they focus mainly on A in the ABC model. On the other hand, REMT therapists do pay distinct attention to these problems particularly in the 'overcoming marital disturbance' stage of therapy. Here the focus is on B in the ABC model. Although Treacher, more than most systems therapists, shows that he does focus on partners' maladaptive cognitions, he again, like BMT therapists, does not make clear distinctions between absolutistic evaluations and distorted inferences as advocated by REMT therapists. Second, systems-oriented practitioners consider that it is very important to conduct therapy with a back-up team of consultants on hand to give immediate supervisory feedback. These consultants typically observe the therapeutic interaction behind a one-way mirror or via closed-circuit television and thence make direct contact with the therapist, helping him or her to make effective interventions. REMT therapists tend not to conduct therapy in this way, preferring to video or audio-tape their sessions, in order to gain feedback on the therapeutic process *after* the event. Third, REMT therapists are probably more willing to treat the marital subsystem in isolation from other parts of the whole system than systems therapists even if the situation indicates the involvement of other family members. Fourth, REMT therapists tend to be more open with their clients in sharing the rationale for their interventions than systems-oriented therapists, particularly those that favour strategic interventions. Finally, unlike those systems therapists who favour the structural perspective of marital/family therapy, REMT therapists are not generally guided by ideas about what constitute 'healthy' or unhealthy family structures. Although, in this latter respect, Woulff (1983) has attempted to synthesize rational-emotive and structural approaches to family therapy.

Because it has distinct features, rational-emotive marital therapy is bound to differ from other approaches to working with couples in a number of respects. REMT's major distinct features are that it:

(1) places a unique emphasis on the role of devout absolutistic cognitions (musts, shoulds etc.) in emotional disturbance, a focus which leads to specific therapeutic interventions (including a wide range of cognitive, behavioural and emotive methods) designed to help partners change these to non-devout relative cognitions (wants, desires etc.);

(2) makes a clear distinction between marital disturbance and marital dissatisfaction and the importance of tackling, in most cases, disturbance issues before dissatisfaction issues in marital therapy if both are present;

(3) seeks to make contracts with each individual partner rather than with

'the couple'. As Harper (1981) has argued, it is difficult to have a contract with an abstraction. When contracts are made with the couple, each partner willingly subscribes to the conditions of the contract.

Enhancing rational-emotive marital therapy: contributions from the other approaches

RET is antiabsolutistic in nature and is thus against the use of dogma in psychotherapy as well as in other human endeavours. Thus, while REMT favours certain therapeutic strategies and methods and is against others, it recognizes that under certain conditions with certain clients such strategies and techniques that it does not favour may have some merit.

Ellis (1977) has argued that the rational-emotive therapist 'for the most part ignores connections between the client's early history and his present disturbances. He does not believe that the client was made neurotic by his past experiences, but by his own unrealistic and over-demanding *interpretations* of these experiences' (p. 27). However, there are times when partners do seek to make such connections and do derive benefit from understanding these (Dryden 1979). Here some of the insights and practices of psychodynamic marital therapists may be helpful (Dryden 1981). However, after such exploration, the rational-emotive marital therapist would wish to stress to clients that: 'Whatever irrational messages were communicated to them by significant others, they are still responsible for determining their own emotional disturbance by the communication of equally irrational messages to themselves' (Dryden 1984, p. 94). Another danger of exploring the past is that partners may begin to severely blame significant others for supposedly causing them their problems. Since REMT therapists consider that blame is a prime ingredient of marital disturbance, they would seek to help clients to accept these significant others as fallible humans rather than to damn them as subhumans.

Daniell has underscored the importance of understanding partners' use of projective identifications in disturbed marital relationships. She argues that a partner may project into the spouse unwanted bits of self that are unacceptable.

While REMT therapists agree that partners often defend themselves against the self-damnation that would result if they did acknowledge these unwanted aspects, they do not frequently refer to such projections when discussing marital problems. Yet the concept is certainly an intriguing one and merits further investigation. It is unfortunate that Daniell does not refer to research evidence supporting the wide use of this defence mechanism in marital disturbance. However, should such evidence be forthcoming, a focus on this mechanism could add appreciably to the rational-emotive conceptualization of marital disturbance.

I have already noted both in my chapter and in the above section the fact that REMT therapists utilize behavioural methods mainly in the 'overcoming marital dissatisfaction' stage of marital therapy to teach couples appropriate skills, and occasionally in the overcoming disturbance stage as an adjunct to cognitive disputing techniques. As such, it is important for REMT therapists to keep abreast of developments in BMT to enable them to apply new, validated methods. As BMT recently seems to be 'going cognitive' (Hahlweg and Jacobson 1984), mutual collaboration between the two approaches seems increasingly likely.

There are signs that rational-emotive therapists are already incorporating insights derived from systems approaches into their work. For example, Woulff (1983), writing about family therapy, suggests that insights from structural-strategic therapy can help rational-emotive therapists to identify dysfunctional aspects of family or marital systems. Having discovered these she then challenges the irrational beliefs of members of the system that impede structural reorganization. My personal difficulty with this approach has already been discussed; namely, it suggests that the therapist sets goals (of structural reorganization) for the members of the system rather than helping them to set their own goals for change. Perhaps on-going dialogue between REMT and systems therapists is needed to resolve some of these ideological problems.

I have argued elsewhere that systems theory offers REMT therapists a wider perspective in understanding how marital problems may be perpetuated (Dryden 1981). Using Feldman's (1976) diagram – see p. 262 of this book – I argued that viewing entire interactional cycles can help REMT therapists intervene in a way that avoids unforeseen and undesired consequences, a result which may occur if only a portion of these cycles are addressed. Finally, rational-emotive marital therapists could well benefit from using the live supervision methods that are a standard feature of the work of systems therapists.

I close with the conclusion to my 1981 paper since it is still apt: 'I am sure that the incorporation of procedures from object relations, behavioural and systems theory would enrich the practice of rational-emotive marital therapy without it losing its unique focus of aiding spouses in dysfunctional marriages to change their individually held beliefs' (Dryden 1981, p. 84). I am biased enough to consider that this enrichment process can also be reciprocal!

References

Dryden, W. (1979) Past messages and disputations: the client and significant others. *Rational Living*, *14(1)*, 26–28

Dryden, W. (1981) Rational-emotive therapy in marriage. *New Forum: The Journal of the Psychology and Psychotherapy Association*, 7, 82–84

Dryden, W. (1984) *Rational-emotive therapy: fundamentals and innovations.* Beckenham, Kent: Croom-Helm.

Ellis, A. (1976) The biological basis of human irrationality. *Journal of Individual Psychology*, *32*, 145–168.

Ellis, A. (1977) A rational approach to interpretation. *In* A. Ellis and R. Grieger (eds) *Handbook of rational-emotive therapy.* New York: Springer.

Ellis, A. (1982) Rational-emotive family therapy. *In* A. M. Horne and M. M. Ohlsen (eds) *Family counseling and therapy.* Itasca, Illinois: F. E. Peacock.

Ellis, A, (1984) The essence of RET-1984. *Journal of Rational-Emotive Therapy*, *2(1)*, 19–25.

Feldman, L. B. (1976) Depression and marital interaction. *Family Process, 15*, 389–395.

Hahlweg, K. and Jacobson, N. S. (eds) (1984) *Marital interaction: analysis and modification.* New York: Guilford.

Harper, R. A. (1981) Limitations of marriage and family therapy. *Rational Living*, *16(2)*, 3–6.

Woulff, N. (1983) Involving the family in the treatment of the child: a model for rational-emotive therapists, *In* A. Ellis and M. E. Bernard (eds) *Rational-emotive approaches to the problems of childhood.* New York: Plenum.

A SYSTEMS THERAPIST'S POINT OF VIEW – ANDY TREACHER

In the course of reading the very interesting and thought-provoking contributions of Diana Daniell, Windy Dryden and Dougal Mackay I realized, once again, how important it is for me to try to develop a more sophisticated approach to the marital work I undertake. There is a well-known folk tale about how a group of blindfolded wise men attempt to discover the nature of an unknown object (an elephant) which has been placed in front of them. One wise man fastens onto the elephant's trunk and is immediately convinced that he has discovered a snake; another discovers the elephant's tail but thinks the animal is a horse; yet another dicovers a leg and decides the object is a tree.

It seems to me that all four of us are essentially in the same position as the so-called wisemen. We each have important strengths in our approaches to marital therapy but I am sure that none of us is actually capable of solving the crucial task that faces all therapists – of being able to genuinely fit our approach to the idiosyncratic needs and problems of the couples that we have in therapy. In practice what we do is to force our couples onto the Procrustean bed of a rather limited approach – we then enjoy working with the couples that find the bed comfortable and moan about the couples that do not, labelling them 'unmotivated' or 'too fearful of changing'.

So above all else I want to avoid the trap of justifying *my* approach by criticizing the other three. I am much happier exploring each of the other approaches in order to say what ideas I would personally like to take from their approaches so that my own approach can be enriched and strengthened.

Factors influencing the formation of the marital relationship

Turning first to Diana Daniell's contribution – I am basically sympathetic to the idea that we all absorb models of partnership and parenting from the family context in which we have grown up (as Daniell argues) but I feel we must be careful not to adopt a naive 'recapitulationary' position on this issue. For example, because my father was aloof and did not parent me as closely as I would (in retrospect) have liked does not mean that I inevitably recapitulate the same aloofness when I parent my son.

Daniell's specific exploration of Bowlby's ideas about the influence of childhood experience on the formation of adult relationships is also of interest to me. An infant's experiences of how her parents maintain (or fail to maintain) that relationship with her may well play a crucial part in the way she will later organize her own adult-to-adult relationships. But at a practical level, when working with a given couple, I would not want to make any dogmatic statements about possible links unless I was able to actually collect convincing evidence from interviewing the couple directly.

Dougal Mackay's exploration of the factors that are operative when a couple decide to get married is much more prosaic and straightforward than Daniell's – 'perceived potential reinforcers' (such as regular sexual activity, starting a family, and parental approach) are stressed. I would wish to incorporate many of Mackay's ideas into my integrated theory but at the same time I am sure there is plenty of mileage in applying Bandura's social learning framework to the process of couple formation. For example it is to be expected that modelling processes can be influential in determining the choice of marital partner and that Mackay's use of Thibaut and Kelley's social exchange model is too limiting.

Unfortunately, neither Windy Dryden nor myself explore the area of couple formation in our chapters. I would guess that Dryden would be happy to accept Mackay's position (in much the same way as I do) but I would suspect that he might be more sympathetic to accepting the idea that the choice of a partner can be influenced by scripts derived from one's family of origin. As I have already hinted, my own position seeks to combine here-and-now explanations with explanations (such as scripting) which are prepared to explore the social learning histories of the individuals involved. I am also sympathetic to Daniell's insistence that there are other factors involved. For example I would largely accept the terms in which she discusses the example of Mr and Mrs Grey – the projective processes that seem to be of crucial importance in this relationship are convincingly traced back to the families of origin of the two partners. The complementary nature of the current relationship is, therefore, not merely observed (and left at that) but explained in terms of the experiences that the couple underwent earlier in their life histories.

The origins of marital disturbance

Daniell's explanation of the origins of marital disturbance is both sophisticated and complicated, and I suspect my summary will not really do justice to it. The essence of her position is to argue that there are powerful unconscious factors that determine the choices that marital partners make. Strong unconscious ties bind individuals to their first love objects (their parents) and it is these ties which help to determine the choice of a partner with whom earlier experiences can be compulsively reenacted.

So the seeds of marital disturbance are implanted in the relationship from its very beginning. Obviously it is not a foregone conclusion that marital dysfunction will inevitably follow – for, according to Daniell, partners often pick each other 'judiciously' since they both share a common level of emotional immaturity. Their marriage can then become a 'container' in which the partners are able to give each other enough time, space and trust to work through their shared area of difficulty.

Daniell's explanation is further complicated by mobilizing the concepts of shared fantasy and shared defence. These are useful quasi-interactional concepts which are helpful in explaining some of the collusive characteristics of certain marital relationships. The emotional distance that a couple adopt in relation to each other is a very tangible feature of any marital relationship. Daniell argues that this distance is determined by a shared fantasy about the feared outcome that will occur if feared impulses in the self or in the partner are actually allowed to emerge. Normally the process of couple formation generates enough material trust for these shared fantasies to be openly explored (and hopefully exploded as myths) but in a situation of marital disturbance these distorted perceptions are not accessible and cannot, therefore, be modified even in the light of current benign experiences.

I find much of what Daniell says both interesting and convincing but I feel there is too great an emphasis on unconscious processes and too little on the direct conscious processes that also influence behaviour. Interestingly Daniell points out that marital disturbance typically occurs when major transitions are occurring within the family life cycle (e.g. the arrival of a first baby can often trigger off a marital crisis), but it is strange that she does not explore the theoretical implications of this point in any depth. For example, while she correctly points out that all these transitional events appear to have a factor in common, i.e. that the couple must define themselves and each other in new ways, she fails to take the argument any further than this observation. It is one of the undoubted strengths of systems theorists that they are genuinely sensitive to these issues because it is systems theory that insists that it is the emergent properties of newly developing systems that must be adequately explored and understood if successful therapeutic interventions are to be made.

Dougal Mackay's explanation of marital disturbance is markedly different from Daniell's. Daniell's explanation largely ignores here-and-now factors whereas Mackay's is very much embedded in the here and now. As he succinctly puts it . . . 'Marital disharmony . . . arises when the costs of remaining married exceed the rewards. Factors which cause and maintain this state of imbalance include the withdrawal of favours, futile attempts to force compliance, failure to communicate properly, inability to solve problems collectively and the presence of inappropriate expectations regarding the relationship'.

Mackay's apparently prosaic approach contrasts with Daniell's highly theoretical one but his insistence on actually examining the parameters that are known to influence marital harmony and disharmony cannot be easily ignored. Research evidence that shows that the tendency of one partner to withhold rewards leads to the other partner reciprocating in kind is significant enough but his inventory of self-defeating change strategies is equally important since it insists that we continually examine the specific nature of the on-going processes in which the couple are caught up. His stress on the significance of communication and problem-solving skills is also an integral part of his approach but recent developments in behaviour therapy have also ensured that the crucial cognitive aspects of couple relationships are no longer ignored. For example, Eidelson and Epstein's (1982) five major irrational beliefs which can commonly bedevil marital relationships are precisely the sort of beliefs which need to be confronted if a marital relationship is to be significantly changed.

Obviously Windy Dryden's approach overlaps strongly with Mackay's at this point — both correctly place a strong emphasis on challenging the disabling cognitive frameworks that distressed couples typically adopt. However, I would hasten to add that much of Daniell's work can be reinterpreted within a cognitive framework. The myths and fantasies talked about by Daniell are not in principle different from Mackay's and Dryden's irrational beliefs. But the thrust of Dryden's position concerning marital disturbances is, nevertheless, different from Mackay's because it is consistently more cognitive in its stance than Mackay's.

Dryden's useful distinction between marital dissatisfaction and marital disturbance is central to his approach. Marital dissatisfaction is a universal, non-problematic, often transitory situation experienced by all couples at one time or another, but marital disturbance arises when marital partners become emotionally disturbed about the marital dissatisfaction they are experiencing. The emotional disturbance they experience in turn prevents them from mobilizing constructive communication, problem-solving and negotiating skills which would normally help them solve the marital dissatisfaction problem that arose in the first place. The thrust of the approach is, therefore, to seek to attack the processes that lead to the couple being emotionally disturbed. The four main methods of creating emotional disturbance (musturbation, I-can't-stand-it-itis, awfulizing and damning) are therefore singled out for replacement by rational information-processing procedures.

Reading Dryden's chapter has reawakened my interest in RET but, despite the elegance of the theory and the personal benefits I have derived from applying RET to some of my own personal problems, I am ultimately sceptical about using it as a general method. My clients tend to be caught up in family systems which give them little time and space to individuate. I might well use an RET or cognitive behaviour therapy approach with an individual client when I have made other interventions which have produced movement within the family system, but I feel it would be extremely time-consuming to adopt an RET approach from the very beginning of therapy.

Therapy

I will not attempt to deal with all the facets of therapy discussed in the four chapters, but I will attempt to come to grips with the differing stances that are adopted. Daniell's approach is clearly less structured than the other three – the therapist's task is to create a safe context in which the couple can work through their problems. The therapists themselves need to be drawn into this process – transference and countertransference processes are therefore accepted as the essential vehicles for producing change. Such an approach inevitably takes time and issues of pace are crucial. The clients must feel able to adopt the pace that suits them and the task of the therapists is to be mainly facilitatory, although, Daniell argues, they also need to be 'penetrating'. However, she does not elaborate the point in any detail.

My own reaction to this stance is somewhat mixed – for some couples I am sure the approach has a lot of possibilities, but I am sceptical about its overall suitability. The approach is too one-dimensional for me – I suppose I lack the patience to work at such a slow pace, but I am also convinced that different couples respond best to different approaches so it is necessary to attempt to match the style of the couple to the therapy. Since most of my marital work takes place in conjunction with therapy that is undertaken with both the nuclear and the extended family of the couple, I prefer to adopt a style of therapy that is generally much more directive. But I am willing to acknowledge that the types of couple that come to an agency such as the IMS may be well suited to the style and pace of Daniell's approach.

Turning to Mackay's approach to therapy, I am immediately attracted to his insistence on the necessity for adequate assessment as an initial stage of therapy. (Many systems theorists suffer from an overdeveloped ability to hypothesize from a minimum of rather poorly collated data but in general it is best to remember the adage that 'when you hear hooves, think first of horses not zebras'.) I am also attracted to a related point – Mackay argues that assessment must be balanced by careful attention to forming and maintaining a therapeutic alliance with the couple in therapy. However, despite these points of agreement, I find that I diverge from Mackay's position on one important point. This may appear at first sight to be an unimportant stylistic difference but I feel it is a crucial issue that may reflect, ultimately, a major philosophical difference.

First of all let us consider the following quotation from Mackay: 'In certain respects, it is actually easier to assess a troubled marriage than an individual's problem since the therapist can directly observe the relevant antecedents and consequences of the target responses, during the treatment sessions, rather than rely on self-reports.' Obviously I am in agreement with this but why should we just limit our assessment to the couple system? Why not see how the couple relate to their children (if they have any) or to the wider systems (parents, friends and neighbours). Mackay points out how myopic behaviour therapists have been in concentrating too much on the individual when it was the marital system that required attention, but I would have thought that he needed to extend his argument to include other systems as well. (I would see Dryden falling into the same trap because both approaches have their origins in individual psychotherapy.)

The actual treatment techniques used by Mackay are ones that I am happy to adopt – they have an essentially commonsense ring to them and create a crucial 'atmosphere' in the therapy, which suits my philosophy – marriage, like so many aspects of life, is something that needs to be worked out – just as a car needs maintenance work, so does a marriage.

I am sure that Dryden would be happy with this metaphor too, since the RET approach to marital therapy is essentially one of exploring myths and getting down to the basics of getting a marriage to work through getting each partner to ask what they want from a marriage and helping them to negotiate ways of getting it. However, the appeal of Dryden's approach is more subtle than this – REMT is a well-thought-out approach which places a great premium on assisting the individuation of both partners. I am not sure whether there is any basic difference between Mackay's and Dryden's approaches as far as this dimension of therapy is concerned, but my understanding of the difference between the two approaches is that Mackay's is basically more eclectic with the treatment plan being dependent on the inital assessments that are made, whereas Dryden's approach adopts a more 'single method' stance: the 'overcoming marital disturbance' phase is a phase in which the RET philosophy and method of therapy are actively taught; the 'enhancing marital satisfaction' phase can afford to be more variegated and custom-built since it draws upon the particular strengths and weaknesses of the couple in therapy.

Mackay's essentially problem-solving method is in many ways closest to the more pragmatic forms of family therapy which adopt the stance that the therapist's task is to help solve the presenting problem that is brought to therapy. RET is closer (paradoxically) to more humanistic forms of family therapy that stress the necessity for setting goals that attempt to directly achieve growth and individuation in therapy. My own form of therapy (as I think my case illustration demonstrates) in fact combines both approaches.

Before concluding this contribution it is necessary to add one final point about my own approach. I tried to select a case illustration which demonstrated the range of techniques which I am capable of utilizing when working with a given case. While my orientation is generally that of a systems theorist, I am very willing to integrate approaches that are taken from other psychotherapy approaches. This might well be called the tool-shed approach, i.e. a given tool is selected and worked with according to the particular requirement of therapy at the time the choice of tool is made.

Conclusion

Having reviewed the four chapters as best I can I have created a lot of confusion in my own mind about how to proceed as a marital therapist. I am quite happy with this confusion since I have felt a strong need to concentrate more of my attention on this element of my therapeutic work. The effect of reading and commenting on my colleagues' work is to force me to reexamine the work of therapists such as Feldman and Pinsof (Feldman 1979; Feldman and Pinsof 1982) and Berman, Lief and Williams (1981) who have made important contributions to developing coherent, integrated models which draw on the strengths of psychodynamic, behavioural and systems approaches. At a broader level I also realize that I need to look more closely at the McMaster 'school' of family therapy which has as yet not developed much of a following in this country. This school of family therapy is perhaps the most universal in its appeal since it seeks to integrate ideas developed from several schools of psychotherapy (Epstein and Bishop 1981).

I am sure, from my own experience with clients, that successful marital therapy requires blending these elements but this in practice means that therapists from different schools need to share their work far more than we do. We tend to hive off from each other – perhaps it is time for an ecumenical movement to be started? I am happy with my tool-shed approach but I often get the impression that I either have selected the wrong tool or I am working with the right tool at the wrong time. What I badly need to develop is an integrated theory which guides and strengthens my approach.

References

Berman, E., Lief, H. and Williams, A. M. (1981) A model of marital interaction. *In* G. Pirooz Sholevar (ed.) *The handbook of marriage and marital therapy.* Lancaster: MTP Press Ltd.

Eidelson, R. J. and Epstein, N. (1982) Cognition and relationship maladjustment: development of a measure of dysfunctional relationship beliefs. *Journal of Consulting and Clinical Psychology*, 50, 715–720.

Epstein, N. B. and Bishop, D. S. (1981) Problem-centered systems therapy of the family. *In* A. S. Gurman and D. P. Kniskern (eds) *Handbook of family therapy*. New York: Brunner-Mazel.

Feldman, L. B. (1979) Marital conflict and marital intimacy: An integrative psychodynamic–behavioural–systemic model. *Family Process*, 18, 69–78.

Feldman, L. B. and Pinsof, W. (1982) Problem maintenance in family systems: An integrative model. *Journal of Marital and Family Therapy*, 8, 295–308.

A BEHAVIOURAL THERAPIST'S POINT OF VIEW – DOUGAL MACKAY

Similarities with other approaches

So far as the nature of marital disturbance is concerned, the behavioural formulation is most similar to that put forward by rational-emotive therapists. Both schools maintain that communication skills deficits and cognitive dysfunctions are the primary causes of marital distress. The main difference between the models is largely one of emphasis. In REMT, the inability of the couple to interact constructively, negotiate compromises and solve problems together is regarded as relevant largely to marital dissatisfaction. Marital disturbance, on the other hand, is attributed to beliefs, held by one or both partners, which are absolutistic in nature. In BMT, no such clear distinction is made between dissatisfied and disturbed marriages. In other words, the therapist is not influenced by the severity of the relationship problems when conducting the behavioural analysis. With all couples, it is assumed that the negative reciprocity which has developed is largely a function of poor interpersonal skills on the part of one or both partners. Although inappropriate expectations, perceptions and attitudes often contribute to marital disturbance, it is conjectured that a crisis would not have emerged if the couple had been able to express their feelings appropriately and listen empathically to each other.

According to the behavioural model, much of the anger and hostility experienced by the distressed marital partner can be attributed to his feelings of frustration: at being unable to express clearly his thoughts and emotions, or with his spouse who consistently fails to acknowledge the points he is making. This raises the interesting question of whether or not these feelings of frustration are justified. In other words, is the marriage disturbed because the couple cannot communicate effectively or because they have unrealistic expectations about how well they *should* be able to communicate? From a strictly theoretical viewpoint, BMT and REMT would part company at this point. However, in clinical practice, therapists from both schools would recognize the complexity of the interactions between cognitions and behaviour and take account of both sets of factors when designing a treatment programme.

An aspect which is common to BMT, REMT and the systems approach is the notion that marital disturbance is perpetuated through a process of negative reciprocity. In other words, both partners are exerting stimulus control over each other's behaviour and thereby contributing equally to the self-defeating patterns of interaction which lie at the core of their relationship problems. Naturally REMT emphasizes the role of dysfunctional beliefs in maintaining these vicious circles while both the systems approach and BMT, in their traditional forms at least, focus more on overt responses. As Treacher points out in his reference to Feldman's work, the models are not antagonistic to each other on this issue and can easily be integrated to produce a comprehensive account of the persistence of maladaptive interactional patterns.

With regard to therapeutic context, only BMT and the psychodynamic approach argue strongly that the treatment contract should be made with both partners and that work should be carried out primarily on a conjoint basis. However the rationales for so doing are rather different. The behaviour therapist does not regard the marriage as a 'psychic entity' which amounts to more than the sum of the two parts. Rather he views the marital relationship as a complex set of behavioural interchanges which have been well rehearsed over the years. Conjoint therapy provides him with a perfect opportunity for observing, analysing and ultimately modifying the maladaptive stimulus–response sequences in an 'in vivo' setting. Seeing individuals separately would decrease his effectiveness in accomplishing this task while introducing other family members, without good reason, would unneccessarily complicate the whole process.

Both REMT and the systems approach incorporate such behavioural techniques as interpersonal skills training, with particular emphasis on negotiation and problem-solving, in their treatment repertoires. The rational-emotive therapist employs them primarily to facilitate cognitive change while the systems therapist is more concerned to disrupt the couple's mode of reacting to each other. As is the case in BMT, homework tasks are set in order to effect generalization from the therapeutic to the domestic situation. However, while therapists from both these schools are mainly interested in global patterns of interaction, the behaviour therapist works with very specific communication skills and coaches the couple in these through modelling, behaviour rehearsal and feedback.

There is an obvious similarity between BMT and the systems approach with regard to therapeutic style. In both schools, it is important that the therapist should be prepared to interrupt the couple when a discussion seems futile, confront them when they are resisting change, alter direction when a session is becoming aimless, and suggest different ways of behaving to effect more constructive interactions. In behaviour therapy, the main purpose of such directive interventions is to ensure that the couple keep to their contract by working on the issues initially agreed upon and in the manner decided by all parties. In the systems approach, the situation is rather different in that the therapist adopts certain tactics and employs particular techniques in response to the phenomena he is observing. In other words, formulation is an on-going process in this approach with interventions being used both to facilitate change and to understand better the couple's problems. Nevertheless, it is important that practitioners of both approaches should be seen to be confident in what they are doing and be prepared to be appropriately assertive with their clients.

Major differences from other approaches

Traditional BMT and psychodynamic therapy provide sharply contrasting views of the nature of marital disturbance. The social exchange model, which regards relationship satisfaction in terms of ratios between rewards and costs, implies that individuals are essentially hedonistic. Since their primary motive is to increase pleasure and decrease pain, they naturally feel disinclined to continue to function in an environment which frustrates them in these endeavours. Attempts by the couple to restructure their marital environment will fail, according to BMT, unless they carry out negotiations on a rational adult-to-adult basis. The psychoanalytic therapist, on the other hand, maintains that the choice of partner and the expectations of marriage are bound up with ambivalent feelings toward love-objects from childhood. One implication of this is that the individual is motivated, at an unconscious level, to compulsively reenact early experiences within the marital context. It is this, so it is argued, which leads the unhappily married person to behave in ways which lead to marital conflict, rather than ineffective change strategies or poor communication skills. In other words, the reason why he is not able to relate to his partner on an adult-to-adult basis is because his feelings towards her are bound up with his arrested emotional development.

Behaviour therapists would not quarrel with the proposition that the role one adopts in marriage is directly affected by relationships with parents in childhood. In fact, one of the main tenets of social learning theory is that, since parents act as models for their children, all kinds of disturbed behaviour can be passed on from generation to generation. However, there is a marked difference between learning discrete reponses through imitation and acquiring diverse patterns of behaviour, some of which may be symbolic, through identification. Moreover, the notion of discrete phases of emotional development, each associated with a succession of positions of ambivalence towards significant others, is outside the frame of reference of the traditional behavioural model. Although many bold attempts have been made to translate psychoanalytic concepts into learning theory terms, none have proved totally satisfactory.

Although BMT and REMT present similar formulations of marital disturbance, and incorporate both cognitive and behavioural techniques in their therapeutic repertoire, they differ significantly with regard to contextual considerations and the therapeutic contract. While the behaviour therapist insists on working with the couple, the rational-emotive therapist prefers to discuss with the clients the arrangement they would prefer. Moreover, should they choose to enter into conjoint therapy, the therapist will spend much of the time working with each individual in turn.* This is in contrast to BMT where the therapist is concerned exclusively with the couple's interactions. Should dysfunctional beliefs emerge as relevant variables, the therapist will not explore their origins with the particular individual concerned nor examine ways in which these cognitions may be interfering with his effectiveness in other life settings. Similarly he will not pursue disclosures from either partner that a particular communication difficulty is not confined to the marriage. Should a client wish to engage in more extensive personal explorations, he would be advised to enter into a separate therapeutic contract with another therapist.

One implication of this restricted agenda is that the therapist's responsibility is to the couple rather than to two individuals. In other words, when both partners actively seek help for their marital difficulties, he will attempt to facilitate changes in an endeavour to improve the quality of their relationship, even though privately he might suspect that the continuation of

---

Editors' note: This is particularly so in the overcoming disturbance stage of REMT.

the marriage is not in the interest of one or both partners. However, if either partner had sought individual therapy instead, the therapist would have considered himself freer to explore, in depth, all aspects of the individual's life-style. One of the many issues that could have arisen is whether or not the individual was being rational by continuing to expend energy on a relationship which had been a constant source of distress to him. Since what is best for the couple may not always coincide with what is best for the individual, the BMT therapist chooses to avoid potential role conflicts by establishing a clearly defined marital therapeutic contract from the outset.

So far as treatment is concerned, the most striking contrast is between BMT and psychodynamic marital therapy. In behaviour therapy it is important to arrive at a comprehensive formulation of the marital problems as early as possible in treatment. Only when all parties share a common conceptualization of the difficulties is it possible to stipulate goals, decide on methods, and enter into a treatment contract. As a result, the agenda for each session is relatively fixed and it is the therapist's task to ensure that discussions of other issues do not interfere with the work which has to be done. This is not to imply that the approach is unnecessarily rigid. If one or both parties seem resistant to change, or if treatment gains do not lead to a corresponding increase in marital satisfaction, then the therapist must be prepared to reformulate the problem and negotiate a new contract.

In the psychoanalytic approach, lack of structure is considered to be an essential feature of the therapeutic process in that it facilitates the development of transference and countertransference feelings. In view of the assumption that behaviour is governed by both conscious and unconscious factors, the interactions between clients and therapists are considered to be important in that they reflect unresolved conflicts which need to be made explicit and worked on. Were the therapists to coach the couple in communication skills, or set them homework assignments, such symbolic material would not present itself to the same degree. Thus, given the major differences between the two approaches in terms of the way they make sense of problems, it is inevitable that they should be in such sharp contrast to each other with regard to methods for facilitating change.

Aspects of other models which could be usefully incorporated into BMT

The fundamental assumption in BMT, that *all* marital difficulties are due to the inability of the couple to negotiate compromises in order to maximize their reward/cost ratios, is open to question. Although empirical and clinical evidence would suggest that this is true for many distressed marriages, it cannot easily account for all the phenomena. For example, the case of the divorced man who reenacts his marital dramas with a series of different partners is unlikely to have a minor communication skills deficit as his major problem. The psychoanalytic model is alone in providing an explanation of why it is that certain individuals engage in disastrous relationships with partners who have certain personality characteristics in common. Moreover it provides plausible hypotheses as to why the conflicts which arise in such relationships are so similar in nature. Thus, although psychodynamic concepts are not easily translated into social learning theory terminology, the behavioural marital therapist would be ill-advised to exclude them altogether from his formulation of complex cases.

However, although the psychoanalytic model may provide useful insights into certain relationship difficulties, it does not automatically follow that an unstructured therapeutic context is essential for facilitating change in such cases. Behaviour therapists would continue to argue that the most effective way of modifying maladaptive habitual responses is to make these explicit and explore alternative ways of behaving. Thus, the main contribution which psychoanalytic theory can make to BMT is to help the therapist to understand better the underlying processes and to take these into account when planning treatment programmes.

A second shortcoming of the traditional behavioural model is that it places undue emphasis on interpersonal behaviour at the expense of cognitive factors. Although helping the couple to exchange 'pleases' can be a useful device for promoting attitude change and modifying attributions, REMT therapists would rightly argue that the effects will only be short-lived if one or both parties are holding on to absolutistic beliefs about marriage. To take a simple example, the wife who believes that 'in order to be happily married my husband must always put me first' may well feel satisfied when he agrees to spend Saturday afternoons at the supermarket rather than at the golf-course. However, if six months later he is required to spend one night each week away on business, the conflict will probably reemerge. Rather than return to their therapist for some booster sessions in negotiation and problem solving, it would clearly be more appropriate to work on the belief which is giving rise to such strong negative feelings. As pointed out in the chapter on BMT, cognitive interventions have been shown to be a very effective component of treatment packages. However, compared with REMT, the behaviour marital therapist is unlikely either to analyse irrational thinking processes in great depth or to modify fundamental beliefs. To do so would place the therapist in the dilemma, mentioned above, as to whether his contract is with the relationship or with the two individuals. Since undoubtedly there are cases where a more penetrating cognitive approach is called for, the behavioural marital therapist might well consider whether or not he is being excessively rigid by insisting on working exclusively in a conjoint context.

Thus, although BMT has proved itself to be an extremely cost-effective approach to resolving marital difficulties, its range of convenience could be extended by accommodating concepts from psychoanalytic theory and techniques from REMT. This could be easily achieved without sacrificing the main elements of this model. The formulation process would be enriched if underlying dynamics were to be incorporated into the behavioural analysis, and the inclusion of sophisticated cognitive interventions in the clinician's repertoire would not interfere with his need for structure in the therapeutic process.

CHAPTER THIRTEEN Marital Therapy
A Behavioural-Systems
Approach – Indications for
Different Types of Intervention
Michael Crowe

General introduction

Within the field of marital therapy there are several theoretical frameworks
and associated intervention approaches which may at first sight appear
unconnected and irreconcilable. Thus, in the seminal book edited by
Paolino and McCrady (1978), the differences and contrasts between psychodynamic, behavioural and systems approaches to both marriage and marital
therapy are made very clear. It may indeed be that the opposite ways of
conceptualization represented by the behavioural and the psychoanalytic
schools are practically irreconcilable, although Segraves (1982) has made a
brave attempt to combine them. However, I will be presenting in the present
chapter the case that, if one uses a basically behavioural framework and
retains an empirical and observational approach to marital problems, it is
possible to enhance the effectiveness of basic behavioural marital therapy
by the use of selected 'systems' techniques at suitable stages in therapy
(Crowe 1982).

Behavioural approaches to marital therapy

These have been widely used and researched in the past fifteen years, since
the pioneering work of Stuart (1969) and Liberman (1970). Behavioural
marital therapy (BMT) has been shown in a variety of studies (see Hahlweg
and Jacobson 1984) to be an effective method for the treatment of marital
problems, especially those involving arguments, power struggles, resentment and anger. BMT is effective in short-term trials in comparison with
no-treatment or placebo control procedures (Jacobson 1978) and this effectiveness is maintained at follow-up to eighteen months after therapy (Crowe
1978).

BMT can be neatly divided into two types of approach (Jacobson and
Martin 1976). These are usually termed reciprocity negotiation (RN) and
communication training (CT) and both will be described in detail in later
sections. RN is usually treated as the more basic approach to marital prob-

lems, with CT being used where negotiation is difficult or communication skills are poor.

Systems approaches to marital therapy

It is well known that some problems appear to resist the simplistic approaches to BMT (Hahlweg 1984). What these problems are and how to identify them will be explored in later sections of this chapter. It is in the face of these problems (e.g. where one partner is firmly labelled as the patient, where one partner places the other on a pedestal or where a rather disturbed relationship is seen as 'perfect') that systems techniques appear to have value. The techniques I shall be describing are in many cases simplifications of those used in family therapy (see Hoffman (1981) for a theoretical exposition of family systems approaches) but in advocating them I shall avoid some of the more abstruse systemic explanations of their use and treat them rather as empirical methods to be used in specific situations. These 'systems' techniques seem to be effective in (a) moving couples from seeing their problems in symptom terms to seeing them in terms of disturbed relationships and (b) removing some of the symptomatic behaviour itself.

The three sources of systems techniques to be mentioned are Structural Therapy (Minuchin 1974), Strategic or Problem-Solving Therapy (Haley 1976) and Systemic Therapy (Selvini Palazzoli et al. 1978). The techniques are, of course, much more widely used in family therapy than in marital therapy. However, Sluzki (1978) summarized quite clearly and succinctly his systems-oriented approach to marital therapy, which includes both structural and strategic elements. In addition, Treacher in the present volume describes a systems approach to working with couples.

Many fascinationg case reports have been published on the application of systems techniques to specific marital problems. For example, Teismann (1979) used some paradoxical and strategic interventions in a case of morbid jealousy with a successful outcome. In a more wide-ranging article, again on jealousy within marriage, Im et al. (1983) describe a range of interventions from cognitive and rational-emotive to structural and paradoxical. However, there is a dearth of published controlled trials of systems marital therapy. The study by Emmelkamp et al. (1984) is one of the few to compare behavioural and systems marital therapy and it is of interest to note that there were no significant differences in outcome. In spite of the lack of outcome studies, clinical experience in the use of both systems and behavioural techniques within the same couple have reinforced for me the notion that some systems techniques will 'unlock' a relationship which appears stuck, and will make it possible at a later stage of therapy to apply behavioural techniques such as RN.

The behavioural-systems approach

What I will be advocating in this chapter is, therefore, an eclectic but primarily behavioural approach to marital therapy. There are some similarities with the approach described by Spinks and Birchler (1982) under the title of Behavioural-Systems Marital Therapy, and it is interesting that Weiss, one of the pioneers of BMT, was also instrumental in developing the approach they describe. Broadly speaking, their approach combines BMT techniques and systems techniques in the assessment period, but they predominantly use BMT during therapy, with some paradoxical and other interventions of a systems type in response to 'resistance' by the couple – e.g. lack of completion of homework tasks or emergence of new symptoms during therapy.

The approach I will be describing is quite similar, but relies on some aspects of individual diagnosis in addition to the degree of inflexibility and individual symptom-orientation in the relationship as the guide whether to use BMT or systems interventions. All these issues will be dealt with in more detail in the subsequent sections.

The techniques basic to the behavioural systems approach

Reciprocity negotiation

Technique of reciprocity negotiation This behavioural approach was originally termed 'operant-interpersonal treatment' (Stuart 1969) and has also been loosely termed 'marital contract therapy'. However, the fact that operant conditioning principles are seldom employed, and the absence of any binding contract between the two marital partners, has led to a gradual abandonment of these two terms in favour of the more general term 'reciprocity negotiation'. The simple-minded concept behind Stuart's approach is derived in part from the social learning theories of Thibaut and Kelley (1959). These, in Stuart's formulation, suggest that in successful marriages there is a fairly high level, and a fairly even division between partners, of rewarding interpersonal behaviour. In marriages which are unsuccessful there is thought to be a low level or a very uneven distribution of such behaviour.

In RN the couple are asked to use the therapist as a kind of diplomatic interpreter, who will help them to reach a negotiated settlement of their differences. The therapist also works from an assumption that the couple recognize that they have difficulties in negotiation, and are prepared to learn from an 'expert' the skills involved. They are each asked to state their complaints about the behaviour of the other partner. The complaints are then examined by the therapist and the partners are asked to restate these complaints as wishes for a change in each other's behaviour so as to eliminate the complaints. Thus negative is converted into positive and past to future.

For example if a man continually returns home later than he has stated, and is unpredictable in this, his wife might say, 'I never know when he's coming home.' The therapist might ask her to say how she wants him to behave, for example: 'I would like him to come home when he has said he would and, if he's going to be late, to 'phone me in time for me to delay my cooking.' The therapist would commend the phrasing of this last statement, which is positive, constructive and future-orientated. He would check with the husband whether the course of action requested is acceptable and practicable, and if so would ask the wife to monitor, during the interval until the next session, whether the husband has complied with her request. A similar sequence of negotiation would take place with the husband's complaints about the wife's behaviour. The key steps in this process are as follows:

(a) complaints become wishes;
(b) wishes become tasks;
(c) tasks are imposed reciprocally;
(d) the carrying out of the tasks is monitored by the one who requested them.

The key transformations in concepts involved are:

(a) past to future;
(b) negative to positive;
(c) general to specific;
(d) destructive to constructive.

The precautions to be taken in task-setting are:

(a) they must be reciprocal;
(b) they must be accepted by both partners;

(c)   they must be practicable;
(d)   they must apply to regularly repeated behaviour

Advantages of reciprocity negotiation   There are some marital problems that lend themselves very easily to this approach. Where both partners have complaints about each other, for instance, RN is probably the approach of first choice. Where one partner is complaining and the other is passively non-compliant with the first partner, the therapist can introduce RN concepts: for instance the passive partner is asked to comply with the wishes of the complaining partner while the complaining partner is asked to address the passive partner in a different way so as to avoid complaining. The therapist may have to work on the communication to some extent in the session to make clear to both partners the kind of positive and constructive comments which are to take the place of complaining. Even where one partner is quite depressed, it is not impossible at times to introduce negotiation on some issues of marital discord. However, this is clearly more difficult than when both partners are having a fairly evenly matched argument about each other's behaviour. The depressed mood and the 'well' partner's response to it mean that the degree of flexibility in negotiation is reduced.

An important principle stated by Stuart (1969) and repeated many times since is that each partner must take responsibility for his/her own behaviour. They should not wait for the other partner to change before changing their own behaviour, but should rather carry out an act of faith by changing themselves first.

Reciprocity negotiation is a reliable and well-researched method of improving marital interaction, and is probably capable of improving some 50 percent of all presented marital problems. Problems which respond well could be characterized as follows:

(a)   arguments, resentment and power struggles;
(b)   some sexual motivation problems;
(c)   problems recognized as marital by the couple themselves;
(d)   problems where the partners are able and willing to negotiate.

Limitations of reciprocity negotiation   Three difficulties arising with this approach can be dealt with by communication training, i.e. where

(a)   both partners put the blame firmly on the same partner – 'it's all my fault' – 'yes, it's all his fault';

(b) the partners cannot communicate constructively, but instead go into digressions, monologues, complaints about past misdeeds, or continually use negative statements about each other's motives;

(c) the partners appear to be unable to use the therapist's positive reframing of complaints as tasks and continue instead to blame the other partner and to expect the other partner to 'change first'.

Communication Training

Technique of communication training This is the next stage of sophistication in marital therapy. It is still a branch of BMT and aims, in a similar way to RN, at improving a couple's negotiating and communicating skills. It is well described in a little manual by Gottman et al. (1976). As in RN, the therapist and the couple both enter the transaction on the understanding that the couple have a lack of communications skills, and are prepared to learn those skills from the therapist.

The principles of CT are quite similar to those of RN. Each partner has to take responsibility for his/her own behaviour, words and feelings. Destructive criticism is converted to constructive, past to present or future, general to specific, negative to positive. The couple must keep to the point of what is being discussed and should try to reach a negotiated conclusion on the topic they are discussing. In order to achieve this, the therapist has to perform an 'audience' function or 'decentre' himself while the couple talk to each other. From time to time he may stop the discussion to point out that one or other partner is being destructive, or vague, or repetitive, and will usually suggest a different way in which they could put the same point. The therapist should remain impartial in this as far as possible and should use the same rules in communicating to the couple as he is asking them to use towards each other; his interventions should be positive, constructive, future-oriented and very specific.

For example, a wife was continually blaming her husband for his insensitivity to her during an episode six years earlier. At first she was inclined, as he was, to call this an obsessional thought and demand medical treatment for it. I gradually helped them to take it more seriously, not as a complaint about the past but as a comment on their present relationship: she continually had to remind him of the past because she thought he was still insensitive to her needs. She was encouraged to ask him to take a different approach to her complaints, which he was prone to dismiss as 'silliness' or 'obsessions'. She asked him to show in the session that he understood how she had suffered six years ago. He said, 'I understand that you were hurt, but I had no intention of hurting you.' To her this was an improvement, but still gave her the impression that she had been wrong in blaming him, and she still thought the second part of his statement showed his defensiveness. I asked him to put the statement the other way round: 'Although I had no intention of hurting you, I understand that you were hurt at the time.' This was more satisfactory to her, and went as far as he could go along the road of accepting responsibility for his own actions and their consequences. It also illustrates the advantages of bringing past grievances as far as possible into the present, and of renegotiating attitudes to such events as a way of improving present communication. Some ground rules for communication training as used by me are as follows:

(a) change destructive to constructive criticism;
(b) partners to suggest alternative behaviours to those complained of;
(c) general complaints to become specific (e.g. not 'you are always putting me down' but 'last Saturday at the party I felt hurt when you mentioned my weight problem');
(d) take the 'I' position (see the above example);
(e) neither partner to go on in monologues – the therapist should insist on a rapid exchange and accurate feedback;
(f) neither partner to assume knowledge of the other's 'real' motives (I often term this activity 'mind-reading' and discourage it);
(g) if possible the partners should end a statement on a positive note (see the example above of changing the order of the sentence) and avoid the 'sting in the tail';
(h) the partners should be aware of each other's sensitive points, and if possible avoid hurting each other in their interaction. Thus a retaliation is reframed by the therapist as showing that that person has been hurt, and one explores the nature of the sensitivity rather than who is to blame for what.

Advantages of communication training Throughout CT, as in RN, the therapist remains the expert, the teacher, never stirring up arguments, always encouraging compromise and understanding, and assuming that the only reason communication problems exist is that the couple have not learned better methods. The problems it is useful for are quite similar to those mentioned above under RN, where there are arguments, resentment, power struggles, sexual motivation problems, and where the marital focus is accepted. CT is useful over and above RN where:

(a) the couple cannot negotiate well;
(b) there are overinclusive discussions;
(c) communication is characterized by misunderstandings and repetition.

Limitations of communication training CT appears to be less effective in the presence of other factors. These include:

(a) where the couple are not ready to accept the focus on interaction as an agenda for the sessions;
(b) where there are great inequalities in power or other important aspects of the relationship;
(c) where one partner is firmly designated by them both as 'the problem';
(d) where there is a constant avoidance of argument;
(e) in the presence of clear neurotic or other psychiatric symptoms.

If these factors are present, or if empirically the couple seem unwilling or unable to accept communication training, or if in the sessions and during 'homework' there is no progress in BMT, then the behavioural-systems approach suggests recourse to either structural or strategic approaches as outlined in the following sections.

Structural marital therapy

Structural techniques Theoretical assumptions for this form of therapy are more speculative and less easily deduced from observation than those of BMT. In place of the simple concept of trying to increase rewarding behaviour between the partners, structural therapy uses concepts such as the boundaries between individuals, their personal territory, dependency, overprotection, enmeshment, symmetry and complementarity. Minuchin (1974) has outlined the key techniques in structural therapy as 'actualising transaction patterns (in the session), marking boundaries, escalating stress, assigning tasks, utilising symptoms, manipulating mood and supporting or guiding' (p. 140). In the practical application of structural therapy to marital problems, probably the most frequent intervention used is to focus on an issue, to intensify it, to reframe the problem and to enact the conflict so that the participants find a new solution by their own efforts.

As in the CT approach it is essential for the therapist in structural MT to 'decentre' himself and insist that the couple talk to each other much of the time. It is very easy for a therapist to be 'triangled in' by a couple anxious to obtain medical or psychological help for the symptom presented by one partner, and, therefore, to have greater difficulty in persuading them to talk to each other. Without this ability to decentre himself it is almost impossible for the therapist to achieve any change in the couple's interaction within the session, and this is the main goal of structural interventions.

As an example of structural MT, if a wife is constantly expressing depressed feelings and the husband speaks on her behalf, a good intervention might be for the therapist to say to the wife: 'Your husband is very helpful to you, isn't he? How can you help him not to work so hard on your behalf?' This labels the wife as having some competence, reframes the husband as being in need of help, and sets the scene for a confrontation which will make it more difficult for the old 'complementary' relationship to continue. The therapist will perhaps go on to inflame the ensuing argument, taking sides with one partner, and not allowing either side to give up until a different equilibrium has been reached during the session.

There are many other kinds of structural intervention which may be used in marital therapy. In order to distract the couple's attention from the symptomatic partner, the therapist may draw attention to a problem presented by the other partner and inquire closely as to its impact on the relationship. The therapist may make rules within the session about one partner not trespassing on the 'territory' of the other – the banning of 'mind-reading' is an example of this (although such an injunction could also be seen as part of communication training). It may also be that the couple cannot draw a boundary round their relationship, and the therapist may encourage them to exclude a child or a parent of one partner from discussions that should be private to the couple.

In a structural approach the therapist needs to be quite supportive to both partners: it is even more important to establish a good working relationship with them both in structural work than in BMT where fewer risks are taken with the couple's motivation. At the same time one should be unafraid of conflict, which is the structural therapist's bread and butter and is perhaps the most powerful influence for change. The therapist is not so obviously 'helpful' as in BMT and takes less responsibility for finding the right solution. He is also far less even-handed in dealing with the couple: as opposed to the therapist role in BMT there is more 'unbalancing' of the relationship and more siding with one partner, even up to the end of a session, in order to achieve some change in the interval between sessions.

There is some task setting in the structural approach, but these tasks are different in some ways from those used in BMT. The tasks arise, not from the stated complaints or wishes of the partners, but from the therapist's goal of altering the marital system. Thus tasks might entail a dependent wife making a regular trip out alone, or a couple having a ten-minute argument each night, neither of which they would spontaneously have stated as goals of therapy.

Advantages of structural approaches   It will be seen from the above description of structural techniques that some effort is spent in changing the focus of the problem from an individual symptom to a marital problem. It is not necessarily spelt out by the therapist that this is being done, but there is always an implied assumption that altering the marital interaction will assist the solution of the (often individual) presenting symptom.

Structural techniques are especially useful for couples with the following characteristics:

(a)   the problems are individual, but can be construed as being perpetuated by marital factors – e.g. depression, anxiety, headaches, unspoken resentment or refusal of sex (perhaps labelled 'frigidity');
(b)   the couple will not or cannot argue, despite obvious differences of opinion;
(c)   there are great inequalities of overt power in the relationship ('complementarity') and this may be associated with overprotection by one partner and dependency in the other, or with a situation where one puts the other on a pedestal;
(d)   where BMT has been tried and has failed, perhaps because of failure of task completion or because of inability to accept the marital focus.

Limitations of structural approaches   Problems with structural techniques, however, arise where a couple are unable to argue even when instructed to do so, where symptoms take an even stronger hold of the discussion in the session, or where it is impossible (e.g. through one partner's silence) to orchestrate a different interactional experience for the couple.

There are also some symptoms or syndromes which seem to be associated with failure of structural techniques. More severe depression, for example, hypochondriasis, severe phobic or anxiety symptoms and morbid jealousy are all symptoms which appear to reduce the flexibility and room for manoeuvre in a relationship; and even when the marital factors can be easily identified by a therapist, the couple are often unable to accept this view, or work with a structural approach. If this is the case, in the behavioural-systems approach the next step is to move into a strategic mode of therapy, as outlined in the next section.

Strategic marital therapy

Strategic techniques   The underlying assumptions of strategic marital therapy are similar in many ways to those of structural MT. The habitual interaction pattern between the two partners is summarized in systems terms using similar concepts such as boundaries, enmeshment, complementarity and distance regulation. The key concept in strategic work is, however, homeostasis. This term, borrowed from the physiologist Claude Bernard, indicates the way in which in a relationship each partner uses various communications or pieces of behaviour to ensure that there is no overall change in the 'distance' or power structure between them. The concept is well discussed by Hoffman (1981). In formulating a hypothesis about a marital problem, the therapist (with or without an observation team) tries to construe the symptom of one partner and the reciprocal behaviour of the other as both serving a homeostatic function and keeping the relationship intact and unchanged. Such a hypothesis would also suggest that, if the symptom and the reciprocal behaviour were to disappear, some consequence would occur which is greatly feared by both partners. A deduction from this formulation would be that both partners would resist quite strongly any move by the therapist to initiate changes which would be likely to remove the symptom. This 'clinging' to the symptom may lead to prolonged ineffective attempts by the therapist (e.g. in BMT or structural MT) to change the relationship and/or remove the symptom.

In a couple who show such a resistance to change, strategic interventions may take several forms. Usually, the session is taken up with some kind of questioning of the couple to find out about the symptomatic behaviour, the antecedents and consequences of it in the partner's behaviour, and other issues around the possibilities of change and the feared consequences of change. The questioning may be of a 'circular' variety (Selvini et al. 1980) in which the therapist always asks A about B's behaviour and B about A's behaviour, but never A about A or B about B; in addition the therapist may ask about the comparison of two people (e.g. ask the husband to compare his wife to his mother in a specific respect) and may ask about more distant members of the family. These elements of the 'Milan' approach can be very useful in carrying out strategic interventions, although I am not here advocating the adoption of the complete Milan approach (Selvini et al. 1978).

Whatever the content of the session, whether circular questioning, free-ranging questions, structural manoeuvres or behavioural work, it is possible to give a strategic intervention at the end. Such an intervention will be either a task for a repeated behavioural interaction (a 'ritual') or an instruction which is usually paradoxical in nature and may contain the 'prescription of the symptom', together with a reason why it is important for the couple to behave in this way.

For example, in the case of a wife who continually expresses depressive ideas and who is labelled as the 'problem' by her husband (who persists in speaking for her) the therapist might remain bland and non-committal during the session, asking many questions about the couple's interactional behaviour, cutting short the wife's depressive complaints but instead asking her how the husband reacts to her depression. The exact form of 'prescription' at the end of the session would vary according to the fine details of the case, but would probably include the following elements.

(a) 'It is important for the wife to remain depressed for the present because she believes that in this way she can protect her husband, . . .' (the symptom).

(b) 'It is important for the husband to continue speaking for his wife because rightly or wrongly he feels that she needs looking after,. . .' (the reciprocal behaviour).

(c) 'Try not to change the status quo because you would both be very upset and anxious at the furious arguments you might have if the wife's depression and the husband's protection ceased. . .' (the feared consequence).

It should also be noted that both partners and their behaviour are connoted positively: criticism should be avoided at all costs, and altruistic reasons given for them both to continue the status quo.

The crucial difference in the therapist's attitude, between behavioural and structural interventions on the one hand and strategic interventions on the other, is that in the latter he is usually seen to be advising against change, while in the former he is advising them to do certain things to improve their interaction. Thus in strategic therapy the couple cannot resist change as no change is being requested. They can resist 'no change' but in that case they will change, which is what the therapist covertly wishes them to do. Even if they stay the same (with regard to the symptom and the reciprocal behaviour) they may still experience a change of attitude in thinking that they are doing this consciously and intentionally for altruistic reasons. Alternatively they may become angry with the therapist for making such silly suggestions and thereby take on some responsibility for controlling their own behaviour. Thus many outcomes may result from a paradoxical intervention which is probably best seen as facilitating flexibility in the relationship while reducing dependency on the therapist.

Advantages of strategic approaches   These are quite similar to those of structural techniques. However, whereas some motivation for change is needed for the couple to cooperate with structural work, this is less so in the case of strategic techniques. Couples who need strategic work would probably be more helpless in their attitudes to the problem than those who can be helped structurally. Couples with inability to argue and inequalities of power in the relationship may be helped strategically; and strategic interventions may be useful in couples in which one partner shows psychiatric symptoms, for example morbid jealousy, hypochondriasis, some phobias and obsessions, some types of anorexia, resistant sexual dysfunctions and even quite severe depression. However, perhaps the most common reason for moving to a strategic approach is the failure of behavioural or structural interventions to produce any change in relationship or relief of symptoms.

Limitations of strategic approaches   As with the other approaches, there are also problems which seem to be unsuitable or fail to respond to a strategic approach. What is being offered to the couple is, in effect, disguised marital therapy, and the problem may be seen as so firmly belonging to one partner that the intervention is ignored or persistently fails to elicit change. Problems involving overt psychosis in one partner usually defeat strategic manoeuvres, despite the encouraging anecdotal reports of Selvini et al. (1978) describing improvement in 'families in schizophrenic transaction'. Both in schizophrenic and manic-depressive patients this failure is very frequent and I virtually never attempt marital therapy of a radical kind (BMT, structural or strategic) with such couples. Similarly, in couples where one partner is an inpatient it is usually impossible to carry out effective marital therapy, because (a) one partner is so clearly defined as psychiatrically ill and (b) the couple are together for such a short time in between sessions.

Educative and supportive approaches with psychotic partners

Lowering expressed emotion and intensity of interaction   It has been shown many years ago now that a high level of 'expressed emotion' in the relatives they live with is a poor prognostic factor in schizophrenics (Brown et al. 1972). 'Expressed emotion' (EE) refers to the attitude of the key relative (usually a spouse or parent) to the schizophrenic patient: it is measured by counting the number of critical or hostile comments made by the relative about the patient at a standardized individual interview. The harmful effect of a 'high EE' relative can be reduced if (a) the patient is on phenothiazine medication and (b) the patient and relative spend less than thirty-five hours per week in face-to-face contact. Recently Vaughn and Leff (1976) replicated the work, and on the basis of these findings Leff, Kuipers and Berkowitz (1983) have developed a method of reducing the EE level in key relatives of schizophrenic patients. There are several approaches available to achieve this (McFarlane 1983), but Leff et al. chose a method involving group training of key relatives in the absence of the patients. The relatives are trained to respond to the psychotic speech and behaviour of the patient with bland but supportive comments instead of the critical and often hostile way in which they have previously been used to responding. They are also encouraged to keep away from the patient for considerable periods of the day, either by going out themselves or by encouraging the patient to go out alone. The critical level of contact with a 'high EE' relative above which the patient is likely to relapse is 35 hours face-to-face interaction per week. With married psychotic patients, it is usually the spouse who is the key relative and an approach (not necessarily group-orientated) which seeks to reduce EE and face-to-face interaction within the couple may well improve the prognosis and reduce the rate of relapse.

Behavioural family work with psychotics   Another related approach to families of patients with schizophrenia is that developed by Falloon and Liberman (1983). Rather similar principles are used to those of Leff et al., but with certain additions, including the use of assertive or 'personal-effectiveness' training for the patient, the use of behavioural communication training for the family and an educational workshop for relatives.

Indications for the educative and supportive approach   The indications for this approach are usually clearest at about the time of discharge from hospital of a married schizophrenic patient. There are interview schedules for eliciting EE levels, and this is the best way of determining whether EE needs to be reduced. However, it is also possible to detect criticism and overinvolvement at either an individual meeting with the spouse or a conjoint interview with the couple.

   This approach is in no way a radical form of marital therapy, but merely a method of reducing relapse in the illness by means of environmental manipulation, the environment in question being the spouse. What is true of schizophrenic patients may to a lesser extent apply to manic-depressive patients, some of whom appear clinically to respond badly to an over-involved, critical nearest relative. Other conditions such as paranoid states and severe personality disorders may be amenable to the educative approach, lowering EE and restricting contact to ameliorate the worst consequences of family overinvolvement and criticism.

Abandoning the attempt at marital therapy and using an individual approach

In some cases of couples who have clearly delineated marital problems it is simply not possible to engage the couple in therapy. There are several possible sequences of events that cause this to happen of which the following are examples.

(a) The couple are on the brink of divorce and one partner is unwilling to be involved in marital therapy. It should be said, however, that some useful conciliation work can sometimes be done in such cases, leading to a less bitter and troubled divorce or separation, with better arrangements for custody and access, than would occur otherwise (see Volume 2, Chapters 9 and 10).

(b) One partner is unwilling to attend sessions: here one may be compelled to accept the situation and treat the partner who attends (often the symptomatic one). In cases of divorce, the partner who attends may be experiencing a grief reaction, in which case 'guided mourning' (Ramsay 1977) may be appropriate. In other cases it is possible (as Bennun reports in Chapter 1 of Volume 2) to carry out quite effective communication and negotiation therapy with the couple by seeing one partner and giving instructions for both to follow at home.

(c) All the above approaches have failed. In this case it may still be desirable and in some cases necessary to support one or both partners as outpatients. In a small minority of cases referred to me, I am seeing both partners in a supportive clinic on a two-monthly basis.

(d) There is no apparent interpersonal problem but the symptoms remain. This may occur for instance in cases of organic cerebral disease (e.g. Parkinsonism or Huntington's Chorea), or in cases of psychiatric disorders in which marital factors play little or no part. Suitable follow-up and treatment of the individual may then be arranged.

Obviously not all married patients who are psychiatrically disturbed need marital therapy, and so far there are few guidelines in the literature to identify those who will or will not respond. My approach is often to attempt one or more of the marital therapy approaches outlined above, before concluding that there is no relationship element to the problem which can be treated.

The practice of the behavioural systems approach to marital therapy

Clinical setting

The clinic in which we have developed our behavioural-systems approach is a marital and family therapy clinic with one-way screen supervision. I also run a sexual dysfunction clinic and a routine psychiatric outpatient clinic, and cases are allocated to each clinic on the basis of referral letters, mainly from GPs. Thus in the marital clinic there is a predominance of cases suitable for couple therapy, and not many cases of purely psychiatric problems or sexual dysfunction. Couples are seen by one therapist as a rule, with the others observing and supervising behind the one-way screen with telephone communication to the therapist.

The couples are seen conjointly throughout, with the first part of the first session devoted to eliciting the problem and obtaining a brief family history. The therapist then moves into a more active form of marital therapy, under the direction of the team, and this is the general pattern of subsequent sessions. Occasionally we will ask to see other members of the family in later sessions and may have individual interviews on rare occasions with each spouse.

The sessions last between one and one-and-a-half hours and are separated by two to three-week intervals, although the intervals may extend to four or six weeks towards the end of therapy. The usual number of sessions is between four and eight.

Basic marital therapy principles

In carrying out marital therapy, it is useful to apply certain basic principles, which are not derived from any theoretical school, but arise from experience and common sense. These are as follows:

(a) Try always to get away from individual focus and concentrate on the relationship. Thus if one partner is 'labelled', ask about similar problems in the other, or ask the labelled partner about the reaction of the other to the problem.

(b) Avoid the trap of treating one partner as the spokesman: if one partner adopts this role, or is put into it by the other, try to engage the silent partner in discussion, ask that partner's opinion, or insist that the partners talk to each other.

(c) Avoid becoming the judge in an adversarial situation where both sides are putting their cases. Either turn the complaints into tasks, or get them to argue (with therapist as referee to insist that they play fair), or cut the sequence short with a different line of questioning.

(d) Avoid becoming the expert who answers their questions on medical or technical matters. Such questions should be politely ignored, or declared to be off limits, or referred to other agencies such as the general practitioner.

(e) Avoid polite conversation. If one perceives that the session is beginning to resemble dinner-table talk, then one is failing as a therapist and being 'triangled in' to the marital system, thus losing one's chance to change it.

(f) Avoid taking sides – except as an intentional manoeuvre in structural therapy.

(g) Check continually, especially at the beginning of sessions, whether both partners still agree on the goals of therapy.

(h) Occasionally one can be overenthusiastic in trying to produce change. It is important to balance what the therapist wants to achieve with what the couple will accept (this applies particularly to structural and strategic moves, which can lead to dropping out from therapy if the expected change is too great).

The application of the therapeutic approach

The characteristic feature of our approach is the practice of moving from one type of marital therapy to another according to the problems presented, the resistance encountered and the stage of therapy which the couple are in at the time. Thus in a single session it is possible to move from a behavioural negotiating approach to provoking an argument between the partners, and to end the session with a paradoxical task. However, it is quite a common experience after a paradoxical task has been given to find that the couple have become much more flexible in the next session and, therefore, to move back to structural or behavioural interventions. The key is always to balance the couple's wish to change against their resistance to exploring the interpersonal problems, and, along with the latter, their tendency to look passively to the therapist to 'treat' the symptom.

Many couples will receive a mixture of techniques as above, but some may be treated exclusively with one method. It is thus possible to use purely RN or CT techniques in one's work with a couple, or structural or strategic techniques alone. The choice of therapeutic approach will depend on a number of factors, as shown in the following section.

The indications for different therapeutic techniques

Figure 13.1 shows in diagrammatic form the way in which one may select the appropriate therapeutic approach for a particular couple at a particular time. Many of the indications for each approach have been encompassed in previous sections dealing with the advantages and limitations of each of the specific approaches. The indications given in the present section are in part a summarized version of the 'advantages and limitations' sections and in part an integrated guide to our total behavioural-systems approach.

RN is the simplest, most robust and well-validated approach, and it is best suited to the couple who have a clearly stated marital problem which is fairly evenly balanced between the two partners. Thus couples with resentments and power struggles expressed in terms of arguments and rows are well suited to this approach. The partners have to be prepared and able to negotiate, given a good deal of assistance and rephrasing by the therapist, and the communication between them needs to be fairly clear and unequivocal. It was also found during a research study (Crowe 1978) that RN was *better* suited to those with low educational attainments than those with higher educational backgrounds: this is in marked contrast to most forms of psychotherapy. However, the presence of significant degrees of psychiatric symptomatology and the presence of an individual focus to the problem with marked resistance to change in the relationship renders RN less useful as an approach.

CT can be used as an effective adjunct to RN in those couples who show the same kinds of resentment, arguments and power struggles as those who

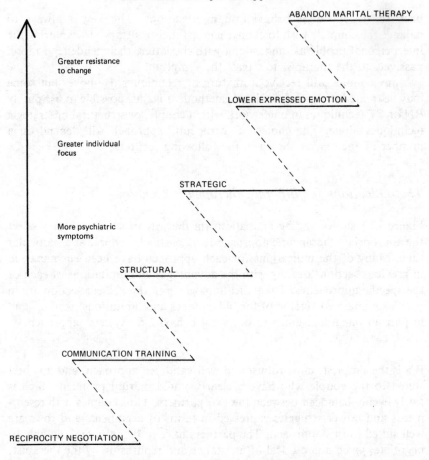

Figure 13.1 A diagrammatic representation of the behavioural-systems approach. (It is usual to start at the lowest suitable level of the hierarchy and only to move to a higher level if resistance to change, individual focus or psychiatric symptoms make work at the lower level unproductive.)

respond to RN; but it is more useful than RN in those cases where there are misunderstandings, overinclusive discussions and difficulties in negotiation. The problem has still to be recognized by both partners as marital for CT to be effective, and as in RN the presence of individual focus, psychiatric symptomatology and resistance to relationship change renders CT less effective.

Structural techniques as an adjunct to the behavioural approaches can be helpful in cases where the relationship focus of the problem is less clear (but still present) and where there is more psychiatric symptomatology. Thus in a couple with marked inequality (one partner the undisputed spokesman, one partner placed on a pedestal, one partner labelled as irresponsible by both, one partner anxious or depressed in response to marital strains) a structural approach can restore the interactional focus, and help the couple to a lesser insistence on the symptom and its 'cure' and a greater equality of responsibility within the relationship. It may also allow the formation of appropriate boundaries around the couple, for instance excluding children or the couple's parents from decisions which should be taken by the couple alone.

Structural techniques are probably unnecessary in the simpler marital problems which are well treated by RN and CT. I prefer not to indulge in speculative theorizing when there appears to be a common-sense solution to a problem: and in some ways it seems insulting to a couple who are trying hard to negotiate a power struggle if the therapist moves quickly away from the problem they are presenting and delves into another area of work.

Structural techniques may, however, be too weak to alter a really rigid system in which a couple insist on the psychiatric focus and resist strongly any relationship change.

Strategic techniques are probably most effective when the system is quite rigid and there is strong resistance to relationship change or even denial of the existence of a relationship problem. Such systems are often encountered in the presence of psychiatric problems such as depression or low self-esteem, anxiety, hypochondriasis, severe phobias (accompanied by collusion by the spouse), eating disorders, morbid jealousy and some sexual dysfunctions which resist the straightforward Masters and Johnson approach. In addition, strategic approaches are useful in couples where the attempts at negotiation, communication training and structural therapy have been unsuccessful.

One might reasonably ask why, if strategic therapy is successful in such difficult cases, one should use BMT and structural therapy at all. It is not completely clear to me that strategic approaches would be successful with the simpler cases in which there is no 'symptom' and 'reciprocal behaviour' to use as the basis for a paradoxical injunction. However, the main reason against using such techniques except where really necessary is that they are based on speculative theories and are far removed from common sense.

Where 'radical' marital therapy is not possible   In the cases where all 'radical' forms of marital therapy (i.e. BMT, structural and strategic) seem to fail, there may be a case for giving up the struggle to label the problem as marital, and therefore adopting an individual supportive, psychotherapeutic or pharmacological approach. In some specifically behavioural problems, such as phobias and compulsions combined with marital problems, it may, in any case, be inappropriate to use marital therapy alone without individual behaviour therapy (Cobb et al. 1980).

However, in cases with psychosis in one partner there may be a case for the approach used by Leff et al. (1983) in which it may be possible, through education of the other partner, to lower stress in the relationship (lowering EE and reducing face-to-face contact); other similar, educational approaches may be used here (Falloon and Liberman 1983).

Therapist role in the different approaches

In the approach of RN, the therapist is clearly and identifiably acting as an agent of change, using the wishes and goals identified by the couple. In CT, he moves a little away from this stance, and imposes his own communication rules in order to help the couple to communicate more effectively; however, he is still working openly and with no hidden agenda, and is still making the (perhaps naive) assumption that the couple are simply not very good at communicating and that, if they can improve their technique, the marital relationship will improve.

In structural therapy, it is less clear to the couple just what the therapist is trying to do, and he shares less of his thinking directly with them. Sometimes he may be seen by them as acting mischievously, as provoking unnecessary arguments and as making a happy relationship less happy. Certainly the outcome of such therapy is more difficult to measure, and a couple assumed by a structural therapist to have improved their marriage, and indeed to have lost the symptom that one of them suffered, may possibly rate their marriage as worse after therapy than before.

It is in strategic therapy that these issues are most problematic. The therapist, in order to overcome or circumvent the couple's 'resistance to change' expresses impotence, advises against change, positively connotes the symptomatic behaviour and may be seen by the couple as being illogical and inconsistent. When the couple return after a two to three-week interval, it does not seem to matter whether the paradoxical task has been carried out or resisted and the only outcome measures of any importance are the rather vague ones of increased flexibility and reduced 'enmeshment' or dependency.

In spite of these differences and anomalies, it seems possible in my experience to combine, either simultaneously or in sequence, elements of all four approaches, as is shown in the following case example.

Case example

The case presented is one which illustrates the behavioural-systems approach to marital therapy with a couple who presented, at least at the beginning of therapy, a fairly clear individual focus to their problems. We began therapy with a generally strategic or paradoxical approach, moved briefly to a structural attempt, but remained broadly strategic for the first four sessions. Thereafter there was a mixture of strategic and structural interventions, and in the last three sessions some reciprocity negotiation was used.

Therapy lasted a year, and during that time the couple were seen eleven times. The first nine sessions were at two to three-weekly intervals and the last two at three-monthly intervals. Each session was supervised by a seminar group watching closed-circuit television and the sessions lasted one and a half hours.

The couple were in their early 50s with two daughters aged 27 and 21. The wife (Mary) was a primary school teacher and the husband (George) a chemical engineer who had a year before taken voluntary redundancy because, as a conservationist, he did not approve of his company dumping chemical waste.

The presenting problem was the husband's depression, which he said he had had for the past twenty-one years. He had had disappointing results from antidepressant treatment, which he was still taking at the time of referral, but the depressive episodes took a rather atypical form. He would become irritable and have temper tantrums, and would often get drunk and say very hurtful things to his wife and family, for which he would apologize the next day. There was very little in the way of sleep, appetite or energy disturbance. Sex was satisfactory to both partners. The referral letter from the GP outlined his previous treatment and mentioned the many types of antidepressant drugs that had been tried. It also mentioned a course of conjoint group therapy that the couple had received at another hospital.

The couple attended together, and requested a conjoint session because the husband said, 'I have a very poor memory, and Mary remembers things for me.' In fact, Mary became the spokesman for the couple, and showed in the first session an almost overwhelming urge to talk about George's behaviour. I tried several times to change the focus of discussions to either

Mary's problems or the relationship itself, but both partners resisted the change. Mary revealed that twenty years before, when George first became depressed, she had read a lot of psychiatric books on the subject and was continually trying to help and understand his problems. Faced with the impossibility of changing the focus in the session (structural approach) or getting the couple to negotiate (behavioural approach), I gave a fairly simple strategic intervention: 'Don't try to alter your depression, George, and don't try to reduce your worry about his depression, Mary, until I see you next.' The husband replied that they would be unable to change even if they wanted to.

In the second session, some more background information emerged. Both partners were members of the peace movement and had also both been involved in left-wing politics at the time of their marriage. They insisted that they never had bad rows, but related one such occasion when they were on holiday on a Mediterranean Island. They had gone almost all the way round the island to a picnic spot: George had known the quick way back to the hotel but Mary had insisted on 'playing for safety' by going back the way they had come. George went with her, but then caused an angry scene blaming her for not believing him, which shocked Mary, who felt she had done nothing wrong. At the end of this session, I suggested that there was a hidden power struggle going on between them, but that open conflict should at all costs be avoided. In their relationship, peace and equality could not exist together, since equality would mean arguments and rows: they should, therefore, opt for peace, with George remaining depressed for Mary's sake, and Mary restraining her emotions so as to look after George and not stir him up.

This was a good example of strategic therapy. The tasks given to both partners involved prescribing the symptom (depression) and the reciprocal behaviour (the wife looking after him and restraining her emotions), with both behaviours positively labelled. The reasons for both partners to do what they were instructed to do were *altruistic* – i.e. 'for your partner's sake' – but also at another level likely to be unpalatable.

The next session, George said, 'I feel worse than ever. My depression is really bad.' Mary too was feeling a great strain in holding back her feelings, and was very worried that George's evening half-pint of beer in the pub was leading him into alcoholism. This admission by Mary of her own problems encouraged me to adopt a more open (structural) approach to them. I encouraged George's assertiveness, saying that probably beer would do him more good than his antidepressants. I also advised Mary to stop psychoanalysing him, but look rather to her own distress.

In this session I was for the first time able to work directly with the couple's behaviour in the session. We had hypothesized that there was a boundary problem between husband and wife, with the wife intruding into his territory in attempting to 'psychoanalyse' him or read his mind, and the husband overtly welcoming this intrusion, perhaps because he was too weak to resist it or perhaps because he enjoyed the lack of responsibility it brought him. My aim was, therefore, to make him more assertive in order to alter the balance and strengthen the interpersonal boundaries in the relationship. As will be seen, I was unsuccessful in strengthening the boundaries, but managed to alter the balance.

The next session, Mary had been to her doctor and had been advised to have two surgical consultations (for spinal trouble and for a possible hysterectomy). George had stopped all tablets (after discussion with his doctor) and was looking after Mary in her 'illness'. He was sure that her visit to the doctor had been occasioned by his own sense of confidence following the discussion in the previous session. Mary confirmed that previously she had avoided the possible operations 'until George was better'. I was pleased with the change but (in a strategic intervention) warned them that the pendulum had simply swung the other way and that open arguments should still be avoided by maintaining the inequality (with George looking after Mary this time).

Two visits later, more open arguments were taking place, and Mary was much less tense than before (she had meanwhile discovered that neither operation was necessary). But she complained that in their arguments George would tend to walk away because of 'the rise in decibels'. I advised George (structural intervention) to stay with the arguments until there was a conclusion, and they managed to argue a point successfully in the session.

Two more sessions later, George was sitting up and looking confident. He had had some depressed days, but was able, in this session, to request Mary to 'leave him to himself' more at these times, as he always came out of them in a few hours. I asked Mary what she wanted of George when she felt tense or tired, and he was able to offer the increased involvement and comfort that she requested (this is an example of reciprocity negotiation). I reinforced the necessity for both of them to argue the points of difference, which neither now appeared afraid of (structural approach).

At this point I was at last able to address myself to the marital relationship overtly and with the couple's full cooperation. Up to this time the focus had always been on George and his depression or Mary and her physical symptoms, but now it was possible to ask them to translate their complaints into wishes and their wishes into tasks for each other, and subsequent enquiries showed that they had remembered and carried out those tasks.

Eighteen months later, at follow-up, George had found a job: Mary had taken early retirement from her school work. George had not taken any antidepressants, and had only had a few periods of mild depression. He continued the evening half-pint of beer. Mary was well, and was often involved in baby-sitting for her granddaughter. Arguments arose at times, but were not a major problem. The improvement in both George's and Mary's symptoms had been achieved partly by prescribing the behaviour complained of, partly by encouraging healthy argument, and partly by negotiation of their relationship patterns. George's depressions (whatever their cause) no longer caused marital difficulties, and the marital strains no longer prolonged the depressions. The case, then, illustrates the gradual progression from strategic to structural and reciprocity negotiating interventions as the system gradually became more flexible and the couple began to focus on interaction rather than individual symptoms.

Conclusions

Marital therapy is becoming a widely accepted form of treatment for many types of problem. For perhaps 50 percent of presenting cases in my experience RN is effective. I prefer to use this approach whenever possible because it makes few assumptions, is based firmly on observed and reported behaviour, and treats the couple at their own valuation. However, it is not always possible to obtain change in interaction by this approach, and some of the couples in whom change does not result may be helped by the therapist adopting a more dictatorial position in insisting on altered communication by CT or structural approaches. Some couples will resist even these methods, and then the therapist has to adopt the more detached and apparently impotent attitude that change would be undesirable for various good reasons which he proceeds to give (strategic approach).

In some cases where the interaction is altered by functional psychoses such as paranoia or schizophrenia it may be impossible to alter the interaction even by paradoxical or strategic approaches, and here it is possible in some cases to improve the prognosis of the patient and to prevent relapse and return to hospital by adopting the 'low EE' approach. Here the key relative is trained to react in an unemotional but accepting way towards the behaviour of the patient, and the patient is encouraged to spend less than thirty-five hours per week in direct face-to-face contact with the key relative.

There are other cases where either there is no marital/family relationship to deal with, where the partner or family member refuses to join the therapy, or where the therapist sees the patient as having an individual problem in which there is no indication for conjoint therapy. It is reasonable in such cases (see Figure 13.1) to abandon marital therapy and (in my own setting) take the patient on as an individual in a different clinic.

References

Brown, G. W., Birley, J. L. T. and Wing, J. K. (1972) Influence of family life on the course of schizophrenic disorders: a replication. *British Journal of Psychiatry, 121,* 241–258.

Cobb, J. P., McDonald, R., Marks, I. and Stern, R. (1980) Marital vs. exposure therapy: psychological treatments of co-existing marital and phobic-obsessive problems. *Behaviour Analysis and Modification, 4,* 3–16.

Crowe, M. J. (1978) Conjoint marital therapy: a controlled outcome study. *Psychological Medicine, 8,* 623–636.

Crowe, M. J. (1982) The treatment of marital and sexual problems: a behavioural approach. *In* A. Bentovim, G. Gorell Barnes and A. Cooklin (eds) *Family therapy: complementary frameworks of theory and practice.* London: Academic Press.

Emmelkamp, P., van der Helm, M., Macgillavry, D. and van Zanten, B. (1984) Marital therapy with clinically distressed couples: a comparative evaluation of system-theoretic, contingency contracting and communication skills approaches. *In* K. Hahlweg and N. S. Jacobson (eds) *Marital interaction.* New York: Guilford Press.

Falloon, I. R. H. and Liberman, R. P. (1983) Behavioral family interventions in the management of chronic schizophrenia. *In* W. R. McFarlane (ed.) *Family therapy in schizophrenia.* New York: Guilford Press.

Gottman, J., Notarius, C., Gonzo, J. and Markman, W. (1976) *A couple's guide to communication.* Champaign, Illinois: Research Press.

Hahlweg, K. (1984) Predicting outcome in behavioural marital therapy. Paper read at the 14th Congress of the European Association for Behaviour Therapy, Brussels.

Hahlweg, K. and Jacobson, N. S. (1984) *Marital interaction: analysis and modification.* New York: Guilford Press.

Haley, J. (1976) *Problem solving therapy.* San Francisco: Jossey-Bass.

Hoffman, L. (1981) *Foundations of family therapy.* New York: Basic Books.

Im, W. G., Wilner, R. S. and Breit, M. (1983) Jealousy: interventions in couple therapy. *Family Process, 22,* 211–220

Jacobson, N. S. (1978) A review of the research on the effectiveness of marital therapy. *In* T. J. Paolino and B. S. McCrady (eds) *Marriage and marital therapy.* New York: Brunner/Mazel.

Jacobson, N. S. and Martin, B (1976) Behavioral marriage therapy: current status. *Psychological Bulletin, 83,* 540–566.

Leff, J., Kuipers, L. and Berkowitz, R. (1983) Intervention in families of schizophrenics and its effect on relapse rate.*In* W. R. McFarlane (ed.) *Family therapy in schizophrenia.* New York: Guilford Press.

Liberman, R. P. (1970) Behavioral approaches to family and couple therapy. *American Journal of Orthopsychiatry, 40*, 106–118.

McFarlane, W. R. (1983) *Family therapy in schizophrenia.* New York: Guilford Press.

Minuchin, S. (1974) *Families and family therapy.* Cambridge, Mass: Harvard.

Paolino, T. J. and McCrady, B. S. (1978) *Marriage and marital therapy.* New York: Brunner/Mazel.

Ramsay, R. W. (1977) Behavioural approaches to bereavement. *Behaviour Research and Therapy, 15*, 131–135.

Segraves, R. T. (1982) *Marital therapy: a combined psychodynamic-behavioral approach.* New York: Plenum Medical.

Selvini Palazzoli, M., Boscolo, L., Cecchin, G. and Prata, G. (1978) *Paradox and counter-paradox.* New York: Aronson.

Selvini Palazzoli, M., Boscolo, L., Cecchin, G. and Prata, G. (1980) Hypothesising – circularity – neutrality: three guidelines for the conductor of the session. *Family Process, 19*, 3–12.

Sluzki, C. E. (1978) Marital therapy from a systems theory perspective. *In* T. J. Paolino and B. S. McCrady (eds) *Marriage and Marital Therapy.* New York: Brunner/Mazel.

Spinks, S. H. and Birchler, G. R. (1982) Behavioral-systems marital therapy: dealing with resistance. *Family Process, 21*, 169–185.

Stuart, R. B. (1969) Operant-interpersonal treatment for marital discord. *Journal of Consulting and Clinical Psychology, 33*, 675–682.

Teismann, M. W. (1979) Jealousy: systematic, problem-solving therapy with couples. *Family Process, 18*, 151–160.

Thibaut, J. W. and Kelley, H. H. (1959) *The social psychology of groups.* New York: Wiley.

Vaughn, C. E. and Leff, J. P. (1976) The influences of family and social factors on the course of psychiatric illness: a comparison of schizophrenic and depressed neurotic patients. *British Journal of Psychiatry, 129*, 125–137.

Index of Names

Note: *Only authors discussed in the text are included; see References section for all authors mentioned.*

Index of Subjects

Note: *The word 'marriage' has been abbreviated to 'm.' throughout the subject index.*